P9-EDO-594

Israel Tour Study Manual

A Resource for Christian Pilgrims to the Land of the Bible

Compiled, Written & Edited by
JoAnn G. Magnuson

Walk About Zion
Count Her Towers
Consider Her Ramparts

Psalm 48:1-2

JoAnn Magnuson

Curator, Jewish-Christian Library & Center

Living Word Christian Center/Maranatha Christian Academy

PO Box 24307

Minneapolis, MN 55424

952-994-7545

jgmagnuson@mac.com

www.jclibrarycenter.com

INDEX

Maps courtesy of Regal Books
The Bible Visual Resource Book, Copyright 1989, Regal Books, Ventura, CA 93009, Used by permission

I am pleased to present this material

to our friends.

I trust this information will help to enrich

your Israel trip.

I want you to share your insights with others

But

Please do not copy the materials

without permission

Copyright 1999©

JoAnn G. Magnuson

ISRAEL STUDY MANUAL INTRODUCTION

The Bible is rooted in the geography and history of the Near East, especially in that part known as Israel. Over 90% of the biblical events took place in this tiny land. In the days of the Bible it was approximately 150 miles long and 50 miles wide! Today it is still 50 miles wide but from Mount Hermon to Eilat is closer to 300 miles. The biblical writers assume their readers are familiar with the land and its history, geography, feasts, customs, culture and language. For this reason they rarely explain these things. This often leaves readers in the 21st century without a complete understanding of the background of the text.

As we learn about the setting of the Bible, we will see that there is a hidden life in the prophets, the disciples and Jesus — a life which can only be understood when we see these writings in their proper context. As Fr. Bargil Pixner, an explorer and archeologist once said, the land itself is like a "fifth gospel." It gives special insights to the other portions of scripture.

Western readers will find a new depth of understanding as they become familiar with the history and geography of the Bible lands. This Study Manual, along with other recommended study aids, will help students to bridge the barriers of time and to understand the context of the biblical world.

This book will help you to interact seriously with the Bible through specially prepared materials. A comprehensive list of Bible references is found in the first pages of the Reference section. A detailed description of the sites we will visit is found in the Site description section. As you study, refer to your Bible Atlas and the map section frequently.

The object of this course is to help you feel at home in the land of the Bible. Our goal is to prepare you for an intelligent experience in Israel. Far too many tourists invest their money to pay for the trip but do not invest the time to prepare for a meaningful experience. Many travelers feel lost and confused for most of their stay. This will not happen to you if you commit yourself to study this manual before you board the plane. We want you to have an adventure that is exciting, life-changing and FUN!

Some students find it helpful to highlight various points and places, especially on the maps, with colored markers. It is good to trace the route you are taking day by day so you can refer to it later. Feel free to make notes in the margins and to add blank pages for your own comments. Read for pleasure, don't try to memorize everything. Your Study Manual will mean much more to you when you get home.

Your Study Manual is intended to deepen your walk with the Lord and introduce you to His Land and His people. You don't have to become a biblical scholar in the few short months before the trip, but you will be a better Bible student when you return. Relax and enjoy!

Objectives

You will soon be visiting the land that served as the geographical stage for almost all the biblical events. You are going to Israel to better understand God's Word and His message for today's world – a serious but pleasurable task for every Christian. You will see the Bible come alive in a new and exciting way!

You will be relating directly with the Lord, the Land, and the People of Israel. By working through this Study Manual you will lay a foundation for a more thorough understanding of God's Word in its geographical context. You are building your own personal library of impressions which books alone can never provide.

Some Objectives are:

To experience and enjoy the Land of Israel

To learn important regional aspects of the land and understand their bearing on settlement, defense and historical developments in Bible times.

To appreciate the geographical and historical perspectives from which the Patriarchs, the Psalmists, the Prophets and the Evangelists wrote.

To develop an intercessor's heart for Israel – and all her people.

Bring Along

A complete Bible in an easy-to-read translation

This Study Manual

A set of colored markers for highlighting

A notebook

Small zip-lock bags – for collecting pottery, rocks, shells, etc.

Pens & 3x5 cards. Insert cards in bags to identify finds and treasures

A lightweight tote or day pack for carrying study aids, Bible, camera, etc.

Water bottle, either bring or plan to buy day by day – remember, the desert is hot – drink lots of water!

Preparation for Israel Travel

Our pilgrimage to Israel is about to begin and we can assure you it will be a marvelous adventure. Perhaps a few thoughts from an adventurer of a generation past will help us to keep our expectations in perspective.

On the back of this page you will find some comments copied from a book called *Palestine Speaks*. It was written by a gentleman named Antonia Fredrick Futterer who explored the land of Israel in the l920s, back in the days of the British Mandate when the country was known as "Palestine." Mr. Futterer was searching for the Lost Ark long before Indiana Jones and Steven Spielberg popularized it! In his book he recounts his adventures in the land and shares some travel tips — some of which seem humorous today but most are still very applicable. You will enjoy them as you prepare to travel to the same places some eighty years later.

You will be glad to know that you no longer need to be subjected to a chemical bath or have your clothing fumigated. You can skip the deck chair and the woolen underwear. But Mr. Futterer is still on target when he advises us to prepare for inconveniences and to learn to be content under all conditions. That advice is as sound today as it was when the Apostle Paul wrote it to the saints at Philippi (Philippians 4:11,12).

Those involved in planning our tour have worked very hard to schedule things as carefully as possible. The airlines, the hotels and the travel agencies all want you to have a wonderful time and to return home safe and happy. But some circumstances are beyond human control. There may be minor changes in the itinerary. Airplanes are sometimes late, sometimes overcrowded. It is important to set our minds to be flexible. Culture shock, jet-lag and language barriers can help us expand our horizons if we decide to receive them as opportunities rather than difficulties.

Mr. Futterer's book reminds us of the amazing changes that have occurred in our lifetime. We will see Israel in a style and a level of comfort unknown a generation ago. Let's pray for each other that we will be worthy of the experience God is providing for us. As we pray for the "peace of Jerusalem" let's prepare to bring our own inner peace along with us. Americans have an unfortunate reputation for making unfavorable comparisons as they travel. By being swift to hear and slow to speak, we can bring blessing to the people we meet and to ourselves.

Experienced travelers always tell us to "travel light." The best things to leave at home are our preconceived notions. If we come with minds and hearts open to the Holy Spirit, we will return home with priceless treasures, treasures that can't be lost, stolen, or taxed!

Palestine Speaks

TRAVEL TIPS FROM 1920

YOUR STEERAGE TREATMENT UPON LANDING AT JAFFA

You and your suitcases will be taken from the steamer into a rowboat, which will land you at a cost of about 75 cents. You will then be taken to *Quarantine*, where you will be subjected to a severe *Chemical Bath*, while your clothes are being fumigated. You will be given a thin bathrobe to stand around in till you get back your suit, which is hardly recognizable, so be sure you land in your worst suit. After this you will be vaccinated, and be ordered to report to the Health Office every third day. When you hear the Officer say "*Finish*" you know you are free for at least three months, which gives you time to collect yourself together again.

A. F. Futterer
Ark Explorer

Your suitcases in the meantime have been taken to the Custom House, which are examined while you wait. Be very obedient and tell what you have. Usually there is no duty to pay, unless you have more than personal effects.

YOUR STEAMER EQUIPMENT

Take a warm Steamer Rug. Rent on ship, or buy a Deck Chair at wharf before sailing, and write your name upon it with ink pencil. Take two strong suits of clothes, one heavy, the other light. Two suits of underwear, all wool, one heavy the other light. A strong pair of shoes, well broken-in, light pair of slippers. A Panama soft hat, and a felt hat and a Steamer Cap. Your Deck Chair may be sold at Port of landing, or else given away to one worthy. Rug is always handy to keep for journeying.

YOUR COMPANION IN TRAVEL

Unless you are thoroughly convinced that you have a sure and tried friend as traveling companion, better travel alone. If you are compelled to travel with someone, be not tied together, each should be free from the other, and ready to help anybody who cannot help themselves.

YOUR COUNTING THE COST WELL

In two ways you must count well the cost. What it will cost in cash, and in not being able to get all you *WANT* during your travels. **Prepare for many inconveniences! Learn to be content under all conditions.** Some have failed in this and ruined their trip, either for want of cash, or want of patience, or self denial.

These 1920 travel tips are from **Palestine Speaks** by A.F. Futterer, published in 1931. This fascinating book is out of print and in short supply. One copy is available in Minneapolis at the Jewish-Christian Library & Center (JCLC). Call JoAnn Magnuson, 952-994-7545.

Guidelines For Ministry In Israel

A trip to Israel is a unique experience. You will walk not only in the footsteps of Jesus but also in the footsteps of those Christian pilgrims who followed after Him. To understand the reaction of Israelis – and Jewish people generally – to Christians, you need to realize that some of Jesus' followers have left a misleading set of footprints on the road.

If you have studied at all about the history of Church antisemitism, you are grieved to discover that many people who claimed to follow Jesus did not express His heart of love to the Jewish people. Many Christians have come to Israel with hatred and violence and their version of the "Good News" was very bad news for the Jews.

The Jewish people are back in their own land after nearly twenty centuries of dispersion. The event which moved world opinion to allow this return was the Nazi Holocaust in which one third of the world Jewish community was brutally murdered. Israel occupies a tiny piece of real estate and the Jewish right to it is regularly contested by their neighbors. Israel is the world's only Jewish State – the only place on earth where Jews are free to be fully Jewish.

Given the sad history of Christian persecution, we should not be surprised to discover resistance to missionary activity in Israel. Many Jewish leaders fear that the conversion of the Jews to Christianity could "give Hitler a posthumous victory," effectively eliminating the Jewish people by assimilation rather than annihilation. Most modern Jews have not rejected Jesus – they have never seen Him. At least they have rarely seen Him portrayed in a way that would cause them to give a second thought to the possibility of His Messiahship.

Before real discussion of Jesus as Messiah can take place, however, much healing needs to occur in relation to the past. While we may feel that no true Bible-believing Christian would consider persecuting the Jewish people, history does not support our feelings. Many Christians who have spoken warmly of their love for Jesus, have spoken and acted hatefully toward His brothers after the flesh. As followers of Jesus we must learn to observe the warning of Rabbi Saul of Tarsus who cautioned against arrogance toward the natural branches in his letter to the Romans. God is beginning a healing process. Only Satan wins when Christians and Jews see each other as enemies. One of the main reasons for work we are doing is to further that healing process.

In view of the misunderstanding that has characterized Jewish-Christian relations, we ask those who travel with us to observe the following guidelines:

- Do not bring Christian tracts to Israel with the intention of handing them out or leaving them to be found by others. This is not an effective method of communication.

- Be very sensitive in sharing your beliefs. Please note, we are not saying "don't share." We are saying please observe I Peter 3:15-16: "...in your heart acknowledge Christ as the holy Lord. Always be prepared to give an answer to everyone who *asks* you to give the reason for the hope that you have. But do this with gentleness and respect..."

- Sometimes we have the opportunity to sing either in the airport or other times when we are together with Jewish friends. Each trip is different, we seek God's direction for each group. If we sing, we usually do not sing "Jesus songs" in these situations. The Old Testament scripture songs are best, especially those we know in Hebrew. In doing this we are able to exalt the Word of God, which creates faith wherever it is spoken, and to express our respect for the Hebrew scriptures. Remember, we are guests of the State of Israel and are often flying on their airplanes. While touring Christian sites we will spend much time in worship of our Lord Jesus. We can honor Him by honoring the sensitivities of His chosen people. There is a fine line of balance between sensitivity and compromise. Pray that all of us will be led by the Spirit of God.

- You may have heard that it is illegal to witness in Israel. This is not actually true. It is illegal to give anyone "material inducement to convert from one religion to another." It is not illegal to talk to anyone who wants to talk about anything. Honest discussion is acceptable – gimmicks are out.

Thank you for taking the time to read these guidelines. We ask that you pray about these things and let the Lord minister to you as to how to walk them out. We would never ask anyone to compromise their belief in the Lord Jesus. We do believe that Jesus will be most honored as we walk in love with listening ears and hearts toward the people of Israel, the apple of God's eye.

Security Procedure

As a passenger traveling to the Middle East, you must be prepared to pass through a security clearance when you check in at the airport in your departure city. On European carriers, the most intense security check will be in their European stopover city enroute to Israel. The purpose of the security check is to make sure that your flight is safe, which is something you surely want too!

The security agents are not employees of the airline but law enforcement officers. Their manner is very business-like and may seem a bit threatening to you. They don't smile a lot. Their job is to keep people with evil intentions off the aircraft which you are about to board. Therefore be prepared to answer their questions and assist them in every way. Sometimes they will ask you to open your luggage. At times, their questions may seem irrelevant or repetitious. Don't get irritated, don't offer information not asked for, just answer and remember they are trying to protect you. You will be asked if you have accepted gifts to bring to Israel. The only gifts you should be carrying are those previously inspected and cleared by your group leader. Do not bring anything which has not been cleared by your group leader! The rules for what may be carried on change often since September 11, 2001.

Check this web site: http://www.tsa.gov/travelers/airtravel/prohibited/permitted-prohibited-items.shtm

So, enjoy your trip and consider your security check as a part of the adventure of traveling abroad. Even if it is less than pleasant, it makes a great story when you get home!

Ten Commandments for Travelers

1. Thou shalt not expect to find things precisely as they are at home — for thou hast left home to find different things.
2. Thou shalt not take things too seriously — for a carefree mind is the basis for a good vacation.
3. Thou shalt not let other tour members get on thy nerves — for thou art paying thy money to enjoy thyself.
4. Thou shalt not worry — he that worrieth hath little joy.
5. Thou shalt not judge all the people of a country by the one person with whom thou hast had a problem.
6. Blessed are those who can wait and smile — for they shall surely enjoy themselves.
7. Thou shalt do somewhat as the natives do — but remember to use American friendliness.
8. Thou shalt carry thy passport at all times — a man without a passport is a man without a country.
9. Thou art welcome where thou treatest thy host with respect.
10. Blessed is the man who seeks to speak a few words in the local language.

A Few Useful Words & Phrases

Shalom = general greeting (peace)	Hasherootim = restroom	B'vakasha = please & you're welcome
Shalom, shalom = nicer than shalom	Ayefo = where?	Boker tov = good morning
Cham = hot	Yafeh = nice	Lila tov = good night
Kar = cold	Yakar = expensive	Erev tov = good evening
Ken = yes	Zol = inexpensive	Metzuyan = excellent
Lo = no	Gadol = large	Todah = thank you
Mayim = water	Kattan = small	Todah rabah = thank you very much
Kesef = money	L'chayim! = to life!	
W.C. = restroom	Mazal tov = good luck!	
	S'licha = excuse me	

Kosher Food – What Is It?

Most hotels and many restaurants in Israel serve kosher food. Jewish dietary laws prescribe which foods are allowed and which are taboo. They try to follow the Biblical laws as to which animals are clean and how the meat is to be prepared. Meat must come only from animals that have cloven hoofs and chew the cud, such as cows, sheep, goats and deer, to mention only the most popular. Fish must have fins and easily removable scales, for instance carp, trout, salmon or herring. This leaves sea creatures such as shrimp, squid, lobster and oysters out of the kosher Jewish diet. The common varieties of poultry, such as chicken, duck, and turkey, are permitted and a popular staple in Israeli diet.

A crucial point in kosher cooking and serving of food is the strict separation of meat and milk. These must not be cooked together, eaten together, or served together and all utensils used in their preparation and consumption must be kept strictly separate. The separation of meat and milk extends to all dairy products as well. This means that you cannot sprinkle grated cheese on a meat lasagna, or have cream in your coffee after a meat meal. (Non-dairy creamers are sometimes available.) The larger hotels have two dining rooms, one for meat meals and the other for dairy dishes, of which Israel has an enormous variety.

The reason for the strict separation of meat and milk is found in Deuteronomy 14:21 which says, "You shall not boil a kid in its mother's milk." To assure that this law is not broken, preparation and consumption of meat and milk is kept entirely separate.

Those restaurants that meet the standards of the Ministry of Industry, Trade and Tourism, where hygiene, cooking and service are concerned, are listed as such and display the tourism emblem.

Middle Eastern Food

In Israel you can eat your way around the world. About half of the population has its roots in over 100 different countries. Some of them have brought their original cuisine with them and dish it up in their own distinctive restaurants. The native born are not to be outdone either, and they are represented by restaurants serving the food of the region – the Middle East.

When going to a Middle Eastern restaurant, make sure to have cash or credit card. Not that they are expensive — on the whole they are not — but you would have to wash a lot of dishes if you ran out of money. Before you have a chance to look at the menu, every inch of table space is taken up by a dozen different salads, depending on the season. Some of the more notable are cucumber in yogurt, pumpkin salad, fried eggplant and eggplant with a sesame sauce, and of course, the Middle Eastern staple, humus, a paste of chick-peas with olive oil. To attack these in true style, you wipe them up with pita – pieces of flat, round bread or a piece torn from a sheet of table-sized thin bread neatly folded on a plate.

When the waiter spies a flagging interest in the panoply of salads, he appears once more, balancing a new array of dishes. Now it's the turn of the stuffed vegetables. If you succeed in polishing off vine leaves, eggplant, artichoke stalks, carrots and peppers, all stuffed with rice, you will be stuffed yourself. Leave room for a special delicacy sometimes accompanying this course: kubeh, a spheroid meat ball coated with cracked wheat.

The meat lovers, who have been neglected up to this point, get their chance now. They have a choice of kebab, shish kebab, roast lamb, lamb chops and even lamb testicles, all served with steaming rice.

Then comes the moment when the gourmands regret their gluttony. The more prudent eaters will have kept an eye on the luscious display of sweets and regulated their intake accordingly. Baklava is only one of these delicious confections made with nuts, almonds, dates and honey. The traditional conclusion of this mideast feast is a tiny cup of Turkish coffee spiced with cardamom. Even if you wanted to wash dishes, you wouldn't have the strength after this repast.

Money, Currency Exchange & Shopping

As you travel in Israel we encourage you to get to know the people of the land. One good way to do this is by shopping. You will enjoy talking to shop keepers, absorbing the sights and sounds of the busy streets, roaming through the Oriental bazaar, spending some leisure time indulging in a pastry and coffee at a sidewalk cafe and seeking out that special gift or antiquity for a friend or relative back home. Of course, all this requires money, so, the most often-asked questions are concerns about money.

Only you know your spending habits and limits. The tour price provides your necessities. You will need pocket money for lunches, snacks, beverages that are not included with meals, soft drinks along the way, candy bars, ice cream and an occasional falafel. We suggest that you carry between $50 to $150 in small US bills. You will be able to use these to buy small items not requiring currency exchange. You can spend U.S. dollars quite easily but don't expect to receive U.S. change in return. We would recommend you take at least $200-$500 in US currency and/or travelers checks. Cash is easier to use, travelers checks are safer but are discounted. If you wish to carry travelers checks for your protection and peace of mind they

can be used to purchase higher priced items or exchanged for Israeli currency. Personal checks are sometimes accepted, with proper identification, at many Jerusalem stores. Major credit cards are also accepted almost everywhere are easiest and safest way to pay. However, BE SURE THAT YOU TAKE THE CARBON AND SAVE YOUR RECEIPT. THIS WILL PROTECT YOU IN CASE OF A PROBLEM. ALSO be sure to call your credit card company – number is found on the back of your card – and notify them that you will be traveling overseas. Sometimes they refuse to honor your card if they think someone is using your card without permission. This is intended to protect you but can be a problem if you really need to use your card.

Also remember, everything takes longer than you are used to in the USA. It is not as easy to get cash on your credit card as it is here. You may have to stand in line for half an hour to cash travelers checks in a bank. Sometimes the hotel can do it, sometimes they are short of cash. So it is good to plan ahead and cash checks when you have the most time to wait. It is best to cash checks as you make purchases. You will want to exchange some dollars into Israeli currency, which is now called the New Israeli Shekel. We do not recommend getting Israeli shekels from a US bank, the rates are never good.

Until recently the shekel was worth about 25¢ or about 4 shekels to $1, but with the changes in the world economy this can vary greatly. Every shekel is divided into 100 agorot, just like pennies to a dollar. Check the rate of exchange shortly before you leave on the tour.

Don't be afraid to use the shekel. Be adventurous and you will feel more like a native. If you make a few mistakes on small purchases it won't matter. In making change, learning directions, and speaking the language, it is impossible to learn without making mistakes.

As for shopping, you will find a variety of items to buy in Israel, from diamonds, leather goods, jewelry, art, and antiquities (finds from archaeological digs) to olive wood manger scenes, beads and camels. If you teach school consider a trip to the Israeli Poster Center located at 29 King George Street, 100 yards from Ben Yehuda Street Mall in the center of Jerusalem. Enjoy — and remember some of the best souvenirs are the pictures you will carry home on your digital camera and in your head and your heart.

There are fine stores which guarantee their work and are endorsed by the Israel Government Tourist Office. Others – well, you get what you pay for. We would not recommend buying serious jewelry in the Old City bazaars. Experience teaches us that gold sometimes turns green and stones are glass — and the merchant has vanished. Ask your tour host for recommendations.

The rate of exchange between US dollars and Israeli New Shekels varies. It usually runs between three and four shekels per US dollar. You can check this web site for exchange rates. http://www.ask.com (ILS stands for Israeli New Shekel.)

If you enter "images of new Israeli shekel" in Google you will see photos of the coins and bills.

Some Suggestions For Your Spare Time

OLD CITY

- Shop, very carefully of course. Remember, merchants expect you to bargain. If you don't, you will spoil their day. It is poor form, however, to begin bargaining if you do not intend to buy.

- If you want to be safe, not sorry, do not eat anything in the Old City unless the place is okayed by your guide or tour host. You probably won't take that advice so the next safest thing is to stick to bread, pastry or fruit you can wash and peel. It's not that the bacteria in Israel are worse than our's – just different.

- Don't accept an offer from a local resident who wants to "be your guide" as you walk around the city. They usually want money, or other favors. "Lah" is No in Arabic, "Lo" is No in Hebrew.

- For a good view in the Old City, climb the steps in the bell tower of the Lutheran Church of the Redeemer. Small fee, long climb. Also you can walk on the roof tops by climbing a staircase in the Jewish Quarter.

- At Jaffa Gate there is a museum with very interesting selection of displays and a film. Small fee.

- Go under the wall near Herod's Gate to see the quarries (may be Zedekiah's or Solomon's). Take your flashlight. Be careful not to slip.

- Go to the Western Wall and pray.

- Explore the Southern Wall excavations. If you want to experience Hezekiah's Tunnel, don't go alone. Take a companion, bring a flashlight, wear waterproof shoes, be prepared to get wet above the knees.

- Investigate the Jewish Quarter.

NEW CITY – West Jerusalem

- Buy coffee and pastry and eat outdoors in Zion Square or along Ben Yehuda Street.

- Attend Shabbat services at Hechel Shlomo Synagogue.

- Go up in the bell tower of the YMCA, across from the King David Hotel. You must go up in groups of two or more (Pay elevator man a small tip).

- Attend a folklore evening. Music and dance from many different Jewish communities.

- Ride a public bus. Explore local shops – used book stores are lots of fun!

- Sit in the lobby of the Plaza, King David, Hilton or other major hotels. Watch people, drink coffee and take advantage of their scheduled events.

- Go to a Hebrew movie, not American.

- Sit in a park, people watch, converse with Israelis.

- Take advantage of all the opportunities for home hospitality you can find.

- Visit the many museums, Biblical Zoo, Ammunition Hill, Tourjeman Post, the City of David, or the museum in the Jaffa Gate Citadel.

- Shop at the *Super Sol* on Agron Street, it is open all night. Take Israeli soup mix or spices home as souvenirs.

NOTE: You will receive your Jerusalem map when you arrive.

General Information For Israel Tours
A Jewish Traveler's Prayer

The Lord bless thee and keep thee. The Lord make His face to shine upon thee and be gracious unto thee; the Lord turn His face to thee and give thee peace. May it be Thy will, Lord of Heaven and Earth, to lead us to peace and safety, to fly us in peace and safety to our desired destination to find life, joy and peace. Guard and watch us who fly the air routes and cross the seaways and travel the overland passes. Make firm the hands that guide the steering and sustain their spirit, so that they may lead us in peace and safety. For in You alone is our shelter from now unto eternity. Amen.

HOW TO PACK

Luggage restrictions change often so we will not discuss details here. Our travel professionals will give us the current regulations with your other documents.

Your luggage should be sturdy and light-weight. Current security regulations do not permit you to lock your luggage. They will break the locks in order to check contents. Don't take anything on a trip that you can't afford to lose! Always put your name on the inside as well as the outside of your luggage. Tags can fall off.

Pack in layers. Start with the heavier and odd-shaped items. Fill in empty spaces with small items. Tissue or plastic between garments eliminates unnecessary creasing. Pack the items you are going to need first in the most accessible places in your bag.

In packing your carry-on bag, consider what items you would be lost without and put them into your carry-on. Usually you and your luggage will arrive at the same time, but it is best to be prepared for the worst! Medications, glasses, clean shirt, change of socks and underwear, curling iron, should go with you into the cabin. Make sure your tickets, passport and money are with you at all times! At the present time, liquids, including cosmetics, are not permitted on the aircraft. However you may bring on an empty water bottle and ask to flight attendent to fill it when you are in the air.

For more info visit this web site:

http://www.tsa.gov

It is wise to bring a small shoulder bag to carry as you tour. (A small backpack works well, if you like them.) Just carry the necessities daily.

CLOTHING SUGGESTIONS

Most people take too much – decide what you think you must have, and leave half of it at home! Choose easy-care fabrics and colors that resist showing dirt. Choose garments you are comfortable in. Allow yourself enough time to pack and re-pack before you go. Practice carrying your luggage to see if you can manage it. Normally, it will be handled for you on a guided tour, but it is good to be able to manage by yourself if necessary.

Israel is very informal. Even government officials seldom wear ties. You may want one good dress or sport coat for a man, in case your tour includes a banquet on the final night. Bring garments that mix-and-match so you can add or subtract layers for changes in weather.

BOTH:

Raincoat or wind-breaker (Jerusalem is cool at night)
Bathrobe (not bulky)
Slippers or socks to wear on the plane. Feet tend to swell on long flights.

WOMEN:
   3 or 4 pair slacks - 1 pair of jeans if you wear them.
   1 skirt or dress, preferably 2-piece so top can be
      used separately; in summer 2 pair of shorts
   4-6 tops, combination of T-shirts, short & long-
      sleeved blouses, turtle-necks
   2 sweaters (cardigan is more useful than a
      pullover) &/or 1 blazer.
   Underwear & stockings (bring liquid soap to wash
      these items in hotel sink)
   1 or 2 nightgowns
   Accessories: scarves, jewelry (not expensive,
      please) shawl, belts
   2 pair good, well-broken-in walking shoes. (Sore
      feet can ruin a trip!)
   1 pair dress shoes, not formal or very high heels.
      Sandals are good.

MEN:
   3-4 pair slacks or slacks & jeans
   1-2 pair shorts
   4-6 shirts (combination of short or long-sleeved,
      dress, knit, turtlenecks, etc)
   1 sports jacket, if desired, not necessary
   1-2 ties (not necessary unless you enjoy wearing
      them)
   2 sweaters and/or sweater vest
   Underwear & socks (Laundry soap)
   2 pair comfortable walking shoes. Tennis shoes ok
      – an extra pair of old tennies or sandals are
      handy for walking through Hezekiah's Tunnel &
      on rocks at Dead Sea.
   Pajamas

Wear loose-fitting clothes on plane, some like jogging suits.
Swim suit
Rain hat or warm cap
Lightweight boots –if you plan to hike during rainy season

OTHER USEFUL ITEMS:

• Alarm clock (quartz or wind-up)
• Umbrella (not necessary in Israel during summer months)
• Washcloth (often not supplied in hotels)
• Hair dryer & curling iron - Israel has 220 volt, direct current so you will need a transformer and an adapter plug to use your U.S. appliances. Many manufacturere make dryers and curling irons with built-in converters. You just flip a small switch on the appliance for use in Israel. If you have these types, you will need only an adapter plug – the 2-prong, small, round type. Israeli hotels usually have an outlet in the bathroom which will operate U.S. electric razors - but they are NOT powerful enough to run heating elements.
• Small flashlight & extra batteries
• Small sewing kit
• Toiletries & cosmetics. (These are available but much more expensive in Israel)
• Sunglasses & sunscreen (Sun on sand and stone is very bright!)
• Small canteen or water bottle
• Inflatable hangers for clothing. Not necessary, but useful for drip dry.
• Sleep mask &/or ear plugs – if you are sensitive to light or noise when sleeping.
• Liquid laundry soap
• Extra pair of glasses &/or copy of your prescription
• Any equipment needed to clean contact lenses
• Any medication you take regularly, good to have copies of prescriptions.
• Aspirin, Kaopectate, Imodium, cough drops. (There is no cause for concern about food or water in Israel but some people have a bit of discomfort from any change in water.)
• Small packets of Kleenex and handi-wipes are very useful.

BIBLE

A small edition is easier to carry. You will want both Testaments. Be sure your name, address and phone number is in it

NOTEBOOK, or journal, pens & pencils

THIS MANUAL with maps & Hebrew phrase section

CAMERA

Most people use digitable cameras today. If you are using a film camera bring all the film you will need.

TRAVELERS CHECKS, CURRENCY, CREDIT CARDS

The Israeli shekel changes value often, we will give you the current rate of exchange just before departure. You may cash US travelers checks as you shop in most shops that serve tourists. Keep records of your check numbers separate from checks and leave a list of numbers at home also. Travelers checks are a safe way to carry money BUT you will lose money on the discounted transaction.

Many experienced travelers make it a practice to carry about $30 to $50 in single dollar bills. These are acceptable almost everywhere and are useful for small or last-minute purchases.

Credit cards from American Express, Bank America, VISA and Mastercard are generally acceptable in Israel. In recent years cash cards are becoming more common in Israel. Also remember it is impossible to rent a car without a credit card.

Banks and public offices close at noon on Friday and days preceding holidays. Everything closes for Shabbat, Saturday, the Jewish Sabbath. This is frustrating for Americans who are used to seven days a week convenience, but remember, God did give Moses some pretty specific instruction on the subject. It is probably good for us to be forced to rest one day a week.

PASSPORTS, TICKETS, TRAVEL DOCUMENTS

Generally your airline tickets, name tags, tour itinerary and flight information will be included in your "passenger kit" which will be sent to you by your travel agent or tour host. Today e-tickets are very popular and you can print them out at home.

It is your responsibility to obtain a valid passport. You will need a copy of your birth certificate for this procedure and some people run into difficulties at this point. Start the procedure as soon as you think you may be planning to travel. Notify your tour host if you are having trouble. *YOU CANNOT TRAVEL OVERSEAS WITHOUT A PASSPORT!!* Make sure you have it with you when you leave home. Do not place it in your checked luggage! You will need to show it several times during the trip. U.S. passports are good for ten years.

Do not be intimidated by the security procedures – they are for your protection. Answer questions as briefly as possible and do not offer unnecessary information. You will receive a boarding pass showing your seat assignment. Keep this handy, with your ticket and passport. An airline representative will collect this card from you as you board. If you are flying via other gateways specific instructions will come from our travel agency and your tour host.

It is not necessary to obtain a visa in advance. An Israeli visa will be stamped on your passport when entering Israel. If you plan to visit an Arab country later, (other than Jordan or Egypt which now have diplomatic relations with Israel) it is wise to ask the passport control to stamp a separate paper which you can carry in your passport while in Israel.

VACCINATIONS

Currently, no vaccinations, shots or inoculations are required for travel to Israel. If you are planning to include other Middle East countries on your itinerary, check with your travel agent or public health service. It is a good time to check with your doctor to be sure your basic inoculations are up to date.

DISEMBARKATION CARDS

While in flight, just before arrival, the cabin attendants will give each individual a card to fill out. This is standard procedure. You will present the card to the immigration authorities as you go through passport control in Israel. Having the card filled out in advance speeds the entrance process. Keep the card in your passport since it will be collected when you leave. One question often asked is, "where are you staying in Israel?" Put either the last hotel where you will stay or simply write, Jerusalem.

TIME DIFFERENTIAL

Israeli Standard Time is two hours ahead of Greenwich Mean Time, 7 hours ahead of Eastern Standard and 8 hours ahead of Central Standard time. Flying time, non-stop to Tel Aviv from N.Y., is about 11 hours. The time goes surprisingly fast as you enjoy dinner, watch a movie and sleep a bit. You will be served breakfast and a snack before landing.

TOUR GUIDE AND BUS DRIVER

We will be met at the airport in Tel Aviv by our Israeli guide. He/she and your tour host will work together to make your visit an unforgettable experience. Guides are licensed by the Israeli government and are considered to be among the best in the world. They are trained in both Old & New Testament background as well as the geography, sociology, art, history, archaeology and culture of the land. You will develop a rapport with your guide and he will respond to individual and group needs. Your guide has the final authority on the bus. Feel free to ask questions. ***Do as the guide directs! Stay with the group! Listen when the guide is talking!!***

YOUR RESPONSIBILITY

Keep up with the schedule, keep track of your own belongings, ***Be On Time!*** Much valuable time can be lost by one person being late for the bus each morning. Generally, the bus tour begins at 8 A.M. You are welcome to be creative and choose to do optional things. But let the tour host know what you are doing and where to find you. You **must** be on the bus on time on the days we are traveling between cities.

SHOPPING

Israel provides you with a wide range of shopping experiences. The Ministry of Tourism symbol (spies carrying grapes) indicates that the shop has been certified by the government. This means you have someone to whom you can address complaints if you feel you've been cheated. Of course, bargaining is a tradition and your own skill will dictate the final price. In the "shuk" (Old City market) you usually pay 30-50% less than the asking price. If you don't get your price at one shop try the next. Olive wood, ceramics, glass from Hebron, jewelry, handicrafts, leather-wear and carpets are things to look for. Save your sales slips to receive refunds on VAT (value added tax). If you pay in U.S. currency, you are sometimes exempt from local taxes. VAT refunds are only given on purchases exceeding $100 from one store, and from a store that is certified. They will give you the proper receipt. Check with your tour host for current rules, these change often due to security concerns.

FOOD

Leave your American tastes at home and adventure a bit. Israeli breakfast is great! Just don't be surprised to see a salad bar-type spread for breakfast. Remember, kosher rules allow no ham or bacon and meat and milk cannot be served together. This means no coffee cream except at breakfast. (Non-dairy creamer may be provided). Water is safe and fruits and vegetables are available and delicious. Be sure to wash fruit carefully if you buy it on the street. You may want to bring packets of instant coffee from home, also sweetener and other things you enjoy, but don't bring fresh fruits or vegetables, stick to packaged snacks.

COMMUNICATION WITH HOME

Before departure you will receive a list of the hotels in which you will be staying and their phone numbers. It is easy to dial direct to Israel – numbers will be provided. Your travel agency will also assist your family in contacting you if an emergency should arise at home. Mail is rather slow, post cards in particular often arrive home after you do. It is good to type a list of names and addresses of those you wish to write to on sticky mailing labels and have them ready to stick on cards or letters. Remember, U.S. postage won't work outside of the USA. We will help you buy stamps in Israel.

LANGUAGE

Almost everyone speaks English so Israel is easy on American visitors. You will have to listen a bit more carefully, accents differ. (Our American accents are not necessarily "right," they are merely the ones we are familiar with.) Try to master some of the Hebrew phrases we have given in the book. Israelis will appreciate your efforts and correct your pronunciation. Be sensitive to Arab shop keepers who say "Salaam" rather than "Shalom." If in doubt about whether you are speaking to a Jew or an Arab, just say, "Hi!".

HEAD COVERINGS

Coverings are not required for ladies, you may do as your own tradition indicates. Men must wear a head covering in synagogues and Jewish holy sites. These are almost always provided at the sites. (The small cloth or paper skull cap is called a *yarmulke* in Yiddish and a *keyppah* in Hebrew.) Women must cover legs and upper arms at holy places. It is useful to take a light-weight shawl or sweater along. Everyone must remove shoes before entering a Moslem mosque.

TELEPHONES

Cell phones may be rented, check with your tour host for current details. Also check with your cell provider for their rules on overseas use.

TAXIS

Taxis abound in Israel. They can be hailed in the street or found outside the hotels. Ask the driver to turn on the meter. Meters are sometimes inside the glove compartment so ask to see it, if in doubt. There is also a large taxi called a *sheroot*. These charge a fixed rate. Ask the rate to your destination before entering cab.

EXTRAS

Beverages are usually not included with meals except with breakfast. Ask your tour host what the arrangements are for this tour. Extras will be charged to your room. Any charges for food, laundry, phone or beverages should be paid directly to the hotel before you check out.

TIPPING

Your tour cost includes a 15% service charge. You may wish to leave a dollar or so per day for the room maid if you are staying in the hotel for more than two days. If you are on a group tour tips for guides, drivers, dining room staff and bell persons are usually pre-paid. Ask your tour host. Generally tips are included in your final billing.

LAST MINUTE THOUGHTS

Zip-lock bags have 1001 uses, bring a bunch along. Also **super glue** which fixes many various breakdowns. (We've used it on everything from glasses to teeth!) Scotch tape, small screwdriver, extra toothbrush, nail polish for runs in nylons and anything else you might find useful. Duct tape is also useful for repairing torn luggage.

BIBLE READINGS

The Gospels, Genesis, Joshua, 1 & 2 Samuel, 1 & 2 Kings and Zechariah 12-14 will help refresh your memory on places you will be seeing. Pray for direction in your reading.

WARS AND RUMORS OF WAR

Media reports often exaggerate and misinterpret the situation in Israel. Your tour hosts have made many trips to Israel and have friends living in the land. We can assure you that Israel takes very good care of her tourists. Since God's Word says that "Jerusalem is a burdensome stone" we can expect some unrest in the region as history moves forward. But tourists often come expecting anxiety and are amazed at the measure of peace and the sense of God's presence they feel. Pray through Psalm 91 with your family and lay fears aside. (You can almost depend on some unsettling news just before you leave for Israel – if you feel led to go, don't let anyone discourage you.) Obey the instructions, give thanks for Israeli security procedures, and ENJOY, ENJOY!

*"Hey, Moses,
we gotta get this group to wear their name tags!"*

Apply for your passport early, always carry it with you while in transit!

Choose luggage that you can handle easily.
Pack prescriptions & necessary items in your carry-on bag. It must fit in overhead or under seat.
Currently only 3 oz bottles of liquids that will fit in a 1 quart zip lock bag may be carried on.

| Temperature Chart | | | | | | | | | | | |
	Jan	Feb	Mar	Apr	May	Jun	Jul	Aug	Sep	Oct	Nov	Dec
Jerusalem	42-50	43-57	47-60	53-69	59-77	63-81	65-83	65-85	64-81	60-77	54-66	46-56
Tel Aviv	48-64	47-65	51-68	54-72	63-77	66-82	69-86	71-86	68-88	59-83	54-76	47-66
Haifa	45-63	47-64	46-70	54-77	58-76	63-81	68-85	70-86	67-85	59-81	55-73	48-64
Tiberias	48-64	48-67	51-72	55-80	62-89	68-94	73-97	74-98	70-95	65-89	58-78	53-68
Safed	37-49	40-51	42-55	48-65	58-76	61-81	65-84	65-85	61-81	58-75	53-66	43-53
Eilat	49-70	51-73	56-79	62-87	69-94	75-98	77-103	78-103	74-97	68-91	60-82	51-74
Sedom	52-68	55-71	60-77	72-89	73-92	84-99	83-102	84-101	81-96	74-89	65-80	56-71

Introduction to Reference Section

We have divided the references into three sections:

• **Bible References**, which includes lists of various biblical passages relating to Israel and two pages of prayer guidelines and suggestions.

• **Israel History References**, a collection of timelines and maps which will help you to place the sites we will be visiting in their historical context.

• **Jewish Customs & Holidays Section,** charts and background information about the Jewish Bible, information about the calendar, the feasts, customs, symbols and ritual objects.

We are always in the process of adding and reorganizing this material. It is not intended to be an exhaustive presentation of Jewish history and customs. It is just an effort to give our pilgrims a bit of background and some "hooks on which to hang the history."

New books keep appearing each time we go to print. You have a limited amount of time to read before the trip begins. We would suggest the following books & films as good choices for pre-tour reading, bearing in mind that there are thousands of other great choices.

Hammond's Atlas of Bible Lands, Edited by Harry T. Frank, Hammond Inc., Maplewood, NJ, 1990

The Bible Then and Now, Rose Publishing

With Jesus in Jerusalem & **With Jesus in Galilee**, Fr. Bargil Pixner, Corazin Publishing 1996

Biblical Archaeological Review, BAR (magazine)

This is My God, The Jewish Way of Life, Herman Wouk, Doubleday & Co., Inc., Garden City, NY, 317 pages

My Heart Is a Violin, Shony Alex Braun & Emily Cavins

The Case for Israel, Alan Dershowitz, John Wiley & Sons, 2003

God in Search of Man (or anything by this author), Rabbi Abraham Joshua Heschel, Farrar, Straus and Giroux, 1976

Israel, A History, Sir Martin Gilbert, Morrow, 1998 (He has authored many historical map books and books of Jewish history, all good)

Why the Jews, The Reason for Antisemitism, Dennis Prager & Joseph Telushkin, Simon & Shuster, 1983

Biographies of various Israeli leaders are available and are very helpful in understanding the early years of Israel.

Films:

Masada

Exodus (Return of Jews to Israel after WWII)

Cast a Giant Shadow (War of Independence)

Weapons of the Spirit (Holocaust rescue in France)

The Chosen (insights on Orthodox Judaism)

Israel Inside

Welcome to a field of learning that will last a lifetime and will yield wonderful fruit!

References For Biblical Sites In Israel

LOD — Lydda – location of modern airport

I Chronicles 8:12	Built by sons of Benjamin
Ezra 2:33	Restored after Babylonian captivity
Acts 9:32-45	Peter healed Aeneas & went from there to Joppa where Dorcas was raised

TEL AVIV

Nehemiah 6:2	Modern city built on Biblical site of Plain of Ono

YARKON RIVER Biblical boundary of tribe of Dan

JAFFA — Joppa or Yafo; name either from "yafe" beautiful, or"Yephet," Noah's son

II Chronicles 2:16	Hiram sent timber from Lebanon to Jerusalem via Jaffa to build Temple
Jonah 1:3	Where Jonah set sail for Tarshish
Ezra 3:7	Port during time of restoration
Acts 9:36	Home of Dorcas (Tabitha)
Acts 10:5	Where Peter was praying when Cornelius called for him

CAESAREA MARITIME

Began as small port; built by Phoenicians – 3rd century BCE

Rose to greatness under Herod; named for Caesar Augustus

Acts 8:40	Philip preached there
9:30	Paul rescued & sent to Tarsus
10:17	Conversion of Cornelius, first Gentile believer
12:19-23	Death of Herod
18:22	Paul greeted church & went to Antioch
21:8	Paul's visits
24:1-25	Paul's trial before Felix
25:1-12	Paul's trial before Festus
26	Paul's hearing before King Agrippa

SHARON PLAIN

I Chronicles 27:29	King David's herds pastured in Sharon
Isaiah 33:9	Like a desert in time of judgment
Isaiah 35:2	Majestic when God restores
Isaiah 65:10	Pasture for flocks
Song of Sol 2:1	Rose of Sharon

NETANYA — Built in 1928, named for Nathan Strauss, American philanthropist

I Kings 4:10	Emek Hefer at time of Solomon

HADERA — Young town; established 1891, at dawn of modern Zionism

Psalm 126:5	Emblem of the city – picture of citrus Reference – Biblical fruit & words: "They that sow in tears shall reap in joy." In territory of Manasseh

CARMEL RANGE

Vineyard of God, Kerem El, Valley of Zebulun

Amos 9:3	No place to hide from God, even on Carmel
I Kings 18-19	Elijah and the prophets of Baal
Song of Solomon 7:5	Head is like Carmel

HAIFA — Israel's main port and 3rd largest city; center of industry and technology; not mentioned in Bible, first mention in 3rd century Talmudic literature; name may be contraction of "Hof Yafe" (beautiful coast)

KISHON RIVER At the foot of Carmel

Judges 4:7,13	Battle of Deborah & Barak vs Sisera
Judges 5:21	Deborah's song of victory
I Kings 18:40	Elijah killed prophets of Baal at Kishon

ACCO — Also spelled Akko & Acre. Greeks and Romans called it Ptolemais, after Ptolemy II Philadelphus, King of Egypt, who ruled and fortified Acco in 261 BCE. Main Crusader seaport in 1100 CE. Napoleon defeated there in 1799. In 1165, the great Jewish philosopher, Maimonides, landed there on his way to Jerusalem. During British Mandate period, the Citadel served as the central prison of Palestine. Many Zionist underground fighters were executed there.

Acts 21:7	Paul visited brethren on journey from Tyre to Caesarea

JEZREEL VALLEY

Also called Esdraelon; in Hebrew, Emek Israel; largest valley in Israel; name means: God sowed

Joshua 17:16	Tribal area of Ephraim & Manasseh

Judges 6:33	Battle of Gideon with Amalekites & Midianites. Story of the fleece.
I Kings 21	Naboth's vineyard; Elijah vs Ahab
II Kings 9 & 10	Death of Jezebel & Ahab's family
Hosea 2:21-23	The Lord's response as He restores His people

MEGIDDO — Mentioned in ancient Egyptian writings of 1478 BCE. Strategic location at opening of a narrow pass on the great highway connecting Egypt & Assyria. Derekh Hayam, Via Maris, the way of the sea. In 1918, British successfully invaded through this pass.

Joshua 12:21	One of 31 kings of Joshua's time
Joshua 17:11	Held by Canaanites, tribe of Manasseh not able to occupy; also Judges 1:27
I Kings 9:15 & 10:26	One of Solomon's chariot cities; extensive excavations
II Kings 9:27	Death of Ahaziah, king of Judah
II Chronicles 35:22	Death of King Josiah
Zechariah 12:11	Weeping in Jerusalem
Revelation 16:16	Prophecies of end-time events

MOUNT TABOR — Means "Mt. of Height"– 1700 ft. above sea level; northern edge of Jezreel Valley. Meeting point of 3 tribal areas: Zebulun – west; Issachar – south; Naphtali – north

Judges 4:4-16	Gathering point for Barak's army in battle against Sisera
Psalm 89:12	"...Tabor and Hermon joyously praise Thy name."
Hosea 5:1	God's judgment comes as a net spread upon Tabor
Matthew 17; Mark 9	Transfiguration of Jesus. Exact site is uncertain, scripture doesn't identify. "A high mountain apart." 1st church building erected on summit by Helena in 326 CE. By 7th century there were 3 shrines dedicated to Jesus, Moses & Elijah. All destroyed by Saladin 1187 CE

NAZARETH — Meaning of name uncertain. Settled in prehistoric times, it is first mentioned in the New Testament as the boyhood home of Jesus. The modern town is a trade center and pilgrimage site. Population: 63,700. Until recently it was populated mainly by Arab Christians. Upper Nazareth settled in 1957 by Jewish immigrants.

Luke 1:28-33	Annunciation
Matthew 1:20-21	Angel spoke to Joseph
Luke 2:39	Family returned to Nazareth
Luke 2:51	Jesus subject to parents in Nazareth
Matthew 2:22,23	Called Nazarene
Luke 4:16-22	"The Spirit of the Lord is upon Me" cf. Isaiah 61:1, 2
Luke 4:29	Attempt to throw Him off the hill upon which city was built
Matthew 13:53-58	A prophet not respected in his own house
Matthew 21:11	"It is the prophet Jesus of Nazareth"
Mark 14:67	"You also were with Jesus of Nazareth"
John 19:19	Title on the Cross: "Jesus of Nazareth, King of the Jews"

CANA — Near Gath-hepher, birthplace of Jonah the prophet; also Horns of Hattin

John 2:1-11	Wedding at Cana in Galilee; Jesus' first miracle
John 4:46	Where Jesus was when called to heal the official's son
John 21:2	Home of Nathanael

NAIN — About 2 miles south of Mt. Tabor; meaning: pleasant

Luke 7:11-17	Widow's son raised from the dead

TIBERIAS — About 2000 years old, begun by Herod Antipas on ruins of ancient town of Rakkat. Became seat of great academies of rabbinic learning. Mishna - 200 CE; Jerusalem Talmud - 400 CE; vowels and punctuated Hebrew script originated here. Today is hub and capital of Galilee, 680 ft. below sea level.

John 6:23	Boats from Tiberias

SEA OF GALILEE — Earliest name: Kinneret, meaning *harp* because sea is harp-shaped. Also called Ginosar, Gennesaret and Sea of Tiberias. 690 ft. below sea level, 13 miles long, 8 miles wide at widest point, 32 miles in circumference, 170 ft. deep at deepest point; Jordan River enters at north & flows through to south.

Mark 1:16-20	Call of first disciples
Mark 3:7-9	Jesus taught from Peter's boat

Luke 5:1-11	Miraculous catch of fish
Matthew 8:23-27	Calming of the storm
Matthew 14:22-23	Jesus walks on the water
John 21:1-14	Jesus prepares breakfast on the beach for disciples

MAGDALA — Migdal: Hebrew for tower

Luke 8:2	Mary Magdalene, out of whom went seven demons

TABGHA — Northeastern shore of Sea of Galilee

Mark 4:1-2	Multiplication of loaves and fish cf. Matthew 14:19-21
Mark 6:53	Healing sick
John 21:15ff	To Peter: "Feed My sheep"

MOUNT OF BEATITUDES

Northwestern shore of the Sea of Galilee, near Capernaum

Matthew 5-7	Beatitudes

CAPERNAUM — Village of Nahum. No evidence that this was the Prophet Nahum

Matthew 4:12-17	Move from Nazareth to Capernaum
Mark 1:29-31	Healing of Peter's mother-in-law
Matthew 9:1	His own city
Mark 9:33	Discussion with disciples on "greatness"
Matthew 17:24-27	Tax – shekel in mouth of fish
Luke 5:27-32	Call of Matthew
Matthew 11:20-24	Woe to Chorazin, Bethsaida & Capernaum
Mark 1:21-38	Sermon in the synagogue, man with evil spirit
Mark 3:31-33	Jesus' mother and brothers
Luke 7:1-10	Healing of centurion's servant
John 6:22-40	Discourse on Bread of Life

CHORAZIN & BETHSAIDA

Matthew 4:23	Jesus teaches and heals
Matthew 11:20	Unbelieving towns
Mark 8:22-26	Healing of blind man

ROSH PINNA — Modern town, founded in 1882; 1st settlement in Galilee, name means "chief cornerstone."

Psalm 118:22	The stone which the builders rejected becomes the chief cornerstone

HAZOR — Hebrew for courtyard or enclosure for flocks. Site of Canaanite excavations

Joshua 11:10	Joshua captures, burns the clty

Joshua 19:36	Given to tribe of Naphtali
I Kings 9:13	Strengthened by Solomon
II Kings 15:29	Captured by Tiglath-Pileser, king of Assyria, in days of Pekah
Judges 4:2	Headquarters of Jabin, Canaanite king who fought Deborah & Barak

KIRYAT-SHMONA, TEL-HAI, METULLA

Modern towns & kibbutzim. Eight young people, including Joseph Trumpeldor, were killed in 1920 defending settlement at Tel-Hai. Metulla is gateway to Lebanon.

CAESAREA PHILLIPI - BANIAS - DAN

Genesis 14:14	Abraham pursued the kings to rescue Lot
I Kings 12:26-30	Golden calf at Dan, Jeroboam
Matthew 16:13-23	Peter's confession of Jesus as Messiah
Mark 8:27ff	"Who do men say that I am?" Announcement of coming suffering

GOLAN HEIGHTS — Mountain range rising on north and east of Sea of Galilee and running north to Mt. Hermon

Deuteronomy 4:41-43	Moses separated 3 cities beyond Jordan River; Golan in Bashan was City of Refuge for tribal area of Manasseh

MT. HERMON — Name means prominent, rugged

Deuteronomy 3:8,9	Boundaries of Promised Land
Joshua 11:17	Valley of Lebanon
Psalm 89:12	Tabor & Hermon praise Thy name
Psalm 133:3	As the dew on the mountains of Hermon that descends on the mountains of Zion...

QUNITRA — Syrian border town on road to Damascus

Acts 9:1-19	Paul on road to Damascus
Galatians 1:12-22	Paul's history in area

GADARA — Capital of Perea, east of Jordan River opposite Tiberias

Mark 5:1ff	Man who lived in tombs, out of whom Jesus cast legion of demon; cf. Luke 8:26

EIN GEV — Pioneer kibbutz on east side of Sea; founded in 1937; home of Teddy Kollek, former mayor of Jerusalem; settler's were first Jewish fishermen in modern times to cast nets into the Sea of Galilee

YARDENIT	Baptismal site for Christians prepared by Israeli government on southern end of Galilee, where Jordan Rivers flows south.

South via the Jordan Valley Route

BEIT SHEAN	In tribal area of Manasseh
I Samuel 31:10	Bodies of King Saul & his sons hung on wall by Philistines; his armor put in shrine to Ashtoreth

MT. GILBOA

I Samuel 28:4	Battle of Saul
II Samuel 1:17-24	David's lament over death of Saul & Saul's sons; curse on land

EIN HAROD

Judges 7:7	Spring where Gideon's army was formed

MEROZ

Judges 5:23	Deborah's curse

GILGAL	Joshua's base of operations after Israel crossed the Jordan
Joshua 4:9	God rolled away the reproach of Egypt (Gilgal means "to roll")
Joshua 5:9	1st Passover in Canaan
Joshua 14:6	Allotment of tribal areas
Judges 2:1	God's angel went from Gilgal to Bochim in judgment
I Samuel 11:14	Saul's kingship confirmed
I Samuel 15:12ff	Samuel and Saul parted after Saul's disobedience
II Samuel 19:15, 40	David welcomed back after Absalom's revolt
II Kings 2:1	Elijah & Elisha
Nehemiah 12:29	Gathering place for singers and musicians for dedication of wall

JERICHO	Ancient, warm wintering place for wealthy of Jerusalem
Deuteronomy 34:3	City of palm trees, Moses viewed it from Moab
Joshua 5:13	Joshua & Commander of the Lord's army
Joshua 6	Capture of city
Joshua 6:26 & I Kings 16:34	Curse on Jericho & fulfillment
II Kings 2:19	Elisha purified the spring
Matthew 20:30	Healing of blind man, cf. Luke 18:35
Luke 19:5	Zacchaeus
Matthew 4:1ff	Mt. of Temptation

MA'ALE-ADUMIM

	The Red Ascent; road from Jericho to Jerusalem; marked border of Judah on south and Benjamin on north; large, new Jewish settlement, suburb of Jerusalem
Luke 10:30	Good Samaritan
Leviticus 16:10	Somewhere along this road, the scapegoat was sent on the Day of Atonement

BETHANY	Village on south side of Mt. of Olives (Arabic: el-Azariyeh)
Matthew 26:6-13	Mary anoints Jesus
Luke 10:38-42	Mary & Martha and the choice of the "better part"
John 11:1-44	Resurrection of Lazarus

BETHPHAGE	Beginning of Palm Sunday procession
Luke 19:29-40	Jesus enters Jerusalem

MT. OF OLIVES	Small range of 4 summits, overlooking Jerusalem and Temple Mt from east
II Samuel 15:30	David went up weeping after Absalom's revolt
Ezekiel 11:23	Glory of the Lord in Ezekiel's vision
Zechariah 14:4	Mount will split from east to west when Messiah's feet stand there
Matthew 21:1-16	Palm Sunday
Matthew 26:30ff	Gethsemane cf. Mark 14:26 & Luke 22:39
Luke 22:47	Betrayal & arrest
Luke 24:50	Ascension of Jesus cf. Acts 1:4-12
	(Olivet discourse - Mark 13:3-37; Matt. 24 & 25; Luke 21:5-36 - End-time teaching)

TEMPLE MOUNT	Mount Moriah
Genesis 22:2	Abraham comes to sacrifice Isaac
II Samuel 7:1-17	David desires to build a house for God
II Samuel 24: 18ff	David buys the threshing floor of Araunah (Ornan) the Jebusite cf. I Chron. 21:18
I Kings 5-6	Construction of Solomon's Temple
I Kings 8 & II Chronicles 7	Dedication of the Temple
Isaiah 6:1-8	Isaiah's vision of the Temple
II Kings 11	Murder of Queen Athaliah of Judah outside the Temple
II Kings 12	Restoration under King Joash
II Kings 22	King Josiah, re-discovery of the Law
Ezekiel 8	Vision relating to idolatry

Ezekiel 10:18	Glory of the Lord leaves the Temple
II Kings 25	Destruction of the Temple by Nebuchadnezzar
Ezra 4:24ff	Reconstruction and dedication of Temple, 300 BCE
Deuteronomy 6:4-9	The Sh'ma – "Hear, O Israel"

TEMPLE SACRIFICES

Exodus 29:38	Daily offerings

THE TEMPLE IN THE NEW TESTAMENT

Luke 1:5-25	Birth of John the Baptist
Luke 2:22-38	Presentation of Jesus in the Temple
Luke 2:40	Boy Jesus in the Temple
Luke 4:9ff	Pinnacle - temptation of Jesus
Matthew 21:12-27	Money-changers
John 2:19-21	"Destroy this temple and in three days..."
John 5:19	Man healed at pool of Bethesda
John 7:14ff	Jesus teaches in Temple
John 8:2ff	Woman caught in adultery, the Light of the world, discussions
John 11:45ff	Plot against Jesus
Matthew 12:41	Widow's mite
Matthew 24:1-25	Prophecy of the destruction of the Temple
Matthew 27:3-10	Judas returns 30 pieces of silver
Matthew 27:52	Veil of Temple torn in two
Acts 3	Lame man healed
Acts 21:15ff	Paul in Temple

CITY OF DAVID

II Samuel 5:5-9	Stronghold of Zion captured by David

GIHON SPRING Beginning of Hezekiah's Tunnel

I Kings 1:38,45	Solomon anointed king
II Chronicles 32:30	Hezekiah digs tunnel into city

POOL OF SILOAM

	End of Hezekiah's Tunnel
Isaiah 7:3	Isaiah sent to Ahaz
Isaiah 22:9	"You made a reservoir, but didn't depend on Him who made it..."
John 9:6	Healing of man born blind

ENROGEL

II Samuel 17:15-22	David is warned and escapes

VALLEY OF HINNOM

Stretches from foot of Mount Zion east to Kidron. Called Gei-Hinnom or Gehenna – became synonymous with place of wicked in world to come.

Jeremiah 7:31-33	"They built the high places of Topheth... to burn their sons and daughters, which I did not command."
Mark 9:42	Offense to little ones
Matthew 27:7-10	Field of the potter
Acts 1:19	Field of blood - judgment on Judas

GALLICANTU Church of Cock Crowing

John 18:15-27	Peter's Denial

CENACLE Upper Room

Matthew 26:26-35	Institution of the Lord's Supper; cf. Mark 14:22; Luke 22:9; I Corinthians 11
John 20:19ff	Jesus appears to the disciples
Acts 1:12ff	Disciple's first prayer meeting
Acts 2:1-4	Pentecost, cf Acts 1:4 - Holy Spirit often appears when we, with one mind, devote ourselves to prayer

VIA DOLOROSA

The Way of the Cross. Begins at Ecce Homo Convent, ends at Church of Holy Sepulchre. (Whether this or the Garden Tomb is the actual burial place of Jesus, is uncertain. The Garden Tomb has a more satisfying atmosphere. The important thing is that Jesus is not in either place, He is Risen!)

Read the accounts of the Passion and Resurrection in the four Gospels.

BETHESDA St. Anne's Church

John 5:1-18	Healing of man crippled for 38 years

KIDRON VALLEY

	Valley between Temple Mount & Mount of Olives
II Samuel 18:18	Absalom's Pillar
II Chronicles 24:20	Zechariah's tomb
Joel 4:1-2	Valley of Jehoshaphat

MOUNT ZION

Refers to larger area than mount of that name today; sometimes refers to the whole city of Jerusalem.

Psalm 9:11-14	Sing praise to God who dwells in Zion
Psalm 48	Beautiful for situation, joy of the whole earth
Psalm 125	Those who trust in the Lord are as

	Mount Zion, which cannot be moved
Psalm 132:13	The Lord has chosen Zion for His habitation
Psalm 133	Dew of Mount Hermon comes down upon mountains of Zion
Psalm 137	Remembrance of Zion in Babylon
Micah 4:7	Lord will make outcasts a strong nation & reign over them in Zion
Hebrews 12:22	Heavenly Jerusalem

HILL OF EVIL COUNSEL

II Kings 11:7	Where Solomon's wives sacrificed to false gods (Today is location of U.N. headquarters)
Matthew 27:3-5	Traditional place of the suicide of Judas Iscariot

BETHLEHEM

Genesis 35:16-20	Death & burial of Rachel
Judges 17:7-13	Country of the Levite, servant of Micah
Book of Ruth	History of Ruth, Boaz & line of David
I Samuel 16	David anointed king by Samuel
II Samuel 23:14	Occupied by Philistines
II Chronicles 11:6	Fortified by Rehoboam
Micah 5:1ff	Prophecy of Messiah's birth
Luke 2:1-5	Birth of Jesus
Matthew 2:1-18	Bethlehem, voice heard in Rama...
Matthew 2:16	Herod's massacre of baby boys in Bethlehem
Luke 2:8-21	Shepherd's field – Beit Sahour

TEKOA
Site of modern settlement

II Samuel 14:2ff	Joab, woman, David & return of Absalom
Amos 1:2	Birthplace of prophet Amos

HEBRON
Kiryat Arba during time of Patriarchs; 1st portion of Promised Land

Genesis 13:18	Abram settled at the oaks of Mamre & built an altar to the Lord
Genesis 18:1-18	Lord appeared to him and the three men announced the birth of Isaac
Genesis 23:2	Death of Sarah
Genesis 23:9ff	Purchase of Cave of Machpelah
Genesis 25:8	Death of Abraham
Genesis 35:27	Meeting of Isaac & Jacob
Genesis 50:13	Death & burial of Jacob

Numbers 13:22	Visit of spies sent by Moses
Joshua 20:7	City of Refuge
Judges 1:10-15	Caleb's claim to the territory
II Samuel 2:1-11	David's capital of Judah for 7-1/2 years
II Samuel 15:7-10	Absalom's revolt (II Sam 3:3 - birthplace of Absalom)

BEERSHEVA
Well of the Oath or Well of the Seven Ewe Lambs

Genesis 21:25-33	Covenant between Abraham & Abimelech; planting of tamarisk tree
Genesis 26:23-25	Isaac renews covenant and builds an altar to the Lord
Genesis 46:1-5	The Lord calls Jacob to go to Egypt
Genesis 21:14ff	Hagar & Ishmael; God hears
I Samuel 8:2	Sons of Samuel judges in Beer-sheva
I Kings 19:1-8	Elijah takes refuge there
II Kings 23:8	Destruction of high places by Josi-ah
Nehemiah 11:25ff	Occupied by Israel after the exile

ARAD

Numbers 21:1-2	Battle against the Canaanite
Joshua 12:14	One of 31 kings defeated by Joshua
Judges 1:16	Descendants of Kenites lived south of Arad

MASADA
Not mentioned in the Bible, but dates to NT time, built by Herod; last stand of Zealots; destroyed by Romans 70 CE

EIN GEDI
Spring of the Kid, shore of Dead Sea

I Samuel 21:29	David's hiding place when pursued by Saul
I Samuel 24	David spares Saul's life
Song of Solomon	1:14 Beloved as a cluster of blossoms in vineyards of Ein Gedi
Ezekiel 47:8-12	Healing of waters of Dead Sea

QUMRAN
Location of caves where Dead Sea Scrolls were found

SODOM & GOMORRAH

Genesis 13:10-13	Separation between Abram & Lot – Lot moves to Sodom
Genesis 18:20-33	Abraham's intercession
Genesis 19	God destroys the cities and rescues Lot

EILAT

Deuteronomy 2:8	Path to the Promised Land
I Kings 9:10	Solomon's fleet of ships at Etzion-Geber, near Eilat on Red Sea
I Kings 22:48	Jehoshaphat's ships

MOUNT SINAI — Mountain between gulfs of Suez & Aqaba, 3 large peaks

Exodus 3:1	Moses & Jethro
Exodus 19	Israel camped before the mountain
Exodus 20	10 Commandments
Exodus 24	Glory of the Lord upon the mountain
Exodus 34	2nd set of tablets
Psalm 68:8,17	Lord is among us, as at Sinai
Galatians 4:21ff	Allegory
Hebrews 12:18ff	2 covenants

GAZA STRIP - PHILISTINE TERRITORY
Cities of Gaza, Gath, Ekron, Ashdod, Ashkelon

Joshua 10:41	Joshua's victory
Joshua 11:22	Anakim left in Gaza only
Joshua 13:3	Five lords of the Philistines
Joshua 15:45-47	Cities allotted to the tribe of Judah
Judges 16:21	Samson imprisoned & blinded
Amos 1:7	Amos prophecies defeat of Gaza
Zephaniah 2:4	Woe upon all residents
Acts 8:26	Philip & Ethiopian

VALLEY OF ELAH — Between Socoh & Azekah

I Samuel 17:2	Battle of David & Goliath

EIN KEREM

Luke 1:39, 80	Possible birthplace of John the Baptist

North From Jerusalem via the Hills of Samaria

GIBEAH — Saul's capital, King Hussein of Jordan started to build a hotel on this site before Six-Day War interrupted

I Samuel 10:26	Valiant men joined Saul
I Samuel 14:16	Saul's watchmen

GIBEON

Joshua 9:3ff	Strategy of Gibeonites
II Samuel 21:1-7	Revenge of Gibeonites in David's time
I Kings 3:5	Solomon prays for wisdom

RAMALLAH — Hill of God - I Samuel 10:5,6

BETHEL — House of God

Genesis 28:12-18	Jacob's dream
Genesis 35:14	Set up pillar

SHILOH

Joshua 18:1	First center of worship in Promised Land; dividing of tribes
Joshua 22:12	Misunderstanding with tribes of Reuben, Gad & Manasseh
Judges 18:31	Location of House of God
Judges 21	Wives for the tribe of Benjamin
I Samuel 3:21	Lord reveals Himself to Samuel
I Samuel 4:20	Death of Eli, the High Priest
I Kings 14:4	Prophet Ahijah and Jeroboam
Jeremiah 7:12	I will do as I have done to Shiloh

LEBONA

Judges 21:19	Benjaminites looked for wives; between Bethel & Shechem

MOUNT GERIZIM & MOUNT EBAL

Deuteronomy 11:29	Moses commands reading of blessings & curses
Deuteronomy 27:13	Repeats command
Joshua 8:30ff	Joshua obeys Moses' command, divides tribes, blessings read on Gerizim, curses on Ebal; altar of sacrifice built on Ebal
John 4:4-40	Woman at well of Samaria

SHECHEM — In Roman times called Neapolis (new city; Now called Nablus; Levitical city of Refuge

Genesis 12:6,7	Abram came to the land, to the Oak of Moreh; God spoke to him
Genesis 37:12ff	Joseph & brothers pastured flocks near Shechem
Joshua 24:1	Joshua gathered tribes
Joshua 24:32	Bones of Joseph buried there
Judges 9	Jotham's parable
I Kings 12	Division between Jeroboam & Rehoboam
I Kings 12:25ff	Jeroboam set up false altars & substitute feasts
Psalm 60:6	God's authority over area cf. Psalm 108:7
Jeremiah 41:4	Murder of Gedaliah

TIRZAH — First capital of Northern Kingdom

Joshua 12:24	One of 31 kings defeated by Joshua
1 Kings 16:8-11	Murder of King Elah by servant Zimri

DOTHAN — City of Manasseh, near Mount

	Gilboa
Genesis 37:17	When brothers conspired to sell Joseph
II Kings 6:13ff	Elisha, Syrians and vision of spiritual support system

JENIN   Ein Gannim, Spring of the Gardens

Joshua 19:20	Tribal area of Issachar
Joshua 21:29	Levitical city
Luke 17:11-19	Possible site of healing of lepers

The Biblical area of Judea and Samaria is mainly in the area often called "The West Bank." Most of the events recorded in the Bible took place there.

From Jerusalem to the airport at Lod...

NEPHTOAH   Stream N.W. of Jerusalem

Joshua 15:9	Tribe of Judah

MOTSA   Tribe of Benjamin; called Mozah

Joshua 18:26

BROOK OF SOREK

Judges 13-16	Stream runs from this area to near Ashkelon; Samson & Delilah story

KIRYAT YEARIM   Abu Ghosh, City of forests; 8 miles west of Jerusalem

Joshua 9:17	Tribal area
I Samuel 6:21	Philistines return Ark
I Samuel 7:1,2	Ark lodged there 20 years
I Chronicles 13-15	Return of Ark to Jerusalem

EMMAUS   Several possible sites

Luke 24:13-31	Disciples on road meet Jesus

VALLEY OF AYALON   Scene of many battles

Joshua 10:11ff	Sun stood still at Joshua's bidding

GEZER

Joshua 10:33	Ancient city of Canaan whose king Horam was slain by Joshua; town marks boundary of Ephraim on western limit of the tribe; allotted to Kohath, sometimes called Gimzo.
I Kings 9:15	One of Solomon's 3 chariot cities
I Chronicles 20:4	War with Philistines

SHA'ALVIM

Joshua 19:42	Shaalabbin, a town in Dan's inheritance
II Samuel 23:32	Birthplace of one of David's mighty men

SCRIPTURES REGARDING GOD'S COVENANT WITH ISRAEL

1. Gen. 12:1-3 First promise to Abraham (Abram at the time), 'I will bless those who bless you and the one who curses you I will curse.'

2. Gen. 15:1-21 Second promise to Abraham. The land from River of Egypt to Euphrates given to Abraham. Includes promise of a son and many descendants, prophesy of captivity in Egypt, promise of the land.

 Gen. 16:12 Ishmael's descendants described: "...a wild donkey of a man, his hand against every man, and every man's hand against him."

3. Gen. 17:1-21 Third promise to Abraham. Covenant of circumcision. Verse 8: promise of land as an everlasting possession.

4. Gen. 18:10-19 Fourth promise to Abraham. Birth of Isaac promised in a year. Renewal of promise of descendants becoming mighty nation.

5. Gen. 22:16-18 Fifth promise to Abraham. After God tested him by requiring the sacrifice of Isaac, God again promises many descendants. Promise includes descendants possessing the gates of Abraham's enemies and the blessing of all nations through Abraham's seed.

6. Gen. 26:2-4, 24 God's promises to Abraham repeated by God to Isaac.

7. Gen. 27:28-29 God's promises passed by Isaac to Jacob, includes 'Cursed be those who curse you, and Blessed be those who bless you.'

8. Gen. 28:13-15 God renews his promises directly to Jacob including the promise of the land.

9. Gen. 32:24-29 Jacob wrestles with what is described as a man and God changes his name to Israel.

10. Gen. 35:9-12 God again calls Jacob Israel and again renews the promises given to Abraham and Isaac.

11. Gen. 46:2-4 God reassures Israel telling him not to be afraid to go to Egypt and join Joseph. Promises to make him a great nation while in Egypt.

12. Ex. 3:2-17 The burning bush. Moses is promised that God will deliver the people from Egypt to a land flowing with milk and honey.

13. Ex. 6:8 God promises Moses to bring the people to the land promised to Abraham.

14. Ex. 23:20-31 God explains how he will deliver the land to the people of Israel and names the boundaries.

15. Lev. 26:1-13 Blessings God will bestow on Israel for obedience.

16. Lev. 26:14-39 Penalties for disobedience. Includes being driven from the land and scattered among the nations.

17. Lev. 26:40-45 God's promise not to reject Israel even in disobedience and his promise to remember his covenant with Abraham, Isaac and Jacob.

18. Num. 34:1-12 God gives specific boundaries for the apportioning of the promised land among the tribes.

19. Num. 4:26-28 Moses warns of disobedience. Tells Israel they will quickly perish from the land for disobedience.

20. Num. 4:29-31 Moses reaffirms that God will not forget his covenant even in the face of Israel's disobedience.

21. Deut. 11:1-32 Rewards for obedience to God recounted. Note: verse 21 where the land is described as being given to Israel for 'as long as the heavens remain above the earth.'

22. Deut. 28:1-68 Blessings for obedience and consequences of disobedience given in fearsome detail. Includes prophesies of Israel's captivities.

23. Deut. 30:1-6 Promise of restoration to the land after captivity.

24. Deut. 32:8-9 God set the boundaries of the nations based on His relationship with Israel.

25. Josh. 1:1-6 Promise to Joshua to deliver the land to Israel, includes boundaries.

26. 1Kg. 9:6-9 God promises Solomon that Israel will be cut off from the land for disobedience.

27. Ps. 102:13-16 "Thou shalt arise, and have mercy upon Zion, for the time to favor her, yea, the set time has come. When the Lord shall build up Zion, He shall appear in His glory."

28. Isa. 11:10-12 One scattering, one regathering. A second scattering (70 AD/CE) and second regathering now in process. Verse 12 - 'He will assemble the scattered people of Judah from the four quarters of the earth.'

29. Isa. 35:1 'The desert shall rejoice and blossom as the rose.' The theme of the restoration of the Negev.

30. Isa. 49:14-26 God promises the land (Zion) that He will return His people to it after their captivity and scattering among the nations. Note verse 25 'for I will contend with him who contends with you.'

31. Isa. 54:1-17 God promises Israel never will be forsaken. Note particularly verses 10 and 17. (Verse

17 ... 'no weapon that is formed against you shall prosper...')

32. Isa. 62:1-12 God again promises full restoration of Israel.

33. Isa. 66:5-10 Prophecy of a land 'born in one day,' a nation 'brought forth in a moment.' Literally fulfilled May 14, 1948. An event like this has never happened in all of history involving any other people. Note: also God's statement concerning his following through on a thing he once sets in motion.

34. Jer. 3:17 Jerusalem to be the throne of the Lord, and all nations shall gather to it.

35. Jer. 16:14-16 First exodus was from Egypt, second (still in process) from ends of earth. Verse 16, fishers and hunters sent to find the people of Israel.

36. Jer. 18:1-7 God's dealings with Israel compared to potter's work on wheel. Pressure forms the pattern the potter desires. Out of the pressure, Israel to be saved and restored.

37. Jer. 30:7 Time of Jacob's trouble, Israel shall be saved out of time of great distress.

38. Jer. 31:35-40 God promises to never cast off the offspring of Israel for any reason, but they shall remain a nation before him 'throughout the ages.' Includes prophecy of rebuilding of Jerusalem with details as to borders.

39. Eze. 36:1-38 RECOMMEND THOROUGH AND CAREFUL READING! God commands Ezekiel to prophesy to the mountains of Israel concerning the restoration of the land and of the people. Note His reason. He twice says that He will do this NOT for their sake, but for His Holy Name's sake.

40. Eze. 37:1-28 The 'dry bones' prophecy concerning the regathering of Israel to the land. (At Masada 2000-yr-old scroll found containing this text.)

41. Eze. 38:8-12 God tells Gog that he will 'come into the land that is restored from the sword, whose inhabitants have been gathered from many nations to the mountains of Israel which had been a continual waste'... 'and they are living securely,'

42. Joel 3:1-2 God's judgment on all nations for their treatment of His people, Israel. Specifically for 'dividing up His land.'

43. Amos 9:14 'I will bring back my exiled people Israel; they will rebuild the ruined cities and live in them. They will plant vineyards and drink their wine; they will make gardens and eat their fruit. I will plant Israel in their own land, never again to be uprooted from the land I have given them,' says the Lord your God.

44. Oba. 1:18-21 Lands that will be possessed by the children of Israel.

45. Zeph 2:4-10 More lands to be possessed by the children of Israel. Note especially verse 10, 'because they have taunted and boasted against the people of the Lord of hosts.'

46. Zech. 2:14-17 God is jealous for Jerusalem and Zion. And angry with the nations that 'added to the calamity of Israel.'

47. Zech. 8:1-8 God again tells of his restoration of the fortunes of Israel.

48. Zech. 10:5-10 More of the restoration. Note the reference to the might of the fighters of Israel. We have seen much of this come to pass in our time.

49. Zech. 12:1-9 Prophesy of the turmoil among nations to be caused by the existence of the nation of Israel, and of the destruction of all nations who come against her.

50. Luke 2:30 'For my eyes have seen your salvation, which you have prepared in the sight of all people, a light for revelation to the Gentiles and for glory to your people Israel.' The child's father and mother marveled at what was said about him. Then Simeon blessed them and said to Mary, his mother: 'This child is destined to cause the falling and rising of many in Israel.'

51. Luke 21:24 Jesus says, 'Jerusalem shall be trodden under foot by the gentiles UNTIL the time of the gentiles is fulfilled.

52. Acts 1:6-8 In answer to disciple's question about restoration of Israel Jesus does not say it will not occur. He indicates a timing element: 'It is not for you to know the times of the seasons, which the Father hath put in His own power. But you shall receive power, after that the Holy Ghost is come upon you: and you shall be witnesses unto Me both in Jerusalem, and in all Judea, and in Samaria, and unto the uttermost part of the earth.'

53. Acts 15:13-16 'Simeon hath declared how God at the first did visit the Gentiles, to take out of them a people for His name. And to this agree the words of the prophets; as it is written, After this I will return, and will build again the tabernacle of David, which is fallen down; and I will build again the ruins thereof, and I will set it up.'

54. Acts 17:26 God has determined the location for all nations beginning with Israel. If Israel is not rightly placed, other nations are out of order, and there is disorder in the world. There will be no real peace in the world until the world is reconciled to Israel and Israel is properly reconciled both to its land and to God who gave them the land.

55. Rom 11:1-32 Paul forcefully puts down the notion that God has rejected Israel, states that they have been temporarily blinded for the sake of the salvation of the Gentiles. Verses 17-21 talks of the Gentiles being grafted into the olive tree that is Israel. Note also verse 18 where he speaks of refraining from arrogance toward the Jews because of present unbelief, and verses 23 and 24 where he speaks of the Jews being grafted back in again, more easily than the Gentiles.

AN OBSERVATION:

While only a few of the preceding references deal with God's blessing those who bless Israel and cursing those who curse Israel, it is interesting to note that no great nation or empire has long survived its opposition to Israel.

Egypt went into decline almost immediately after the Exodus and has never regained a fraction of its former glory. Babylon was destroyed after their captivity of the Jews. The empires that arose after Alexander also faded away after conquering Israel. Rome was in its heyday until it destroyed Jerusalem in 70 A.D., later, Rome itself was destroyed. Great Britain had an empire on which the sun never set until it opposed the return of the Jews to their homeland. The Soviet Union was an empire feared throughout the world, that also persecuted the Jewish people and opposed Israel. The Soviet Union is no more.

Finally, it should be noted that this particular promise is given by God with no conditions of any kind attached to it. In other words, whoever opposes or curses Israel or the Jewish people, regardless of the justification, God will oppose or curse, and whoever blesses Israel, deserved or not, God will bless. This does not mean that God does not judge and discipline His chosen people. But it should serve as a warning to non-Jews who often in history have thought they were called as God's arm of judgment.

Promises To Israel

THE WORD OF GOD

Psalm 18:30
> As for God, His way is perfect, the word of the Lord is flawless.

Isaiah 40:8
> The grass withers, and the flowers fall, but the word of our God stands forever.

THE PROMISES OF GOD
> The Holy Scriptures contain hundreds of prophecies about Israel and the Jewish People. Although written thousands of years ago, many prophecies have been fulfilled since 1948 in the State of Israel.

Psalm 121:4

Behold, He that keepeth Israel shall neither slumber nor sleep.

Deuteronomy 7:6

For you are a people holy to the Lord your God. The Lord your God has chosen you out of all the peoples on the face of the earth to be His people, His treasured possession.

Genesis 12:3

I will bless those who bless you and whoever curses you I will curse; and all the people on earth will be blessed through you.

Isaiah 60:12

For the nation that will not serve you will perish; it will be utterly ruined.

GOD'S COVENANT

Genesis 12:1-2

The Lord said to Abram, "Leave your country, your people and your father's household and go to the land I will show you. I will make you into a great nation and I will bless you; I will make your name great, and you will be a blessing."

Genesis 13:14-15

And the Lord said to Abram, after Lot had separated from him, "now lift up your eyes and look from the place where you are, northward and southward and eastward and westward; for all the land which you see, I will give it to you and to your descendants forever."

Genesis 15:18

On that day the Lord made a covenant with Abram saying, "To your descendants I have given this land, from the river of Egypt as far as the great river, the river Euphrates."

Genesis 17:8

And God said, "The whole land of Canaan, where you are now an alien, I will give as an everlasting possession to you and your descendants after you, and I will be their God."

Genesis 17:20-21

And God said to Abraham, "And as for Ishmael, I have heard you; I will surely bless him; I will make him fruitful and will greatly increase his numbers. He will be the father of 12 rulers, and I will make him into a great nation, But my covenant I will establish with Isaac, whom Sarah will bear to you by this time next year."

Genesis 16:12

The angel of the Lord spoke to Hagar before the birth of Ishmael, "He will be a wild donkey of a man; his hand will be against everyone and everyone's hand against him, and he will live in hostility toward all his brothers."

DIASPORA

Deuteronomy 28:64

The Lord will scatter you among all nations, from one end of the earth to the other.

REGATHERING

Deuteronomy 30:3-4

Then the Lord your God will restore your fortunes and have compassion on you and gather you again from all the nations where He scattered you. Even if you have been banished to the most distant land under the heavens, from there the Lord your God will gather you and bring you back.

Isaiah 43:5-6

"Do not be afraid for I am with you; I will bring your children from the east and gather you from the west. I will say to the north, give them up; and to the south, do not hold them back; bring my sons from afar and my daughters from the ends of the earth."

Ezekiel 11:17

"I will gather you from the nations and bring you back from the countries where you have been scattered, and I will give you back the land of Israel again."

Ezekiel 34:13

"And I will bring them out from the people and gather them from the countries and bring them to their own land."

Isaiah 11:12

He will assemble the scattered people of Judah from the four quarters of the earth.

SURVIVAL

Psalm 124:1-3

Let us now say, Had it not been the Lord who was on our side when men rose up against us, then they would have swallowed us alive, when their anger was kindled against us.

Jeremiah 31:11

For the Lord will ransom Jacob and redeem them from the hand of those stronger than they.

RESTORATION

Ezekiel 36:34-35

The desolate land will be cultivated instead of lying desolate in the sight of all who pass through it. They will say, "This land that was laid waste has become like the garden of Eden; the cities that were lying in ruins, desolate and destroyed are now fortified and inhabited."

Isaiah 49:11

"I will turn all my mountains into roads and my highways will be raised up. See, they will come from afar, some from the north, some from the west."

Ezekiel 36:30

"And I will multiply the fruit of the tree and the produce of the field, that you may not receive again the disgrace of famine among the nations."

Isaiah 43:19

"Behold I will do a new thing; now it shall spring forth; shall you not know it? I will even make a way in the wilderness and rivers in the desert . . . to give drink to my people, my chosen."

Isaiah 35:1

The desert shall rejoice and blossom as the rose.

Isaiah 41:18

"I will make rivers flow on barren heights, and springs within the valleys. I will turn the desert into pools of water and the parched ground into springs."

Jeremiah 31:12

They will come and shout for joy on the heights of Zion; they will rejoice in the bounty of the Lord – the grain, the new wine and the oil, the young of the flocks and herds. They will be like a well-watered garden, and they will sorrow no more.

Isaiah 61:5

And strangers shall stand and feed your flocks, and the sons of the alien shall be your plowmen and your vinedressers.

Isaiah 41:20

"I will set pines in the wasteland, the fir and the cypress together, so that the people may see and know, may consider and understand that the hand of the Lord has done this, that the Holy One of Israel has created it."

Amos 9:14

"I will bring back my exiled people Israel; they will rebuild the ruined cities and live in them. They will plant vineyards and drink their wine; they will make gardens and eat their fruit. I will plant Israel in their own land, never again to be uprooted from the land I have given them," says the Lord your God.

Nahum 2:4

The chariots storm through the streets, rushing back and forth through the squares. They look like flaming torches, they dart about like lightning.

JERUSALEM

Zechariah 8:8

"I will bring them back to live in Jerusalem; they will be my people and I will be faithful and righteous to them as their God."

Isaiah 65:18-19

"But be glad and rejoice in what I will create, for I will create Jerusalem to be a delight and its people a joy. I will rejoice over Jerusalem and take delight in my people; the sound of weeping and of crying will be heard in it no more."

Psalm 128:5-6

May the Lord bless you from Zion all the days of your life; may you see the prosperity of Jerusalem and may you live to see your children's children. Peace be upon Israel.

Isaiah 62:6-7

"I have posted watchmen on your walls, O Jerusalem, they will never be silent day or night. You who call on the Lord, give yourselves no rest and give Him no rest until He establishes Jerusalem, and makes her the praise of the earth."

LEBANON
Isaiah 29:17-21

In a very short time, will not Lebanon be turned into a fertile field and the fertile field seem like a forest? In that day the deaf will hear the words of the scroll, and out of gloom and darkness the eyes of the blind will see. Once more the humble will rejoice in the Lord; the needy will rejoice in the Holy One of Israel. The ruthless will vanish, the mockers will disappear, and all who have an eye for evil will be cut down.

WHY AND HOW TO PRAY FOR ISRAEL?

Because Christians owe a great debt to the Jewish people. From them we have received the prophets, the apostles, the Bible, the Messiah and salvation.

Because there is a divine purpose through them of bringing world-wide blessing. Through them God will work out His plan of redemption.

Because Israel is loved by the Father in heaven. Romans 9:10-11, Jeremiah 31, Isaiah 62, Isaiah 40, Psalm 135:4.

Because, according to the Abrahamic covenant, God will treat us as we treat the Jewish people. Genesis 12:3

Because "Now is the time to favor Zion...the set time has come." Psalm 102:13

Because we are to "speak tenderly to Jerusalem" and "comfort God's people" Isaiah 40:1.

BEFORE YOU BEGIN, REMEMBER . . .

Intercession is warfare; sometimes there may be casualties. The warfare requires teamwork, enabling us to cover one another. Put on the whole armor of God.

Be single-minded. Meet specifically to pray for Israel and the Jewish people.

The real "battle for Israel" is between principalities and powers in the heavenlies. The spirit behind Islam is one of the strongest opponents. This is not a spirit to be casually challenged.

Praying for Israel is not an option; it is a command. Psalm 122:6 does not refer to spiritual Jerusalem only, and there is certainly no need to pray for peace in the heavenly Jerusalem!

True intercession is far more than pleading with God as though we were trying to get Him to do something He is unwilling to do. It is rather His project of getting us to the place where we understand His will and can speak it into reality. This requires intimacy with God.

Only when we are prepared to lay down our lives – spirit, soul, and body – can we become real intercessors.

When you begin to pray seriously and regularly for Israel, the Jewish people and related issues, you become a "watchman on the walls," Isaiah 62. The 2400 years separating you from Nehemiah fade into insignificance and you become part of a noble procession of God's faithful ones who have prayed, fasted and wept over those ancient walls.

Though the walls surrounding Jerusalem today are not the same ones Nehemiah walked on, the city is still in the same place and the concerns on the heart of God and His intercessors have not changed much either. God still wants to rebuild and restore both His city and His people that His Word might go forth from Jerusalem and His glory might be seen there.

Become familiar with the scriptures dealing with Israel and God's purposes for her. The end-time references in Ezekiel, Daniel, Zechariah, Joel, Matthew 24, Mark 13, Luke 21, and Revelation are especially significant.

Become familiar with current issues as they concern the areas you are praying about:

- Judea & Samaria – the West Bank
- U.S. support of Israel
- Jews remaining in Eastern Europe and the former Soviet Union
- Antisemitism and the Church
- Islam
- Spiritual renewal in Israel

Remember, we are to watch, keep alert and be vigilant according to scripture. We are not to be unaware and uninformed. The enemy has always been aware of Israel's significance and has inspired pharaohs, kings and fuhrers with satanic hatred, believing that wiping out the Jewish people as a nation could thwart God's plan for planet earth. You may come up against strong opposition. Count the cost! We believe, however, that God's benefits to prayer warriors will far outweigh the enemy's assaults.

The most repeated promise in the Bible is the restoration of Israel – it is a subject of much importance to God.

There is a link between Israel and the Church. God deals in a similar manner with both of His covenant people – often at the same time.

Jesus, for Christians, the greatest Jew of all, forsook all divine privileges to become a servant of the House of Israel – by His life and His death. God has constituted the Church to be His body, His instrument of action and mercy on earth – having ourselves tasted God's mercy, we are bidden to be merciful.

Hebrews 11 gives an account of some of the Jewish martyrs who laid down their lives for our sake. God is calling us now to be ready to repay that debt, to stand in the gap for Israel.

One of the leading causes of the Holocaust was the deafening silence of the church worldwide. That silence still exists. Unless the Christian voices are heard, the ignorance among Christians and non-Christians alike will continue.

Although God calls Zion "the apple of His eye," in the world's eyes Zion is called "an outcast for whom no one cares," Jeremiah 30:17.

We must not sit on the fence at this time of history but rather stand together with the Lord for His people.

How to Pray for Israel

"Pray for the peace of Jerusalem: May those who love you be secure. May there be peace within your walls and security within your citadels." – Psalm 122:6-7

In this day no prayer is more important than prayer for Jerusalem; no place, closer to God's heart. Within the answer to our prayers for Jerusalem's peace is the salvation and the healing of the nations.

The following brief outline is only a suggested beginning to prayer for Jerusalem and Israel. As we obey God's command to pray for the City of David, He enlarges our understanding of its position and importance through scripture. He then also opens our eyes to new excursions in prayer for this chosen city and nation.

HOW TO PRAY FOR JERUSALEM

1. Pray specifically. The following items are examples for general areas of prayer. Keep abreast of current events and pray for each new situation in as much detail as possible.

2. Read your Bible and pray those scriptures relating to Israel's well-being. Isaiah 62:6,7 exhorts us to do this.

3. Pray in song and praise – Use the Psalms as examples. Some are Psalm 84, 122, 128, 129, 132, 133, 134, 147, 148, 149. Note David's praise in II Samuel 6 and remember prayers for Jerusalem are prayers for the dwelling place of the Lord.

4. Pray in intercession – take Israel's burdens and lift them up to the Lord. Receive the administration of God's grace personally for yourself to pray for Israel. Allow God to use you as an inter-

cessor. (To understand this role better, read Lamentations and Daniel.)

WHY PRAY FOR JERUSALEM?

1. God tells us to! (Psalm 122:6)

2. We are called to be watchmen. (Isaiah 62:6-7) "You who call upon the Lord, give yourselves no rest, and give Him no rest till He establishes Jerusalem and makes her a praise in the earth."

WHAT TO PRAY FOR JERUSALEM

ITS PEACE – Pray for:

1. Security for those who love Jerusalem, in whose hearts Jerusalem holds a special place: Their welfare, their health, their families, their homes, their businesses, their enterprises, their activities so they will be free and at peace to pray for Jerusalem.

2. Those who support Israel financially. (There are many Jews and Gentiles who buy Israeli bonds and support Israeli charitable causes. They need rich blessings from God in order to continue their support.)

3. The internal affairs of the city. Honest and fair dealings among its citizens. No cheating, lying, stealing. That evil forces would be kept from the city. The city's government to have the mind of God in its administration in accordance with God's laws; no oppressive laws or taxes on the people. Adequate food and water supplies. Proper maintenance of city services and utilities.

4. Defenses – Protect Israel from specific enemies, (Hamas, Hezbollah, hostile Arab nations) and from attacks on Jerusalem; request angelic protection over the city. Strengthen the defenders. Keep radar and other communications equipment in efficient operating order. Give citizens eyes and ears to perceive possible attacks or other terrorist tactics. Encourage the men and women on patrol around the city, specifically for Jerusalem, but also for Israel in general, especially those isolated settlements of Judea and Samaria. Bless the nations that support Jerusalem as Israel's capital. (Remember the Jebusites in I Chronicles. 11:4.)

ITS PROSPERITY – Pray for:

1. Trade and commerce. Israeli industries to thrive. The days of the citrus groves are gone, modern Israel is a major producer of high tech and medical devices. But tourism is still a major income producer. Pray for increased tourist trade and God's protection over all tourists.

2. Economy. That Israel, financially speaking, will become the head and not the tail; that she will lend to many nations and not borrow (Deuteronomy. 28:12-13). That the many other financial blessings of Deuteronomy. 28:1-14 would come to her.

3. That she would return to her former glory as under David and Solomon's reign (I Kings 10 is a good example of Israel's wealth).

ITS PEOPLE – Pray for:

1. The President and Prime Minister. God promises, "their governors shall proceed from the midst of them and I will cause him to draw near, and he shall approach unto me" (Jeremiah 30:21). "I will make the governors of Judah like a hearth fire...and they shall devour all the enemies round about..."(Zechariah 12:6).

2. Safety. For the security and welfare of the Jewish people everywhere, especially those in Iran, Syria, Russia and places where their security and safety is questionable.

3. Aliyah (Return). That Jews wishing to return to their historical homeland will find no hindrances. Pray especially for those from Ethiopia, Russia and Syria.

CHRISTIAN ACTIVITY IN ISRAEL

1. Pray for Christians in Israel that they might have a spirit of meekness toward the Jews and not boast against the natural branches. Romans 11:20. Pray that the voices of those truly called of God would be heard in the land.

2. Pray against false theology and theories that would discredit Israel's place in God's current plan. This includes the *Replacement theology*, *Supersessionism* and various similar beliefs.

3. Pray for Arab Christians, both those who are friendly to Israel and those who aren't. Pray that all will see the value of living in peaceful relationship.

4. Pray for organizations that seek to build Christian-Jewish relations. Pray for harmony as each one fulfills their own unique calling.

Reference Section
History – Timelines

Time-Line of Events in Jewish, Christian & Muslim History

Note: BCE: before the common era, BC: before Christ, CE: common era, AD: Anno Domini, the year of our Lord

Archaeological Periods

Neolithic	c. 5000 BCE
Chalcolithic	c. 4000
Early Bronze I	c. 3150
Early Bronze II	c. 2850
Early Bronze III	c. 2600
Early Bronze IV	c. 2300
Middle Bronze I	c. 2150
Middle Bronze IIA	c. 2000
Middle Bronze IIB	c. 1750
Late Bronze I	c. 1550
Late Bronze IIA	c. 1400
Late Bronze IIB	c. 1300
Iron Age - Israelite period	c. 1200

The Dawn of History as we know it (Sumer, Egypt) c. 3000 BCE

Early Dynastic period (Akkad)	c. 2800
Old Kingdom period (Egypt)	c. 2700-2400
Ebla flourishes	c. 2500-2200

World of Ancient Israel c. 2000-587 BCE

Middle Kingdom period (Egypt)	2100-1780
Old Babylonian period c.	2000-1750
Israel's Patriarchal period	c. 2000-1700
Abraham, Isaac & Ishmael	c. 1850/1750/1700
Old Assyrian period	c. 1900-1400
Hammurabi	c. 1792-1750
Hittite empire	c. 1750-1200
Hyksos in Egypt	c. 1700-1550
Kassite period (Babylonia)	c. 1600-1150
New Kingdom period (Egypt)	c. l570-1085
Ugaritic texts	c. 1500-1200
Middle Assyrian period	c. 1400-900
Amarna period (Egypt)	c. 1400-1300
Mosaic period (Israel);	c. 1300-1200
Exodus from Egypt & Canaan Entry	c. 1250-1200
Sea Peoples invade Egypt and Syro-Palestine	c. 1200
Period of the Judges	c. 1200-1050/1000
Middle Babylonian period	c. 1150-900
Hebrew prophets (Samuel-Malachi)	c. 1050-450
Monarchical period in Israel	c. 1000-587
Saul (transitional king)	c. 1030-1010
David - made Jerusalem his capital	c. 1010-970
Solomon - building of the Temple	c. 970-931

Split between Israel & Judah	c. 931
Neo-Assyrian period	900-612
Israelite Prophets Amos, Hosea, Isaiah	750-725
Northern Kingdom (Israel) destroyed	722/721
Neo-Babylonian period	612-538
Josiah (Judean King)	620
Judean Prophets Jeremiah and Ezekiel	c. 600-580
Southern Kingdom (Judah) and Temple destroyed – Babylonian exile	587/586

Judaism after Babylonian Exile c. 538 BCE-70 CE

Persian Period	538-333
Edict of Cyrus (first return from Exile)	538
Jerusalem Temple rebuilt	520-515
Judean Prophet Haggai	520
Reformation led by Ezra and Nehemiah	450-400
Torah (Pentateuch recognized as Scripture)	c. 450

Hellenistic (Greek) period 333-63

Alexander the Great	333/331
Judaism under Ptolemies & Seleucids	c. 320-168
Septuagint translation of Torah into Greek	c. 250
Rome comes to Mediterranean world	c. 230-146
Prophets Nevi'im (2nd division of Jewish Scriptures) recognized as Scripture	c. 200
Qumran community	c. 200 BCE-135 CE
Maccabean revolt & Hasmonean rule	168/167-63 BCE
Rome (Pompey) annexes Palestine	63 BCE
Rule of Rome	c. 146 BCE-400 CE
Herod the Great	37-4 BCE
Hillel & Shammai (Jewish sages)	turn of the era
Rome establishes rule in Judea	6 CE
Jesus	before 4 BCE-c. 30 CE
Gamaliel I (Jewish leader-scholar)	c. 40 CE
Paul, the apostle	36-64 CE
Josephus (Jewish historian)	c. 37-100 CE
Christian Testament (NT) writings	c. 50-125 CE

Early Christian Period 30-311 CE

Talmudic Development 70-400/600 CE

First Jewish Revolt against Rome	66-73
Destruction of Jerusalem & 2nd Temple	70
Jewish center for study at Yavneh (Yohanan ben Zakkai)	c. 73
Gamaliel II excludes sectarians from synagogues	c. 90-100

Writings Ketuvim (3rd & last division of Jewish Scriptures) accepted as sacred scripture c. 90-150

Jewish Revolts vs Rome outside Palestine 114-117

Akiba consolidates Rabbinic Judaism 120-135

Bar Kokhba rebellion (Second Jewish Revolt) Jerusalem renamed, Jews forbidden 132-135

Mishnah compiled/edited under Judah the Prince c. 200

Persecution of Christianity by Rome to 311

Origen (Christian scholar) 200-254

Babylonian Jewish Academy at Sura c. 220

Babylonian Jews flourish under Persians c. 250

Early development of Christian monasticism in Egypt 250-330

Eusebius (Christian author, historian) 263-339

Christian persecution by Emperor Diocletian 303

Emperor Constantine embraces Christianity 312/313

Classical Christianity **325-1517**

First Ecumenical Church Council, at Nicea 325

Jerusalem Christian construction under Constantine, Helena 330

Jerome c. 325-420

Augustine 354-430

Christianity becomes religion of Roman Empire 380/391

Palestinian Talmud edited c. 400

Babylonian Talmud edited c. 400-600

Rome sacked by Visigoths 410

Jewish office of Nasi/Prince abolished by Rome 425

Christian Ecumenical Council of Chalcedon 451

Medieval Period in the West **c. 600-1500**

Growth of Muhammad's Message **610-1258**

Muhammad (the Prophet of Islam) c. 570-632

Prophetic call & start of Koranic revelations c. 610

The hijra (emigration) from Mecca to Medina 622

Mecca becomes capital of Islam 630

Pope Gregory the Great 590-604

Period of Jewish Rabbinic Geonim c. 600-1300

The 4 "rightly guided caliphs" of Islam 632-661

Jewish return to Jerusalem under Islam 638

Assassination of Ali (last of the four) 661

Umayyad Dynasty of Islam in Damascus 661-750

Muslim Attacks on Constantinople 669, 674

Muslim Forces Successfully Attack Spain 711

Islam repulsed at Tours, gateway to Europe 732

Karaism (reaction to Rabbinic Judaism) c. 760

Charlemagne (Holy Roman Empire) 742-814

Abbasid Dynasty - Baghdad

(Golden Age of Islamic culture) 750-1258

Caliph Harun al-Rashid rules c. 800

Translation of Greek learning into Arabic c. 825

Shiite Movement begins 874

Continuation of Umayyad rule in Spain to 12th century

Saadia Gaon (Rabbinic Jewish sage) 882-942

Golden Age in Spain (Umayyad dynasty) c. 950-1150

Founding of Cairo by the Shiite Fatimid dynasty in Egypt 969

Avicenna - Muslim Platonist philosopher ??-1037

Final split of Latin (Roman) and Greek (Byzantine) Churches 1053/54

Norman conquest of England 1066

Rashi (Rabbi Solomon ben Isaac) 1040-1105

Crusades 1095-1291

Crusaders capture Jerusalem 1099

Judah Halevi (Jewish author) 1085-1140

Bernard of Clairvaux (Christian mystic) 1090-1153

Averroes; Muslim Aristotelian philosopher ??-1198

Maimonides (Rabbi Moses ben Maimon) 1135-1204

Saladin (1138-1193) overthrows Fatimid dynasty in Egypt 1171

Saladin recaptures Jerusalem from Crusaders 1187

Francis of Assisi c. 1181-1226

Pope Innocent III 1198-1216

The Zohar (Jewish Kabala) c. 13th century

Death of Genghis Khan 1227

Spanish Inquisition c. 1230

Thomas Aquinas 1225-1274

Mamluk Islamic rule in Egypt 1254-1517

Fall of Islamic Abbasid dynasty to Mongols 1258

Rebuilding of Political Islam 1258-1500

Expulsion of Jews from England 1290/1291

Expulsion of Christian Crusaders from Syria 1291

Italian Renaissance 1300-1517

Expulsions of Jews from France 1306-1394

John Wycliffe 1328-1384

Rise of the Ottoman Muslim dynasty in Turkey 14th century

Tamurlane, Turkic ruler in central Asia 1336-1405

Damascus sacked by Tamurlane 1400

Fall of Constantinople to Ottomans 1453

Gutenberg Bible printed (invention of printing press) 1456

Expulsion of Muslim Moors from Spain 1492

Expulsion of Jews from Spain, Portugal	1492, 1496
Islamic Dominance as far East as India	c. 1500-1920
Reformation and Post-Reformation Christian Period	1517-present
Jewish Transition towards Modernity	c.1550-1700
Ottoman Muslim Empire in Turkey	1500-1920
Victory of (Ottoman) Selim I over Egypt	1517
Suleiman I, the Magnificent, rules	1520-1566
Safavid Shiite Muslim dynasty in Iran	c. 1500-1800
Mughal Muslim dynasty in India	c. 1500-1800
Protestant Christian Reformation	c. 1500-1650
Martin Luther	1483-1546
Luther posts 95 theses in Wittenburg	1517
Luther preaches against Jews	1542-1546
Thomas Cranmer	1489-1556
William Tyndale	c. 1494-1536
John Calvin	1509-1564
Jewish ghettos instituted (Venice, Rome)	1516, 1555
Shulhan Aruk (code of Jewish law)	1567/1571
Rene Descartes	1596-1650
Christian Puritans to America	1620
Shabbatai Zvi (Jewish "messianic" leader)	1626-1676
Arrival of Jews in New Amsterdam	1654
Jews readmitted to England by Oliver Cromwell	1655
Jews expelled from Vienna	1670

Toward Modern Period   c.1700-present

Israel Baal Shem Tov (founder of Jewish Hasidism)	1700-1760
John and Charles Wesley	1703-1791 & 1707-1788
Wahhabi "fundamentalist" movement arises in Islam	c. 1750
Moses Mendelssohn (Jewish "enlightenment" scholar)	1729-1786
Napoleon (France)	1769-1821
American Revolution; religious freedom guaranteed	1775-1781
French Revolution	1789
French Jews given citizenship	1790-1791
Napoleon, battle of the Pyramids in Egypt	1798
Muslim Wahhabis capture Mecca & Medinah	1801-1804
Rise of Jewish Reform movement in Europe	mid-19th century
American Civil War	1861-1865
Ghettos abolished in Italy	1870

Reform Judaism in US establishes Union of American Hebrew Congregations	1873
Mass migrations of eastern European Jews	1881
French occupation of Muslim Tunisia	1881
British occupation of Muslim Egypt	1882
Reform Jewish Pittsburg Platform	1885
Founding of Conservative Judaism, in US (Solomon Schechter)	1886
Theodore Herzl publishes *The Jewish State*	1896
First Jewish Zionist congress	1897
Founding of the Modern Jewish Orthodox movement	early 20th century
Revolution by "young Turks" under Ottomans	1908
Tel Aviv founded as Hebrew-speaking Jewish city	1909
World War I	1914-1918

20th Century Realignment in the Middle East   c. 1914-present

Beginning of Arab revolt against Ottoman Turkish rule	1916
British capture Baghdad	1917
Balfour Declaration favors Jewish National home	1917
Damascus taken by T.E. Lawrence and Arabs	1918
Egyptian revolution	1919
Kingdoms of Iraq and Jordan established	1921
Overthrow of Ottoman Muslim rule by "young Turks" (Kemal Ataturk)	1923
Caliphate officially abolished	1924
Pahlevi dynasty in Persia/Iran	1925-1979
Kingdom of Saudi Arabia established	1932
Adolph Hitler becomes Chancellor of Germany	1933
Jewish rights in Germany rescinded by Nuremberg laws	1935
Reform Jewish Platform (Zionism, etc.)	1937
Kristallnacht - German synagogues burned	9 Nov 1938

World War II   1939-1945

The Nazi Holocaust against Jews	1933-1945
Partition of India and Pakistan	1947
Israeli Declaration of Independence	1948
Libya proclaims independence	1952
Egyptian republic under Nassar	1953-54
Sudan & Tunisia independence, Pakistan Republic	1956
United Arabic Republic established	1958
Founding of the Jewish Reconstructionist movement; Mordecai Kaplan)	1960s
Six Days War reunites Jerusalem	

under Israeli control	1967	Oslo Agreement	1993
Yom Kippur War in Israel	1973	Israeli-Jordanian treaty	1994
President Sadat of Egypt visits Jerusalem	1977	Oslo Accords	Sept. 28, 1995
Camp David Peace Treaty	1979	Nov. 4, Yitzak Rabin assassinated	1995
Knesset votes Jerusalem as the undivided capital of Israel	1980	Benjamin Netanyahu elected Prime Minister	1996
		Ehud Barak elected Prime Minister	1999
Intifada - Palestinian uprising	1987-1993	Ariel Sharon elected Prime Minister	2001
Gulf War	1991	Ehud Olmert replaced ailing Sharon	2005
Madrid Peace Conference	1991		

The Time of Abraham

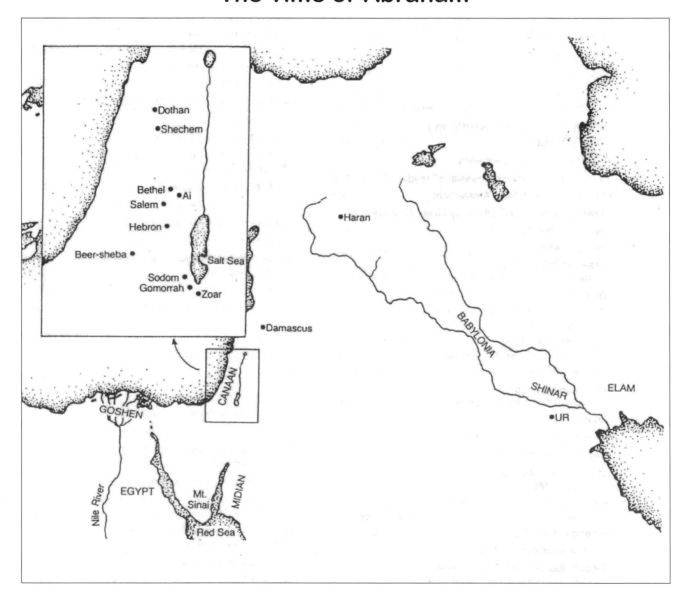

The Bible Visual Resource Book, Copyright 1989, Regal Books, Ventura, CA 93009, Used by permission

Map of the Exodus

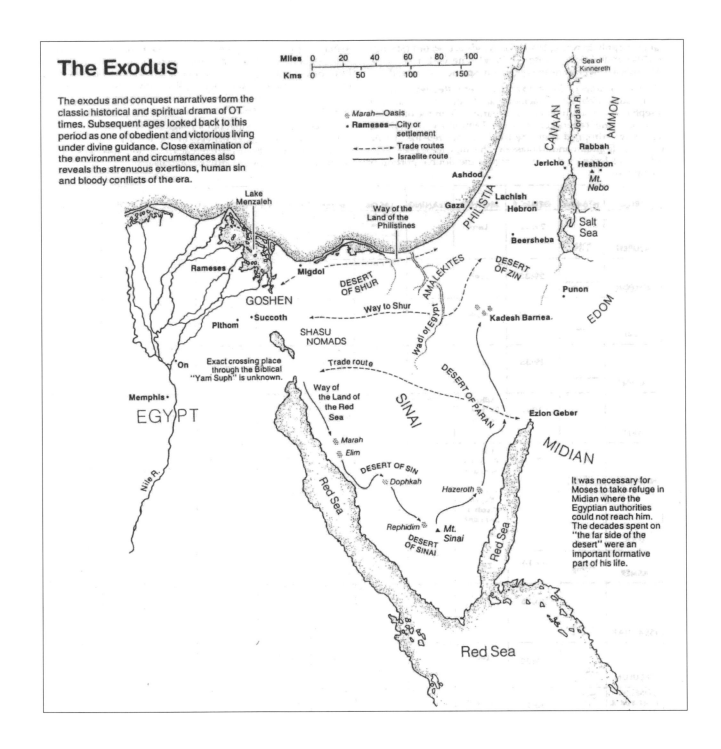

The Exodus

The exodus and conquest narratives form the classic historical and spiritual drama of OT times. Subsequent ages looked back to this period as one of obedient and victorious living under divine guidance. Close examination of the environment and circumstances also reveals the strenuous exertions, human sin and bloody conflicts of the era.

Miles 0 20 40 60 80 100

Kms 0 50 100 150

✧ Marah—Oasis
• Rameses—City or settlement
- - - → Trade routes
——→ Israelite route

Sea of Kinnereth

CANAAN

Jordan R.

AMMON

Rabbah

Jericho · Heshbon
▲ Mt. Nebo

Ashdod

PHILISTIA

Lachish

Gaza

Hebron

Salt Sea

Way of the Land of the Philistines

Beersheba

Lake Menzaleh

Rameses

Migdol

DESERT OF SHUR

AMALEKITES

DESERT OF ZIN

Punon

GOSHEN

Way to Shur

Wadi of Egypt

Kadesh Barnea.

EDOM

Succoth

Pithom

SHASU NOMADS

On

Exact crossing place through the Biblical "Yam Suph" is unknown.

Trade route

Way of the Land of the Red Sea

DESERT OF PARAN

Ezion Geber

Memphis

EGYPT

SINAI

MIDIAN

Nile R.

Red Sea

✧ Marah
✧ Elim

DESERT OF SIN

✧ Dophkah

Hazeroth ✧

Rephidim ▲ Mt. Sinai

DESERT OF SINAI

Red Sea

It was necessary for Moses to take refuge in Midian where the Egyptian authorities could not reach him. The decades spent on "the far side of the desert" were an important formative part of his life.

Red Sea

The Bible Visual Resource Book, Copyright 1989, Regal Books, Ventura, CA 93009, Used by permission

The Tribes Of Israel

In the Bible the word "tribe" usually refers to the 12 tribes of Israel, the sons of Jacob. Two Hebrew words are used for tribe, seemingly interchangeably. Both mean rod, staff or scepter and probably first referred to a chief leading with a rod. The word came to apply to whole tribe. The words are: *matteh* (Strong's # 4294) and *shebet* (Strong's # 7626). The verb form *natah* (Strong's # 5186) means to stretch out, spread out, extend.

The twelve sons of Jacob (Yaacov) were: Reuben, Simeon, Levi, Judah, Zebulun, Issachar, Dan, Gad, Asher, Naphtali, Joseph and Benjamin. Levi was separated from the others for service in the Tabernacle and the Temple (Num. 1:47-53). Joseph was dropped from the tribal list but replaced by his two sons, Ephraim and Manasseh. This may have been a fulfillment of Joseph's dream, receiving the double portion of the first son.

The tribes of Reuben, Gad and half of Manasseh were settled on the east side of the Jordan (Num. 32:33). Joshua 15-19 records the settlement of the other tribes on the west of the Jordan. The borders of Benjamin and Zebulun are carefully defined. The others list the cities, but the borders are not so clear. Benjamin, Judah and Simeon were in the south, as was Dan, before moving north. Ephraim and half of Manasseh were in the hill country north of Benjamin. The other four were north of the Jezreel Valley with Asher on the coast and Naphtali by the Kinneret.

The tribes were united in one kingdom through the reign of Solomon. After the division under Rehoboam and Jereboam the northern 10 tribes were headquartered at Tirzah and later Samaria. Judah was always headquartered at Jerusalem.

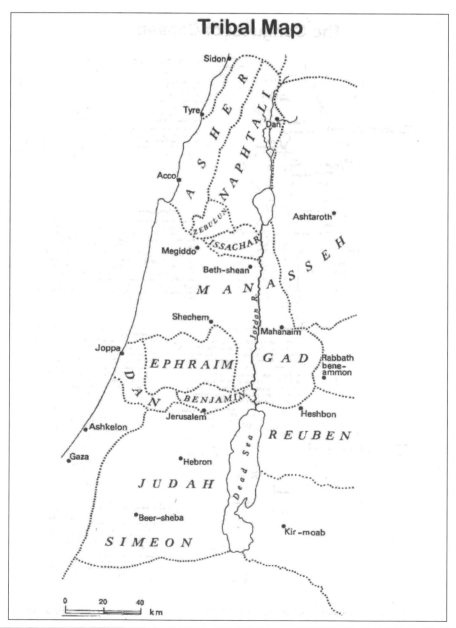

Tribal Map

Tribal Chart

TRIBE	HEBREW	GENESIS	MOTHER	MEANING	JACOB	MOSES	DEBORAH	FULFILLMENT	MEMBERS	STONE	LOCATION
REUBEN		29:32	LEAH	BEHOLD, A SON	GEN 49:3, FIRST-BORN, POWERFUL, BUT UNSTABLE, SHALL NOT EXCEL	DT 33:6, LET HIM LIVE & LET NOT HIS MEN BE FEW	JDG 5:16, TARRIED IN SHEEPFOLD, BUT SEARCHED HEARTS	LOST RIGHTS AS FIRST-BORN, NEVER CAME TO LEADERSHIP		SARDIS	EAST OF JORDAN, NEAR DEAD SEA
SIMEON		29:33	LEAH	HEARING	GEN 49:7, VIOLENT, TO BE DIVIDED & SCATTERED	NO MENTION, ABSORBED IN JUDAH	NO MENTION	SMALLEST TRIBE, NUM 26		TOPAZ	CENTRAL NEGEV
LEVI		29:34	LEAH	JOINED	GEN 49:7, SAME AS SIMEON	DT 33:8-11, HAD PRIESTLY TEACHING ROLE	NO MENTION	SCATTERED OCCUPIED PRIESTLY CITIES	MOSES, AARON, ELI, SAMUEL, JEREMIAH, EZEKIEL, EZRA, JOHN	CARBUNCLE	NO TERRITORY
JUDAH		29:35	LEAH	PRAISE	GEN 49:8, PRAISED BY BROTHERS, SCEPTRE NOT TO DEPART	DT 33:7, PRAYER FOR GOD'S HELP	NO MENTION	FROM DAVID'S TIME, LARGEST & IN LEADERSHIP	OTHNIEL, ACHAN, DAVID, SOLOMON, JESUS	EMERALD	NORTHERN NEGEV
DAN		30:6	BILHAH, LEAH'S SERVANT	JUDGE	GEN 49:16, JUDGE HIS PEOPLE, SERPENT WHO BITES ENEMY	DT 33:22, LION'S WHELP, LEAPS FROM BASHAN	JDG 5:17, DID NOT HELP DEBORAH, STAYED WITH SHIPS	BOTH JUDGE & ATTACKER	SAMSON	SAPPHIRE	SOUTH OF JAFFA, THEN NORTHERN GALILEE
NAPHTALI		30:8	BILHAH, LEAH'S SERVANT	WRESTLE	GEN 49:21, HIND LET LOOSE, BEARS GOODLY FAWNS	DT 33:23, FULL OF GOD'S BLESSING, POSSESS THE SEA	JDG 5:18, HELPED BATTLE ON HGTS	ISA 9:1, MAKE GLORIOUS THE WAY OF THE SEA	BARAK, JUDGES 4	DIAMOND	NORTHERN GALILEE, ALONG KINNERET
GAD		30:11	ZILPAH, LEAH'S SERVANT	FORTUNE, SEER, ARMY	GEN 49:19, RAIDERS OVER-COME HIM BUT HE RAIDS THEM	DT 33:20, BLESSED WARRIOR, EXECUTED GOD'S DECREE	JDG 5:17, CALLED GILEAD, DID NOT SUPPORT DEBORAH	GOD'S HISTORY FILLED WITH WARS		JACINTH, LIGURE	EAST OF JORDAN
ASHER		30:13	ZILPAH, LEAH'S SERVANT	HAPPY	GEN 49:20, RICH FOOD, ROYAL DAINTIES	DT 33:24,25, FAVORED, DIP FOOT IN OIL	JDG 5:17, SAT STILL AT SEA COAST	SETTLED IN FERTILE AREA	ANNA, LUKE 2	AGATE	SOUTHERN & WESTERN GALILEE
ISSACHAR		30:18	LEAH	REWARD	GEN 49:14, SAW LAND WAS GOOD, BECAME SERVANT	DT 33:18, 19, JOINED W/ ZEBULUN, HIDDEN TREASURES OF SAND	JDG 5:15, SUPPORTED DEBORAH, FAITHFUL TO BARAK	MAY HAVE BEEN ENSLAVED BY CANAANITES	DEBORAH, MEN OF ISSACHAR, 1 CHR 13-32	AMETHYST	EASTERN JEZREEL
ZEBULUN		30:20	LEAH	DWELLING	GEN 49:13, SHALL DWELL AT HAVEN OF THE SEA	DT 33:18, REJOICE IN GOING OUT, SEAFARING	JDG 5:18, RISKED LIFE FOR ISRAEL	LOCATED BETWEEN MEDITERRANEAN & GALILEE, TRADERS		BERYL	WESTERN JEZREEL, REACHING TO SEA
JOSEPH, EPHRAIM & MANASSEH		30:24	RACHEL	ADDING, DOUBLE FRUIT, CAUSE TO FORGET	GEN 49:22, FRUITFUL BOUGH, SHOT AT BY ARCHERS, STRENGTHENED BY GOD	DT 33:13-17, GREATLY BLESSED BY GOD	JDG 5:14, EPHRAIM MAIN HELP TO DEBORAH	2 TRIBES; EPHRAIM HOUSED SANCTUARY AT SHEHEM, SYMBOL FOR ALL NORTHERN TRIBES	JOSHUA, GIDEON, JEPHTHAH	ONYX	HIGHLANDS OF SAMARIA, HALF MANASSEH ON EAST OF JORDAN
BENJAMIN		35:18	RACHEL	SON OF RIGHT HAND OR SOUTH	GEN 49:27, RAVENOUS WOLF, DEVOUR IN MORNING, DIVIDE IN EVENING	DT 33:12, BELOVED, SECURE, DWELLS BETWEEN SHOULDERS	JDG 5:14, MARCHED TO BATTLE	MILITARY RENOWN, LIVED IN BUFFER ZONE	EHUD, SAUL, ESTHER, MORDECAI, PAUL	JASPER	NORTH OF JERUSALEM

Israel Study Manual 2012 © JoAnn Magnuson

Five Cities of the Philistines

1. Gaza 2. Ashkelon 3. Ashdod 4. Ekron 5. Gath

Each was a commercial center with important connections reaching as far as Egypt along the coastal plain, the ancient Via Maris. The ships of Phoenicia, Cyprus, Crete and the Aegean called at Philistia's seaports, which included a site today known as Tel Qasila. On the Yarkon River, just north of Tel Aviv, it is today on the grounds of the Eretz Museum on the Tel Aviv University campus. A Philistine temple was discovered there.

The arid, sandy plain borders the desert to the south and the foothills of the plateau of Judah to the east. The western foothills called, the *Shphela*, was the site of many biblical battles.

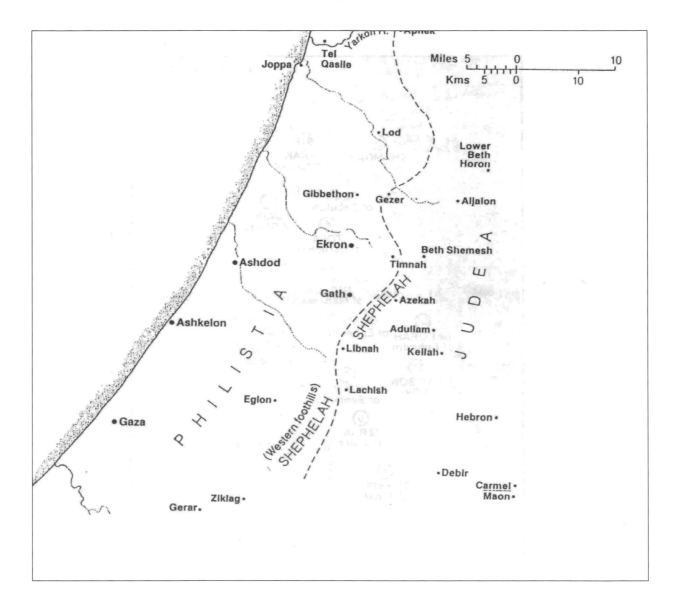

The Bible Visual Resource Book, Copyright 1989, Regal Books, Ventura, CA 93009, Used by permission

Rule of the Judges

1. Othniel of Judah defeated King Cushan of Mesopotamia, who had ruled Israel for 8 years, Judges 3:7-11.
2. Ehud of Benjamin defeated King Eglon of Moab who had ruled for 18 years, Judges 3:12-30.
3. Shamgar defeated the Philistines, Judges 3:31.
4. Deborah & Barak defeated Jabin of Hazor who had ruled Israel "with cruelty and violence for 20 years," Judges 4-5.
5. Gideon drove out the Midianites and Amalekites who had oppressed Israel for 7 years, Judges 6-8.
6. Tola of Issachar, Judges 10:1-2.
7. Jair of Gilead, Judges 10:3-5.
8. Jephthah of Gilead defeated the Ammonites, who had ruled for 18 years, Judges 10:6-12:7.
9. Izban of Judah, Judges 12:8-10.
10. Elon of Zebulun, Judges 12:11-12.
11. Abdon of Ephraim, Judges 12:13-15.
12. Samson of Dan did great exploits against the Philistines, who ruled Israel for 40 years, Judges 13-16.

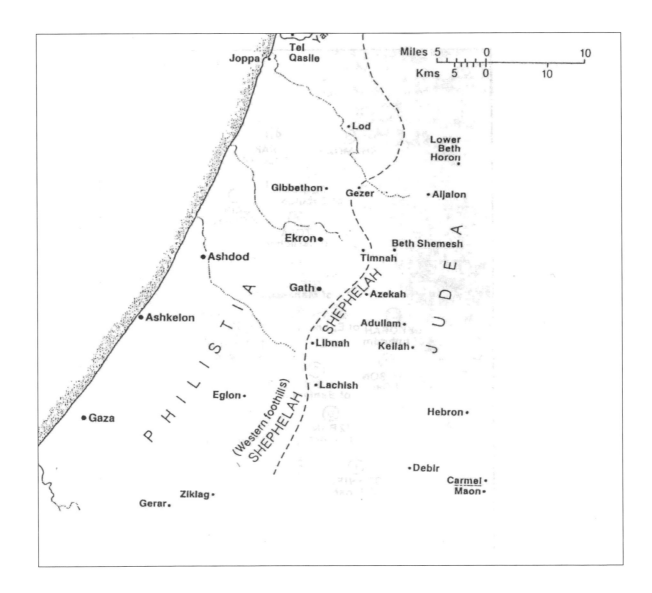

The Bible Visual Resource Book, Copyright 1989, Regal Books, Ventura, CA 93009, Used by permission

Kings of Israel

United Monarchy

SAUL *Asked* (pre-1004 BCE)

The handsome and humble Benjamanite whom the prophet Samuel anointed as Israel's first king, Saul came into his own when he rallied the nation to defend Jabesh. He united the tribes for the first time since Joshua and scored impressive victories over the Philistines and other enemies pressing on Israel's borders. Early achievements were overshadowed by his personal torment and demonic insanity, his clashes with Samuel and his love/hate relationship with David. After a reign of twenty years, he killed himself after being wounded in the battle of Gilboa (1 Sam 9-31; 2 Sam; 1 Chr 5:10; 8:33; 9:39;10; 15:29; 26:28).

DAVID *Beloved* (1004-965)

Anointed king by Samuel when he was a young shepherd boy, David came to the throne at age thirty, after years of running from Saul. A charismatic and brilliant leader, he made Israel a major power. He conquered Jerusalem and made it the national capital, secured territory between Dan and the Brook of Egypt that included the major trade routes, strengthened his borders with treaties and vassal states, and gave Israel an army. His later years were saddened by an attempted coup by his son Absalom, famine, pestilence and other problems. Before he died he made Solomon, his son by Bathsheba, his successor (1 Sam 16-31; 1 Kgs 1-2).

SOLOMON *Peace* (965-928)

Famed for his wisdom, Solomon built on the foundations laid by David, organizing the kingdom for tax and administrative purposes, developing commerce and shipping, launching a lavish building program to embellish the kingdom, and establishing an extravagant court life. Although his subjects were proud of him his splendid court and building projects drained much of the new wealth, and he fell under foreign influence through his many wives and their gods. Toward the end of his reign there was discontent over taxation and forced labor, as well as unrest at the borders of the kingdom, and the united kingdom failed to survive after his death. (1 Kgs 2-11)

Kings of Judah (928-586)

REHOBOAM *Freer of the people* (928-911)

Son of Solomon, Rehoboam was unable to hold his father's kingdom together and ruled only in Judah. He wasted Judah in wars with Israel. When Pharaoh Shishek I invaded, Rehoboam lost his Red Sea outlet and had to pay heavy tribute to save Jerusalem. He built fifteen border fortifications, leaving only the north open in hopes of reconciliation with Israel. As did his father Solomon, he became snared in idolatry through his many foreign wives (1 Kgs 11-12; 2 Chr 9-13).

ABIJAM *Father of light* (911-908)

Attempted to conquer Israel but advanced only a few miles, to Bethel (1 Kgs 14:31; 15:1-8; 2 Chr 11:20,22; 12:16;13).

ASA *Physician* (908-867)

Israel tried to invade Judah, and Asa asked help of Ben-hadad of Aram-Damascus, who attacked Israel. As soon as Israel withdrew, Asa fortified the border between them. Later he repelled an invasion by Zerah the Ethiopian. Asa was a religious reformer who tried to stamp out idolatry, but was accused of relying too heavily on doctors instead of on God for curing his own ills (1 Kgs 15, 16; 2 Chr 14-17:2; Jer 41:9).

JEHOSHAPHAT *God is Judge* (867-846)

Toured the kingdom to institute religious and judicial reform, strengthened fortifications and army, revived commerce. Renewed friendship with Israel by marrying his son to their royal family and by joining in common wars. Defeated Moab by sending the choir in front of the army. Alliance with Israel brought God's judgment (1 Kgs 15:24;22; 2 Kgs 1:17;3; 8; 12:18; 2 Chr 17-21).

JEHORAM *God is High* (846-843)

Jehoshaphat bequeathed shares of his wealth to seven sons, but gave the kingdom to Jehoram, the first-born. Jehoram killed his six brothers to make his rule secure. Fell into idolatry after marrying daughter of Ahab and Jezebel of Israel to seal relationship between the two nations. Lost Edom. His family, except for youngest son, Ahaziah, was wiped out in a Philistine invasion that reached Jerusalem. Prophet Elijah wrote to him of God's displeasure with his actions. The Bible says he died of bowel disease. Since he was not mourned or buried in royal tombs, he may have been murdered, poisoned perhaps (2 Kgs 1:17; 8 & 12; 2 Chr 21:1-22:1-11).

AHAZIAH *God holds, possesses* (843)

Trying to aid Israel's war with Aram-Damascus, listened to evil counsel of his wicked mother, Athaliah. Ahaziah was caught in Jehu's coup and was killed as part of Jehu's program to wipe out Jezebel's descendants (2 Kgs 8:-11:1-2; 12:18; 2 Chr 22).

ATHALIAH *God is Strong* (842-836)

Daughter of Jezebel, she was the only queen either kingdom ever had. Promoted worship of Baal. She seized power after her son Ahaziah's death by massacring heirs to the throne – only Ahaziah's infant son, Joash, escaped when he was hidden in the Temple by the priest Jehoiada. When he was seven, Joash was crowned king in the Temple under armed guard. Athaliah, hearing the singing and trumpeting, dashed in, yelling, "Treason, treason." She was dragged from the Temple and killed (2 Kgs 8:26; 11:1-20; 2 Chr 22-23).

JOASH *God Supports* (836-798)

Although he had been saved and enthroned by Jehoiada, the priest, and restored the Temple, Joash allowed idol worship after death of Jehoiada. Ultimately came under God's judgment for murder of Zechariah, son of the priest. Joash lost the Temple treasures when King Hazael of Aram-Damascus threatened Jerusalem. He was killed by his own officers (2 Kgs 11-13:1; 2 Chr 22:11,24).

AMAZIAH *God has strength* (798-769)

Amaziah, age 25, took a census to conscript an army. In a successful war against Edomites he recovered trade routes to the Gulf of Aqaba. Then he erred by challenging Israel. He was defeated by King Jehoash of Israel, who destroyed part of Jerusalem's walls and took hostages and spoils. Amaziah turned from following the Lord and his people killed him at the fortress of Lachish (2 Kgs 12:-15:3; 2 Chr 24:27; 25; 26:1).

UZZIAH *God is Strong* (769-758)

Taking the throne at age sixteen, Uzziah made Judah more prosperous than it had been since Solomon. He repaired relations with Israel and reorganized Judah's army to reconquer all lost territory. Uzziah recovered Edom and repaired the port of Ezion-geber, annexed Philistine cities on the coast, and built fortifications along highways and borders. Jerusalem was refortified and became a busy commercial center. But after Uzziah developed leprosy he lived in seclusion in the palace, having his son Jotham execute his orders. Because of his leprosy, he was not buried in the royal tomb (2 Kgs 14:21-22; 15:1-8; 2 Chr 26; Amos 1:1).

JOTHAM *God is perfect* (758-733)

Well trained by his father, Jotham maintained Judah's prosperity and military advantage. The Bible says he did right in the sight of the Lord but the people continued acting corruptly (2 Kgs 15:5, 7, 30-38; 2 Chr 26:21-23; 27).

AHAZ *He holds* (733-727)

A weak king who inherited the throne at age 20, Ahaz indulged in pagan cults that involved child sacrifice and burned his son as an offering. He was unable to control Edom or the Philistine coast, both of which broke away. When he was invaded by a coalition of Israel and Aram-Damascus, appealed to Tiglat-pileser, saying "I am thy servant." The Assyrians obliged by crushing Damascus and most of Israel, but in return Ahaz had to pay Tiglat-pileser heavy tribute. He, too, was denied burial in the royal tombs (2 Kgs 15:38; 16:1-20; 23:12; 2 Chr 27:9; 28:1-27;29:19; Isa 7:1-12, 14-28).

HEZEKIAH *God is strength* (727-698)

Judah was no more than an Assyrian vassal when able Hezekiah came to the throne at age 25. As Assyrian power was declining, he risked restoring Israelite worship in Jerusalem and inviting the people of Israel to participate, acts that gave him strong backing from the prophet Isaiah. Knowing war was inevitable, Hezekiah produced large numbers of weapons, constructed storehouses for staples, and improved the capacity of Jerusalem's water supply to withstand siege. Against Isaiah's advice, he joined an anti-Assyrian coalition that resulted in the destruction of Lachish and heavy tribute being imposed on Jerusalem. Despite a siege, Jerusalem was spared (2 Kgs 16:20; 18-20; 2 Chr 28:27,29-32; Isa 36-39; Jer 26:18-19).

MANASSEH *Causing forgetfulness* (698-642)

Made king at age 12, he is noted for the restoration of pagan cults, continued tribute to Assyria and generally being one of Judah's worst kings. However, later in life he called on God in distress, repented and ordered the people to worship God. Rebuilt the wall of City of David (2 Kgs 20-21; 2 Chr 32:33; 33; Jer 15:4).

AMON *Workman* (641-640)

Continued idolatrous practices. Was assassinated by his own officers (2 Kgs 21:18-26; 2 Chr 33:20-25).

JOSIAH *God supports* (639-609)

Became king at age eight, instituted religious reform after finding book of the law. Listened to prophetess Huldah. Celebrated Passover. Killed in battle when he foolishly tried to prevent Egyptian army from crossing his land to get to Assyria (2 Kgs 21:24-26;22-23; 2 Chr 33:125-35).

JEHOAHAZ *God upholds* (609)

Tried to be king after his father's death, but Pharaoh Necho II sent him in chains to Egypt, where he died (2 Kgs 23:30-40; 2 Chr 36:1-4).

JEHOIAKIM *God sets up* (608-598)

His name was Eliakim, but it was changed by Pharaoh Necho, who appointed him puppet ruler of

Judah. Jeremiah said he deserved the burial of an ass because he built himself a palace when his people were heavily taxed to pay Egyptian tribute. In 605, Babylonia won Judah from Egypt. After three years of their rule, Jehoiakim rebelled and then promptly died, leaving his son to cope with Babylonian revenge (2 Kgs 23:34-37; 24:1-6; 2 Chr 36:4-8; Jer 22:18-24; 26:21-23; 36; 46:2; Dan 1:1-2).

JEHOIACHIN *God Established* (597)
Came to throne just as Nebuchadnezzer arrived in Jerusalem. After a three-month siege, he was taken captive to Babylon. Judah kept hoping for his return. After 37 years in prison, he was freed, but never returned to Jerusalem (2 Kgs 24:6-17, 25:27-30; 2 Chr 36:8-9; Est 2:6; Jer 24:1; 52:31-34).

ZEDEKIAH *God is might* (597-586)
Appointed to throne by Nebuchadnezzar, who changed his name from Mattaniah, Zedekiah ruled under a handicap, his subjects considered Jehoiachin their king. Moreover, the land was desolate, and most skilled laborers had been deported to Babylon. Nevertheless, he rebuilt Jerusalem's defenses and saved the city from the Edomites. He then conspired against Babylon so that Nebuchadnezzar laid siege and destroyed Jerusalem. Zedekiah was taken in chains to Nebuchadnezzar, who forced him to watch the execution of his sons and then blinded him and sent him in chains to Babylon, where he died (2 Kgs 24; 2 Chr 36:11-20; 34:37-39; 52; Ezk 17:15-20).

KINGS OF ISRAEL (928-723)

JEROBOAM *Enlarger* (928-907)
Son of Nebat of Ephraim who served Solomon. Jereboam was promised rule of ten tribes by prophet Ahijah as God's judgment on Solomon for idolatry. After an unsuccessful plot to overthrow Solomon, he had taken asylum with Pharaoh Shishek I. He returned to rule Israel on Solomon's death, built a new capital at Tirzah, and was condemned for setting up gold calves at new sanctuaries in Bethel and Dan to keep his people from worshipping in Jerusalem. He reigned only four years before Pharaoh Shishek overran Israel. Border wars with Judah began (1 Kgs 11:26-40; 12-15, 2 Kgs 3:3; 9:9; 10:29; 13:2; 14:24;17:21;23:15; 2 Chr 10:-13:1-10).

NADAB *Liberal, Willing* (907-906)
Continued battles with Judah over borders and idolatrous practices of his father. While he was warring with Philistines, Baasha killed him and seized the throne (1 Kgs 14:20; 15:25-31).

BAASHA *Boldness* (906-883)
Unsuccessfully invaded Judah and was, in turn, invaded by Damascus. Lost much of Galilee and continued idolatry (1 Kgs 15-16; 21:22; 2 Kgs 9:9; Jer 41:9).

ELAH *Oak* (883-882)
Ruled only until he was murdered by Zimri, one of his officers, while "drinking himself drunk" (1 Kgs 16:8-10).

ZIMRI *Celebrated* (882)
Ruled seven days. The army, angered by his treason, proclaimed Omri king and surrounded the capital. Zimri set fire to the palace and let it collapse on him (1 Kgs 16:9-20).

OMRI *God apportions* (882-871)
From a human viewpoint, Omri was an effective king. He made peace with Judah and won back Moab and other lost territories. To cement ties with Tyre, he married his son Ahab to Jezebel, daughter of the king of Tyre. She introduced Baal worship to Israel. Because of this Omri was denounced by the prophets. However he brought peace and prosperity to the northern kingdom and established a strategically located new capital, Samaria, to guard the Via Maris and to rival Jerusalem. Omri died after only 12 years on the throne but he so impressed contemporary leaders that Israel was afterward known as the Land of Omri (1 Kgs 16:21).

AHAB *Father's brother* (871-852)
Continued his father's policies, politically effective, spiritually decadent. Completed construction in Samaria, rebuilt Jericho. Jezebel's promotion of Phoenician cults brought the wrath of the prophet Elijah upon him. Ben-hadad of Aram-damascus launched two attacks that Ahab repelled, but Ahab was criticized for sparing Ben-hadad's life. Meanwhile, Moab revolted. Ahab was killed in final battle against Ben-hadad (1 Kgs 16-22; 2 Chr 18).

AHAZIAH *God possesses* (852-851)
Son of Ahab and Jezebel. His first act as king was to injure himself by falling from a second story. He lived only long enough to fail twice; he tried to kill Elijah, who had predicted his death; and he tried to start a navy, which apparently sank (1 Kgs 22:51; 2 Kgs 1; 2 Chr 20:35-37).

JEHORAM *God is high* (851-842)
Also a son of Ahab and Jezebel. Made an abortive attempt to recover Moab. Samaria was besieged by Arameans but survived. In an Aramean battle he was wounded and while he recuperated turned the army over to his general, Jehu. Elisha commanded a revolt against Jehoram, anointing Jehu as king, urging him to kill the descendants of Jezebel, including Jehoram (2 Kgs 3; 8:28-29; 2 Chr 22:5-7).

JEHU *God is He* (842-814)

Founder of the longest-lived dynasty in Israel. Son of Jehoshaphat. Killed the House of Ahab, including wicked Jezebel, but allowed worship of God to be linked with Baal worship. Ignored crumbling economy and foreign alliances. Lost territory east of Jordan to Damascus. Black Obelisk depicts his submission to Shalmaneser III of Assyria (1 Kgs 19:16-17; 2 Kgs 9-10; 15:12; 2 Chr 22:7-9; 25:17; Hos 1:4).

JEHOAHAZ *God upholds* (814-800)

His spiritual and political behavior caused the Northern Kingdom to lose even more territory. Syrians under Hazael and Ben-hadad took heavy toll. Near end of his life Jehoahaz prayed for help (2 Kgs 10:35 13:1-10; 22-25; 14:1,8; 2 Chr 25:17,25).

JEHOASH *God supports* (800-784)

His father's prayer answered as war with Syria turned in Israel's favor. Recovered territory lost by his father. Attacked by Amaziah of Judah, so Jehoash punished Jerusalem by breaching the walls and taking captives and treasures (2 Kgs 13:9-25; 14:1-27; 2 Chr 25:17-25).

JEROBOAM II *Enlarger* (784-748)

A strong ruler, made peace with Judah and recovered territory until Israel was larger than it had been since David's time. (cf. Jonah's prophecy: 2 Kgs 14:25). Freedom from foreign attack brought prosperity, also extremes of wealth and poverty, empty religious ritual and false security condemned by the prophet Amos (2 Kgs 13:13; 14:16-29; 15:1-8; Amos 1:1; 7:9-11).

ZECHARIAH *God is renowned* (748-747)

Reigned six months before being assassinated by Shallum (2 Kgs 14:29; 15:8-9).

SHALLUM *Recompenser* (748-747)

Leader of conspiracy that overthrew dynasty of Jehu, fulfilling prophecy of 2 Kgs 10:30. Reigned a month, murdered by Menahem (2 Kgs 15:10-15).

MENAHEM *Comforter* (747/6-737/6)

Military governor of Tirzah, old capital of Israel. Proclaimed king after killing Shallum, he suppressed a rebellion with great cruelty. Became more unpopular by imposing heavy taxation to pay tribute to Tiglat-pileser to keep Assyrian forces out. Last king to be succeeded by his son (2 Kgs 15:14-22).

PEKAHIAH *God watches* (737/6-735/4)

Continued collecting tribute for Assyria until murdered by one of his army officers in second year of his reign (2 Kgs 15:22-26).

PEKAH *Watchfulness or Opening* (735/4-733/2)

Seized throne after murdering Pekahiah at Samaria. Allied with Rezin of Syria, tried to get Judah to join coalition against Assyria. Isaiah advised Uzziah against this course. When Judah refused, Pekah attacked Judah and carried off captives. Judah called on Assyria for aid, and Tiglat-pileser responded by conquering all of Israel and deporting much of its population to Assyria leaving Pekah only the hill country of Samaria. Pekah was murdered by Hoshea. (2 Kgs 15:25-32, 37; 16:1-5; 2 Chr 28:6; Is 7:1).

HOSHEA *God is help* (733/2-724/3)

Puppet king who collected tribute for Assyria until Tiglat-pileser died. Then he tried to rebel, expecting support from Egypt. This brought Shalmaneser V of Assyria down to capture Samaria and deport its population, ending the kingdom of Israel. (2 Kgs 15:30; 17:1-6; 18:1, 9-10).

Map of Divided Kingdom

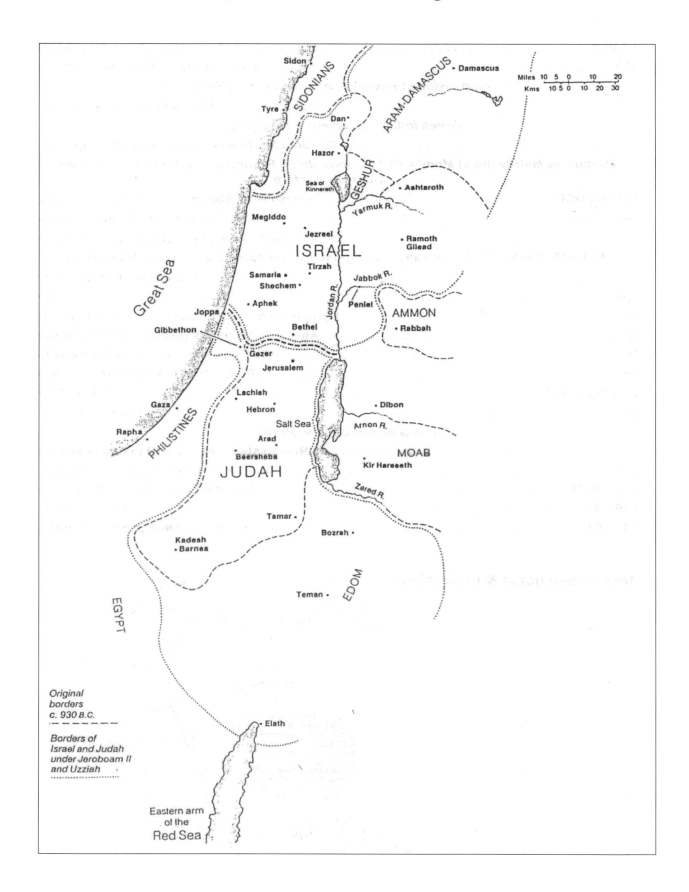

Sidon

Tyre

SIDONIANS

Damascus

ARAM-DAMASCUS

Dan

Hazor

GESHUR

Sea of
Kinnereth

Ashtaroth

Yarmuk R.

Megiddo

Jezreel

ISRAEL

Ramoth
Gilead

Tirzah

Samaria

Jabbok R.

Shechem

Aphek

Jordan R.

Peniel

AMMON

Joppa

Bethel

Rabbah

Gibbethon

Gezer

Jerusalem

Great Sea

Lachish

Gaza

Hebron

Dibon

Arnon R.

Rapha

Salt Sea

PHILISTINES

Arad

Beersheba

MOAB

Kir Hareseth

JUDAH

Zared R.

Tamar

Bozrah

Kadesh
Barnea

Teman

EDOM

EGYPT

Original
borders
c. 930 B.C. — — —

Borders of
Israel and Judah
under Jeroboam II
and Uzziah ·········

Elath

Eastern arm
of the
Red Sea

Miles 10 5 0 10 20
Kms 10 5 0 10 20 30

The Bible Visual Resource Book, Copyright 1989, Regal Books, Ventura, CA 93009, Used by permission

Timeline of the Maccabean Period

333-63 BCE . . . . Hellenistic (Greek) period
333/331 . . . . Alexander the Great conquers Israel

Greek Kingdom divided between Ptolemies/Egypt & Seleucids/Syrians

320-168 . . . . Judaism under Greek Ptolemies & Seleucids

Greek influence Hellenized many Jews

167 . . . . Seleucid Antiochus IV enforced worship of Zeus

Mattathias/Mattityahu at Modi'in (d.166, sons: John, Simon, Judas, Eleazar, Jonathan)
Guerrilla warfare

168/167-163 BCE . . . . Jewish Maccabean revolt & Hasmonean rule
164/December . . . . Rededication of Temple (Hanuka)
163 . . . . Battle w/Lysias - Syrian, death of Eleazar

100,000 infantry, 20,000 cavalry, 32 elephants - approached Jerusalem from south

142 . . . . Simon became high priest
134-104 . . . . John
104-103 . . . . Hyrcanus son, Aristobulus I, called himself King
104-76 . . . . Alexander Janneus (brother of Aristobulus I)
67 BCE . . . . Hyrcanus II vs Aristobulus II
63 BCE . . . . Rome (Pompey) annexes Palestine
ca. 146 BCE-400 CE . . . . Rule of Rome
37-4 BCE . . . . Herod the Great

Hillel & Shammai (Jewish sages)

6 CE . . . . Rome establishes rule of prefects in Judea
5/4 BCE? . . . . birth of Jesus, the Messiah
active ca. 40 CE . . . . Gamaliel I (Jewish leader-scholar)
active 36-64 CE . . . . Paul, the apostle
ca. 37-100 CE . . . . Josephus (Jewish leader, historian)

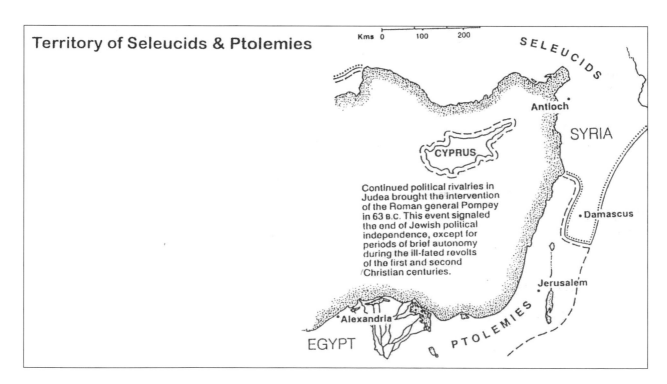

Territory of Seleucids & Ptolemies

Kms 0   100   200

SELEUCIDS

Antioch

SYRIA

CYPRUS

Continued political rivalries in Judea brought the intervention of the Roman general Pompey in 63 B.C. This event signaled the end of Jewish political independence, except for periods of brief autonomy during the ill-fated revolts of the first and second Christian centuries.

Damascus

Jerusalem

Alexandria

EGYPT

PTOLEMIES

The Bible Visual Resource Book, Copyright 1989, Regal Books, Ventura, CA 93009, Used by permission

House of Herod

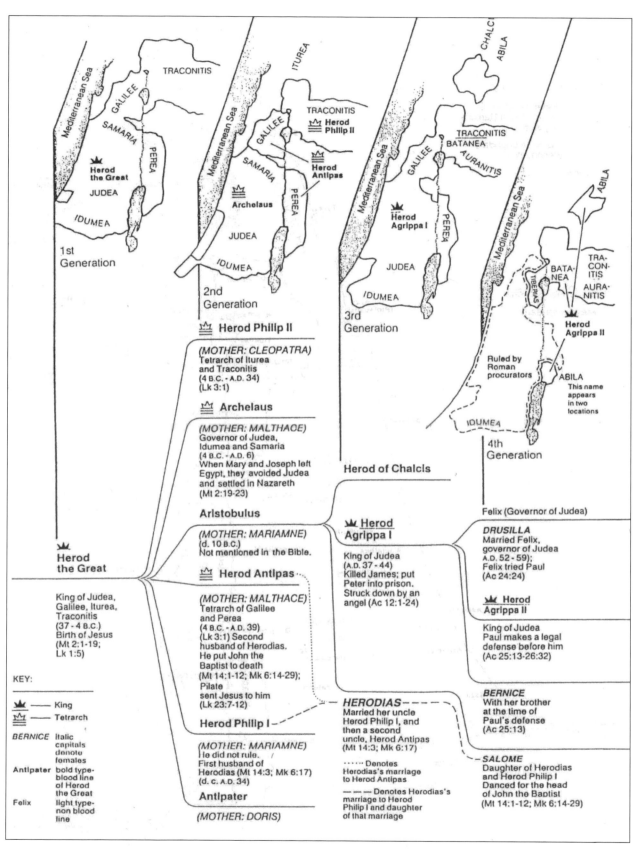

1st Generation

2nd Generation

3rd Generation

4th Generation

☥ **Herod Philip II**

(MOTHER: CLEOPATRA)
Tetrarch of Iturea
and Traconitis
(4 B.C. - A.D. 34)
(Lk 3:1)

☥ **Archelaus**

(MOTHER: MALTHACE)
Governor of Judea,
Idumea and Samaria
(4 B.C. - A.D. 6)
When Mary and Joseph left
Egypt, they avoided Judea
and settled in Nazareth
(Mt 2:19-23)

Aristobulus

(MOTHER: MARIAMNE)
(d. 10 B.C.)
Not mentioned in the Bible.

☥ **Herod Antipas**

(MOTHER: MALTHACE)
Tetrarch of Galilee
and Perea
(4 B.C. - A.D. 39)
(Lk 3:1) Second
husband of Herodias.
He put John the
Baptist to death
(Mt 14:1-12; Mk 6:14-29);
Pilate
sent Jesus to him
(Lk 23:7-12)

Herod Philip I

(MOTHER: MARIAMNE)
He did not rule.
First husband of
Herodias (Mt 14:3; Mk 6:17)
(d. c. A.D. 34)

Antipater

(MOTHER: DORIS)

☥ **Herod
the Great**

King of Judea,
Galilee, Iturea,
Traconitis
(37 - 4 B.C.)
Birth of Jesus
(Mt 2:1-19;
Lk 1:5)

Herod of Chalcis

♛ **Herod
Agrippa I**

King of Judea
(A.D. 37 - 44)
Killed James; put
Peter into prison.
Struck down by an
angel (Ac 12:1-24)

HERODIAS
Married her uncle
Herod Philip I, and
then a second
uncle, Herod Antipas
(Mt 14:3; Mk 6:17)

Felix (Governor of Judea)

DRUSILLA
Married Felix,
governor of Judea
A.D. 52 - 59);
Felix tried Paul
(Ac 24:24)

♛ **Herod
Agrippa II**

King of Judea
Paul makes a legal
defense before him
(Ac 25:13-26:32)

BERNICE
With her brother
at the time of
Paul's defense
(Ac 25:13)

SALOME
Daughter of Herodias
and Herod Philip I
Danced for the head
of John the Baptist
(Mt 14:1-12; Mk 6:14-29)

KEY:

♛ ——	King	
☥ ——	Tetrarch	
BERNICE	Italic capitals denote females	
Antipater	bold type- blood line of Herod the Great	
Felix	light type- non blood line	

····· Denotes
Herodias's marriage
to Herod Antipas

— — — Denotes Herodias's
marriage to Herod
Philip I and daughter
of that marriage

The Bible Visual Resource Book, Copyright 1989, Regal Books, Ventura, CA 93009, Used by permission

Israel under Herod the Great
37-4 BCE

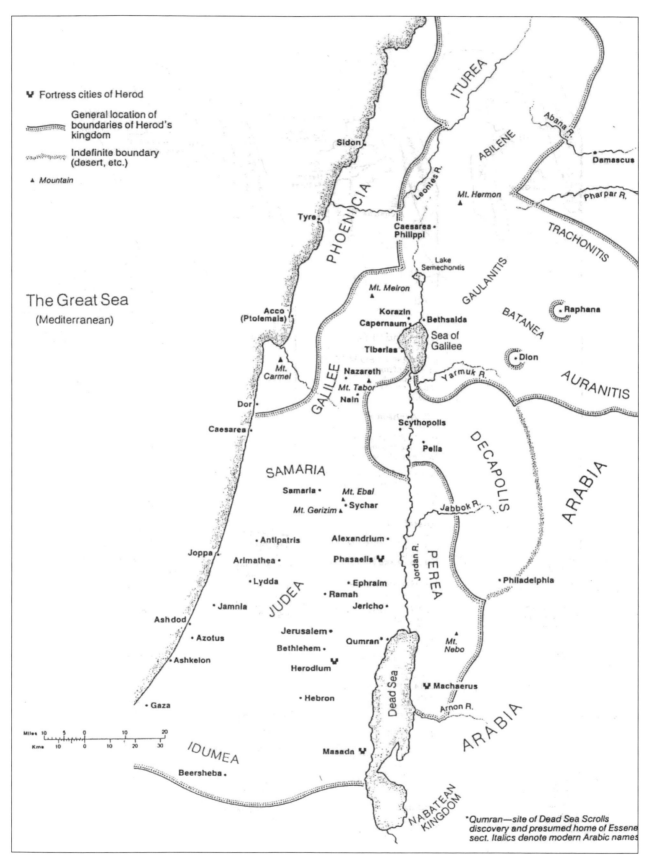

Legend:
- **Ⴣ** Fortress cities of Herod
- General location of boundaries of Herod's kingdom
- Indefinite boundary (desert, etc.)
- ▲ Mountain

ITUREA

ABILENE

Abana R.

Damascus

Sidon

Leontes R.

Mt. Hermon

Pharpar R.

TRACHONITIS

PHOENICIA

Tyre

Caesarea Philippi

Lake Semechonitis

GAULANITIS

BATANEA

Raphana

The Great Sea
(Mediterranean)

Acco (Ptolemais)

Mt. Meiron

Korazin

Capernaum • Bethsaida

Sea of Galilee

AURANITIS

Tiberias

Dion

Mt. Carmel

GALILEE

Nazareth

Mt. Tabor

Nain

Yarmuk R.

Dor

Scythopolis

Caesarea

Pella

DECAPOLIS

SAMARIA

Samaria • Mt. Ebal ▲
Mt. Gerizim ▲ • Sychar

Jabbok R.

ARABIA

Antipatris

Alexandrium

Joppa

Arimathea

Phasaelis Ⴣ

Jordan R.

PEREA

Lydda

Ephraim

Philadelphia

Jamnia

Ramah

Jericho

Ashdod

JUDEA

Azotus

Jerusalem

Qumran

Mt. Nebo

Ashkelon

Bethlehem

Herodium Ⴣ

Dead Sea

Ⴣ Machaerus

Hebron

Gaza

Arnon R.

ARABIA

Miles 10 5 0 10 20
Kms 10 0 10 20 30

IDUMEA

Masada Ⴣ

Beersheba

NABATEAN KINGDOM

*Qumran—site of Dead Sea Scrolls discovery and presumed home of Essene sect. Italics denote modern Arabic names

The Bible Visual Resource Book, Copyright 1989, Regal Books, Ventura, CA 93009, Used by permission

Beginning of the Life of Jesus/Yeshua
Journey to Bethlehem, Flight to Egypt, Return to Nazareth

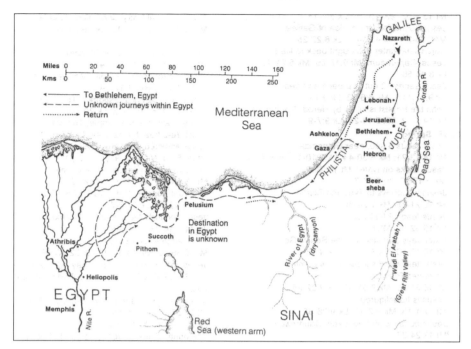

New Testament Events

6/5 BCE
Birth of Jesus, Bethlehem, Mt. 1:18-25, Lk 2:1-7

6/5 BCE
Visit of the Shepherds, Bethlehem, Lk 2:8-20

6/5 BCE
Presentation in the Temple,Jerusalem,
Lk 2:21-40

? Visit by the Magi, Bethlehem, Mt. 2:1-12

? Escape to Egypt, Mt 2:13-18

? Return to Nazareth, Mt 2:19-23

5/10? CE Birth of Saul of Tarsus,

7/8 CE Visit to Temple, Jerusalem, Lk 2:41-52

Beginning of Jesus' Ministry

26 CE
Jesus Baptized by John, Mt 3:13-17, Mk 1:9-11,
Lk 3:21-23, Jn 1:29-39
Jesus tempted by Satan, Judean Wilderness, Mt
4:1-11, Mk 1:12-13, Lk 4:1-13
Jesus' First Miracle, Cana, Jn 2:1-11

27 CE
Jesus' cleansing of Temple, Jn 2:14-22
Meeting with Nicodemus, Jerusalem, Jn 3:1-21
Samaritan Woman, Samaria, Jn 4:5-42
Healing Nobleman's son, Cana, Jn 4:46-54
At Synagogue in Nazareth, Lk 4:16-31
Fishermen become Disciples,
Capernaum, Mt 4:18-22, Mk 1:16-30, Lk 5:1-11
Healing of Peter's mother-in-law, Capernaum, Mt

8:14-17, Mk 1:29-34, Lk 4:38-41
Jesus begins his first preaching trip through
Galilee, Mt 4:23-25; Mk 1:35-39; Lk 4:42-44
Matthew decides to follow Jesus, Capernaum,
Mt 9:9-13; Mk 2:13-17; Lk 5:27-32

28 CE
Choosing of the 12 disciples, Mk 3:13-19;
Lk 6:12-15
Jesus preaches "Sermon on the Mount,"
Mt 5:1-7; Lk 6:20-49
Dinner at home of Pharisee, Capernaum,
Lk 7:36-50
Jesus travels again through Galilee, Lk 8:1-3
Jesus tells parables about the kingdom,
Mt 13:1-52; Mk 4:1-34; Lk 8:4-18
Jesus calms the storm, Sea of Galilee.
Mt 8:23-27; Mk 4:35-41; Lk 8:22-25
Jairus's daughter is brought back to life by
Jesus, Capernaum, Mt 9:18-26; Mk 5:21-43;
Lk 8:40-56
Jesus sends 12 out to preach and heal,
Mt 9:35-11:1; Mk 6:6-13; Lk 9:1-6
John the Baptist is killed by Herod, Machaerus,
Mt 14:1-12; Mk 6:14-29; Lk 9:7-9

29 CE, Spring
Jesus feeds 5,000, near Bethsaida,
Mt 14:13-21; Mk 6:30-44; Lk 9:10-17, Jn 6:1-14
Jesus walks on water, Mt 14:22-23;
Mk 6:45-52; Jn 6:16-21

The Bible Visual Resource Book, Copyright 1989, Regal Books, Ventura, CA 93009, Used by permission

Jesus withdraws to Tyre and Sidon,
Mt 15:21-28; Mk 7:24-30
Jesus feeds 4,000 people,
Mt 15:32-39; Mk 8:1-9
Peter says that Jesus is the Son of God,
Mt 16:13-20; Mk 8:27-30; Lk 9:18-21
Jesus tells His disciples of His coming death,
Caesarea Philippi,
Mt 16:21-26; Mk 8:31-37; Lk 9:22-25
Jesus is transfigured,
Mt 17:1-13; Mk 9:2-13; Lk 9:28-36
Jesus pays his temple taxes, Capernaum,
Mt 17:24-27

YEAR OF OPPOSITION

29 CE
October, Jesus attends the Feast of
Tabernacles, Jerusalem, Jn 7:11-52
Jesus heals a man who was born blind,
Jerusalem, Jn 9:1-41
Jesus visits Mary and Martha, Bethany,
Lk 10:38-42

29 CE, Winter, Jesus raises Lazarus from the dead,
Bethany, Jn 11:1-44

30 CE
Jesus begins his last trip to Jerusalem,
Lk 17:11
Jesus blesses the little children, across the
Jordan, Mt 19:13-15; Mk 10:13-16; Lk 18:15-17
Jesus talks to the rich young man, across the
Jordan, Mt 19:16-30; Mk 10:17-31; Lk 18:18-30
Jesus again tells about his death and
resurrection, near the Jordan,
Mt 20:17-19; Mk 10:32-34:Lk 18:31-34
Jesus heals blind Bartimaeus, Jericho,
Mt 20:29-34; Mk 10:46-52; Lk 18:35-43
Jesus talks to Zaccheus, Jericho, Lk 19:1-10
Jesus returns to Bethany to visit Mary and
Martha, Bethany, Jn 11:55-12:1

THE LAST WEEK
Sunday, The Triumphal Entry, Jerusalem,
Mt 21:1-11; Mk 11:1-10; Lk 19:29-44;
Jn 12:12-19
Monday, Jesus curses the fig tree,
Mt 21:18-19; Mk 11:12-14
Monday, Jesus cleanses the Temple,
Mt 21:12-13; Mk 11:12-14
Tuesday, Authority of Jesus questioned,
Mt 21:23-27; Mk 11:27-33; Lk 20:1-8
Tuesday, Jesus teaches in the temple,
Mt 21:28-23:39; Mk 12:1-44; Lk 20:9-21:4
Tuesday, Jesus anointed, Bethany,
Mt 26:6-13; Mk 14:3-9; Jn 12:2-11
Wednesday, The plot against Jesus, Mt 26:14-
16; Mk 14:10-11; Lk 22:3-6
Thursday, The Last Supper, Mt 26:17-29;
Thursday, Mk 14:12-25; Lk 22:7-20; Jn 13:1-38
Jesus comforts the disciples

Jn 14:1-16:33
Thursday, Gethsemane, Mt 26:36-46; Mk 14:32-
42; Lk 22:40-46
Thursday night and Friday, Jesus' arrest and
trial, Mt 26:47-27:26; Mk 14:43-15:15; Lk 22:47-
23:25; Jn 18:2-19:16
Friday, Jesus crucifixion and death, Golgotha, Mt
27:27-56; Mk 15:16-41;
Lk 23:26-49; Jn 19:17-30
Friday, The burial of Jesus, Joseph's Tomb, Mt
27:57-66; Mk 15:42-47; Lk 23:50-56;
Jn 19:31-42

POST-RESURRECTION
Sunday, The Empty Tomb, Jerusalem,
Mt 28:1-10; Mk 16:1-8; Lk 24:1-12;
Jn 20:1-10
Sunday, Mary Magdalene sees Jesus in the gar-
den, Jerusalem, Mk 16:9-11; Jn 20:11-18
Sunday, Jesus appears to the two going to
Emmaus, Mk 16:12-13; Lk 24:13-35
Sunday, Jesus appears to 10 disciples,
Jerusalem, Mk 16:14; Lk 24:36-43; Jn 20:19-25
Jesus appears to the 11 disciples, Jerusalem,
one week later, Jn 20:26-31
Jesus talks with some of his disciples, Sea of
Galilee, one week later,Jn 21:1-25
Jesus ascends to His Father in heaven, Mt of
Olives, 40 days later, Mt 28:16-20;
Mk 16:19-20; Lk 24:44-53

35 CE
Martyrdom of Stephen, Acts 7:57-60

35 CE
Saul meets Jesus on road to Damascus,
Acts 9:1-19

35-38 CE
Trip to Arabian desert, Gal 1:17

38 CE
Visit to Jerusalem, Acts 9:26-29, Gal 1:18-19

38-43 CE
Ministry in Syria & Cilicia, Acts 9:30, Gal 1:21

43 CE
Arrival in Syrian Antioch, Acts 11:25-26

43/44 CE
Famine, Acts 11:27-30, 12:25

44 CE   Death of Herod Agrippa I, Acts 12:19

46/48 CE
First Missionary Journey, Acts 13:2-14:28

48/49 CE
Writing of Galatians (?) from Syrian Antioch

49/50 CE
Jerusalem Conference, Acts 15:1-29;
Gal 2:1-10

51/52 CE
Appearance before Gallio, Acts 18:12-17

51 CE
Writing of 1 Thessalonians from Corinth

50

51/52 CE
Writing of 2 Thessalonians from Corinth

52 CE
Return to Jerusalem & Syrian Antioch, Acts 18:22

50/52 CE
Second Missionary Journey, Acts 15:40-18:23

53/57 CE
Third Missionary Journey, Acts 18:23-21:17

53/55 CE
At Ephesus, Acts 19:1-20:1

55 CE
Writing of 1 Corinthinians from Ephesus

55 CE
Writing of 2 Corinthinians from Macedonia

57 CE
Writing Romans from Corinth or Cenchrea

57/59 CE
Paul imprisoned at Caesarea, Acts 23:23-26:32

59 CE
Shipwreck on voyage to Rome, Acts 27:1-28:16

59/61 CE
First Roman imprisonment, Acts 28:16-31

60 CE Writing of Ephesians from Rome

60 CE Writing of Colossians from Rome

60 CE Writing of Philemon from Rome

61 CE Writing of Philippians from Rome

62 CE
Release from Roman imprisonment

62/67 CE
Fourth Missionary Journey, Titus 1:5

63/65 CE
Writing of 1 Timothy & Titus from Philippi

67/68 CE
Second Roman imprisonment, 2 Tim 4:6-8

67/68 CE
Writing of 2 Timothy from Mamertime dungeon, 2 Tim 4:6-8

67/68 CE
Trial & execution of Paul

Galilee and the North of Israel

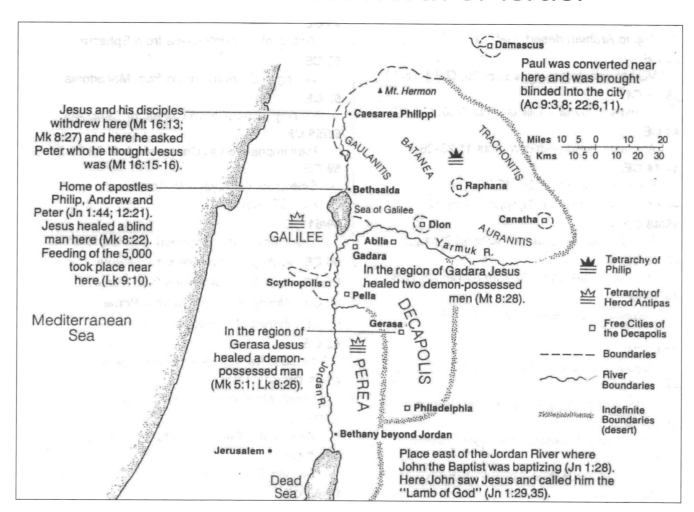

The Bible Visual Resource Book, Copyright 1989, Regal Books, Ventura, CA 93009, Used by permission

Jerusalem during the Time of Jesus

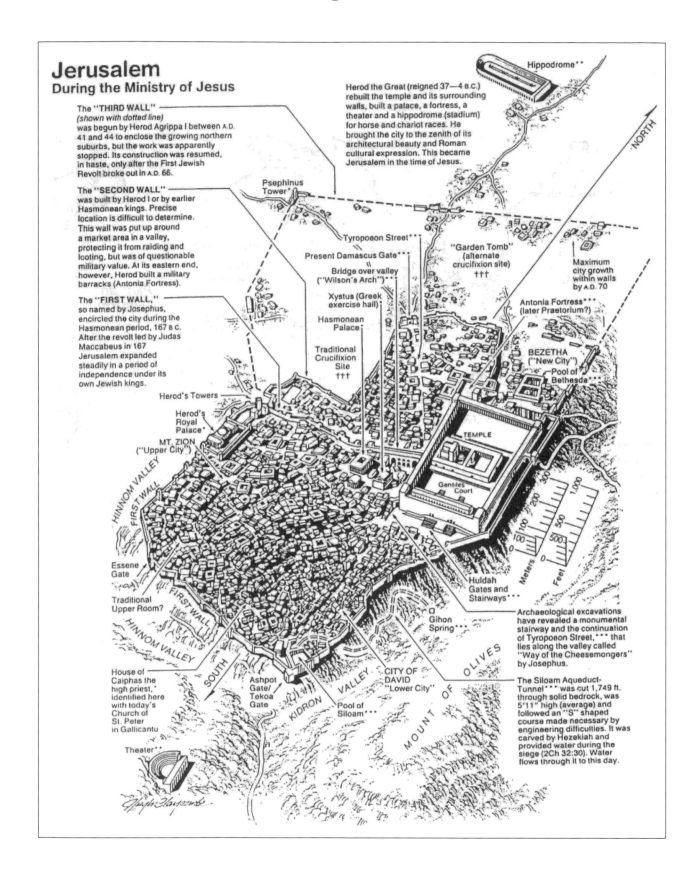

Jerusalem
During the Ministry of Jesus

The "THIRD WALL" (shown with dotted line) was begun by Herod Agrippa I between A.D. 41 and 44 to enclose the growing northern suburbs, but the work was apparently stopped. Its construction was resumed, in haste, only after the First Jewish Revolt broke out in A.D. 66.

The "SECOND WALL" was built by Herod I or by earlier Hasmonean kings. Precise location is difficult to determine. This wall was put up around a market area in a valley, protecting it from raiding and looting, but was of questionable military value. At its eastern end, however, Herod built a military barracks (Antonia Fortress).

The "FIRST WALL," so named by Josephus, encircled the city during the Hasmonean period, 167 B.C. After the revolt led by Judas Maccabeus in 167 Jerusalem expanded steadily in a period of independence under its own Jewish kings.

Herod the Great (reigned 37—4 B.C.) rebuilt the temple and its surrounding walls, built a palace, a fortress, a theater and a hippodrome (stadium) for horse and chariot races. He brought the city to the zenith of its architectural beauty and Roman cultural expression. This became Jerusalem in the time of Jesus.

Hippodrome **

NORTH

Psephinus Tower *

Tyropoeon Street ***

Present Damascus Gate ***

Bridge over valley ("Wilson's Arch") ***

Xystus (Greek exercise hall)

Hasmonean Palace

Traditional Crucifixion Site †††

Herod's Towers

Herod's Royal Palace *

MT. ZION ("Upper City")

"Garden Tomb" (alternate crucifixion site) †††

Maximum city growth within walls by A.D. 70

Antonia Fortress *** (later Praetorium?)

BEZETHA ("New City")

Pool of Bethesda ***

TEMPLE

Gentiles Court

HINNOM VALLEY

FIRST WALL

Essene Gate

Traditional Upper Room?

FIRST WALL

HINNOM VALLEY

House of Caiphas the high priest, * identified here with today's Church of St. Peter in Gallicantu

Theater **

SOUTH

Ashpot Gate/ Tekoa Gate

KIDRON VALLEY

Pool of Siloam ***

CITY OF DAVID "Lower City"

Gihon Spring ***

Huldah Gates and Stairways ***

MOUNT OF OLIVES

Meters
Feet
100 200 300
500 1,000

Archaeological excavations have revealed a monumental stairway and the continuation of Tyropoeon Street, *** that lies along the valley called "Way of the Cheesemongers" by Josephus.

The Siloam Aqueduct-Tunnel *** was cut 1,749 ft. through solid bedrock, was 5'11" high (average) and followed an "S" shaped course made necessary by engineering difficulties. It was carved by Hezekiah and provided water during the siege (2Ch 32:30). Water flows through it to this day.

The Bible Visual Resource Book, Copyright 1989, Regal Books, Ventura, CA 93009, Used by permission

Nations Mentioned at Pentecost

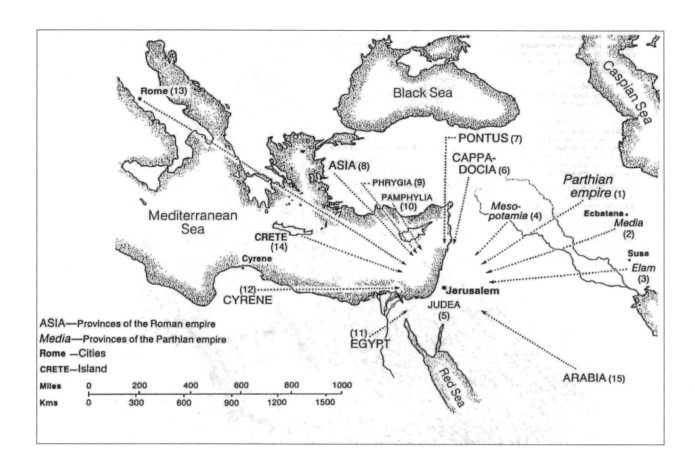

Rome (13)

Black Sea

Caspian Sea

PONTUS (7)

CAPPA-
DOCIA (6)

ASIA (8)

Parthian
empire (1)

PHRYGIA (9)

PAMPHYLIA
(10)

Meso-
potamia (4)

Ecbatana
Media
(2)

Mediterranean
Sea

CRETE
(14)

Susa
Elam
(3)

Cyrene

Jerusalem

(12)
CYRENE

JUDEA
(5)

ASIA—Provinces of the Roman empire
Media—Provinces of the Parthian empire
Rome—Cities
CRETE—Island

(11)
EGYPT

ARABIA (15)

Red Sea

Miles	0		200		400		600		800		1000
Kms	0	300		600		900		1200		1500	

The Bible Visual Resource Book, Copyright 1989, Regal Books, Ventura, CA 93009, Used by permission

Spread of the Christian Message

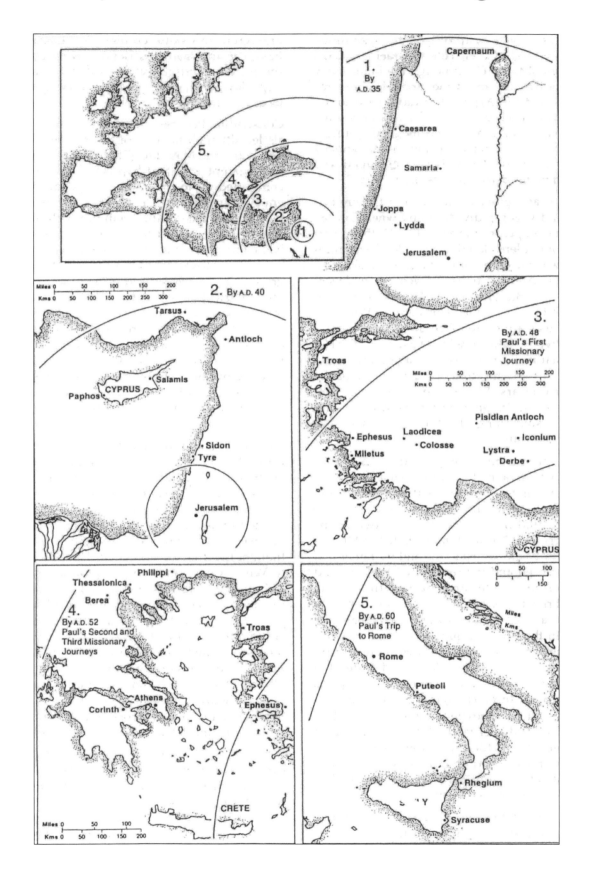

The Bible Visual Resource Book, Copyright 1989, Regal Books, Ventura, CA 93009, Used by permission

Reference Section
Historical Background

The Byzantines

You will not travel far or long in Israel before you begin to hear of the exploits of the Byzantines. The time period of their rule in Israel is usually dated from 324–638 CE although the founding of the city of Byzantium on the straits between the Black Sea and the Aegean Sea dates back to 658 BCE. A Greek colony under a leader named Byzas, Byzantium maintained its good commercial position and managed its own affairs under a series of ancient rulers. It was besieged and destroyed by Emperor Severus about 196 CE.

The power and glory of the Roman Empire had peaked and was rapidly declining when Diocletian became emperor in 285 CE. By 311, there were at least four rulers claiming the title. Constantius Chlorus was the emperor in charge of Gaul, Spain and Britain. About 270, he married a humble servant girl from Bithynia named Helena. In 274, she gave birth to a son named Constantine. When her husband was appointed Caesar he was encouraged to divorce Helena, which he did in 292. (Her humble status did not make her a political asset.) He then married Theodora, the daughter of one of the other Caesars. When Constantius was sent north to rule in Britain, Constantine was left with Diocletian, something of a hostage to guarantee his father's loyalty.

In 295, Constantine accompanied Diocletian to Palestine where he met the Christian leader Eusebius, who was to become his friend and future biographer. Constantine became a Caesar when his father died in 306. He defeated two of the other rulers in 312 at the famous Battle of Milvian Bridge near Rome. Constantine and his father had been influenced and impressed by Christians and had opposed Diocletian's persecution of the Church. Prior to the battle, Constantine is said to have seen a cross in the sky and have heard the words, "In this sign conquer." Whatever his personal beliefs may have been, he became a champion of the Christian cause. He soon defeated the other contenders for the throne and set up his capital in Byzantium, changing its name to Constantinople. He immediately made Christianity a legal religion and later made it the official religion of the State. This sudden shift from a position of a persecuted minority to a place of political power greatly affected the history of the Church. The effect was not altogether positive.

At this point in history, we see a major move away from Christianity's Jewish roots. The Gospel had come to the Greeks but Greek thought had also seeped into the Church. The calendar was arranged to avoid connecting Easter with Passover and many restrictions were placed on the Jewish community. The Church took more steps down the misguided path of trying to honor Jesus by harassing the Jews.

Constantine became a leading force in Christian circles although he did not receive baptism until nearly the end of his life. (This may have been due to a current idea that baptism forgave all sins committed up to the point of baptism, therefore encouraging people to postpone it as long as possible.)

Constantine seems to have had real affection and respect for his mother, Helena. He had coins made in her honor, re-named the city of her birth Helenopolis and in 324 sent her on a pilgrimage to the Holy Land. Exactly what she did on this trip is unclear. Facts and legends have mixed over the years. She was nearly eighty at this time and is credited with locating sites of significance in New Testament history as well as giving alms to the poor and needy. She identified the cave in Bethlehem where Jesus was born and the place on the Mount of Olives where He ascended into heaven. Churches were soon built on these sites.

The stories about the Holy Sepulcher are less certain. During the years of Roman occupation Hadrian had built a temple to Venus on a site outside the city wall. He had barred Jews from the city and renamed it Aelia Capitolina. Constantine wanted to identify and build a church on the site of Jesus' crucifixion and resurrection. It was thought that this site was under Hadrian's temple to Venus. Constantine wrote to Macarius, Bishop of Jerusalem, ordering a church built "worthy of the most marvelous place in the world." Legend has it that Helena herself found three crosses in a cistern just east of Calvary and miraculous occurrences indicated which one was the "true cross." Eusebius of Caesarea, one of the major biographers of the era, does not mention Helena being personally involved with the locating of the Holy Sepulcher but St. Ambrose and Rufinus, who wrote sometime later do mention the story.

Whatever her contributions may have been to early archaeology, it seems that Helena was truly a pious Christian lady who prayed regularly, helped the needy and sincerely wanted to honor the Lord by identifying the holy places. Unfortunately her efforts started a trend that would make future generations wonder if Jesus had said, "Go into all the land and build churches," instead of "Go into all the world and preach the gospel."

In 325, Constantine played a leading role in the Council of Nicaea which was called to arbitrate the Arian controversy that had divided Christians in Egypt and North Africa. The dispute involved questions about the nature of Christ and the persons of the Trinity. The differences between the parties seem to include personality conflicts as well as theological differences. One wonders, in retrospect, if it would have been better had the Church emphasized the things the Bible made clear and resisted the temptation to define things the Bible left vague.

We can appreciate the Byzantines for their support of Christianity while questioning the direction that support took. Most modern Israelis are charitable in their assessment of Constantine and Helena, pointing out the advantage for us of having the biblical sites marked in some way. And yet, as we enter the many dark structures filled with icons we can imagine the confusion of Jewish Israelis who know the clear Bible commands against idols and graven images. Many think that Christians are polytheists who obviously worship various idols.

We cannot change the negative aspects of Byzantine influence, but we can be aware of the problems added to Jewish-Christian relations by this era of history. As we grow in understanding, we can pray that God will use us as agents of healing in our time.

The Byzantine Empire was one of the greatest of European civilizations. The Byzantine civilization, if not the Empire, really began in the year 324 CE. This is the year Constantine became Emperor. Constantine ruled over a united Empire but moved his capital from Rome to Byzantium. He spent a great deal of time and money preparing the city to be the future capital. The city was renamed Constantinople but is also often called "New Rome."

Like most political entities the history of the Byzantine Empire can be categorized into three parts, a beginning, middle and end or an ascension period, a golden period and a period of decline and fall. There are subcategories but we will not get into that here.

The early period is marked by a separation of identity of the Empire. This period is usually marked from 395 CE when the Eastern Roman Empire and the Byzantine Empire, formally separated with the death of Emperor Theodosius I. Theodosius's son, Arcadius, age 17, ruled the Eastern Empire from Constantinople, his other son, 10 year old Honorius, ruled the Western Empire from the city of Milan. At the time everyone thought that this was going to be a temporary setup but it turned out to be permanent.

Notable events in the early period are the building of walls around Constantinople, a rising threat from Barbarians in the west, the eruption of religious debate and conflict after Christianity became a dominant force in the Empire, and the birth of Islam.

The Golden Period of the Byzantine Empire is considered to have begun in 641 CE. The golden period was marked by massive border changes, constant warfare with the Arabs and to a lesser extent Bulgars, a final split between the Roman Catholic Church and the Eastern Orthodox Churches and a renaissance in the arts.

The final period began 1025 CE and ended with the fall of Constantinople in 1453 CE. This period was marked by the loss and reconquest and then another loss of Constantinople, constant civil war and the splintering and fall of the Empire.

The Church, as an institution, continued to grow. At the time of Constantine there were five leading cities which were the headquarters of church leaders called metropolitans or archbishops. These cities were Jerusalem, Alexandria, Antioch, Constantinople and Rome. Eventually the Church became a religious monarchy with the Bishop of Rome recognized as the pope or the "Father of the Church." From the early years, there had been disagreements between the Eastern and the Western Church, and in 1054, the final split or schism divided the Latin and Greek branches of Christianity. The Bishop of Rome and the Patriarch of Constantinople excommunicated each other and the division has persisted ever since.

You will find churches of both eastern and western traditions represented in Israel. These ancient Christian groups may seem quite foreign, extremely formal and spiritually cold in the eyes of many Americans – both Catholics and Protestants. The religious and political power-playing down through the centuries seems a far cry from Jesus' call to simple discipleship.

Before we judge too quickly or harshly, however, we should remember that the churches of the Protestant Reformation have also learned to play power politics. In only four- or five-hundred years, Protestants have also learned the fine art of empire-building. A close and honest look will show areas needing repentance and renewal in everyone's tradition.

Where Does Islam Fit Into the Historical Drama?

As the Roman world declined and broke apart, it split into three main areas: the West, Byzantium and Islam. The weakening of Byzantine defenses after Emperor Justinian's military campaigns opened the way for an invasion from Arabia. The Arabs or Saracens, as the Romans called them, were barbarians at the beginning of the seventh century. They were mainly polytheists and nature worshippers. Mohammed, an illiterate camel-driver, married to an older and rather wealthy woman, was a seeker after spiritual truth. He knew both Jews and Christians and absorbed bits and pieces of both religious teachings. When he was about forty, he turned from merchant life and became a religious ascetic. He spent days in lonely meditation and experienced visions that he believed to be direct revelations from Allah, the Arabic name for God.

Rejected in Mecca, Mohammed fled north to Medina where he preached and gathered a growing band of disciples. The year of his flight to Medina (Hejira), 622 CE, marks the first year of the Moslem era. Mohammed intended to wipe out primitive superstitions and unite the Arabs under a single pure faith. The new religion was called Islam, meaning submission or surrender. The followers are called Muslim, those who are submitted. Themes drawn from the Judeo-Christian scriptures appeared in rewritten form in some cases. Abraham's spiritual heritage is said to pass to Ishmael rather than Isaac. Friday is the day of worship.

The basic duties of Muslims are called the Five Pillars of Faith. They are:

1. The profession of faith: there is no god but Allah and Mohammed is his Prophet.

2. Daily prayer – at dawn, midday, midafternoon, sunset and nightfall. At these appointed times the muezzin (criers) give the call from the tall, slender minarets or towers. (Today tape recorders are sometimes used.)

3. Giving to the poor. In Islamic countries it is collected through regular taxes, about 40% of income.

4. Fasting during the holy month of Ramadan, the ninth month of the lunar calendar. No food or drink may be taken from sunrise to sunset.

5. Every Moslem, who can possibly afford it, must make a pilgrimage to the shrine of Mecca at some time during his or her life. One who has made the journey is called a Haj (male) or Haja (female).

Also in early time a sixth duty was required of all able-bodied men: participation in the jihad (holy war). This was the spark that ignited the early Moslem conquest.

You may have noticed this trend reappearing with the rise of modern militant Islam.

The Arab period begins with the birth of Mohammed in 570 CE. When he died in 632, he had already established Islam as a world power, welded the desert tribes together and gained control of much of the Middle East. He was succeeded by his friend and father-in-law, Abu Bekr, who died in 634, and was followed by the fiery Omar, who conquered Jerusalem in 637 and Egypt in 644. Later a split developed between the Sunnis, associated with the Ommiad Dynasty, who had moved the capital of Islam from Medina to Damascus, and the Shiites, connected with the Abbassid family who gained power in 750 and moved the capital again to Baghdad.

The ninth and tenth centuries saw the height of Muslim civilization. Although the Arabs were themselves rather culturally backward, Islam provided a unifying faith, a common language and relative political and economic stability which brought about something of a renaissance of various traditions, especially Hellenistic, Syrian and Persian. Greek scientific and philosophical works were translated into Arabic and Arabic numerals (actually developed in India) changed the world of mathematics. Christian Europe discovered Plato and Aristotle via the great study centers in Spain and the Moslem world. Islamic-style architecture, with its intricate geometric and floral designs, developed out of Mohammed's prohibition of human and animal figures in art.

Islam might have conquered the known world had the Saracen horsemen not been defeated at the Battle of Tours by Charles Martel, grandfather of Charlemagne, in 732 CE. This outside danger brought about the alliance of the Franks and the Papacy which also changed the course of history, but that is another story. To sum up the Islamic period, we see the Moslem caliphs in secure control of the lands of the Bible until the Crusader Period began.

Since September 11, 2001 Americans have been awakened to a rising tide of a very militant form of Islam in our modern world. While as Christians we are committed to loving our enemies and doing good to those who harm us we must also be aware of the dangers to our civilization and the Judeo-Christian values upon which it is built. We must find ways to live at peace with the many decent Muslims who also want peace while being alert to the danger from militant Muslims bent on control of the world.

Films like *Obsession* are important contributions to our understanding of militant Islam. Check their web site,

http://www.obsessionthemovie.com/

The Crusader Period (1099-1263)

The Crusades were sparked by Caliph Hakim's assault on the Church of the Holy Sepulcher and other Christian sites in 1009. The idea began to grow in Europe that it would be pleasing to God if they expelled the "infidel Turk" from the Christian holy sites.

I want to make it clear that there were legitimate reasons for the Crusades. Islam has contained a militant streak from its inception and Caliph Hakim was an extreme example. In 1005, he ordered the killing of all the dogs in Egypt and discarded them in the desert. He forced the inhabitants of Cairo to work at night and sleep at morning, and whoever caught violating his orders was punished severely. In 1014, he ordered women not to go out at all and ordered the shoemakers not to make any women's shoes. He killed his tutor Abul Qasim Said ibn Said al-Fariqi and the great majority of his viziers. Most of those viziers were Christians. Some of them served as physicians as well. Al-Hakim also killed many other officials, high-ranking as well as lowly ones. These include viziers, judges, poets, physicians, bathhouse keepers, cooks, cousin, soldiers, Jews, Christians, intelligence gatherers, and even cut the hands of female slaves in his palace. In some cases, he did the killing himself. In 1009, he destroyed the Church of the Holy Sepulchre in Jerusalem, then under Fatimid control. He made Christians and Jews wear a black hat. He made the Christians wear wooden crosses, half a meter long by half a meter wide, around their necks. The Jews were ordered to wear a wooden calf hanging around the neck, so as to remind them of the sin of the golden calf. Although Christians were not allowed to buy slaves, male or female, and had few other privileges, they were allowed to ride horses on the condition that they ride with wooden saddles and unornamented girths. Towards the end of his reign he became increasingly erratic and feared by his officials, soldiers and subjects alike. Muslim and Christian dignitaries alike went to his palace kissing the ground and stood at the palace gates asking him for forgiveness and promising not to listen to any rumors that were spreading. Then they raised a petition to al-Hakim and he forgave them.

He offered gifts for youths to jump from a high place in the palace in a water pool. About 30 of them died because they missed the water pool and hit the rocks.

He forbade musical instruments, singers, and musicians. Al-Hakim burned the entire Jewish quarter in Cairo. He burned the town of al-Fustat after the people circulated a statement saying he had abandoned Islam by proclaiming that he was divine. He forbade women to weep at funerals.

Al-Hakim disappeared in 1021 while on a donkey trip without any guards. The donkey was later found near a well covered with blood. It is believed that his sister hired assassins to kill him because of a dispute between them. Although he presumably died, the Druze believe he had been hidden away by God and will return as the Mahdi (Islamic messiah figure) on Judgment Day.

In 1095, at the Council of Clermont in France, Pope Urban II announced the launching of the First Crusade. The background of this call is a bit complex and several motives can be considered. The militant Seljuk Turks had been making inroads into the Byzantine Empire in Asia Minor. Although the eastern and western Christian leaders had already excommunicated each other, Byzantine Emperor Alexius appealed to the Pope for help. Urban saw that a holy war against the Turks would have several advantages. In addition to opening roads of pilgrimage and capturing the Holy Sepulcher, the Byzantine east might be compelled to recognize the supremacy of the Pope. And, of course, foreign wars are always an economic boon and would keep the lesser nobility from fighting among themselves at home. So off went the Crusaders.

Godfrey of Bouillon was the main leader of the First Crusade which took Jerusalem on June 7, 1099. The Crusaders went on an orgy of killing and looting of both Muslims and Jews. They frequently murdered Jews in Europe along the way. It is hard to imagine true Christians thinking that this carnage was in any way honoring to the Lord Jesus Christ, but human capacity for self-deception is amazing!

At its height, the Latin Kingdom of Jerusalem under various Crusaders controlled the coastal cities from Beirut to Ashkelon and the interior, including the Negev, as far as the Jordan River. In the north three other Crusader states were formed: the county of Tripoli – much of modern Lebanon; the principality of Antioch – in modern Turkey; and the county of Edessa in Syria. Various knightly orders were started in Jerusalem: the Templars, the Hospitalers of St. John and the Teutonic Order.

The Crusader control weakened after their defeat by the Moslem leader, Saladin, at the Horns of Hattin, near the Sea of Galilee, in July of 1187. The Crusaders learned that it is unwise to fight uphill battles in the Galilee in July, wearing heavy armor and having a short supply of water. Whether anyone learned anything else is unlikely.

The third Crusade included romantic figures such as: Richard the Lion-Hearted, Philip of France and Frederick Barbarossa of Germany. Richard and Philip hated each other and Frederick drowned before reaching the Holy Land. At the end of this period, the Crusader Kingdom had shrunk noticeably and Akko or

Acre became the principle headquarters.

You will see remains of Crusader castles throughout the lands of Israel, Jordan and Lebanon. The architecture is impressive. But again, we see why both Jews and Moslems in the Middle East think of Christians as empire-builders rather than relationship builders. Our task is to change that perception.

Crusader Kingdom

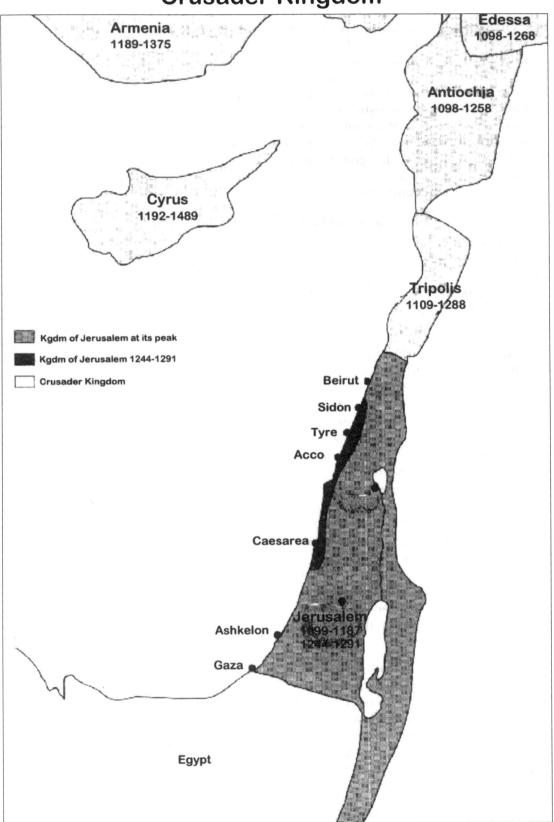

Armenia
1189-1375

Edessa
1098-1268

Antiochja
1098-1258

Cyrus
1192-1489

Tripolis
1109-1288

▨ Kgdm of Jerusalem at its peak
■ Kgdm of Jerusalem 1244-1291
□ Crusader Kingdom

Beirut

Sidon

Tyre

Acco

Caesarea

Jerusalem
1099-1187
1244-1291

Ashkelon

Gaza

Egypt

The Mameluke Period (1250-1517 CE)

The Crusaders were driven from Jerusalem by Moslem Ayyubid troops in 1244. Less than a decade later a political assassination in the Nile Delta brought to power a military caste of freed slaves, who became known as the Mamelukes. They were to rule the Middle East for over 250 years (1250-1517). The Mamelukes were of diverse ethnic stock, Turks, Tartars, Kurds, Armenians and even some West Europeans. They were also usually converts to Islam, as a result of their initial enslavement as children. Their caste was not hereditary, but rather perpetuated by recruitment. The descendants of the Mamelukes generally took civilian positions in the Egyptian bureaucracy. Mameluke politics were, frequently, violent. Many officers experienced periods of disgrace, sometimes punished by exile to Jerusalem, and imprisonment, although it did not necessarily end their careers; few Mameluke rulers died in their beds.

Jerusalem under the Mamelukes had the paradoxical position of being politically and economically neglected, while being religiously revered and even glorified.

The political status of Jerusalem declined sharply under Mameluke rule. Jerusalem had been called the capital of the "Crusader Kingdom" but under the Mamelukes Jerusalem was not even a provincial capital and became subject to two other cities, Cairo and Damascus. Cairo was the seat of the sultan and as such capital of the empire. "Greater Syria," subject to Cairo, was divided into seven mamlakas or regions; the largest of which was the mamlaka of Damascus; Jerusalem was a minor subdistrict (wilaya) in this mamlaka.

The lower political status also meant that the city was protected by only a small garrison of troops. Also the city was not connected to the imperial communications network. This system of roads, constructed by the Sultan Baybars in the mid-13th century was meant to connect the cities of Greater Syria with Cairo and facilitate the efficient passage of government communications. These roads extended as far as the Euphrates, but never included Jerusalem.

The disgraced officers sometimes exiled to Jerusalem produced some of Mameluke Jerusalem's most ornate buildings. Apparently these officers were concerned about how history would remember them. Consequently, they constructed religious academies (madrassas) with ornate facades. The madrassas, hostels and charitable institutions, are characterized by the alternate use of red and white stones, geometric black and white stone interlace ("ablaq"), softening of angles by means of stalactites and domes, and the elaboration of facades with carved stone "picture-frames.

One such building is the Tashtimurya at 106 Street of the Chain in the Moslem Quarter. The Tashtimurya was built in 1382 by the Emir Tashtimur, a former governor of Damascus. It contains the tombs of Tashtimur and his son, which are visible beyond the barred window. The building's entrance stands out for its decorative niche high above the doorway. Another nearby madrassa, the Tazya, (111 Street of the Chain) was built by the exiled Emir Taz in 1362. His former position as court cup-bearer is indicated by two goblets, carved on either side of an ornate Arabic inscription above a window. Above this inscription are interlocking, clover shaped stones, typical of Mameluke period architecture in Jerusalem.

The Mameluke period stands out as one of the few times in Jerusalem's history that the city had no wall. This too reflected the reduced political status of the city. Its previous wall had been destroyed in 1219 by the Ayyubid ruler of Damascus El Malik El Muathim Isa and there exists no archeological evidence of a city wall until the present walls were constructed by Suleiman the Magnificent in the mid-16th century. Apparently no Mameluke ruler had ever considered their reconstruction sufficiently important. In addition to the city's declined prestige this probably also reflected the geopolitical/military reality at the time. All the serious external military threats to the Mamelukes were far from Jerusalem's ruined ramparts. In 1310 the Sultan El Nasir Muhamed bin Qala'un ordered that the citadel be rebuilt. It provided a line defense for Jerusalem's governor and the small Mameluke garrison stationed there, but afforded little protection for the rest of the city's inhabitants.

The lack of a wall was a source of great distress to Jerusalem's Jewish visitors, who saw this as a sign of the city's desolation. In 1488 Rabbi Ovadia of Bartenura wrote: "Jerusalem is almost desolated and it goes without saying that it has no wall around it."

Meet the Ottomans

To understand the modern Middle East, one has to know something about the Ottoman Empire. It is also important to remember that the land of the Bible has not been ruled by the people who lived there since the Roman conquest in 63 BCE, and the existence of Israel as a Jewish commonwealth ended in 70 CE. The Ottoman Turks were the penultimate "absentee landlords," ruling from 1520 to the end of World War I in 1917, when the British took over as the "mandatory" power.

The Ottomans where descendants of the Western Turks who were called the Oghuz. They came from the region of Anatolia in the west of Turkey and came primarily as settlers during the reign of the Seljuks in 1098-1308. Some of them were warriors of the Muslim faith carrying out jihad, or "holy struggle," to spread the faith among hostile unbelievers.

The Ottomans soon ruled a small military state in western Anatolia by 1300, about the time the Seljuk state was crumbling apart. This small state was in conflict with several other small Muslim states, each preying on the other for territory. By 1400, however, the Ottomans had managed to extend their influence over much of Anatolia and even into Byzantine territory in eastern Europe: Macedonia and Bulgaria. In 1402, the Ottomans moved their capital to Edirne in Europe where they threatened the last great bastion of the Byzantine Empire, its capital, Constantinople. The city seemed to defy the great expansion of Islam. No matter how much territory fell to the Muslims, Constantinople resisted every siege and every invasion. The Ottomans, however, wanted to break this cycle. Not only would the seizure of Constantinople represent a powerful symbol of Ottoman power, but it would make the Ottomans master of east-west trade. In 1453, Sultan Mehmed (1451-1481), who was called "The Conqueror," finally took this one last remnant of Byzantium and renamed it, Istanbul. From that point onwards, the capital of the Ottoman Europe would remain fixed in Istanbul and, under the patronage of the Ottoman sultans, become one of the wealthiest and most cultured cities of the early modern world.

The Ottoman Empire had been started. It expanded greatly under Sultan Selim I (1512-1520), but it was under his son, Sultan Suleiman (1520-1566), called "The Lawmaker" in Islamic history and "The Magnificent" in Europe, that the empire would reach its greatest expansion over Asia and Europe. Suleiman is the Arabic way of pronouncing Solomon.

The Period of Great Expansion

The empire, reunited by Muhammad I, expanded victoriously under Muhammad's successors Murad II and Muhammad II. The victory (1444) at Varna over a cru-

sading army led by Ladislaus III of Poland was followed in 1453 by the capture of Constantinople. Within a century the Ottomans had changed from a nomadic horde to the heirs of the most ancient surviving empire of Europe. Their success was due partly to the weakness and disunity of their adversaries, partly to their superior military organization. Their army comprised numerous Christians—not only conscripts, who were organized as the corps of Janissaries, but also volunteers. Turkish expansion reached its peak in the 16th cent. under Selim I and Suleiman I, also called, the Magnificent.

The reign of Suleiman I began (1535) the traditional friendship between France and Turkey, directed against Hapsburg Austria and Spain. Suleiman reorganized the Turkish judicial system, and his reign saw the flowering of Turkish literature, art, and architecture. In practice the prerogatives of the sultan were limited by the spirit of Muslim canonical law (sharia), and he usually shared his authority with the chief preserver of the sharia and with the grand vizier (chief executive officer).

In the progressive decay that followed Suleiman's death, the clergy (ulema) and the Janissaries gained power and exercised a profound, corrupting influence. The first serious blow by Europe to the empire was the naval defeat of Lepanto in 1571, inflicted on the fleet of Selim II by the Spanish and Venetians under John of Austria. However, Murad IV in the 17th cent. temporarily restored Turkish military prestige by his victory (1638) over Persia. Crete was conquered from Venice, and in 1683 a huge Turkish army under Grand Vizier Kara Mustafa surrounded Vienna. The relief of Vienna by John III of Poland and the subsequent campaigns of Charles V of Lorraine, Louis of Baden, and Eugene of Savoy ended in negotiations in 1699 which cost Turkey Hungary and other territories.

Decline

The breakup of the state continued with the Russo-Turkish Wars in the 18th cent. Egypt was only temporarily lost to Napoleon's army, but the Greek War of Independence and its sequels, the Russo-Turkish War of 1828–29, and the war with Muhammad Ali of Egypt resulted in the loss of Greece and Egypt, the protectorate of Russia over Moldavia and Walachia, and the semi-independence of Serbia. Drastic reforms were introduced in the late 18th and early 19th cent. by Selim III and Mahmud II, but they came too late. By the 19th cent. Turkey was known as the "Sick Man of Europe."

Through a series of treaties from the 16th to the 18th cent. the Ottoman Empire gradually lost its economic independence. Although Turkey was theoretically among the victors in the Crimean War, it emerged from the war economically exhausted. The Congress of Paris (1856) recognized the independence and integrity of the Ottoman Empire, but this event marked the confirmation of the empire's dependency rather than of its rights as a European power.

The rebellion (1875) of Bosnia and Herzegovina precipitated the Russo-Turkish War of 1877–78, in which Turkey was defeated despite its surprisingly vigorous stand. Romania (i.e., Walachia and Moldavia), Serbia, and Montenegro were declared fully independent, and Bosnia and Herzegovina passed under Austrian administration. Bulgaria, made a virtually independent principality, annexed (1885) Eastern Rumelia with impunity.

Sultan Abd al-Majid, who in 1839 issued a decree containing an important body of civil reforms, was followed (1861) by Abd al-Aziz, whose reign witnessed the rise of the liberal party. Its leader, Midhat Pasha, succeeded in deposing (1876) Abd al-Aziz. Abd al-Hamid II acceded (1876) after the brief reign of Murad V. A liberal constitution was framed by Midhat, and the first Turkish parliament opened in 1877, but the sultan soon dismissed it and began a rule of personal despotism. The Armenian massacres of the late 19th cent. turned world public opinion against Turkey. Abd al-Hamid was victorious in the Greco-Turkish war of 1897, but Crete, which had been the issue, was ultimately gained by Greece.

Collapse

In 1908 the Young Turk movement, a reformist and strongly nationalist group, with many adherents in the army, forced the restoration of the constitution of 1876, and in 1909 the parliament deposed the sultan and put Muhammad V on the throne. In the two successive Balkan Wars (1912–13), Turkey lost nearly its entire territory in Europe to Bulgaria, Serbia, Greece, and newly independent Albania. The nationalism of the Young Turks, whose leader Enver Pasha gained virtual dictatorial power by a coup in 1913, antagonized the remaining minorities in the empire.

The outbreak of World War I found Turkey lined up with the Central Powers. Although Turkish troops succeeded against the Allies in the Gallipoli campaign (1915), Arabia rose against Turkish rule, and British forces occupied (1917) Baghdad and Jerusalem. In 1918, Turkish resistance collapsed in Asia and Europe. An armistice was concluded in October, and the Ottoman Empire came to an end. The Treaty of Sèvres confirmed its dissolution. With the victory of the Turkish nationalists, who had refused to accept the peace terms and overthrew the sultan in 1922, modern Turkey's history began.

A Look At The Development of Christian Antisemitism

*I, the Lord your God, am a jealous God, visiting the iniquity of the fathers on the children,
to the third and fourth generation of those who hate Me. Exodus 20:5*

*I and my father's house have sinned. We have acted very corruptly against Thee
and have not kept the commandments. Nehemiah 1:6,7*

Persecution and animosity toward the Jews began early in their national history. Pharaoh, Haman and Antiochus Epiphanes are only a few examples of rulers who tried to destroy God's chosen people. Those of us who believe that there is a personal evil force at work in the world, see Satan behind all of this. He has tried to ruin God's plan for humankind since the Garden of Eden. Since the presence of the Jews in the world reminds us of the God of the Bible who keeps covenant and shows mercy, enemies of God have an innate desire to get rid of this people. However, our concern here is for Christians, who also claim a chosen relationship with God. That persecution of the Jews has arisen from our community is a tragedy and a shame with which we must deal.

I. The Historical Record

A. 30 – 300 CE The Early Church

1. The early Church was Jewish. Conflict of church and synagogue was between brothers.
2. Is there antisemitism in the New Testament?
3. How about Jewish persecution of early Christians?
4. No scriptural basis for retaliation. Luke 6:27-31.
5. Christian accusations against Jews in 2nd century.
6. 144 - Marcion, early Christian Gnostic, tried to de-Judaize Church.
7. 250 CE - 1st charge of Deicide - deliberate killing of God.
8. 3rd century document instructed Christians to pray and fast for the Jews during Passover. (Better than forced conversions, which, unfortunately, continued.)

B. 312 - 1000 CE The Institutional Church

1. Conversion of Constantine. Edict of Milan permitted religious toleration for Christians.
2. As church left its position as persecuted minority and came to political power it took increasingly unbiblical stance in regard to the Jews.
3. Moved from Hebrew to Greek world-view.
4. Rise of the concept of supersessionism.
   a. Says God is finished with the Jews.
   b. Claims the Church is the new Israel, supersedes the Jews.
5. Quotes from Church Fathers: (growing antagonism toward the Jews).
   a. Gregory of Nyssa: "brood of vipers, haters of goodness."
   b. St. Jerome: ". . .serpents, image of Judas, their psalms and prayers are the braying of donkeys."
   c. St John Chrysostom: "Jews are inveterate murderers, possessed by the devil, their debauchery and drunkenness gives them the manners of the pig. They kill and maim one another." "Jews are abandoned by God and for the crime of deicide there is no expiation possible." "God has always hated the Jews."
   d. St Augustine: "Let us preach to Jews in spirit of love, not for us to boast over broken branches." Less condemning, however Augustine's theology tended to allegorize the Hebrew scriptures and minimize God's continuing covenant with Israel.
6. 415 CE – Bishop of Alexandria expelled the Jews and gave their property to a Christian mob.
7. 632 CE – Beginning of forced baptisms.
8. 897 CE – Jews stripped of property rights.
9. 10th century CE – Custom began of hitting a Jew in the face on Good Friday and stoning Jewish homes on Palm Sunday.

C. 1095 –1300 CE Crusades

1. 1096 - 1st Crusade. More than 5,000 Jews in the Rhineland slaughtered as Crusaders made their way to the Holy Land.
2. 1146 – 2nd Crusade. Monk Rudolph vs St. Bernard of Clairvaux. Entire Jewish community of Bloise, France burned at stake in Blood Libel accusation.
3. 1189 - 3rd Crusade. Most violent in England. In York, 150 Jews under siege in a castle committed suicide rather than be burned at the stake.
4. Debts owed to Jews were canceled for Crusaders.
5. 1215 - Jews in many areas forced to wear distinctive dress and live in restricted areas.
6. Star of David as badge of shame and pointed hat required in Poland.
7. 1236 - Burning of Talmud and other Jewish writings.

D. 1300-1500 Inquisition

1. 1320 – Jews accused of poisoning water wells. Along with blood libel and desecration of the host, this marks beginning of Jewish world conspiracy theories.
2. 1347-50 Black Death. Jews blamed again. 200 Jewish communities destroyed.
3. Inquisition was permanent court of the Church established to stamp out heresy. Problem in Spain dealt with so-called Conversos, Jews who had abandoned their faith under duress but still maintained ties with Jewish community and practice.
4. 1483 – Torquemade, Inquisitor General. Thousands of Jews tortured and burned at stake.
5. 1492 – 130,000 Jews forced to leave Spain.

E. 1500-1600 Reformation

1. Luther had sympathy for Jews in early years of his work. Became angry when they didn't quickly convert to his renewed Christianity.
2. 1543 - Published *Of The Jews And Their Lies*. (Main points listed here)
   a. Synagogues should be burned, homes destroyed.
   b. Should be deprived of prayerbooks and Talmuds.
   c. Rabbis forbidden to teach.
   d. Forbid passports and traveling privileges.
   e. Stopped from money-lending & usury. Forced to do manual labor.
   f. "Act so we may be free of this insufferable, devilish burden – the Jews."

F. 1600-1900 Further Developments

1. Poland: Received Jewish refugees from time of Crusaders.

a. Great persecution began 1648 – Cossacks.
b. 1795 - Jews confined to *Pale of Settlement.*
2. Russia: Pogroms - devastation. 1881-1921, Jews began mass migration to US & Argentina.
3. Myth of racial superiority of Aryan race, Hegel, de Gobineau.
4. France: 1894 - Dreyfus case covered by Herzl
5. Protocols of the Learned Elders of Zion – hoax by Russian anti-Semites, 1905. Exposed in 1921 by London Times. Promoted in USA by Henry Ford.

G. 20th Century - Nazi Germany & the Holocaust

1. Hitler becomes Chancellor – 1933.
2. Nuremberg Laws identify & isolate Jewish population – 1935.
3. Kristallnacht – anti-Jewish riots – Nov. 9, 1938.
4. Building of death camps – 1940-42
5. 6 million dead – 1945.

Note: *Nazism is pagan, not Christian BUT most Nazis were members in good standing of Christian churches.*

II. Christian Response

A. Repent – look for hidden areas of prejudice in our own hearts and communities.
B. Accept responsibility. We can't align only with the good in our collective past.
C. Engage in practical acts of concern toward Israel and the Jewish people.
D. Speak truth, correct false impressions.
E. Relate with integrity.

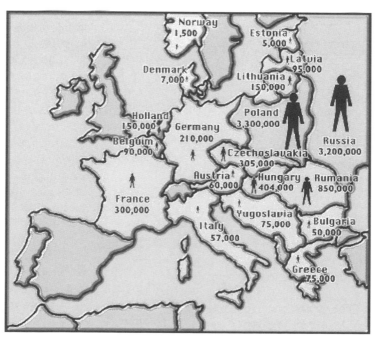

The Holocaust Years

As soon as Hitler came to power in 1933, he began to put into effect various laws and regulations that deprived the Jews, bit by bit, of their rights and property. It was all done legally, because Hitler had absolute power. Dates listed here reflect when various rules were passed. To stifle protest or criticism, from Jews or non-Jews, armed storm troopers were free to use violence and imprisonment. Particularly at the beginning, could anyone be certain where the chain of actions would lead?

This chronology was compiled from *The Destruction of the European Jews* **by Raul Hilberg.**

Chronology of Laws and Actions Directed Against Jews in Nazi Germany 1933-45

1933

Jan. 30 — Adolf Hitler becomes Chancellor of the German Reich. He is the Supreme Leader of the NSDAP (National Socialist German Workers Party) and the SA (storm troopers).

Mar. 5 — Adolf Hitler receives a strong vote of confidence from the German people in the Reichstagswahl (parliamentary elections).

Mar. 24 — The Reichstag empowers Hitler to enact laws on its behalf.

April 1 — Adolf Hitler proclaims a one-day boycott of all Jewish shops. All non-Aryan civil servants, with the exception of soldiers, are forcibly retired.

April 21 — Kosher butchering is forbidden by law.

April 25 — Fewer non-Aryan children are admitted to German schools and universities.

June 16 — There are **500,000 Jews** living in the Third Reich.

July 14 — German nationality can be revoked - for those considered "undesirable" by the government.

1934

Aug. 1 — Paul von Hindenburg, second president of the German Republic, dies.

Aug. 3 — Adolf Hitler declares himself both President and Chancellor of the Third Reich.

1935

Mar. 16 — Compulsory military service is reinstituted in Germany in open defiance of the Versailles Treaty.

Sept. 6 — Jewish newspapers can no longer be sold in the street.

Sept. 15 — Nuremberg Laws deprive Jews of German citizenship and reduce them to the status of "subjects"; forbid marriage or any sexual relations between Jews and Aryans; forbid Jews to employ Aryan servants under the age of 35.

1936

Mar. 7 — Jews no longer have the right to participate in parliamentary elections.

Aug. 1 — The German army reoccupies the Rhineland.

Aug. 1 — The Olympic Games are opened in Berlin. Signs reading "Jews Not Welcome" are temporarily removed from most public places by order of the Fuhrer to present a favorable and misleading picture to foreign tourists and journalists.

1937

July 2 — More Jewish students are removed from German schools and universities.

Nov. 16 — Jews can obtain passports for travel abroad only in special cases.

1938

Mar. 11 — German troops march into Austria.

July 6 — Jews may no longer follow certain occupations such as broker, matchmaker, tourist guide, real estate agent.

July 23 — On this date rule was passed that as of Jan. 1, 1939, all Jews must carry identification cards.

July 25 — On this date rule was passed that as of Sept. 30, 1939, all Jews must have only Jewish first names. If a Jew has a German first name, *Israel* or *Sarah* must be added to it.

Oct. 5 — Jewish passports are marked with a "J".

Oct. 28 — About 15,000 "stateless" Jews are "resettled" in Poland.

Nov. 7 — Herschel Grynszpan, a Jew, attempts to assassinate the German Attache`, vom Rath, in Paris.

Nov. 9 — Vom Rath dies. Goebbels, recognizing the propaganda value, issues instructions that "spontaneous demonstrations" against Jews are to be "organized and executed" throughout Germany – in retaliation! The pogrom, called *Kristallnacht* (Night of Broken Glass) begins.

Nov. 10 — Pogrom continues.

Nov. 11 — Jews may no longer own or bear arms. Synagogues destroyed in entire Reich.

Nov. 12 — Following the Nazi-organized pogrom, "reparations" of one-billion Reichsmarks are imposed on the German Jews, and they must further repair all damages at their own cost.
Jews may no longer head businesses.
Jews may no longer attend plays, movies, concerts and exhibitions.

Nov. 15 — All Jewish children remaining in German schools are removed to Jewish schools.

Nov. 23 — All Jewish businesses are closed down.

Nov. 28	Jews may no longer be in certain districts at certain times.
Dec. 3	Local authorities allowed to bar Jews from the streets on Nazi holidays.
	Jews must hand in their driver's licenses and car registrations.
	Jews must sell their businesses, real estate and hand over their securities and jewelry.
Dec. 8	Jews may no longer attend university.

1939

Mar. 15	German troops march into Czechoslovakia.
April 30	Rent protection for Jews is reduced.
May 17	About **215,000 Jews** still live in the Third Reich.
Sept. 1	Germany declares war on Poland.
Sept. 3	**WORLD WAR II BEGINS.**
	Curfew for Jews is instituted: 9 PM in summer, 8 PM in winter.
Sept. 21	Pogroms against Jews in Poland.
Sept. 23	All Jews must hand in their radios to the police.
Oct. 12	Austrian Jews are beginning to be deported to Poland.
Oct. 19	"Reparations" for German Jews are increased to 1.25 billion Reichsmarks and are now payable by November. 15, 1939.
Nov. 23	Polish Jews must now wear yellow Stars of David.

1940

Feb. 6	Unlike the rest of the German people, Jews do not receive clothing coupons.
Feb. 12	German Jews begin to be taken into "protective custody," that is, deported to concentration camps.
July 29	Jews may no longer have telephones.
Dec. 24	Jews to pay special income tax.

1941

June 12	Jews must designate themselves as "unbelievers"
July 31	Beginning of the "final solution."
Sept. 1	Every Jew in Germany must also wear a Star of David.
	Jews may no longer leave their places of residence without permission of the police.
Oct. 14	The large-scale deportation of Jews to concentration camps begins.
Oct. 24	Friendly relations with Jews prohibited.
Dec. 26	Jews may no longer use public phones.

1942

Jan. 1	Approximately **130,000** Jews now live in the Third Reich.
Jan.10	Jews must hand in any woolen and fur clothing still in their possession.
Feb. 17	Jews may no longer subscribe to newspapers or magazines.
April 17	A Jewish apartment must be identified as such with a Star of David beside the nameplate.
April 24	Jews are forbidden the use of public transportation.
May 15	Jews are forbidden to keep dogs, cats, birds, etc.
May 29	Jews are no longer permitted to visit barber shops.
June 9	Jews must hand over all "spare" clothing.
June 11	Jews no longer receive smoking coupons.
June 19	Jews must hand over all electrical and optical equipment, as well as typewriters and bicycles.
June 20	All Jewish schools are closed.
July 17	Blind or deaf Jews may no longer wear armbands identifying their condition in traffic.
Sept. 9	Jews not permitted to institute civil suits.
Sept. 18	Jews can no longer buy meat, eggs or milk.
Oct. 4	All Jews still in concentration camps in Germany are to be transferred to Auschwitz.

1943

| April 21 | Jews found guilty of crimes are to be conveyed to extermination camps in Auschwitz or Lublin after serving their sentences. |
| July 1 | Property of Jews to be confiscated after their death. |

1944

| Sept. 1 | Approximately **15,000** Jews now live in the Third Reich. |

1945

Jan. 17	Soviet troops liberate Warsaw.
Jan. 27	Soviet army entered Auschwitz, liberated more than 7,000 remaining prisoners, who were mostly ill and dying.
Feb. 4-11	Yalta Conference in the Crimea.
March 5	American troops reach the Rhine river.
April 11	American troops liberate Buchenwald.
April 15	British troops liberate Bergen-Belsen.
April 25	American and Soviet troops meet at the Elbe River.
April 30	Hitler commits suicide.
May 7	Germany surrenders unconditionally. End of the war in Europe.
Aug. 15	Japan surrenders unconditionally. End of WW II.
Nov. 22	Nuremberg War Crimes Tribunal commences. The Nuremberg trials concluded on Oct 1, 1946, which happened to be the Day of Atonement (Yom Kippur), with a judgment in which 12 defendants were sentenced to death, three to life imprisonment, four to various prison terms, and three acquitted.

ANSWERS TO THE TWELVE MOST FREQUENTLY ASKED QUESTIONS ABOUT THE NAZI HOLOCAUST

1. When speaking about the Holocaust, what time period are we referring to?

The term *Holocaust* refers to the period from January 30, 1933, when Hitler became chancellor of Germany, to May 8, 1945 (V-E Day) when the war in Europe ended.

2. How many Jews were murdered during the Holocaust?

While it is impossible to ascertain the exact number of Jewish victims, statistics indicate that the total was over 5,830,000. Six million is the round figure accepted by most authorities. The number murdered in each country and the percentage they constituted of the pre-war Jewish population were as follows:

Austria	40,000	20%
Belgium	40,000	67%
Bulgaria	—	—
Czechoslovakia	315,000	88%
Denmark	500	8%
Estonia	1.500	33%
Finland	8	1%
France	90,000	30%
Germany	170,000	32%
Greece	60,000	80%
Holland	105,000	75%
Hungary	200,000	50%
Italy	8,000	16%
Latvia	80,000	84%
Lithuania	135,000	87%
Luxemburg	700	23%
Norway	750	42%
Poland	2,850,000	88%
Rumania	425,000	50%
USSR	1,252,000	44%
Yugoslavia	60,000	80%

The death camps – those with special apparatus for mass murders – were all located in Poland. Their names were: *Auschwitz-Birkenau, Belzec, Chelmno, Maidanek, Sobibor, Treblinka.*

3. How many non-Jewish civilians were murdered during World War II?

While it is impossible to ascertain the exact number, the recognized figure is approximately 5,000,000. Among the groups which the Nazis and their collaborators murdered and persecuted were: Gypsies, Serbs, Polish intelligentsia, resistance fighters from all nations, German opponents of Nazism, homosexuals, Jehovah's Witnesses, habitual criminals, "anti-socials" such as beggars and vagrants.

4. What does the term *Final Solution* mean, and what is its origin?

The term *Final Solution, Endlosung,* refers to the Germans' plan to physically liquidate all the Jews in Europe. The term was used at the Wannsee Conference (held in Berlin January 20, 1942), where German officials discussed its implementation.

5. How did the Germans define who was Jewish?

On November 14, 1935, the Nazis issued the following definition of a Jew:

- Anyone with three Jewish grandparents;
- Someone with two Jewish grandparents who belonged to the Jewish community on Sept. 15, 1935, or joined thereafter; or one who was married to a Jew or Jewess on Sept. 15, 1935, or married one thereafter;
- Or one who was the offspring of a marriage or extramarital liaison with a Jew on or after Sept. 15, 1935.

6. Did all the Germans support Hitler's plan for the persecution of the Jews?

Although the entire German population was not in agreement with Hitler's persecution of the Jews, there is no evidence of any large-scale protests regarding their treatment. There were Germans who defied the April 1, 1933, boycott and purposely bought in Jewish stores, and there were those who aided Jews to escape and to hide, but their number was very small. Even those who opposed Hitler were in agreement with his anti-Jewish policies. Among the clergy, Provost Bernhard Lichtenberg of Berlin, publicly prayed for the Jews daily and therefore was sent to a concentration camp by the Nazis. Other priests and ministers were imprisoned for their failure to cooperate with the Nazis' anti-Semitic policies, but the majority of the clergy complied with the directives against German Jewry, and did not protest.

7. Did the peoples of occupied Europe know about the Nazis' plans for the Jews? What was their attitude? Did they cooperate with the Nazis against the Jews?

The attitude of the local population – vis-a-vis the persecution and destruction of the Jews – varied from zealous collaboration with the Nazis to active assistance to Jews, and thus it is difficult to make generalizations. The situation also varied from country to country. In Eastern Europe, and especially in Poland, Russia and the Baltic States (Lithuania, Latvia, and Estonia), there was much more knowledge of the final

Solution, because it was implemented in those areas. Elsewhere, the local population had less information on the details of the Final Solution.

In every country they occupied, with the exception of Denmark, the Nazis found many locals who were willing to cooperate fully in murder of the Jews. This was particularly true in Eastern Europe, where there was a long-standing tradition of virulent antisemitism, and where various national groups which had been under Soviet domination (Ukranians, Lithuanians, Latvians) fostered hopes that Germans would restore their independence.

In several countries in Europe, there were local fascist movements which allied themselves with the Nazis and participated in anti-Jewish actions. For example: the Iron Guard in Rumania, the Arrow Cross in Hungary, the Ustasha in Croatia, and the Hinka Guard in Slovakia. On the other hand, in every country in Europe, there were courageous individuals who risked their lives to save Jews. In several countries, there were groups which aided Jews such as Joop Westernweel's group in Holland, "Zegota" in Poland and the Assisi underground in Italy.

8. What was the response of the Allies to the persecution of the Jews? Could they have done anything to help?

The response of the Allies to the persecution and destruction of European Jewry was inadequate. Only in January 1944, was an agency – the War Refugee Board – established for the express purpose of saving the victims of Nazi persecution. Prior to that date, little action was taken.

On December 17, 1942, the Allies issued a condemnation of Nazi atrocities against the Jews, but this was the only such declaration made prior to 1944. Moreover, no attempt was made to call upon the local population in Europe to refrain from assisting the Nazis in the murder of Jews.

Even following the establishment of the War Refugee Board and the initiation of various efforts designed to save Jews, the Allies refused to bomb the death camp of Auschwitz and/or the railway lines leading to that camp, despite the fact that Allied bombers were at that time engaged in bombing factories very close to the camp, and were well aware of its existence and function.

Other practical measures, which were not taken, concern the refugee problem. Many tens of thousands of Jews sought to enter the United States, but were barred from doing so by the stringent American immigration policy. Even the relatively small quotas of visas which existed were often not filled, although the number of applicants was usually many times the number of available places.

Conferences held in Evian, France (1938) and Burmuda (1943) to solve the refugee problem did not contribute to a solution. At the former, the countries invited by the United States and Britain were told that no country would be asked to change its immigration laws. Moreover, the British agreed to participate only if Palestine would not be considered. At Bermuda, the delegates assembled but did not deal with the fate of those still in Nazi hands, but rather with those who had already escaped to neutral lands.

Practical measures which could have been taken to aid in the rescue of Jews included:
- permission for temporary admission of refugees
- relaxation of stringent entry requirements
- frequent and unequivocal warnings to Germany, as well as to local populations all over Europe, that those participating in the murder of Jews would be held strictly accountable
- warnings to Jewish communities on the Nazis' plans to murder them
- the bombing of the death camp at Auschwitz

9. Who are the *Righteous Among the Nations*?

Righteous Among The Nations or *Righteous Gentiles* is a term used to refer to those non-Jews who aided Jews during the Holocaust. There were Righteous Gentiles in every country over-run or allied with the Nazis, and their deeds often led to the rescue of Jewish lives.

Yad Vashem, the Israeli National Remembrance Authority for the Holocaust, bestows a special medal upon these individuals, who also are invited to plant a tree near the memorial to the martyrs of the Holocaust at Yad Vashem. As of 2007, Yad Vashem had honored approximately 22,000 Righteous Gentiles from 44 countries, after carefully evaluating each case.

The country with the most Righteous Gentiles is Poland; the country with the highest proportion (per population) is Holland. The figure of 2,500 is far from complete as many cases were never reported – either because those who were helped died, or other reasons. Moreover, this figure only included those who actually risked their lives to save Jews, and not those who merely extended aid.

10. Did the Jews in Europe realize what was going to happen to them?

Regarding the knowledge of the Final Solution by its potential victims, several key points must be kept in mind. First of all, the Nazis did not publicize the Final Solution, nor did they ever openly speak about it.

Every attempt was made to fool the victims, and thereby prevent or minimize resistance. Thus, deportees were always told that they were going to be "resettled" and were led to believe that conditions where they were going to be sent ("in the East") would be better than those in the ghettos. Moreover, following arrival in certain concentration camps, the inmates were forced to write home about the "wonderful conditions" in their new place of residence. In addition, the notion that human beings – let alone the civilized Germans – could build camps with special apparatus for mass murder, seemed unbelievable in those days. The Germans were regarded by many Jews as a liberal, civilized people since they remembered that German troops had liberated the Jews from the Czar in World War I.

The Germans made every effort to ensure secrecy, and thus it was extremely difficult to escape from the death camps. Escapees who did return to the ghetto frequently encountered disbelief when they related their experiences. Even Jews who had heard of Auschwitz, Treblinka, Sobibor, etc., had difficulty believing what the Germans were doing there. Moreover, the number of places where such information was available was limited as each of the Jewish communities of Europe was in almost complete isolation. Thus, there is no doubt that many European Jews were not aware of the Final Solution – a fact corroborated by German documents and the testimonies of survivors.

11. Was there any opposition to the Nazis within Germany?

Throughout the course of the Third Reich, there were different groups who opposed the Nazi regime or certain Nazi policies. They engaged in resistance at different times and with different scope, methods and aims. Those who were in opposition from the beginning were the leftist political groups and various disappointed conservatives. At a later date, church groups, government officials and businessmen joined as well. After the reversal in the tide of the war, parts of the military played an active role in resistance. At no point, however, was there ever a unified resistance movement.

It is extremely difficult to ascertain the extent of the opposition to the Nazis in Germany. While it was certainly more widespread than Nazi propaganda would have us believe, it should not be exaggerated. Among the groups which attempted to resist the Nazis were members of the Social Democratic Party which included The Red Patrol in Berlin, the Socialist Front in Hanover, the New Beginning, The International Socialist Combat League, etc.; and the communist party (Red Orchestra); isolated church leaders and clergymen – for example, the Confessional Church, founded to counteract the Nazis' attempts to coordinate church and state (Dietrich Bonhoeffer, Martin Niemoller, etc.); assorted civil servants (Carl Goerdeler), members of the armed forces, and military intelligence, students (White Rose), as well as various other groups (Kreisam Circle). A film called "Sophie Scholl" about the White Rose group came out in 2006.

12. Did the Jews try to fight against the Nazis? Where? To what extent were such efforts successful?

Despite the difficult conditions which Jews were subjected to in Nazi occupied territories, there was resistance to the Nazis. This resistance can be divided into four basic types of armed activities:

1) Ghetto revolts
2) Resistance in concentration and death camps
3) Partisan warfare
4) Resistance work.

The Warsaw Ghetto revolt - which lasted for about five weeks, beginning April 19,1943 - is probably the best-known example of armed Jewish resistance, but there were many ghettos in which Jews fought against the Nazis. Among the ghettos in which armed resistance took place were:

Bialystok 8/16/43; Lachwa 9/3/42; Czestochowa 6/25/43; Tatarsk 10/25/42; Kletzk 7/21/42; Nieswiez 7/22/42; Mir, 8/9/42; Krements 9/9/42; Tuchin 9/23/42; Cracow 12/22/42; Lvov 6/43; Bendzin 8/3/43; Tarnow 9/1/43; Stardubsk 10/25/41.

Despite the terrible conditions in the death, concentration and labor camps, Jewish inmates fought against the Nazis in the following camps: *Treblinka 8/2/43; Babi Yar 9/29/43; Sobibor 10/14/43; Janowska 11/19/43; Auschwitz 10/7/44.*

Jewish partisan units were active in the following areas: *Minsk, Vilna, Naliboki Forest, Baranowitz, Liphichan Forest, Zhetel, Parcew Forests, Swienciany, Naroch Forest, Raab Island - Yugoslavia and Kovno.*

Jewish units of the resistance were established in France, Belgium and Slovakia. Jews also played an active role in the opposition to the Nazis in Italy, Greece, Yugoslavia and Bulgaria.

While the sum total effect of the armed resistance by Jews was not overwhelming militarily and did not play a significant role in the defeat of Nazi Germany, these acts of resistance did lead to the rescue of an undetermined number of Jews, as well as the loss of Nazi lives and property.

Christian Zionists

While most of the early Christians were Jews, the church gradually lost interest in its Jewish roots and heritage as it moved to the pagan world. By the 3rd century C.E. few Christians thought of Jesus as a Jewish teacher or rabbi. Fewer still thought of the Jews as God's prophets, priests, kings, and apostles. Some medieval Christian pilgrims related to the ancient Jews as they traveled to the Holy Land, but few felt connected to the contemporary Jews they met along the way. For over 1000 years most of the church believed that Christians had replaced the Jews as God's covenant people. There were isolated instances of Christians who read the scriptures differently but until the Reformation few Christians considered the possibility of a Jewish return to Israel. The translation of the Bible into the language of the common people, particularly the English Bible, produced a radical change. Barbara Tuchman, in her book, "Bible and Sword," says, "...without the background of the English Bible it is doubtful that the Balfour Declaration would ever have been issued..."

We who are 21st century Christian Zionists are proud to follow in the footsteps of many Bible-believers who see overwhelming evidence in scripture for God's continuing covenant with the Jewish people and their right to their ancient homeland. We would like to introduce a few of those who left these footprints:

Henry Finch (1558-1625), Member of British Parliament, jurist and legal writer, a Hebraist wrote in Hebrew. "A true forerunner of a modern non-Jewish Zionist."

Holger Paulli (1644-1714), a Danish pietist, believed whole-heartedly in the Jewish Return to the "Promised Land."

John Toland (1670-1722) an Irish participant in the theological and political debates in England. In 1714 he published his "Reasons for Naturalising the Jews in Great Britain and Ireland on the Same Footing with all Other Nations."

John Calvin (1509-1564) was one of the foremost leaders in the Protestant Reformation in Europe. (as with others, there is a mixed bag - Calvin held a high view of the Abrahamic covenant but expelled Jews from some cities he controlled.)

John Knox (1515-1572) Leader of the Reformation in Scotland. Frederick M. Schweitzer, in his work, *A History of the Jews Since the First Century A.D.*, said: "Scots are very proud that unlike 'the kingdom to the south' their homeland has never been desecrated by anti-Semitism, expulsions, confiscations, or ill-feeling of any kind toward Jews . . ."

Puritan Movement, both in England and America, drew heavily on the Hebrew scriptures as a model for Christian life. Biblical personal and place names abound in early America. The American Thanksgiving celebration is based on the concept of Sukkot. The third oldest chair at Harvard is the Hancock Professorship in Hebrew.

Joseph Eyre, 1771 published, *Observations upon Prophecies Relating to the Restoration of the Jews*. He drew public attention to the ancient biblical promises from the Creator to Abraham.

Warder Cresson, 1798-1870, Quaker, U.S. Counsel in Jerusalem 1848. Established an agricultural settlement in the Valley of Rephaim and worked to form Jewish settlements in the Galilee.

Charles Jerram, 1795, Divinity Student at Cambridge, wrote essay on future restoration of the Jewish people to their land, based on Genesis 12:1-3; 17:8 & Luke 21:24.

Lord Palmerston, British Foreign Secretary, wrote in 1840 to the British Ambassador in Constantinople. Favored British policy keeping Ottoman regime in power to encourage the Sultan to aid the Jews to return and settle in Palestine.

Lord Shaftesbury (Anthony Ashley Cooper, 1801-1885) a man of faith who based his life on literal acceptance of the Bible. He believed the Jews were "God's ancient people," and he accepted them in the same way that he accepted the Bible. In 1838 when Mehemet Ali of Egypt threatened the Sultan, Palmerston and Shaftesbury influenced the Turkish Government to permit the establishment of a British Consulate in Jerusalem.

John Scott, 1777-1834, wrote "Destiny of Israel" promoting return of Jews to their land.

Period of the Enlightenment, French Revolution & Napoleon brought increasing tolerance for the Jews. Napoleon favored Jewish presence in ancient Israel.

George Gawler, 1796-1869, senior commander at the Battle of Waterloo & first Governor or Australia. Worked with Sir Moses Montefiore to develop Jewish settlements in Israel. Projects included Yemin Moshe, first neighborhood outside walls of Jerusalem.

George Eliot, 1819-1880, pen name of author Mary Anne Evans, wrote *Daniel Deronda*, a sympathetic account of Zionist aspirations.

John Nelson Darby, 1800-1882, founder of Plymouth Brethren. Doctrine of dispensationalist pre-millennialism. Divides history into different dispensations in which God works differently. Taught the return of the Jews to their land before the second advent.

William H. Hechler, 1845-1931, British clergyman, tutored the son of Grand Duke of Baden - the future German Emperor. Worked with British Christians to aid Jewish refugees from Russian pogroms. A strong believer in biblical prophecies of the return of the Jews to Israel. In 1885 he was appointed chaplain to British Embassy in Vienna, became a devoted friend of Theodor Herzl and was instrumental in arranging Herzl's first contact with German royalty.

He arranged the audience, in 1898, between Herzl and the Kaiser. Hechler called for, "an end to the antisemitic spirit of hatred, which is most detrimental to the welfare of all our nations." He was an honored guest at the first Zionist conference in Basle.

Laurence Oliphant, 1829-1888, British Protestant and mystic, member of Parliament. Traveled in the Holy Land and wrote a book, "Land Of Gilead," outlining a plan to begin Jewish settlement on the east bank of the Jordan. In Haifa, he employed Naftali Imber, the author of *Hatikva*, as his secretary.

William E. Blackstone, 1860-1929, Chicago businessman, evangelical Christian, wrote several booklets predicting Jewish return to their land. In 1891 he presented Pres. Harrison with a petition with over 400 prominent Christian signatures calling for American support for the Jewish return. Later he influenced Pres. Wilson to accept the Balfour Declaration.

Lord Arthur James Balfour, 1848-1930, British states-man. Both Balfour and Prime Minister Lloyd George were deeply religious and were steeped in the Bible. They were very much in favor of implementing this plan. The Balfour Declaration calls for "the establishment in Palestine of a national home for the Jewish people."

Lt. Col. John Henry Patterson, 1867-1947, Irish Protestant, Bible student. Led the Zion Mule Corps, a group of Jewish volunteers who fought for Britain in WWI. He rejoiced at the Balfour Declaration and wrote: "Christians, too, have always believed in the fulfillment of prophecy and the restoration of the Jewish people...Nothing like this has been known since the days of King Cyrus."

Charles Orde Wingate, 1903-44, British officer, intense Bible believer, always carried a Bible with him. In 1936 he began training the Haganah. He used the Hebrew scriptures as a training manual and created the Night Squads, which included future Israeli commanders Yigal Allon and Moshe Dayan. In 1939 The British transferred him because of his Zionist sentiments. At his farewell he quoted Psalm 137: "If I forget thee, O Jerusalem..." and promised to return. He was killed in action in Burma in 1944. After the birth of the State of Israel in 1948 his widow was flown over the village named for him. She wrote a note to the Jewish defenders and threw his Bible out to the soldiers down below. He is affectionately remembered as, "Hayedid," which means the friend, in Hebrew.

G. Douglas Young, 1910-1980, Founder of the Institute of Holy Land Studies and Bridges for Peace. In 1963 Doug Young and his wife, Georgina, moved to Israel. For almost two decades, he was actively involved in the everyday life of the Jerusalem community and in communicating a positive view of Israel to Christians in America.

During the Six-Day War Dr. Young drove an ambulance through the bombed areas of Jerusalem and his wife fed and sheltered neighbors and visiting soldiers at the Institute of Holy Land Studies. The people of Israel reciprocated his love by awarding him Jerusalem's highest honor, the title "Worthy of Jerusalem." Young's "Dispatch from Jerusalem" still brings news from Israel to the American Christian community. When he died of a heart attack in May 1980, he was mourned by the Jerusalem community and buried on the crest of Mount Zion after a stirring memorial service at St. Andrews's Scottish church. Freda Keet, a prominent newscaster on Israel Radio's English-language program, summed up Young's accomplishments:

"For Israelis, and especially for Jerusalemites, Douglas Young represents the voice of Christianity, that part of Christianity which understands what Israel is, and what Israel does, and what Israel is trying to achieve. For us he has truly been a builder of bridges. And for this we owe him our eternal gratitude."

Many Catholics have also taken a strong stand for Zionism and Christian-Jewish understanding. A sample includes: Fr. Friedrich Heer, author of *God's First Love*; Fr. Edward Flannery, author of *The Anguish of the Jews*; Jacques Maritain, author of *The Mystery of Israel*; Fr. Michel Riquet, author of *A Christian Faces Israel*; The Sisters of Sion; and of course, Pope John XXIII, who shortly before his death composed this prayer:

"We realize now that we no longer see the beauty of Thy Chosen People and no longer recognize in their faces the features of our firstborn brother. We realize that our brows are branded with the mark of Cain. Centuries long has Abel lain in blood and tears, because we had forgotten Thy love. Forgive us the curse which we unjustly laid on the name of the Jews. Forgive us that, with our curse, we crucified Thee a second time."

Christians of many theological backgrounds have been friends of Israel and the Jewish people but those who hold a high view of the authority of the Bible are more likely to see significance in God's covenant promises and God's hand in history. We apologize to thousands of Christian Zionists who do not appear on this list. We offer this simply as a starting point for a very extensive and important study.

Birth of Modern Israel – May 14, 1948

From 1517 until the end of World War I both the Jews and the Arabs living in Eretz Israel – sometimes called Palestine – were under the rule of the Turkish Ottoman Empire. From the destruction of the Temple in 70 C.E., the land formerly known as Israel – changed to Palestine by the Romans – was ruled by absentee land lords. As part of their battle against the Turks, who were allies of Germany. The British made promises of independence to both Jews and Arabs. After the war they did not keep these promises and Palestine became a British protectorate or mandate. British rule had already produced hostilities between Arabs and Jews between the two World Wars. Jewish refugees came in increased numbers as a result of World War II. When the British agreed to withdraw from Palestine, the UN set up an arrangement to divide the land into Arab and Jewish states. The Arabs refused to accept the agreement and began a war to destroy Israel. They were defeated and lost some of the land the UN had awarded to them. This has been the pattern also of subsequent wars. Israel's offers of compromise and co-existence have always been refused.

WHAT IS A KIBBUTZ?

A kibbutz is a cooperative village which is governed by the general assembly of all its members. All property is collectively owned, and work is organized on a collective basis. All members have equal rights and each member contributes his labor and skills, to the best of his ability, towards the economic, social and cultural advancement of the community. In return, the kibbutz assumes full responsibility for the well-being of its members and provides for all their physical, cultural, social and educational needs.

Primarily agricultural, most kibbutzim also have a factory or industry of some sort, as their produce alone will not support the community financially. While families live in separate apartment units, all meals are served in a common dining hall and prepared in a common kitchen. Though each age group of children is cared for in a separate unit, in some kibbutzim the children sleep in the family apartment. This is a more recent development. In the early days, all children slept in the children's house.

The kibbutz is run as a simple democracy. Decisions are made at the General Meeting which is open to all members. Elected committees handle the day-to-day affairs. There is no money used within the settlement, but members are given an annual stipend to be used outside the kibbutz and on vacation. Much like the early church in its attitude about material things, it is unlike Marxism in that life on a kibbutz is the result of a voluntary choice.

Kibbutz Degania, on the southern end of the Sea of Galilee, is called the *Mother of Kibbutzim*. It was started in 1901, and Moshe Dayan was one of the first children born there. During the1930's, European Jews who could see the coming of Nazi persecution, went to Israel in large numbers, and it was during that period of mass immigration that kibbutz society was firmly established. A very strong sense of Zionism prevailed in the kibbutzim, though most of them are not particularly religious. Kibbutzniks are usually work-oriented people, especially members of the older generation. Some of the younger members identify with the kibbutz philosophy, some prefer to try other life-styles. Children of kibbutz members can choose whether or not to stay on as adults. Kibbutz members make up about 3% of the total population, but have contributed about 25% of the Israeli leadership. Early kibbutzniks carved out a homeland from swamps and deserts with a sense of commitment and determination reminiscent of the American pioneers. The kibbutz movement is uniquely Israeli and it would be hard to imagine the vast strides made In agriculture and forestry without kibbutz life. Whether this type of life will continue to draw the next generation of Israelis remains to be seen. There are about 260 kibbutzim in Israel today.

Other Rural Settlements

The Moshav is a cooperative village where each family maintains its own household and works its own plot of land. Supply and marketing are handled cooperatively and capital and equipment are usually owned jointly. The average moshav numbers 60-100 families. There are approximately 450 moshavim, housing about 4% of Israel's population.

Moshav Shitufi is based on collective ownership and economy as in the kibbutz, but each family is responsible for running its own household. Work and pay are adjusted to individual circumstances.

Regional Development Bloc

In the 1950's, many new immigrants were absorbed into Israeli life by being provided with farming opportunities in new villages in parts of the country which were previously uninhabited. Each village was usually settled by people sharing similar ethnic and cultural backgrounds. The need to provide adequate services to these small communities led to the development of the "rural cluster" concept, linking several villages to a local rural center where basic health, education and commercial services are available. This also helps foster social integration of people from different cultural backgrounds. The clusters are administratively linked to a regional town which provides services such as hospitals, high schools, commercial, banking and industrial facilities. The town provides housing and increased employment opportunities for thousands of people.

The Flag Of Israel

Psalm 60:4 reads, "Thou hast given a banner to them that fear Thee, that it may be displayed because of the truth." Israel celebrated her 60th anniversary in 2012 and it is interesting to take a new look at the flag she displays.

The geometrical design of two equilateral triangles, the one imposed in reverse on the other, has been known for hundreds of years in many tribes and countries. Two bars and the star are designed in blue on a white background.

The name "Magen David" or *Shield of David* first appeared in Hebrew literature in the 12th century, when it was used by the Karaite, Yehuda Ben Elia Hadassi, scholars tell us. He said that the six corners represent the four directions of the compass, the earth and heaven. The first to use it officially probably was the Jewish community of Prague in the year 1354 when commanded by Charles IV of Bohemia to have a red flag on which a Star of David was to be emblazoned. However, it did not become an important Jewish symbol until about the middle of the 17th century.

But Theodor Herzl, founder of the modern Zionist movement, did not plan to use this flag. He envisioned a different flag, one with seven golden stars on a white background. However, he compromised for the Magen David with one star in each of the six angles, a seventh star above it and the words, "Arie Yehuda" (Lion of Judah) in the center. This was the first flag of the Zionist movement. Bible students will find it interesting to note that the children of Israel were commanded to make ribbons of blue on their garments in Numbers 15:38, which reads, "Speak unto the children of Israel, and bid them that they make them fringes in the borders or their garments throughout their generations, and that they put upon the fringe of the borders a ribbon of blue...." Blue, the heavenly color, was used on the borders of the priests' garments, showing that these servants of God were to be heavenly in their obedience and character and be separate from earthly things.

It was David Wolfson – later Herzl's successor as leader of the Zionist movement, who first suggested that the parallel line of the Jewish *tallit*, the prayer shawl, be used on the new flag, above and below the Star of David, as the official flag of the State of the people of Israel. He describes the event as follows: "At the behest of our leader, Herzl, I came to Basel to make preparations for the Zionist Congress.... Among the many problems that occupied me then was one which contained something of the essence of the Jewish problem. What flag would we have in the Congress Hall? Then an idea struck me. We (Jews) have a flag - and it is blue and white. The Tallit with which we wrap ourselves when we pray - that is our symbol. Let us take this symbol from its bag and unroll it before the eyes of Israel and of all nations. So, I ordered a blue and white flag with the Shield of David painted upon it. That is how our national flag, that flew over the Congress Hall, came into being."

In 1933, this design was adopted as the flag of the Zionist Organization and the Jewish people by the 18th Zionist Congress.

When the new State of Israel was proclaimed in May 1948, the flag as we know it today was declared the official flag of Israel.

פגילת העצמאות

Declaration of Israel's Independence

Issued at Tel Aviv on May 14, 1948 (5th of Iyar, 5708)

The Land of Israel was the birthplace of the Jewish people. Here their spiritual, religious and national identity was formed. Here they achieved independence and created a culture of national and universal significance. Here they wrote and gave the Bible to the world.

Exiled from Palestine, the Jewish people remained faithful to it in all the countries of their dispersion, never ceasing to pray and hope for their return and the restoration of their national freedom.

Impelled by this historic association, Jews strove throughout the centuries to go back to the land of their fathers and regain their statehood. In recent decades they returned in masses. They reclaimed the wilderness, revived their language, built cities and villages and established a vigorous and ever-growing community, with its own economic and cultural life. They sought peace yet were ever prepared to defend themselves. They brought the blessing of progress to all inhabitants of the country.

In the year 1897 the First Zionist Congress, inspired by Theodor Herzl's vision of the Jewish State, proclaimed the right of the Jewish people to national revival in their own country.

This right was acknowledged by the Balfour Declaration of November 2, 1917, and re-affirmed by the Mandate of the League of Nations, which gave explicit international recognition to the historic connection of the Jewish people with Palestine and their right to reconstitute their National Home.

The Nazi holocaust, which engulfed millions of Jews in Europe, proved anew the urgency of the re-establishment of the Jewish State, which would solve the problem of Jewish homelessness by opening the gates to all Jews and lifting the Jewish people to equality in the family of nations.

The survivors of the European catastrophe, as well as Jews from other lands, proclaiming their right to a life of dignity, freedom and labor, and undeterred by hazards, hardships and obstacles, have tried unceasingly to enter Palestine.

In the Second World War the Jewish people in Palestine made a full contribution in the struggle of the freedom-loving nations against the Nazi evil. The sacrifices of their soldiers and the efforts of their workers gained them title to rank with the peoples who founded the United Nations.

On November 29, 1947, the General Assembly of the United Nations adopted a Resolution for the establishment of an independent Jewish State in Palestine, and called upon the inhabitants of the country to take such steps as may be necessary on their part to put the plan into effect.

This recognition by the United Nations of the right of the Jewish people to establish their independent State may not be revoked. It is, moreover, the self-evident right of the Jewish people to be a nation, as all other nations, in its own sovereign State.

ACCORDINGLY, WE, the members of the National Council, representing the Jewish people in Palestine and the Zionist movement of the world, met together in solemn assembly today, the day of termination of the British Mandate for Palestine, by virtue of the natural and historic right of the Jewish people and of the Resolution of the General Assembly of the United Nations,

HEREBY PROCLAIM the establishment of the Jewish State in Palestine, to be called ISRAEL.

WE HEREBY DECLARE that as from the termination of the Mandate at midnight, this night of the 14th to 15th May, 1948, and until the setting up of the duly elected bodies of the State in accordance with a Constitution, to be drawn up by a Constituent Assembly not later than the first day of October, 1948, the present National Council shall act as the provisional administration, shall constitute the Provisional Government of the State of Israel.

THE STATE OF ISRAEL will be open to the immigration of Jews from all countries of their dispersion; will promote the development of the country for the benefit of all its inhabitants; will be based on the precepts of liberty, justice and peace taught by the Hebrew Prophets; will uphold the full social and political equality of all its citizens, without distinction of race, creed or sex; will guarantee full freedom of conscience, worship, education and culture; will safeguard the sanctity and inviolability of the shrines and Holy Places of all religions; and will dedicate itself to the principles of the Charter of the United Nations.

THE STATE OF ISRAEL will be ready to cooperate with the organs and representatives of the United Nations in the implementation of the Resolution of the Assembly of November 29, 1947, and will take steps to bring about the Economic Union over the whole of Palestine.

We appeal to the United Nations to assist the Jewish people in the building of its State and to admit Israel into the family of nations.

In the midst of wanton aggression, we yet call upon the Arab inhabitants of the State of Israel to return to the ways of peace and play their part in the development of the State, with full and equal citizenship and due representation in all its bodies and institutions—provisional or permanent.

We offer peace and unity to all the neighboring states and their peoples, and invite them to cooperate with the independent Jewish nation for the common good of all.

Our call goes out to the Jewish people all over the world to rally to our side in the task of immigration and development and to stand by us in the great struggle for the fulfillment of the dream of generations—the redemption of Israel.

With trust in Almighty God, we set our hand to this Declaration, at this Session of the Provisional State Council, in the city of Tel Aviv, on this Sabbath eve, the fifth of Iyar, 5708, the fourteenth day of May, 1948.

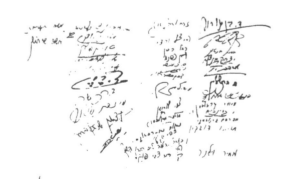

Issued by the Information Department
Embassy of Israel
Washington, D.C. 20008

Israel: Background and Statistics

Location

Israel is located in the Middle East, along the eastern coastline of the Mediterranean Sea, bordered by Lebanon, Syria, Jordan and Egypt. It lies at the junction of three continents: Europe, Asia and Africa. Long and narrow in shape, the country is about 290 miles (470 km.) in length and 85 miles (135 km.) in width at its widest point.

Although small in size, Israel encompasses the varied topographical features of an entire continent, ranging from forested highlands and fertile green valleys to mountainous deserts and from the coastal plain to the semitropical Jordan Valley and the Dead Sea, the lowest point on earth. Approximately half of the country's land area is semi-arid.

Israel's geographic diversity is unique among the countries of the world. Although only about the size of the state of Maryland or New Jersey, and a little larger than Wales, it contains an amazing variety of topographical and climactic features.

Compressed within long, narrow borders, Israel is a country of short distances. It can be crossed by car from west to east in barely two hours, and from north to south in about ten. In the course of either drive, mountains and plains, fertile fields and barren deserts, seacoast and rocky highlands are often minutes apart.

In the Galilee, in the north, forested highlands merge with green valleys. Sand dunes and citrus groves mark the coastal plain bordering the Mediterranean Sea. Deserts, stretching southward through the Negev and Arava, meet the tropical waters of the Gulf of Eilat on the Red Sea.

Climate

Israel's climate is characterized by much sunshine, with a rainy season from November to April. Total annual precipitation ranges from 20-50 inches (50-125 cm.) in the north to less than an inch (2.5 cm.) in the far south. Regional climactic conditions vary considerably: hot, humid summers and mild, wet winters on the coastal plain; dry, warm summers and moderately cold winters, with rain and occasional light snow, in the hill regions; hot, dry summers and pleasant winters in the Jordan Valley; and semi-arid conditions, with warm to hot days and cool nights, in the south.

Flora and Fauna

The rich variety of Israel's plant and animal life reflects its geographical location as well as its varied topography and climate. Over 380 kinds of birds, some 150 mammal and reptile species, and nearly 3,000 plant types (150 of which are native to Israel) are found within its borders. About 150 nature reserves, encompassing nearly 400 square miles have been established throughout the country.

Water

The scarcity of water in the region has generated intense efforts to maximize use of the available supply and to seek new resources. In the 1960s, Israel's freshwater sources were joined in an integrated grid whose main artery, the National Water Carrier, brings water from the north and center to the semi-arid south. Ongoing projects for utilizing new sources include cloud seeding, recycling of sewage water and the desalination of seawater.

Population

Israel is a country of immigrants. Since 1948, Israel's population has grown seven-fold. Its over 7 million citizens comprise a mosaic of people with varied ethnic backgrounds, lifestyles, religions, cultures and traditions. The country's population stands at 7,282,000, according to figures released by the Central Bureau of Statistics. Some 5,499,000 of the population (75.5 percent) are Jews, 1,461,000 (20.1%) are Arabs and the remaining 322,000 (4.4%) are immigrants and their offspring who are not registered as Jews by the Interior Ministry.

Lifestyle

About 90% of Israel's inhabitants live in some 200 urban centers, some of which are located on ancient historical sites. About 5% are members of unique rural cooperative settlements - the kibbutz and the moshav.

Israel In The World

Israel proclaimed its independence on May 14, 1948 in the area designated for a Jewish state by the UN partition plan of November 29, 1947, and since May 1949 has been a member state of the United Nations. It maintains about 80 diplomatic missions abroad, which represent Israel's political, commercial and cultural interests. Its officials participate in most international forums dealing with matters such as world health, environmental control, disarmament, international law and many more. Trade agreements, cultural exchange programs and the like have developed between Israel and many countries over the years. Itself a developing country, Israel shares its experience and expertise with other developing countries in such fields as agriculture, hydrology, regional planning, health, youth leadership and community organization.

The State

Israel's Declaration of Independence of May 14, 1948 lays down some basic characteristics of the State and guiding principles of its policy, among these,*"the natural right of the Jewish people to be master of its own fate, like all other nations, in its own sovereign state. The State of Israel will be open for Jewish immigration and for the ingathering of the exiles; it will foster the development of the country for the benefit of all its inhabitants..."*

Israel is a parliamentary democracy consisting of legislative, executive and judicial branches and structured, according to the principle of division of authority, to ensure checks and balances within the system. All citizens of Israel, regardless of race or religion, are guaranteed equality before the law and full democratic rights. Freedom of speech and assembly, of press and political affiliation, of strike and demonstration, as well as the right of the individual to vote according to his or her conscience, are embodied in the country's laws and traditions.

Political parties in Israel represent the whole spectrum of ideologies, from far-left to far-right. All Israeli citizens over the age of 19 may vote and from age 21, be elected to office. The country is regarded as a single constituency, and voting is universal, secret and proportional on the basis of party lists. Changes are being considered to make the elected officials more directly responsible to the voters, as in the U.S. system.

The Prime Minister & the President

The duties of the President are largely ceremonial and formal. He may serve a maximum of two five-year terms. He accepts the credentials of foreign envoys to Israel and appoints the judiciary and the diplomatic representatives abroad. The Prime Minister is the actual head of government. From 1996 to 2001 citizens voted directly for Prime Minister. Now the PM is chosen by the vote for the party. Term is four years but new elections can be forced by no-confidence vote of the Knesset.

The Cabinet, Israel's executive body, is appointed and headed by the Prime Minister and is responsible to the Knesset. To date, no one party has ever received an absolute majority of the vote so the practice has been for the party receiving the highest vote to form a coalition with other cooperative parties. The Cabinet ministers are assigned portfolios – such as foreign affairs, defense, housing, tourism, education, etc.

The Knesset, Israel's legislative body, is a single-chamber parliament with 120 members. It elects the President and the Speaker of the Knesset, and may dissolve itself and call for new elections before the end of its four-year term. Although Knesset debates are conducted in Hebrew, Arab and Druse members may address the House in Arabic, Israel's other official language. Simultaneous translations are provided. Thus far, Israel has not enacted a formal constitution but there is a code of basic law which will eventually form part of such a document.

The Israeli court system is entirely independent of the executive and legislative branches. Judges are appointed by the President on the recommendation of a public nominations commission. There are three levels of the court. In addition, each religious group has its own courts with full jurisdiction in matters of its own concerns.

Israel In Numbers, 2010:

Population: 7,882,000

Jews: 79%
Non-Jews: 21%
% Israeli Jews in World Jewry: 26%

Presidents of Israel

Hayim Weizmann	1948-52
Yitzhak Ben-Zvi	1952-63
Zalman Shazar	1963-73
Ephraim Katzir	1973-76
Yitzhak Navon	1976-83
Haim Herzog	1983-93
Ezer Weizmann	1993-2000
Avraham Burg	2000
Moshe Katsav	2000-2007
Shimon Peres	2008-

Prime Ministers

David Ben Gurion	1948-54
Moshe Sharett	1954-55
David Ben Gurion	1955-62
Levi Eshkol	1962-68
Golda Meir	1968-74
Yitzhak Rabin	1974-77
Menahem Begin	1977-83
Yizhak Shamir	1983-84
Shimon Peres	1984-88
Yizhak Shamir	1988-92
Yitzhak Rabin	1992-95
Shimon Peres	1995-96
Binyamin Netanyahu	1996-99
Ehud Barak	1999-2001
Ariel Sharon	2001-06
Ehud Olmert	2006-09
Binyamin Netanyahu	2009-

Statistics from Wikipedia

A Few Facts About the West Bank For Your Data Bank . . .

We receive many inquiries of this sort: "I want to be a friend to Israel but the news is so confusing! Israel often looks bad in the press. How can I respond to the questions my family or neighbors are asking?" Nobody has all the answers but we offer this brief list of facts to help you prepare to respond.

- God promised to keep His covenant with Israel as long as the sun, moon and stars endure. The West Bank is Biblical Judea & Samaria.
- Even though other nations have ruled the land since 70 CE, there has always been a Jewish population in the land during the 1900 years of dispersion.
- Jerusalem has never been the capital for any people, other than the Jews.
- A Palestinian Arab state never existed. While Arabs have lived in the land called Palestine since the Moslem conquest, they have never had an autonomous political entity. The land has been governed by absentee rulers from 70 CE to 1948.
- The Ottoman Turks ruled the area from 1517 to 1917. The Turkish territories were divided by the World War I victors and the British were give a mandate over the areas that were to become Israel and Jordan.
- During the years of the British Mandate (1917–1948) many Arabs, as well as Jews, moved to the area called Palestine. Higher wages and living standards drew many Arabs from Syria and Egypt.
- In 1922, 78% of the Mandate area became a Palestinian Arab area on the east bank of the Jordan River – later to be called the Hashemite Kingdom of Jordan.
- In 1948, the Arabs refused the UN Partition Plan which would have given them the state they are asking for today.
- The land of Israel is a geographic unit, from the Jordan River to the Mediterranean Sea. If divided again, as it was before 1967, it would be very difficult to defend. It is also important to remember that the West Bank is the Biblical heartland of Israel, the highlands giving strategic control of the watershed to those who occupy them. Without this territory Israel is only 9 to 15 miles wide along the coast.
- There was no peace when the West Bank and East Jerusalem were in Arab hands from 1948 to 1967. If, as is often suggested, the return of the West Bank to Arab or joint Jordanian and Palestinian control will bring peace to the Middle East, why then was there no peace when these territories were in Arab hands for nearly twenty years? If the Palestinians will be satisfied with autonomy in the "West Bank," why was the PLO formed in 1964 when the West Bank already was under Arab control? Why did the Arab nations declare war on Israel in 1967 when they already possessed the West Bank? Perhaps it was not to liberate the Palestinians, but to destroy Israel.

- There is reason for concern that a Palestinian state in the West Bank could easily become another Lebanon – filled with internal strife, graft, corruption and violence.
- Zionism began as a dream, in the face of a long history of antisemitism, that a homeland would be created where all Jews, who desired to do so, would be able to settle. With continuing evidence of antisemitism in the world today, it would be a tragic mistake should Israel be so reduced in size as to prevent her from being a potential homeland for all the Jews who want to immigrate.
- Israel is the only democratic state in the area. There are at least 20 Arab states in the region and only one Jewish state.
- The Palestinian Authority was formed in 1994, according to the Oslo Accords between the Palestine Liberation Organization (PLO) and the government of Israel, as a five-year interim body, during which final status negotiations between the two parties were to take place. As of 2012, more than seventeen years following the formulation of the PA, a final status has yet to be reached. According to the Oslo Accords, the Palestinian Authority was designated to have control over both security-related and civilian issues in Palestinian urban areas (referred to as "Area A"), and only civilian control over Palestinian rural areas ("Area B"). The remainder of the territories, including Israeli settlements, the Jordan Valley region, and bypass roads between Palestinian communities, were to remain under exclusive Israeli control ("Area C"). East Jerusalem was excluded from the Accords. In the 2006 Palestinian legislative elections Hamas was victorious. Today the PA controls the West Bank and Hamas rules the Gaza Strip – from which rocket attacks are ofte-naimed at nearby Israeli towns.
- Does justice for the Palestinians necessarily mean forming a second Palestinian State? (Such a state already exists in Jordan, where a very large majority of the citizens are Palestinians.) Many Palestinians just want to live in peace and dignity in the country of their choice. All the Arabs who want to make Israel their home should be treated justly by the Israeli authorities, just as God expected the Egyptians to treat the Jews justly when they lived in Egypt. In fact, while there are many legitimate griev-

ances, Israel has generally treated the Palestinian population better than America has treated the Native American Indians, and far better than Jordan, Syria or Egypt has treated the Palestinians. A just solution to the Palestinian problem needs to include guaranteed full rights as co-citizens for the Palestinians in the country of their choice, whether in Jordan, Syria, Lebanon or Israel.

There are no easy solutions to this conflict. Pray for all involved – for Arab Christians who are often caught in the middle, for the young Israeli soldiers who have to make difficult decisions while rocks are flying, for political leaders who need the wisdom of Solomon.

Those of us who take the Bible seriously should consider these thoughts:

Deuteronomy 32:8 says, "When the Most High gave the nations their inheritance, when he divided all mankind, he set us boundaries for the peoples according to the sons of Israel."

Joel 3:1 –2 "In those days and at that time, when I restore the fortunes of Judah and Jerusalem, I will gather all nations and bring them down to the Valley of Jehoshaphat. There I will enter into judgment against them concerning my inheritance, my people Israel, for they scattered my people among the nations and divided up my land."

Gaza & Hamas

Since its founding in 1987 in Gaza by Sheikh Ahmad Yassin, Hamas – an Arabic acronym for Islamic Resistance Movement meaning "zeal" – has been committed to destroying the Jewish state and replacing it with an Islamic state in all of Palestine.

Hamas enjoys strong financial backing from Iran (an estimated $20 - $30 million), private benefactors and Muslim charities in Saudi Arabia and the Gulf states.

Hamas was created shortly before the December 1987 Intifada as a more militant, Palestinian offshoot of the Muslim Brotherhood, a religious, political and social movement founded in Egypt and dedicated to the gradual victory of Islam. Since the mid-1970s, the Brotherhood had been expanding its influence in the West Bank and Gaza Strip through its vast array of social services. Hamas advocacy of an immediate holy war to liberate Palestine rendered the Brotherhood's policy of gradual Islamicization ineffectual.

Hamas preaches and engages in violence and terror in order to destroy the state of Israel and replace it with an Islamic state. Its virulent hatred of Jews and Judaism is deeply rooted in the antisemitic writings of Muslim Brotherhood theologians.

In August 1988, Hamas issued its Covenant laying down its ideological principles and goals. In Hamas' worldview, Islamic precepts forbid a Jewish state in the area known as Palestine and the Jewish people have no legitimate connection to the land of Israel.

In 1993 the Palestinian Authority was set up as an interim administrative body to govern Palestinian population centers, with Israel maintaining control of Gaza Strip's airspace, all but one of its land borders and territorial waters, until a final agreement could be reached. As agreement remained elusive, Israel unilaterally disengaged from Gaza in 2005.

The Gaza Strip is one of the territorial units forming the Palestinian territories. Since July 2007, following the 2006 Palestinian legislative election and Hamas has functioned as the de-facto ruler in the Gaza Strip, forming an alternative Hamas Government in Gaza.

Judea & Samaria
The West Bank

Movements within Judaism

Several denominations have developed within Judaism, especially among Ashkenazi Jews living in English-speaking countries. The Jewish community in these countries is divided into distinct religious denominations, often called "branches" or "movements." Despite the efforts of several of these movements to expand and achieve recognition in Israel, they have remained largely a feature of Judaism in the diaspora.

The three largest denominations, known in in the United States as Orthodox, Conservative, and Reform, originated in the Haskalah (Jewish Enlightenment) and its aftermath, and were shaped by the experience of Jewish immigration to the United States. Several smaller movements have emerged in the years since. In more recent years, all of these movements have been shaped by the challenge of assimilation.

• Common values. The movements share common values such as tikkun olam (a sense of Jewish responsibility to heal or repair the world) and klal Yisrael (a sense of being part of, and responsible for, the universal Jewish community). These Jewish values are the basis for cooperation and interplay among the various movements.

• Sacred texts. The movements share a recognition that the Torah and other Jewish spiritual writings such as Tanakh and Talmud are central to Jewish experience. However they differ in their approach to such texts.

The movements differ in their views on various religious issues. These issues include the level of observance, the methodology for interpreting and understanding Jewish Law, biblical authorship, textual criticism, and the nature or role of the the Messiah (or Messianic age). Across these movements, there are marked differences in liturgy, especially in the language in which services are conducted, with the more traditional movements emphasizing Hebrew. The sharpest theological division occurs between Orthodox and non-Orthodox Jews, such that the non-Orthodox movements are sometimes referred to collectively as the "liberal denominations" or "progressive streams."

Some people reject the term denomination as a label for different groups and ideologies within Judaism, arguing that the notion of denomination has a specifically Christian resonance that does not translate easily into the Jewish context. Other commonly used terms are movements, branches, trends, streams, or even flavors of Judaism. This article uses the terms interchangeably, without purporting to affirm the validity of one term over another.

The Jewish denominations themselves reject characterization as sects. Sects are traditionally defined as religious subgroups that have broken off from the main body, and this separation usually becomes irreparable over time. Within Judaism, individuals and families often switch affiliation, and individuals are free to marry one another, although the major denominations disagree on who is a Jew. It is not unusual

for clergy and Jewish educators trained in one of the liberal denominations to serve in another, and many small Jewish communities combine elements of several movements to achieve a viable level of membership.

Relationships between Jewish religious movements are varied, but are generally marked by interdenominational cooperation outside of the realm of halakha (Jewish Law). The movements cooperate on many issues, often uniting with one another in community federations and in campus organizations such as the Hillel Foundation. Jewish religious denominations are distinct from but often linked to Jewish ethnic divisions and Jewish political movements.

Historic movements and sects

In Roman times, at the time of the destruction of the Second Temple, the Jewish people in Palestine were divided into several movements, sometimes warring among themselves: Saducees, Pharisees, Essenes, and Zealots. Many historic sources, from Flavius Josephus to the Christian New Testament to the recovered fragments of the Dead Sea Scrolls, attest to the divisions among Jews at this time. Rabbinical writings from later periods, including the Talmud, attest further to these ancient schisms. Modern Judaism developed from the Pharisee movement, and became known as Rabbinic Judaism (in Hebrew "Yahadut Rabanit") with the compilation of oral law into Mishna. After the destruction of the Second Temple and the Bar Kokhba revolt, the other movements disappear from historical records.

Modern Judaism has two tiny sects, concentrated primarily in Israel. These remnant communities reflect more ancient divisions in the Jewish people.

• Karaites. Historically, the Karaites appeared after the Islamic conquest of the Middle East, as a schismatic group that rejected the innovations of rabbinical Judaism and the authority of the Exilarch. In their own writings, the Karaites claim descent from the Saducees. Karaism accepts only the written Tanakh (the Hebrew Bible), rejecting the Talmud and other rabbinical writings. At the time of the traveler Benjamin of Tudela in the 12th century, Karaites were still widely dispersed around the eastern Mediterranean, both in Islamic areas and in the Byzantine Empire. Benjamin describes Karaite communities in many of the places he visited. In the early 20th century, small Karaite communities remained in Egypt, Turkey, the Crimea, and Lithuania. Today, a few thousand Karaites remain, mostly living in Israel. Traditionally, rabbinic Judaism has regarded the Karaites as Jewish, but heretical.

• Samaritans. The first historical references to the Samaritans date from the Babylonian Exile. Jewish tradition does not regard the Samaritans as Jews. However, the Samaritan's own history claims descent from the tribe of Joseph in the northern Kingdom of Israel, conquered by Assyria in 722 BCE. Modern DNA evidence supports the Samaritan's claim that they are descended patrilineally from ancient

Israelites.[1] Samaritan scripture preserves a version of the Pentateuch and some writings from Tanakh in slightly variant forms. The Samaritans have dwindled to two communities numbering about 650 individuals. One is located in the Israeli city of Holon, while the other is located near Nablus on Mount Gerizim.

Jewish ethnic and cultural divisions

Traditionally, Judaism is not divided into religious traditions based on theological difference. However, a wide array of Jewish communities have developed independently, distinguishable by their varying practices in matters that are not considered central ideas within Judaism, such as Maimonides' list of the Jewish principles of faith.

Although there are numerous Jewish ethnic communities, there are several that are large enough to be considered "predominant." Ashkenazi communities compose about 42% of the world's Jewish population, and Sephardic communities compose about 37%. Of the remainder, the Mizrahi Jewish communities—the "Arab" and "Persian" Jews—compose the greatest part, with about 16% of the world's Jewish population. Together these ethnic groups compose 95% of the world's Jewish population.

The remaining 5% of Jews are divided among a wide array of small groups (perhaps the Beta Israel group of Ethopian Jews is the most important), some of which are nearing extinction as a result of assimilation and intermarriage into surrounding non-Jewish cultures or surrounding Jewish cultures.

Religiously speaking, most Jewish communities have historically held that there is no relevant role for "dogma"; rather, there Is halakha (Jewish law) only. The extent to which every Jew as an individual adheres to Jewish law has long been regarded as a matter of personal preference, although the idea has always been prominent that every Jew should be as observant of the laws as they are able. The Enlightenment had a tremendous effect on Jewish identity and on ideas about the importance and role of Jewish observance. Due to the geographical distribution and the geopolitical entities affected by the Enlightenment, this philosophical revolution essentially affected only the Ashkenazi community; however, because of the predominance of the Ashkenazi community in Israeli politics and in Jewish leadership worldwide, the effects have been significant for all Jews.

Hasidic Judaism

Hasidic Judaism was founded by Israel ben Eliezer (1700-1760), also known as the Baal Shem Tov or the Besht (the Hebrew and Yiddish acronym of Baal Shem Tov). His disciples attracted many followers among Ashkenazi Jews, and established numerous Hasidic sects across Europe. Hasidic Judaism eventually became the way of life for many Jews in Europe. It came to the United States during the large waves of Jewish emigration beginning in the 1880s.

In the late 18th century, there was a serious schism between Hasidic and non-Hasidic Jews. European Jews who rejected the Hasidic movement were dubbed Mitnagdim ("opponents") by the followers of the Baal Shem Tov, who had previously called themselves Freylechen ("happy ones") and now began to call themselves Hasidim ("pious ones"). Some of the reasons for the rejection of Hasidic Judaism were the overwhelming exuberance of Hasidic worship, their untraditional ascriptions of infallibility and alleged miracle-working to their leaders, and the concern that it might become a messianic sect. Since then all the sects of Hasidic Judaism have been subsumed theologically into mainstream Orthodox Judaism, particularly Haredi Judaism, although cultural differences persist.

Modern divisions or "denominations"

Perhaps the greatest divisions since the time of the division between the Sadducees and Pharisees two millennia ago are the divisions within the Ashkenazic community that have arisen in the past two centuries, ever since the Enlightenment and the Renaissance influenced Jews from northern and eastern Europe.

The first evidence of this great dogmatic schism was the development of the Reform Judaism movement, rejected "ethnic Judaism" and preferred to regard Judaism as a religion rather than an ethnicity or a culture. Over time several movements emerged:

• Orthodox Judaism. Orthodox Jews generally see themselves as practicing normative Judaism, rather than belonging to a particular movement. Within Orthodox Judaism there is a spectrum of communities and practices, including Modern Orthodox Judaism, Haredi Judaism ("ultra-orthodox"), and a variety of movements that have their origins in Hasidic Judaism.

• Conservative Judaism or Masorti Judaism. Founded in the United States after the division between Reform and Orthodox Judaism, to provide Jews seeking liberalization of Orthodox theology and practice with a more traditional and halakhically based alternative to Reform Judaism. It has spread to Ashkenazi communities in anglophone countries and Israel.

• Reconstructionist Judaism. A small, liberal Jewish movement, found primarily in the United States. It began as a liberal movement within Conservative Judaism and formally separated in the 1980s.

• Reform Judaism or Progressive Judaism. Originally formed in Germany as a reaction to traditional Judaism, stresses integration with society and a personal interpretation of the Torah.

• Humanistic Judaism. A nontheistic movement that emphasizes Jewish culture and history as the sources of Jewish identity. Founded by Rabbi Sherwin Wine, it is centered in North America but has spread to Europe, Latin America, and Israel.

Information primarily from Wikipedia

The Jewish Bible
Tanakh: an acrostic for *Torah, Nevi'im, K'tuvim*

Torah (Pentateuch):
1. Genesis ~ *Beresheet*
2. Exodus ~ *Sh'mot*
3. Leviticus ~ *V'Yikra*
4. Numbers ~ *B'midbar*
5. Deuteronomy ~ *D'varim*

Neviim - Prophets:
6. Joshua ~ *Yehoshua*
7. Judges ~ *Shoftim*
8. Samuel I & II ~ *Shmuel*
9. Kings I & II ~ *Melakhim*
10. Isaiah ~ *Yeshayahu*
11. Jeremiah ~ *Yirmiyahu*
12. Ezekiel ~ *Yekhezkel*
13. Book of the Twelve:

Hosea ~ *Hoshea*
Joel ~ *Yoel*
Amos ~ *Ahmos*
Obadiah ~ *Ovadya*
Jonah ~ *Yona*
Micah ~ *Meekha*
Nahum ~ *Nakhum*
Habakkuk ~ *Khabakuk*
Zephaniah ~ *Tzefanya*
Haggai ~ *Khagai*
Zechariah ~ *Zekharya*
Malachi ~ *Malakhi*

Ketuvim - Writings:
14. Psalms ~ *Teheelim*
15. Proverbs ~ *Mishlei*

16. Job ~ *Eeyov*
17. Song of Songs ~ *Shir haShirim*
18. Ruth ~ *Root*
19. Lamentations ~ *Eikha*
20. Ecclesiastes ~ *Kohelet*
21. Esther ~ *Ester*
22. Daniel ~ *Danee-ayl*
23. Ezra ~ *Ezra* & Nehemiah ~ *Nekhemya* (treated as single book)
24. Chronicles I & II ~ *Divrei ha-Yamim* (aleph & bet)

Some Torah Facts:

Chapter & verse divisions were not known until Middle Ages
Scrolls were 24 feet long

Masoretic Text (MT)
masar = to deliver, tradition
Marorites - scribes & scholars pre 800 AD, responsible for MT

Talmud: from root lamed = to learn
The Oral Law
    Mishna, shanah = to repeat
    Gemara, gamar = to complete & to study repeatedly

Halakhah = law, literally "the way to walk"
Aggadah = stories, poetry, "to tell"

Hillel & Shammai: Leaders of two schools of thought from period
    just before time of Jesus
Shammai: Generally more harsh in interpretation.
Hillel said: "What is hateful to you, do not do to your fellow.
       All the rest is commentary. Go & study."

Jewish Calendar

The date of Jewish holidays does not change from year to year. Holidays are celebrated on the same day of the Jewish calendar every year, but the Jewish year is not the same length as a solar year on the Gregorian calendar used by most of the western world, so the date shifts on the Gregorian calendar.

Background and History

The Jewish calendar is primarily lunar, with each month beginning on the new moon, when the first sliver of moon becomes visible after the dark of the moon. In ancient times, the new months used to be determined by observation. When people observed the new moon, they would notify the Sanhedrin. When the Sanhedrin heard testimony from two independent, reliable eyewitnesses that the new moon occurred on a certain date, they would declare the rosh hodesh (first of the month) and send out messengers to tell people when the month began.

The problem with strictly lunar calendars is that there are approximately 12.4 lunar months in every solar year, so a 12-month lunar calendar loses about 11 days every year and a 13-month lunar gains about 19 days every year. The months on such a calendar "drift" relative to the solar year. On a 12 month calendar, the month of Nisan, which is supposed to occur in the Spring, occurs 11 days earlier each year, eventually occurring in the Winter, the Fall, the Summer, and then the Spring again. To compensate for this drift, an extra month was occasionally added: a second month of Adar. The month of Nisan would occur 11 days earlier for two or three years, and then would jump forward 29 or 30 days, balancing out the drift.

In the fourth century, Hillel II established a fixed calendar based on mathematical and astronomical calculations. This calendar, still in use, standardized the length of months and the addition of months over the course of a 19 year cycle, so that the lunar calendar realigns with the solar years. Adar II is added in the 3rd, 6th, 8th, 11th, 14th, 17th and 19th years of the cycle. The new year that began Monday, September 25, 1995 (Jewish calendar year 5756) was the 18th year of the cycle. Jewish year 5758 (which began October 2, 1997) was the first year of the next cycle.

In addition, Yom Kippur should not fall adjacent to a Sabbath, because this would cause difficulties in coordinating the fast with the Sabbath, and Hoshanah Rabba should not fall on Saturday because it would interfere with the holiday's observances. A day is added to the month of Heshvan or subtracted from the month of Kislev of the previous year to prevent these things from happening.

Numbering of Jewish Years

The year number on the Jewish calendar represents the number of years since creation, as calculated by adding up the ages of people in the Bible back to the time of creation. However, it is important to note that this date is not necessarily supposed to represent a scientific fact. For example, many Orthodox Jews will readily acknowledge that the seven "days" of creation are not necessarily 24-hour days (indeed, a 24-hour day would be meaningless until the creation of the sun on the fourth "day").

Jews generally do not use the words "A.D." and "B.C." to refer to the years on the Gregorian calendar. "A.D." means "the year of our Lord," which is a Christian affirmation. Instead, Jews use the abbreviations C.E. (Common Era) and B.C.E. (Before the Common Era).

Calendar Chart

Reli-gious Year	Civil Year	Hebrew Month	Modern Equivalent	Agricultural Seasons	Climate	Special Days
1	7	Nisan	March-April	Barley Harvest	Latter Rains *Malqosh*	14 – Passover, Pesach 21 – First Fruits 27 – Holocaust Day
2	8	Iyar	April-May	General Harvest		5 – Independence Day 18 – Lag b'Omer 28 – Jerusalem Day
3	9	Sivan	May-June	Wheat Harvest Vine Harvest	D R Y S E A S O N	6 – Pentecost, Shavuot
4	10	Tammuz	June-July	First Grapes		
5	11	Av		Grapes, Figs, Olives		9 – Destruction of Temple
6	12	Elul	August-September	Vintage		
7	1	Tishri	September-October	Ploughing		1 – New Year 10 – Day of Atonement 15-21 – Tabernacles
8	2	Marcheshvan	October-November	Grain Planting	Early Rains *Yoreh* Rainy Season	
9	3	Kislev	November-December	July-August		25 – Dedication, Hanuka
10	4	Tevet	December-January	Spring Growth		
11	5	Shevet	January-February	Winter Figs		
12	6	Adar	February-March	Pulling Flax Almonds Bloom		13-14 – Purim
		Adar Sheni	Intercalary Month			

THE MONTHS OF THE JEWISH CALENDAR

Months of the Jewish Year

The "first month" of the Jewish calendar is the month of Nisan, in the spring, when Passover occurs. However, the Jewish New Year is in Tishri, the seventh month, and that is when the year number is increased. This concept of different starting points for a year is not as strange as it might seem at first glance. The American "new year" starts in January, but the new "school year" starts in September, and many businesses have "fiscal years" that start at various times of the year. Similarly, the Jewish calendar has different starting points for different purposes.

Month	Length	Gregorian Equivalent
Nisan	30 days	March-April
Iyar	29 days	April-May
Sivan	30 days	May-June
Tammuz	29 days	June-July
Av	30 days	July-August
Elul	29 days	August-September
Tishri	30 days	September-October
Heshvan	29 or 30 days	October-November
Kislev	30 or 29 days	November-December
Tevet	29 days	December-January
Shevat	30 days	January-February
Adar	29 or 30 days	February-March
Adar II	29 days	March-April

In leap years, Adar has 30 days. In non-leap years, Adar has 29 days.

The length of Heshvan and Kislev are determined by complex calculations involving the time of day of the full moon of the following year's Tishri and the day of the week that Tishri would occur in the following year. The mathematics involved are rather complex but there are plenty of easily accessible computer programs that will calculate the Jewish calendar for more than a millennium to come.

Note that the number of days between Nisan and Tishri is always the same. Because of this, the time from the first major festival (Passover in Nisan) to the last major festival (Sukkot in Tishri) is always the same.

לְשָׁנָה הַבָּאָה
בִּירוּשָׁלַיִם

Next Year in Jerusalem!

The Feasts Of Israel

Many Christians do not realize that the seven feasts which God commanded in Leviticus 23 are still observed by their Jewish neighbors. The feasts, as given to Israel, have a multi-faceted significance. First there was the seasonal aspect of each holiday, involving agricultural activities in the land; then the feasts were to be a memorial of God's dealings with the people of Israel; and, finally, there may be prophetic symbolism. Many Christians see parallels in God's dealings with Israel and with the Church.

A study of the feasts of Israel will not only bring a greater understanding of the Jewish roots of our faith; it will teach Christians much about various themes of God's dealing with humankind throughout the ages. Leviticus 23 lists these seven feasts in order of their seasonal observance: Passover, Unleavened Bread, First Fruits, Pentecost, Trumpets, Day of Atonement, and Booths or Tabernacles. We will also look at the extra-biblical feasts.

Passover

Passover, the first and probably best known feast, comes in the spring, in the Jewish month of Nisan, also called Abib. Passover commemorates the redemption of the Hebrews from Egyptian slavery. On the first Passover each Hebrew household sacrificed a perfect yearling lamb and sprinkled the blood on the crosspiece and sideposts of the door. The "Angel of Death" passed over the houses which were protected by the blood of the lamb, but where there was no blood, the first born was slain. In Christian teaching all persons are seen

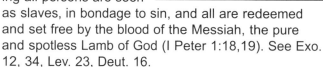

as slaves, in bondage to sin, and all are redeemed and set free by the blood of the Messiah, the pure and spotless Lamb of God (I Peter 1:18,19). See Exo. 12, 34, Lev. 23, Deut. 16.

Modern Jewish observance of **Passover or *Pesach***, in Hebrew, no longer includes the eating of the Paschal lamb but the Seder meal is a great visual aid and the menu items have lovely symbolic meanings. The season begins with a thorough house-cleaning to remove all traces of leaven. The Haggadah – the guidebook used at the meal – contains narratives from the Bible and history, songs, prayers and proper blessings. The food items are the wine, matzah – unleavened bread, karpas – parsley or celery dipped in salt water to represent tears, maror – bitter herb (usually horseradish), haroset – chopped apples and nuts symbolizing the mortar of the bricks in Egypt.

The Feast of Unleavened Bread

The Feast of Unleavened Bread occurs simultane-ously with Passover. It begins the day after the Passover eve, and lasts for seven days. Because they are so closely related in time and purpose, the names are often interchangeable. During Passover and the Feast of Unleavened Bread the Jewish people put away all leaven from their homes and eat unleavened bread or matzah. Leaven in Scripture is usually a symbol of sin. In Christian symbolism the unleavened matzah portrays the sinless Messiah. It is pierced, even as Jesus was pierced by the nails in His hands and feet and the Roman spear in His side; and it is striped in the baking, reminding us that Isaiah said, "But he was wounded for our transgres-sions, he was bruised for our iniquities and with his stripes, we are healed." Isaiah 53:5. However, and this is a big however, the piercing and striping is a much more modern phenomena, caused by modern baking methods and should not be assumed to have existed in biblical times.

First Fruits

The Feast of First Fruits is directly related to Passover and Unleavened Bread, for it is to be cele-brated on "the morrow after the Sabbath," which means the day after the first day of Unleavened Bread. In Bible times this holiday was a feast of thanksgiving for the barley harvest, the first grain of the season. The first harvest is viewed as a promise of the larger harvest to come because the conditions which brought about the first harvest will also bring the rest. Christians see Jesus as Messiah, the First Fruit whom God raised from the dead. Just as the barley har-vest was the promise of more to come, Christians believe that the resurrection of Jesus promises ulti-mate resurrection from the dead. We Christians may appreciate our own interpretation of the symbolism without expecting our Jewish friends to see the same lessons we see in the Feasts.

Shavuot, or the Feast of Weeks

Shavuot, or the Feast of Weeks, also is calculated from the first feast, Passover. It comes 50 days after the Passover sabbath, thus the name Pentecost, which means "fifty." This is a Greek name, but the Jewish people call it "Shavuot," which is the Hebrew word for *weeks*. Shavuot is also a harvest festival, thanking God for the wheat harvest. In Israel today it is customary to adorn the synagogues with plants and flowers, symbolic of the first-fruits. In the syna-gogue it is usual to read from the book of Ruth, and also the Ten Commandments and the account of Mt. Sinai. According to oral tradition, this day is the day that Moses received the Law on Mt. Sinai. On Shavuot, the priests offered two loaves of bread made from the newly harvested grain. Unlike other offerings, these loaves were baked with leaven. These two loaves are seen by some as a type of God's people, both Jews and gentiles, given eternal life and made one. The proper scripture references are: Ex. 19 & 20; Num. 28:28; Deut. 15. Traditions include eating dairy foods and staying up all night studying Torah. The Hebrew date is Sivan 6-7.

After Pentecost, there is a long time lapse before the next feast. Some Christians see in this symbolism of the present age of waiting for the return of the Messiah. Then in the autumn, in the month of Tishri, the seventh month of the Jewish calendar, comes the Feast of Trumpets, more commonly called **Rosh Hashanah**. This marks the beginning of the civil year and is the Jewish New Year's Day. In Leviticus 23:24 God commanded the blowing of trumpets on the first day of the seventh month to call the congregation of Israel together for a very solemn assembly. According to Jewish teachings, Rosh Hashanah is the beginning of ten days of judgment when all the children of men pass before the Creator. The righteous are written into the Book of Life, the wicked are condemned, and those who are not wholly righteous nor wholly wicked are given ten days to repent and thus escape judgment. Many Christians believe that those who are written in the Lamb's Book of Life need not fear final judgment, but look forward to Messiah's return with the trumpet sound and the voice of the Archangel to bring us into His sabbath rest.

Yom Kippur

The ten days of repentance and introspection lead into the most solemn day of the Jewish year, Yom Kippur, the Day of Atonement. It has become a time of fasting and prayer. It was the only time in Bible days when the high priest could enter the Holy of Holies. He went in before the Lord with the blood of a sacrificed animal to beg forgiveness for the sins of the people (Lev. 16, 23, 25; Num. 29). Today there are no animal sacrifices because there is no Temple. The Jewish people rely on repentance and God's mercy for forgiveness of sins. Lev. 17:11 teaches that atonement is in the blood and Christians see the crucifixion of Jesus as a fulfillment of this atonement or covering. The Christian scriptures speak of the veil of the Temple being torn in two, signifying that the way had been opened into the Holy of Holies. Both Jews and Christians expect a great and final Day of Atonement prophesied in Zechariah 12:11 and 13:1 when all people will see the Messiah.

Sukkot

The seventh and final feast is the Feast of Booths or Tabernacles, known in Hebrew as Sukkot. In Bible days this was the final fall harvest festival, a time of ingathering at Jerusalem. The Jewish people built booth-like structures and lived in them during this feast as a reminder of the temporary dwellings the Israelites had in the wilderness. Even today many Jewish people build open-roofed, three-sided huts for this festival. They decorate them with tree boughs and autumn fruits to remind them of harvest. Everyone in Israel who was able, came up to Jerusalem for this harvest festival every year. The Temple worship for the holiday included the ritual pouring of water from the Pool of Siloam, symbolic of the prayers for the winter rains. It was at this time that Jesus cried out, "if any man thirst, let him come unto me and drink." (John 7:37-38) After Israel's final day of atonement, the Feast of Booths will be celebrated again in Jerusalem (Zechariah 14:16). Booths speak of the final rest, as well as the final harvest. In Christian understanding, John wrote in Revelation 21:3, "Behold, the tabernacle of God is with men, and He will dwell with them, and they shall be His people and God Himself shall be with them, and be their God." Christians see this as the fulfillment of His promise, "I am Alpha and Omega, the beginning and the end. I will give unto him that is athirst of the fountain of the water of life freely."(Revelation 21:6)

Simhat Torah

Simhat Torah (rejoicing in the Torah) is the last day of the Sukkot festival, the eighth. On this day the annual cycle of reading from the Torah in the synagogue is completed and a new cycle begun. Lest Satan should tempt one to rejoice because the last words of Deuteronomy are finished, they begin reading Genesis immediately. On Simhat Torah eve, and again during the day, all the scrolls are taken from the Ark and carried in procession around the synagogue, while songs of praise are chanted.

Hanuka

Hanuka, the Feast of Lights, is not commanded in the Bible but it celebrates an important event. According to tradition, this festival was begun by Judah Maccabee and his followers after the successful rebellion against the Greeks of Syria. During the eight days of this festival, one additional light is lit for each day, until on the eighth day eight lights are burning. This is said to commemorate the miracle of the oil which took place after the Maccabees recovered the Temple from the Greeks. It was discovered that the Greeks had defiled all the oil used in the Temple menorah, except for one cruse, which contained only enough to keep the menorah burning for one day. However, a miracle occurred, and the oil lasted eight days, until new supplies could be consecrated. In remembrance, the festival of Hanuka was instituted. Had not the Maccabees or Hasmoneans, as they are sometimes called, taken a stand against the inroads of pagan Greek culture, there might have been no Jewish community for Miriam and Yosef to bring Yeshua/Jesus into.

Other Jewish Holidays

Purim

Purim commemorates the events that took place in the Book of Esther. It is celebrated by reading or acting out the story of Queen Esther and by making noises to drown out every mention of Haman's name. In Purim it is a tradition to masquerade around in costumes and to give Mishloakh Manot (care packages, i.e. gifts of food and drink) to the poor and the needy. In Israel it is also a tradition to arrange festive parades, known as Ad-D'lo-Yada, in the town's main street.

Since the creation of the State of Israel in 1948, the Chief Rabbinate of Israel has established four new Jewish holidays.

Yom HaShoah

Nisan 27, Day of the fall of the Warsaw Ghetto, day to remember the 6 million who died in the Holocaust.

Yom Hazikaron — Memorial Day

4th of Iyar. Day to remember fallen soldiers.

Yom Ha'atzmaut

Israel Independence Day. Occured on May 14, 1948. Celebrated in Israel with dancing in the streets, hitting each other on the head with plastic hammers. In Israel, the previous day is called Yom Hazikaron, remembrance day for soldiers who have died in Israel's wars.

Yom Yerushalayim — Jerusalem Day

28th of Iyar, reunification of Jerusalem.

Lag B'Omer

Thirty-third day between Passover and Shavuot. The day when celebrations may occur during a normally solemn time. Three-year old boys have first haircuts.

Fast of the Fourth Month

The day Moses broke the tablets of the Law. Beginning of three weeks of penitence before the 9th of Av.

Tisha B'Av

Date of the destruction of both First and Second Temples as well as many other Jewish historical tragedies. A fast day.

Tu B'Shvat

New Year for the trees. Like Arbor Day. A day to plant trees.

What Did A Passover Seder (meal) Look Like in the Time of Jesus?

In biblical times laborers and slaves ate hurriedly while squatting on the ground. The affluent, on the other hand, reclined on cushions alongside a low, three-sided table called a triclinium. On the night of Pesach, when there was to be no distinction between rich and poor, everyone reclined at the table in the manner of free men. This would have been the style familiar to Jesus and His talmidim (disciples).

Most of us in the western world are influenced by medieval art as we visualize biblical scenes. The famous painting of Leonardo da Vinci's, "Last Supper" shows thirteen European-style men lined up on one side of a dining room table. Recent scholarship will help us paint a more realistic picture in our minds. When you visit Israel check to see who is presenting a "Biblical Dinner" experience and try to join them.

The experience will look more like this one. For more information check the web site of Dwight Pryor, founder of the Center for Judaic-Christian Studies; www.jcstudies.com

Shabbat ~ The Sabbath ~ The Most Holy Day

It has been said, "More than the Jews have kept the Sabbath, the Sabbath has kept the Jews." Genesis 2:1-3 tells us that God finished His work on the seventh day and blessed and made it holy because it was the day creation was finished.

In the Ten Commandments the 4th commandment calls for Shabbat observance. Exodus 20:8-11 calls on God's people to "remember" the Shabbat and keep it holy. In Deuteronomy we are told to "observe" the Shabbat and keep it holy.

Remember is *zachor* in Hebrew and observe is *shamor*. The use of two words underscores the importance of remembering and doing.

It is a wonderful experience to be in Jerusalem on Shabbat. Most people leave work early to purchase food and flowers for their special Shabbat dinner. As the sunset approaches public transportation stops and you can almost feel the city taking a deep breath and preparing to relax and remember God's commandment. Candlelight appears in windows and families gather together.

Shabbat begins no later than 18 minutes before sundown and is welcomed by reciting several blessings. The first blessing follows the lighting of the candles which are lit by the mother while she draws her hands over the candles, saying: "Blessed are You, Lord our God, Ruler of the universe, who makes us holy with mitzvot and instructs us to kindle the lights of Shabbat."

Next is the *Kiddush*, the blessing over the wine: "Blessed are You, Lord our God, Ruler of the universe, Creator of the fruit of the vine." And then hands are washed and the hallah bread is lifted up for the *Motzi*, the blessing over bread: "Blessed are You, Lord our God, Ruler of the universe, who brings forth bread from the earth."

After the meal is completed and the dishes have been removed from the table, the grace (birkat ha-mazon) is recited. This long responsive prayer praises God for His many blessings.

Other traditions include:

1. Zedakah Box: collecting coins for charity.

2. Husband's praise of his wife based on Proverbs 31.

3. Traditional blessing of the children, while the father places his hands on their heads. For sons, "May God make you like Ephraim and Manasseh." For daughters, "May God make you like Sarah, Rebecca, Rachel and Leah."

4. The blessing of girls from "Fiddler on the Roof" reflects the traditional concepts and is a nice song to sing.

Rabbi Abraham Joshua Heschel wrote a lovely essay on Shabbat
which has been edited by Minnesota poet, Ruth Brin

Eternity Utters a Day

A thought has blown the market place away; there is a song in the wind and joy in the trees.
The Sabbath arrives in the world, scattering a song in the silence of the night:
eternity utters a day.
Where are the words that could compete with such might?
Six days a week we live under the tyranny of things of space;
on the Sabbath we try to become attuned to the holiness in time.
Six days a week we wrestle with the world, wringing profit from the earth;
on the Sabbath we especially care for the seed of eternity planted in soul.
The world has our hands, but the soul belongs to Someone Else.
Six days a week we seek to dominate the world;
on the seventh day we try to dominate the self.
To set apart a day a week,
a day on which we would not use the instruments so easily turned into weapons of destruction,
a day for being with ourselves, a day on which we stop worshiping the idols of technical civilization,
a day on which we use no money,
a day of armistice in the economic struggle with our fellowmen and the forces of nature –
is there any institution that holds out a greater hope for man's progress than the Sabbath?

Havdalah (separation) – the ceremony ending Shabbat. Special braided candle with two wicks is lit, usually held by youngest child. Blessings are said and a full cup of wine and a box filled with spices is passed. The blessing thanks God for the distinction between the sacred and profane. Each person has a sip of wine and a few drops are saved to extinguish the candle. Wish everyone a "shavuah tov," a good week to come.

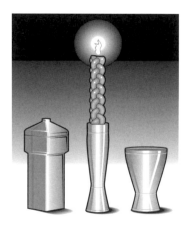

Biblical Sacrifices

Name	Biblical References	Elements	Purpose
Burnt Offering	Lev 1;6:8-13 8:18-21;16:24	Bull, ram or male bird (dove or young pigeon for poor); wholly consumed; no defect	Voluntary act of worship; atonement for unintentional sin in general; expression of devotion, commitment and complete surrender to God
Grain Offering	Lev 2; 6:14-23	Grain, fine flour, olive oil, incense, baked bread (cakes or wafers) salt; no yeast or honey; accompanied burnt offering and fellowship offering (along with drink offering)	Voluntary act of worship; recognition and provisions; devotion to God
Fellowship Offering	Lev 3; 7:11-34	Any animal without defect from herd or flock; variety of breads	Voluntary act of worship; thanksgiving & fellowship (it included a communal meal)
Sin Offering	Lev 4:1-5:13; 6:24-30; 8:14-17; 16:3-22	1. Young bull; for high priest & congregation 2. Male goat; for leader 3. Female goat or lamb: for common person 4. Dove or pigeon: for the poor 5. Tenth of an ephah of fine flour: for the very poor	Mandatory atonement for specific unintentional sin; confession of sin; forgiveness of sin; cleansing from defilement
Guilt Offering	Lev 5:14-6:7; 7:1-6	Ram or lamb	Mandatory atonement for unintentional sin requiring restitution; cleansing from defilement; make restitution; pay 20% fine

Torah Reading Schedule

1. In the Beginning, *Bere'sheet* . . . . Gen. 1:1–6:8 . . . . I Sam. 20:18-42
2. Noah, *No'akh* . . . . Gen. 6:9-11:32 . . . . Isa. 54:1-55:5
3. Go to!, *Lekh Lekha* . . . . Gen. 12:1-17:27 . . . . Isa. 40:27-41:16
4. And he appeared, *Va-Yera* . . . . Gen. 18:1-22:24 . . . . 2 Kgs. 4:1-37
5. Sarah lived, *Hayyei Sarah* . . . . Gen. 23:1-25:18 . . . . 1 Kgs.1:1-31
6. Descendants, *Toledot* . . . . Gen. 25:19-28:9 . . . . Mal.1:1-2:7
7. And he left, *Va-Yeze* . . . . Gen. 28:10-32:3 . . . . Hos. 12:13-14:10
8. And he sent, *Va-Yishlach* . . . . Gen. 32:4-36:43 . . . . Obad. 1:1-21
9. And he dwelt, *Va-Yeshev* . . . . Gen. 37:1-40:23 . . . . Amos 2:6-3:8
10. After, *Mi-Ketz* . . . . Gen. 41:1-44:17 . . . . 1 Kgs. 3:15-4:1
11. And he went up, *Va-Yigash* . . . . Gen. 44:18-47:27 . . . . Ezek. 37:15-28
12. And he lived, *Va-Yekhi* . . . . Gen. 47:28-50:26 . . . . 1 Kgs. 2:1-12
13. Names, *Shemot* . . . . Exo. 1:1-6:1 . . . . Is. 27:6; 28:13; 29:22-23
14. And I appeared, *Va-Era* . . . . Exo. 6:2-9:35 . . . . Ezk. 28:25-28-29:21
15. Go!, *Bo* . . . . Exo. 10:1-13:16 . . . . Jer. 46:13-28
16. When he let go, *Be-Shallach* . . . . . . Exo. 13:17-17:16 . . . . Judg. 4:4-5:31
17. Jethro, *Yitro* . . . . Exo. 18:1-20:23 . . . . Isa. 6:1-7:6; 9:5-6
18. Ordinances, *Mishpatim* . . . . Exo. 21:1-24:18 . . . . Jer. 34:8-22; 33:25-26
19. Offering, *Terumah* . . . . Exo. 25:1-27:19 . . . . 1 Kgs. 5:26-6:13
20. You shall command, *Tetzaveh* . . . . . Exo. 27:20-30:10 . . . . Ezk. 43:10-27
21. When you take, *Ki Tisa* . . . . Exo. 30:11-34:35 . . . . 1 Kgs. 18:1-39
22. And he assembled, *VaYakhel* . . . . . . Exo. 35:1-38:20 . . . . 2 Kgs. 11:17-12:17
23. Sum, *Pekudei* . . . . Exo. 38:21-40:38 . . . . 1 Kgs 7:51-8:21
24. And he called, *Va-Yikra* . . . . Lev. 1:1-5:26 . . . . Isa 43:21-44:23
25. Command!, *Tzav* . . . . Lev. 6:1-8:36; . . . . Jer. 7:21-8:3, 9:22-24
26. Eighth, *Shemini* . . . . Lev. 9:1-11:47 . . . . 2 Sam.6:1-7:17
27. She conceives, *Tazri'a* . . . . Lev. 12:1-13:59 . . . . 2 Kgs 4:42-5:19
28. Leper, *Mezora* . . . . Lev. 14:1-15:33 . . . . 2 Kgs 7:3-20
29. After the death, *Akharei Mot* . . . . . . Lev. 16:1-18:30 . . . . Eze. 22:1-19
30. Holy, *Kedoshim* . . . . Lev. 16:1-18:30 . . . . Amos 9:7-15
31. Speak!, *Emor* . . . . Lev. 21:1-24:23 . . . . Ezk. 44:15-31
32. On Mt Sinai, *Be-Har* . . . . Lev. 25:1-26:2 . . . . Jer. 32:6-27
33. In My Statutes, *Be-Hukkotai* . . . . . . Lev. 26:3-27:34 . . . . Jer. 16:19-17:14
34. In the wilderness, *Be-Midbar* . . . . . . Num. 1:1-4:20 . . . . Hos. 2:1-22
35. Take!, *Naso* . . . . Num. 4:21-7:89 . . . . Jud. 13:2-25
36. When you set up, *Be-Ha'alotkha* . . . Num. 8:1-12:16 . . . . Zech. 2:14-4:7
37. Send!, *Shelach Lekha* . . . . Num. 13:1-15:41 . . . . Josh. 2:1-24
38. Korah, *Korach* . . . . Num. 16:1-18:32 . . . . 1 Sam. 11:14-12:22
39. Statute, *Khukat* . . . . Num. 19:1-22:1 . . . . Jud. 11:1-33
40. Balak, *Balak* . . . . Num. 22:2-25:9 . . . . Mic. 5:6-6:8
41. Phinehas, *Pinchas* . . . . Num. 25:10-30:1 . . . . 1 Kgs. 18:46-19:21
42. Tribes, *Mattot* . . . . Num. 30:2-32:42 . . . . Jer. 1:1-2:3
43. Stages, *Masei* . . . . Num. 33:1-36:13 . . . . Jer. 2:4-28; 3:4
44. Words, *Devarim* . . . . Deut. 1:11-3:22 . . . . Isa. 1:1-27
45. And I besought, *Va-Ethannan* . . . . . Deut. 3:23-7:11 . . . . Isa. 40:1-26
46. Because, *Ekev* . . . . Deut. 7:12-11:25 . . . . Isa. 49:14-51:3
47. Behold!, *Re'eh* . . . . Deut. 11:26-16:17 . . . . Isa. 54:11-55:5
48. Judges, *Shofetim* . . . . Deut. 16:18-21:9 . . . . Isa. 51:12-52:12
49. When you go forth, *Ki Tetze* . . . . . . Deut. 21:10-25:19 . . . . Isa. 54:1-10
50. When you come, *Ki Tavo* . . . . Deut. 26:1-29:8 . . . . Isa. 60:1-22
51. You stand, *Nitzavim* . . . . Deut. 29:9-30:20 . . . . Isa. 61:10-63:9
52. So he continued, *Va-Yelekh* . . . . . . Deut. 31:1-30 . . . . Isa. 55:6-56:8-10
53. Give ear!, *Ha'azinu* . . . . Deut. 32:1-52 . . . . 2 Sam. 22:1-51
54. And this is the blessing, *VeZot HaBerahah* . . . Deut. 33:1-34:12 . . . . Josh. 1:1-18

Jewish Symbols

Magen David – Star of David
An old symbol used by many groups. Both five & six-pointed stars have appeared as religious symbols since ancient times. During times of persecution Jews were often forced to wear this symbol and it is used on the Israeli flag as a badge of honor now that the Jewish people have been restored to their ancient land.

The Chalice – Kiddush Cup
Every Friday night, as the Sabbath – Shabbat – begins, the head of each Jewish household raises a cup of wine and says the blessing: "Blessed art Thou, O Lord our God, King of the Universe, who gives us the fruit of the vine." Jewish blessings bless God for the gifts He gives.

Torah Scroll

The Torah – the first five books of the Bible – is written in Hebrew on a scroll by a specially trained scribe with a special ink and parchment. Men from the congregation are honored by being chosen to come forward and read the proper portion of scripture for that Shabbat. The scroll is treated with great respect.

Shofar – Ram's Horn
In the Bible God told the people of Israel to use a ram's horn as a trumpet to call the people to prayer and worship. The Jewish people have used this type of trumpet ever since. Even today our Jewish neighbors use a highly polished ram's horn to call the congregation to worship on special holidays.

Menorah – 7-Branch Oil Lamp

God told the people of Israel to make a golden lampstand to light the tabernacle and the temple. The menorah is the major symbol of Israel.

Hanukkiah – 9 Branch Lampstand

This menorah is a special lamp for the holiday of Hanukah. This took place about one hundred and sixty years before the time of Jesus and was a time when the Jewish people were being persecuted by the Greeks. The temple had been defiled and a family called the Maccabbees stood against the pagan Greeks and cleansed the temple. A supply of oil which would normally have lasted for one day miraculously lasted for eight days. This is why the Hanukah menorah has eight candles plus one called the servant candle which lights the others.

Dreidel – A Toy for Hanukah

At Hanukah which occurs in December, near Christmas time, Jewish children play a game using this top or draydel. They get money or gifts from family and friends for spinning the top and having it land on the right letter. The letters stand for the words: "A great miracle happened there."

Chai – Hebrew for Life
The letters het and yod make the Hebrew word chai. (Remember, Hebrew is written from right to left.) Chai is the Hebrew word for "life." You are probably familiar with the word through the famous song from Fiddler on the Roof – "To life, to life, l'chaim!" Since Hebrew words always have numerical value, because letters are used for numbers, the numerical value of chai is "18." The symbol is used in many ways. You often see it on jewelry.

The pronounciation sounds like "hi" except the "h" has a gutteral sound from the back of the throat. Don't be misled by the "ch" usage. It is not pronounced as in the "ch" in "church."

Through all their years of persecution, Jewish people have learned to celebrate life. Christians can join in the celebration because we have been grafted into the Jewish root of the olive tree through Jesus our Messiah. By getting acquainted with our Jewish roots, we can learn much about celebration and the joy of life.

Graphics courtesy of Davka

Jewish Customs

Tefillin

Tefillin are two small black boxes with black leather straps attached. Jewish men are required to place one box on their head and tie the other on their arm each weekday morning. This custom is based on the scripture in Deut. 6:8 which says, "Bind them as a sign on your hand and let them serve as a frontlet between your eyes." The words of Ex. 13:1-10;11-16; Deut. 6:4-9; 11:13-21 are hand-written by a scribe and placed inside the boxes. The tefillin are wrapped around the arm seven times and the straps on the head are adjusted so they fit snugly. Right-handed people put them on the left arm, left-handed on the right arm. Putting on tefillin is the first mitzvah assumed by a Jewish male upon his Bar Mitzvah at age 13. Tefillin are worn each weekday morning but not on Shabbat or most Jewish holidays. On the fast day of Tisha B'Av they are worn only during the afternoon prayer service.

Mezuzah

Mezuzah is the Hebrew word for doorpost. (Deut. 6:9) For thousands of years Jews have posted small boxes, also known as mezuzot, on their doorposts. Inside the box is a small scroll, which must be written by a scribe. It contains the first and second paragraphs of the *Sh'ma*, including the commandment concerning the mezuzah. The mezuzah often has the letter "shin" or the word "shaddai" on it. This is one of the names of God. The Jewish person entering or leaving the home is reminded of the high standard of behavior the Torah has taught him and the responsibility to live in a way that honors God. The mezuzah is attached to the upper third of the doorpost, at a slant. Every room in the house, except the bathroom, should have a mezuzah although many people put them only on the outer door.

Procedure for affixing a mezuzah:
Before attaching a mezuzah to a doorpost the following blessing should be recited:

Baruch ata adonai elohainu melech ha-olam asher kidshanu b'mitzvotav v'tzivanu likboa mezuzah.

Blessed art Thou, Lord our God, King of the universe who has sanctified us with His commandments and commanded us to affix a mezuzah.

Fringe and Prayer Shawl

When Yigal Yadin, late Professor of Archaeology at the Hebrew University and Deputy Prime Minister in the Begin administration, made his celebrated discoveries in the caves in the Judean Desert in 1960, his findings included a small, ball-shaped, matted mass of blue-dyed threads. Upon being unravelled, this was found to consist of several knotted fringes – *tseetseeYOT* – apparently the work of a woman's hands, who had conscientiously prepared them in advance for the time they should be needed for the fringes of a prayer shawl.

When any artifact of antiquity is unearthed there is rejoicing; this particular discovery possessed a special significance. In the months that followed many requests came to Professor Yadin from rabbis who wished to examine the tseetsee'yot. Their interest was motivated not by the age of the find alone, but by the earnest desire to learn how the tseetsee'yot were made. For by the time the period of the Gemara (200-500 CE) had succeeded the Mishnaic period (the era of the find) a note of uncertainty had crept into the method for fashioning the tseetsee'yot. Here at last was the opportunity to compare the appearance of the tseetseet as we know it today with one that was 18 centuries old.

What is a **tseetseet**? Literally, it is a fringe. But it is a special kind of fringe, knotted and worn in a special way and possessing a special history and significance.

Today the tseetseet or fringe is attached to two types of garments: to the four corners of the prayer shawl or talleet, and to each corner of a four-cornered garment worn under the clothing and called, because of its shape, "four corners," "arBA kanFOT," as well as a "tallit katan" which means a "little tallit." The tseetseet itself consists of four threads which are drawn through a small hole in the corner of the cloth so that this fringe appears to have eight threads. The threads are wound and knotted five times in a prescribed and traditional manner.

In Matt. 9:20-22 a woman with a hemorrhage was healed when she "touched the hem of Jesus' garment." There is good evidence that what she really touched was the tzeetzeet (tassel) of his *ta-LIT* (mantle). In the time of Jesus, the tallit was part of everyday dress and not a religious article.

Some Suggestions
About the use of Jewish Ritual Objects

Many of us involved in what is known as the "Jewish roots movement" have attempted to interest Christians in learning about the Jewish background of the world of Jesus and the early Church. We have encouraged study of the biblical feasts and learning about the historical experience of our Jewish friends. We want Christians to learn to think "Jewishly" and to build appreciation for Jewish practices.

We appreciate the recent Christian interest in Israeli-style dance and the keeping of the festivals. We endorse efforts to make Christians aware of the Jewish festival cycle and Jewish ways of worship. However, it is vital for Christians to realize that our Jewish friends and neighbors are often puzzled and sometimes frightened and offended by the Christian use of Jewish ritual objects such as the prayer shawl (tallit) and ram's horn (shofar). These articles are used in very specific ways in Jewish worship. For Christians to use them is not necessarily wrong, but it must done discreetly and sensitively, with an understanding of how Jews feel about these items. To use them casually in ways that offend Jewish sensibilities does not serve to build positive relations between our communities.

We believe that Jesus will be honored as his disciples (the Christians) and his brothers and sisters (the Jewish people) come together, listen to each other and learn to understand and appreciate each other. Then the Holy Spirit will be set free to do His own wonderful work. If we unwittingly offend our Jewish brothers and sisters, we can set back the program of God – no matter how good and noble our intentions!

The Shofar

The ram's horn, known as the shofar, is one of the oldest Jewish symbols. The Torah states that the giving of the Ten commandments was preceded by loud shofar blasts on Mount Sinai. Joshua brought down the walls of Jericho with shofar blasts. The Torah calls Rosh Hashanah "a day of blowing" due to the centrality of the shofar to this high holy day. The shofar continues to be used to mark solemn occasions and, in Israel, to inaugurate new presidents and celebrate military victories. The following information, gathered from Jewish sources, will give you an understanding of the shofar and its proper use in its Jewish context:

- The shofar is blown every morning, except Shabbat, during the month of Elul to direct the heart of the Jew towards repentance that comes from the depths of the soul.

- Isaiah prophesied that the shofar will call home to Jerusalem all those who have been dispersed.

- To hear the blast of the shofar on Rosh Hashanah is the primary mitzvah (commandment) of this day, so important that the Code of Jewish Law has determined that one should forsake all other benefits and go to where the the call of the shofar may be heard.

- The blowing of the shofar declares to God that, in a manner similar to Abraham who was willing to sacrifice his beloved son Isaac in order to serve God, so we too are willing to sacrifice our own lives for the sanctification of His holy name.

- The Midrash declares that there are two times that God Himself will blow the shofar: the first at Mount Sinai just preceding the awesome revelation of His Holy Torah to the Jewish nation and in the future, just before the coming of the Messiah.

- The Talmud states that the shofar is blasted in order to frighten and confound Satan.

The Tallit

The tallit is a prayer shawl, the most authentic Jewish garment. It is a rectangular-shaped piece of linen, wool, polyester or silk with special fringes called "tseetseet" on each of the four corners. **The purpose of the tallit is to hold the** tseetseet which are tied and knotted according to a very complex procedure and filled with religious significance. The tallit may be large or small and of any color but it must have four corners with tzitzit at each one.

- The tallit has been called the "robe of responsibility." The Torah commands that the children of Israel make for themselves tassels or fringes on the corners of their garments throughout the generations as a reminder of the commandments of God.

- The purpose of the tseetseet is to serve as a reminder of God's commandments as the Israelites were told in Numbers 15:39 "...That shall be your fringe. Look at it and recall the commandments of the Lord and observe them so that you are not seduced by your heart or led away by your eyes."

- The tallit may not be worn upside down or inside out and the special band called the *Atarah* must always be worn on the top and outside.

- The tallit is only worn at certain times. It is worn for morning prayer during the week as well as Shabbat and other holy days. It is not, however, worn in the evening because of the commandment that one should see the tzitzit. It is believed that it must be seen by the light of day. Only the Shaliach Tzibur (who leads prayer) is allowed to wear a tallit even in the afternoon and evening.

- In most communities, a Jew who has reached the age of majority (Bar Mitzvah age 13) may wear a tallit. In the past it was generally not worn by women – today more women in Reform and Conservative congregations are wearing tallit. In some very traditional communities it is worn only by married men.

Tefillin

The Sh'ma
Scriptures Placed in the Mezuzah

Deuteronomy 6:4-9

Sh'ma Yis'ra'eil Adonai Eloheinu Adonai echad. Barukh sheim k'vod malkhuto l'olam va'ed. V'ahav'ta eit Adonai Elohekha b'khol l'vav'kha uv'khol naf'sh'kha uv'khol m'odekha. V'hayu had'varim ha'eileh asher anokhi m'tzav'kha hayom al l'vavekha. V'hayu had'varim ha'eileh asher anokhi m'tzav'kha hayom al l'vavekha. V'shinan'tam l'vanekha v'dibar'ta bam b'shiv't'kha b'veitekha uv'lekh't'kha vaderekh uv'shakh'b'kha uv'kumekha Uk'shar'tam l'ot al yadekha v'hayu l'totafot bein einekha. Ukh'tav'tam al m'zuzot beitekha uvish'arekha.

Hear, Israel, the Lord is our God, the Lord is One. And you shall love the Lord your God with all your heart and with all your soul and with all your might. And these words that I command you today shall be in your heart. And you shall teach them diligently to your children, and you shall speak of them when you sit at home, and when you walk along the way, and when you lie down and when you rise up. And you shall bind them as a sign on your hand, and they shall be for frontlets between your eyes. And you shall write them on the doorposts of your house and on your gates.

Deuteronomy 11:13-21

V'hayah im shamo'a tish'm'u el mitz'votai asher anokhi m'tzaveh et'khem hayom l'ahavah et Adonai Eloheikhem ul'av'do b'khol l'vav'khem uv'khol naf'sh'khem V'natati m'tar ar'tz'khem b'ito yoreh umal'kosh v'asaf'ta d'ganekha v'tirosh'kha v'yitz'harekha. V'natati eisev b'sad'kha liv'hem'tekha v'akhal'ta v'sava'ta. Hisham'ru lakhem pen yif'teh l'vav'khem v'sar'tem va'avad'tem Elohim acheirim v'hish'tachavitem lahem V'charah af Adonai bakhem v'atzar et hashamayim v'lo yih'yeh matar v'ha'adamah lo titein et y'vulah va'avad'tem m'heirah mei'al ha'aretz hatovah asher Adonai notein lakhem. V'limad'tem otam et b'neikhem l'dabeir bam V'sam'tem et d'varai eileh al l'vav'khem v'al naf'sh'khem uk'shar'tem otam l'ot al yed'khem v'hayu l'totafot bein eineikhem. B'shiv't'kha b'veitekha uv'lekh't'kha vaderekh uv'shakh'b'kha uv'kumekha Ukh'tav'tam al m'zuzot beitekha uvish'arekha. L'ma'an yirbu y'maychem vi-y'may v'naychem al ha-adamah asher nishba Adonai la-avotaychem latayt lahem ki-y'may ha-shamayim al ha-aretz.

And it shall come to pass if you surely listen to the commandments that I command you today to love the Lord your God and to serve him with all your heart and all your soul, That I will give rain to your land, the early and the late rains, that you may gather in your grain, your wine and your oil. And I will give grass in your fields for your cattle and you will eat and you will be satisfied. Beware, lest your heart be deceived and you turn and serve other gods and worship them. And anger of the Lord will blaze against you, and he will close the heavens and there will not be rain, and the earth will not give you its fullness, and you will perish quickly from the good land that the Lord gives you. So you shall put these, my words, on your heart and on your soul; and you shall bind them for signs on your hands, and they shall be for frontlets between your eyes. And you shall teach them to your children, and you shall speak of them when you sit at home, and when you walk along the way, and when you lie down and when you rise up. And you shall write them on the doorposts of your house and on your gates. In order to prolong your days and the days of your children on the land that the Lord promised your fathers that he would give them, as long as the days that the heavens are over the earth.

Numbers 15:37-41

Vayo'mer Adonai el mosheh lei'mor

Dabeir el b'nei Yis'ra'eil v'amar'ta aleihem v'asu lahem tzitzit al kan'fei vig'deihem l'dorotam v'nat'nu al tzitzit hakanaf p'til t'kheilet. V'hayah lakhem l'tzitzit ur'item oto uz'khar'tem et kol mitz'vot Adonai va'asitem otam v'lo taturu acharei l'vav'khem v'acharei eineikhem asher atem zonim achareihem L'ma'an tiz'k'ru va'asitem et kol mitz'votai viyitem k'doshim lei'loheikhe. Ani Adonai Eloheikhem asher hotzei'ti et'khem mei'eretz Mitz'rayim lih'y-ot lakhhem leilohim. Ani Adonai Eloheikhem

And the Lord spoke to Moses, saying...

Speak to the children of Israel and say to them they should make themselves tzitzit (fringes) on the corners of their clothing throughout their generations, and give the tzitzit of each corner a thread of blue. And they shall be tzitzit for you, and when you look at them you will remember all of the Lord's commandments and do them and not follow after your heart and after your eyes which lead you astray. In order to remember and do all My commandments, and be holy for your God. I am the Lord, your God who lead you from the land of Egypt to be a God to you. I am the Lord, your God.

What's Kosher and Why?

The Lord said to Moses and Aaron, "Say to the Israelites: 'Of all the animals that live on land, these are the ones you may eat: You may eat any animal that has a split hoof completely divided and that chews the cud. . . .'Of all the creatures living in the water of the seas and the streams, you may eat any that have fins and scale." Leviticus 11:1-3, 9

Do not eat anything you find already dead. You may give it to an alien living in any of your towns, and he may eat it, or you may sell it to a foreigner. But you are a people holy to the Lord your God. Do not cook a young goat in its mother's milk. Deuteronomy 14:21

Those of us working in the Jewish roots movement have made it a goal to help Christians understand our Jewish background of our faith in order that we might promote and extend Jewish-Christian understanding. For that reason we have presented a variety of articles over the years explaining Jewish traditions and some of the lessons we as New Covenant believers can learn from these things. *Kashrut* – the Jewish dietary laws – is basic to Jewish life even though different branches of Judaism live it out differently. It is important for those of us who want to relate to the Jewish Community to understand the rules and customs involved with food preparation.

Most of us who visit Israel quickly become aware of the Kosher laws as we experience them in hotel dining rooms. Non-Jews are often puzzled by the separate sets of dishes for meat and milk and the frustration of not being able to have coffee with the evening meal lest milk be used in a cup belonging to the meat dishes. We cannot promise to make you into experts on the fine points of kosher law but we will try to define some of the basic elements of this rather complex code of laws.

What is Kosher?

A look at the scriptures quoted above tells us that the tribes of Israel were allowed to eat:

- The front quarters of four-legged land animals with cloven (parted) hooves and a regurgitative digestion (they chew their cud)

- These animals must be slaughtered by one stroke of a sharp knife, severing the windpipe, esophagus and jugular vein.

- Fish that have both fins and scales (other water animals are forbidden)

- Birds, except those expressly forbidden (mostly predators)

- Certain insects

Forbidden are:

- Animals that have died in ways other than official ritual slaughter

- A kid boiled in its mother's milk (the laws separating meat and milk grows out of this)

- Swarming or creeping things like worms with some exceptions

- Any meat with blood remaining in it

Food permissible according to Jewish law is called *kasher* (kosher). The word is used infrequently in the Bible where it is translated as *fit* or *proper*. The opposite of kasher is *terefah*, often pronounced *treif*. Terefah appears in Ex. 22:31 and literally means *something torn*, referring to an animal killed by another beast. The Bible also refers to unclean animals as *tame`* meaning *foul in a religious sense*. The opposite is *tahor* meaning *bright or clean*. Jewish teaching makes it clear that unclean animals are not naturally repulsive but are to be avoided simply because divine commandment forbids them.

The Talmud divides all the commandments into two classes: "those which should have been given had they not been given," i.e., laws whose value is self-evident, and "Those about which Satan and the Gentiles can raise questions," i.e., laws which seem to have no rational explanation. An observant Jew should not say, "I do not like pork!" but rather, "I would like to eat it, but my Father in heaven has forbidden it, and I have no choice." The Orthodox position is that God has set up these laws for His own reasons and the Jews should simply obey.

Why Kosher?

However, many scholars have attempted to find reasonable explanations. Philo of Alexandria says the dietary laws were intended to teach man to control his bodily appetites, to discourage excessive self-indulgence. Philo believed that the prohibition of eating carnivorous beasts and birds was to teach kindness and gentleness. He saw the eating of animals that chew the cud and have divided hooves as meaning that man grows in wisdom only as he repeats and chews over what he has studied and if he learns to divide and distinguish various concepts.

A thousand years later, Maimonides held a similar view. But being a physician, he also saw the possibility of health reasons. Even though no one knew of the health hazards carried by pork, rabbits and shellfish, it is true that avoiding these things probably kept the Jewish community healthier. The same situation appears involving hand-washing. Ex. 30:17ff requires priests to wash their hands before approaching the altar. In the years preceding the Christian era the Pharisees tried to give a priestly character to all Jewish life. They saw the family table as a sort of altar and taught that all persons should wash before breaking bread. While this was done for religious reasons, it had the effect of reducing the spread of communicable disease. This also was behind the ridiculous rumors that abounded in the Middle Ages saying that Jews were poisoning water wells because the Christians seems to be dying of the bubonic plague in greater numbers than the Jews. The medieval Christians had no idea of the value of hand-washing which was protecting the Jews.

While swine are technically no more unkosher than other forbidden animals, pork has become an object of special abhorrence. The attack on Judaism by Antiochus Epiphanes focused on the orders for the Jews to sacrifice swine on the holy altar. Down through history, Gentile enemies have often tried to force Jews to eat pork. In Israel today it is illegal to raise pigs on the land. Some non-kosher kibbutzim have circumvented this law by raising pigs in buildings off the ground. (Pork is euphemistically referred to as *white steak* in Israel!)

New Testament Views

In Mark 5 we find Jesus meeting a demon-possessed man who was living among the tombs in the mountainous area near Gadera. Jesus cast out the demons and sent them into a herd of pigs who ran down the mountain and drowned in the Sea of Galilee. Swine were found in this area because it is the Greek Decapolis – the non-Jewish eastern side of the sea.

When Jesus said, "It is not what enters a man's mouth that defiles him; what defiles a man is what comes out of his mouth," (Matt. 15:11) he was not speaking of the basic dietary laws of the Bible but of the Pharisaic requirement to wash the hands before eating. There is no reason to doubt that Jesus observed the biblical food restrictions. As we have often pointed out, he was an observant Jew from an observant family, with observant friends and followers.

In the early church the Jewish-Christians generally kept the kosher laws but decided at the historic gathering recounted in Acts 15 that the Gentile converts to Christianity need only refrain from meat offered to idols, from blood and from strangled animals. These conditions were lost later as Christianity became more Greek and less Hebrew. Many of us feel this was an unfortunate trend.

Some Details About Kosher Laws Today

Meat: Permitted animals are horned ruminants. This basically means beef, veal, lamb and goat. Of these animals, the hind quarter may be eaten only if certain tendons and nerves are removed by a technique called *porging*. (cf. Gen. 32:32 – the story of Jacob's wrestling with the angel and being touched in the sinew of his thigh.) Usually the hind quarters of kosher meat is sold to nonkosher markets. Slaughter must be done by a *shochet*, a qualified slaughterer, licensed and supervised by the rabbinate of the community. The shochet must examine the animal after slaughtering to look for ritual defects.

Poultry: Only chicken, ducks, geese, turkeys and pigeons are regarded as proper for a kosher diet. They, too, are ritually slaughtered.

Salting: All meat, four-legged or fowl, must be soaked in water for half an hour, then thickly salted. The salt remains for about an hour, then the meat is washed to remove the salt and any remaining blood. This process is not necessary if meat is broiled over an open flame. An egg containing a drop of blood must be thrown away.

Fish: Fish must have fins and scales. This forbids eels, sharks, catfish and sturgeon – as well as shellfish. Fish may be cooked with milk. Frogs and reptiles are forbidden.

Animal Products: Eggs of forbidden fowl and milk of forbidden mammals are forbidden.

Milk and Meat: The Hebrew word for meat or flesh is *basar* and milk is *chalav*. The commandment "You shall not boil a kid in its mother's milk" (Ex. 23:19, 34:26; Dt. 14:21) has been understood by tradition to forbid the mixing, cooking or eating of milk and milk products with meat and meat products. This also applies to fowl but not fish. Talmudic law requires separate utensils for milk and meat if the containers are of porous material. It is usually customary to have separate sets of dishes, tableware and cooking utensils – one for milk and one for meat meals. After eating meat one should wait a period of 72 minutes to six hours before eating milk. Neutral foods, which may be eaten with either meat or milk, are called *pareve*.

Dennis Prager, in his excellent book: *The Nine Questions People Ask About Judaism*, lists some of the major purposes of Kashrut.

1. to limit the number of animals the Jew is permitted to kill and eat.

2. to render the slaughter of the permitted animals as painless as possible.

3. to cause revulsion at the shedding of blood.

4. to instill self-discipline in the Jew.

5. to help sustain Judaism and the cohesion of the Jewish community.

6. to raise the act of eating from an animal-like level.

He believes that man was a vegetarian in the Garden of Eden and will be again in the coming Kingdom of God. However the vegetarian ideal is not enforced now because it is nutritionally difficult and would not be observed since meat-eating seems to be an innate desire. Jewish law did not ban meat but restricted it and made it more humane. He also suggests that the reason for separating meat from milk symbolizes separating death from life. Ancient Egyptian culture was preoccupied with death – their holy book was *The Book of the Dead*. The Jews left Egypt with a preoccupation with life which has characterized them ever since. This may be why a *cohen*, a Jewish priest, could not touch a dead body. He was to concern himself only with life.

Prager concludes: "every time a Jew sits down to eat a kosher meal he or she is reminded that the animal being eaten is a creature of God, that the death of such a creature cannot be taken lightly, that hunting for sport is forbidden, that we cannot treat any living thing irresponsibly, and that we are responsible for what happens to other beings (human and animal) even if we did not personally come into contact with them."

Kashrut is not required for Gentiles. Neither our early Jewish-Christian fathers nor our contemporary Jewish friends are interested in imposing Kosher law upon us. But, as usual, we find our lives and our thinking enriched by understanding the precepts which the Holy One, Blessed be He, gave to His Chosen People. Perhaps these thoughts can sensitize us to opportunities for self-discipline, mercy and everyday holiness that may present themselves in our walk through God's world.

The Thirteen Principles of the Jewish Faith

Compiled by Maimonides – Moses ben Maimon, 1135-1204 CE

I Believe With Perfect Faith:

- That the Creator creates and controls everything. He alone has made, is making, and will make all things.

- That the Creator is one. There is no other unity like His. He alone is our G-d. He was, He is, and He will always be.

- That the Creator is not a physical being. Physical concepts do not apply to Him. Nothing at all resembles Him.

- That the Creator is without beginning and without end; He precedes all existence.

- That it is proper to pray only to the Creator. It is not proper to pray to anything else.

- That the Creator communicates through His prophets.

- That the prophecy of Moses was true. He was the chief of all prophets, both before and after him.

- That the entire Torah (both Oral and Written) which we now have is that which was given to Moses.

- That the Torah will not be changed. The Creator will not give another Torah.

- That the Creator is aware of all of man's deeds and thoughts.

- That the Creator rewards those who guard His commandments and punishes those who disobey His commandments.

- In the coming of the Messiah. Even though he will delay, every day I will expect his arrival.

- That the dead will be brought back to life. The Creator will decree the time for this awakening.

A Brief Introduction to Hebrew Words & Phrases

Alphabet Chart

(1) Pronunciation	(2) Book Print	(3) Final Form	(4) Name of Letter	(5) Book Print	(6) Block	(7) Script
Silent letter	א		Aleph	א	א	אc
B as in Boy / V as in Vine	בבב		Bet	בבב	ב	ב
G as in Girl	גגג		Gimmel	גגג	ג	c
D as in Door	ד		Dalet	ד	ד	ד
H as in House	ה		Hey	ה	ה	ה
V as in Vine	ו		Vav	ו	ו	I
Z as in Zebra	זז		Zayin	זז	ז	ל
CH as in BaCH	ח		Chet	ח	ח	ח
T as in Tall	טט		Tet	טט	ט	6
Y as in Yes	י		Yod	י	י	ו
K as in Kitty / CH as in BaCH	כככ	ך	Kaf	כככ	כך	כ
L as in Look	ל		Lamed	ל	ל	ל
M as in Mother	מ	ם	Mem	מ	מם	N P
N as in Now	נ	ן	Nun	נ	נן	ן ו
S as in Sun	ס		Samech	ס	ס	o
Silent letter	ע		Ayin	ע	ע	8
P as in People / F as in Food	פפ	ף	Pey	פפ	ףפ	פ
TS as in NuTS	צ	ץ	Tsade	צץ	צץ	3
K as in Kitty	ק		Qof	ק	ק	ק
R as in Robin	ר		Resh	ר	ר	ר
SH as in SHape / S as in Sun	שש		Shin	שש	ש	ש
T as in Tall	ת		Tav	ת	ת	ת

Hebrew Words & Phrases

When You're Flying

Welcome . . . . Ba-rukh ha-ba
Airplane . . . . .Ma-toss
Pilot . . . . .Tay-yass
Steward . . . . .Da-yal
Stewardess . . . . .Da-yeh-let
Airport . . . . .S'deh Te-oo-fah
Passport . . . . .Dar-kon
Flight ticket . . . . .Kar-tiss Tis-a
Luggage . . . . .Miz-va-dah
Small bag . . . . .Teek
Bon Voyage . . . . .De-rekh Tzle-kha

Around You

Man . . . . .Ish
Husband . . . . .Ba-al
Woman/wife . . . . .Ish-ah
Boy . . . . .Ye-led
Girl . . . . .Yal-dah
Children . . . . .Yeledim
House . . . . .Ba-yit
Floor level . . . . .Ko-mah
Apartment . . . . .Di-rah
Street . . . . .Re-khov
Town/city . . . . .Ir
Village . . . . .K'far
Collective settlement . . . . .Kib-butz
Country . . . . .Eh-retz
Sky . . . . .Sha-ma-yeem
Sea . . . . .Yam
Sun . . . . .She-mesh
Mountain . . . . .Har
Valley . . . . .E-mek

What's The Time?

Time . . . . .Z'man
Minute . . . . .Re-ga
Hour . . . . .Sha-ah
Day . . . . .Yom
Night . . . . .Lai-lah
Week . . . . .Sha-voo-a
Month . . . . .Kho-desh
Year . . . . .Sha-nah
Today . . . . .Ha-yom
Yesterday . . . . .Et-mol
Tomorrow . . . . .Ma-khar
What's the time? . . . . .Ma ha-sha-ah?
It's 1 o'clock . . . . .Ha-sha-ah E-hat

Getting Along

Tourist . . . . .Ta-yar
Guest . . . . .O-re-akh
New Immigrant . . . . .Oleh/a Kha-dash/a
Hotel . . . . .Ma-lon
Room . . . . .Khe-der
Dining Room . . . . .Kha-dar Ha-okhel
Waiter/ress . . . . .Mel-tzar/it

Meal

Meal . . . . .Aru-khah
Restaurant . . . . .Miss-a-dah
Water . . . . .Ma-yim
Food . . . . .O-khel
Table . . . . .Shul-khan
Chair . . . . .Ki-sey
Ulpan (Hebrew language school) . . . . .Ul-pan
Book . . . . .Se-fer
Map . . . . .Ma-pah
Telephone . . . . .Te-li-fone
Telegram . . . . .Miv-rak
Post Office . . . . .Do-ar
Pen . . . . .Eyt
Pencil . . . . .I-pa-ron
Letter . . . . .Mikh-tav
Stamp . . . . .Bool
Envelope . . . . .Ma-a-ta-fah
Aerogram .I-ge-ret A-vir
Rest room/toilet/WC . . . . .She-ru-tim
Youth Hostel . . . . .Akh-sa-ni-at No-ar

Buying and Traveling

Sherut . . . . .She-rut
Taxi . . . . .Mo-neet
Car . . . . .Me-kho-neet
Bus . . . . .O-to-boos
Driver . . . . .Ne-hag
Train . . . . .Ra-ke-vet
Ticket . . . . .Kar-tees
Road . . . . .K'vish
Money . . . . .Kes-sef
Gift . . . . .Ma-ta-nah
Clothes . . . . .Be-ga-deem
Earrings . . . . .A-gi-lim
Ring . . . . .Ta-ba-at
Shop/store . . . . .Kha-nut
Market . . . . .Shuk
Grocery Store .Ma-ko-let
Receipt . . . . .Ka-ba-lah
Central Bus Station . . . . .Ta-khana Mer-ka-zit
How much is this? . . . . .Ka-mah zeh o-leh?
Where is ___ street? . . . . .Ey-fo re-khov ?
When is the next bus to...? . . .Ma-tai ha-o-to-boos ha-ba?
Tell me when to get off . . . . . . .Ta-gid-li ey-foh la-re-det
Forward . . . . .Ka-dee-mah
Counsellor . . . . .Ma-drikh/ah
Guide . . . . .Mo-reh/rah De-rekh
Group . . . . .K'vu-tzah

Greetings

Hello/Peace/Good-bye . . . . .Sha-lom
Good morning . . . . .Bo-ker Tov
Good evening .E-rev Tov
Good night . . . . .Lei-lah tov
Thank you . . . . .To-dah
How are you? . . . . .Mah Sh'lom-kha/ekh

Fine, thanks . . . . .Tov, todah
Please/you're welcome . . . . .B'va-ka-shah
Excuse me . . . . .Sli-khah
See you soon . . . . .L'hit-ra-ot
My name is . . . . .Shmi
What's your name? . . . . .Ma sheem-kha/shmekh
I live in . . . . .Ani gar b'/gara b'
Wait . . . . .Rega

Simple Words
Yes . . . . .Ken
No . . . . .Lo
Maybe . . . . .Oo-lie
Of course . . . . .Be-takh
Good . . . . .Tov
Bad . . . . .Rah
Where . . . . .Ey-foh
This/that . . . . .Zeh
Who . . . . .Mi
What . . . . .Mah
Why . . . . .La-mah
Here . . . . .Po
There . . . . .Sham
Do you have? . . . . .Yesh l'kha/lakh?
What happened? . . . . .Ma ka-ra
Nothing . . . . .Shoom d'var
Patience . . . . .Sav-la-nute

Doing Things
I am going . . . . .Ani ho-lekh/et
I am traveling . . . . .Ani no-seya/sa-at
I am drinking . . . . .Ani sho-teh/tah
I am writing . . . . .Ani ko-tev/et
I am giving . . . . .Ani no-tain/tenet
I am inquiring . . . . .Ani m'va-kesh/et
I am eating . . . . .Ani o-khel/et
I am talking . . . . .Ani lo-kayakh/kakhat
I see . . . . .Ani ro-eh/ah
I hear . . . . .Ani sho-may-ah/ma-at
I want . . . . .Ani ro-tzeh/tzah

Places
Parliament . . . . .K'nes-set
Cinema . . . . .Kol-no-a
Theatre . . . . .Tey-a-tron
Museum . . . . .Mu-zay-ohn
Synagogue . . . . .Beit K'nes-set
Church . . . . .K'nei-si-yah
Mosque . . . . .Mis-gad
University . . . . .Oo-ni-ver-see-ta

Security Words
Help . . . . .Ez-rah
Bomb . . . . .P'tsa-tsah
Emergency .Khey-room
Shelter . . . . .Mi-klat
Suspicious item . . . . .Kha-fetz Kha-shood
Explosion . . . . .Hit-po-ts'tsoot

Mine . . . . .Mo-kesh
Danger . . . . .Sa-ka-nah
Policeman/woman .Sho-ter/et

Sick?
Nurse . . . . .A-khot
Doctor . . . . .Ro-feh/fah
Infirmary . . . . .Mir-pa-ah
Examination . . . . .B'di-kah
Sick . . . . .Kho-leh/ah
Medicine . . . . .T'ru-fah
Pill . . . . .Ka-door
Injection . . . . .Z'ri-kah
Diarrhea . . . . .Shil-shul

Numbers
One . . . . .E-khad
Two . . . . .Shna-yim
Three . . . . .Shloh-shah
Four . . . . .Ar-bah-ha
Five . . . . .Kha-mee-shah
Six . . . . .Shee-shah
Seven . . . . .Shee-vah
Eight . . . . .Shmoh-nah
Nine . . . . .Tee-shah
Ten . . . . .Assah-rah

An important clue: in Hebrew "ch" or "kh" sounds like the ch sound in Bach, not "ch" like church or chicken.

A useful hint: find out and write down the Hebrew words for all the things in your room and put signs on them. More than learning new words, you'll never forget where you left your bed or night stand.

Some Arabic Phrases
Hello/Peace/Good-bye .Salaam
House . . . . .Bayt
Sun . . . . .Shamesh
Father . . . . .Ab
Apple . . . . .Tuffah
Blessing . . . . .Baraka
Hello .Ah-lan wa sah-lan
How are you? .Keyf hehlak?
Fine . . . . .Kway-yis, il-Ham-du lil-leh
Thank you . . . . .Shuk-ran
Your're wekcome . . . . .Af-wan
Pleased to meet you . . . . .It-shar-raf-na
Goodbye . . . . .Ma-as-sa-leh-ma
Yes . . . . .Ay-wa
No . . . . .La
Fine, ok . . . . .Tay-yib, oh-key
Tomorrow . . . . .Buk-ra
Yesterday . . . . .Im-beh-riH am

Note: masculine Hebrew nouns generally end with "im," feminine with "ot." Where you see a "/" we are showing both.

Glossary of Hebrew & Israeli Terms

Note: Transliterating Hebrew into English allows for a wide variety of spellings. In this book you will find different usages because sections have been written at different times using a variety of resources. We are merely giving you an idea of pronunciation.

Aliyah: Hebrew word meaning *To go up*. Used for immigration to Israel and also the act of being called forward to read scripture in synagogue.

Ashkenazim: Jews from Europe and western countries. Jews from Spain and the Arab countries are called *Sephardim*.

Balfour Declaration: British statement in 1917 calling for establishment of a national home for the Jewish people in Palestine. Written by Sir Arthur Balfour, British Christian Zionist.

Bracha: Blessing. There are proper Jewish blessings for every imaginable occasion.

Chasidim: "Pious ones." Jewish mystics from Poland whose way of life is characterized by religious zeal, prayer and joyful worship.

Chamsin: Arabic word for the hot, dust-laden wind that seems to cause people to behave strangely. Hebrew word is *Sharav*.

Diaspora: Dispersion of the Jews throughout the world following Assyria and Babylonian captivity & particularly after destruction of the Temple.

Druse: An Arab people with a religion somewhat different from Islam, which honors Jethro, father-in-law of Moses. Details of beliefs are secret. 33,000 Druse live in Israel.

Eretz Yisrael: The Land of Israel.

Falafel: Israel's "fast food." Yemenite delicacy made of ground, fried chickpea patties covered with sauce, sandwiched into a pita bread, served with salad & sauces.

Gan: Hebrew word for garden, also used of day-care centers for children.

Haganah: Pre-statehood Jewish defense force in Israel.

Haggadah: "To tell." Used of the text for Passover seder and the non-legal contents of the Talmud & Midrash.

Halakhah: "The way one goes." The legal rules of conduct in Jewish life, in contrast to *Haggadah*

Hatikva: The Israeli national anthem. "The Hope." Written by Naftali Imber, 1878.

Histadrut: Huge Israeli labor union which represents most of Israel's workers. Founded by David Ben-Gurion in 1920 to teach Jews how to become farmers & craftsmen. It owns a chain of department stores – *HaMashbir*, a major dairy – *T'nuva*, a construction company – *Shikkun Ovdim, Solel Boneh* – the firm that builds roads & houses, *Bank*

HaPoalim and *Egged* – the bus cooperative. Ironically, it is one of the largest employers.

Israel Defense Forces: IDF. In Hebrew, the *Tsevah Haganah l'Yisrael* – abbreviated *Tsahal*. Israel's amazing citizen army. Almost everyone serves – men for 3 years, women 2 years.

Ivri: Hebrew word for *Hebrew*. Means "from the other side," used of Abraham who came from across the Euphrates River. The language is called *Ivrit*.

Kaddish: Prayer recited by mourners in memory of those who have died. A hymn of praise to the Creator, it does not mention death nor is it a prayer for the dead.

Kafiyah: Square scarf, tied with a double coil of black wool or goat's hair, worm by Bedouin Arabs as protection from the sun. The red or black checkered type is sometimes a political statement of Palestinian Arab nationalism.

Ketubah: Jewish marriage contract.

Kiddush: *Sanctification*. Prayer recited over cup of wine to set apart as holy the Sabbath and festivals.

Kashrut: Laws of food preparation to insure strictly kosher food.

Kibbutz: Collective agricultural-industrial settlements. Unique Israeli phenomenon. Word means "to group together." Plural *kibbutzim*.

Kippah: Plural is kippot. Traditional head-covering worn by Jewish men. *Yarmulke* in Yiddish.

Knesset: "Assembly." Israeli Parliament, composed of more than 20 political parties.

Kupat Cholim: National Health Service

Kotel: Hebrew for wall. Used of the Western Wall – *Kotel Hamaarivi*, the retaining wall of the Temple Mount, the only remaining portion of the Second Temple. Before Israel controlled the Old City, it was called the *Wailing Wall*.

Magen David: Shield of David – the 6-pointed star. One of the symbols of Israel.

Magen David Adom: Red Shield of David – the Israeli Red Cross-type organization. (Accent last syllable.)

Menorah: Seven-branched lampstand. Ancient symbol of Israel, from tabernacle furnishings.

Mezuzah: Small wood or metal case attached to door frame containing scripture scroll.

Midrash: Sermons or explanations of Scripture.

Mitzvah: Good deed. Action in obedience to the Law. Plural - *mitzvot*.

Mikveh: Plural mikveot. Jewish ritual baths, found in abundance at southern entrance to Temple Mount. Ceremonial washing, forerunner of Christian baptism.

Moshav: Cooperative village in Israel. Plural is *moshvim*.

Nabateans: Arab people who settled in the Negev in 6th century BC. Highly developed methods of agriculture & water conservation.

Olim: Immigrants to Israel. (Related to *aliyah*)

Omer: Sheaf of grain. First sheaf of grain cut during barley harvest, offered in the Temple on 2nd day of Passover. Lev. 23:9-16 commands counting 50 days from Passover to Shavuot known as "counting the omer."

Protocols Of The Learned Elders Of Zion: A notorious forged document based on a fictional account of a plot by Jewish leaders to seize world power. Used by Nazis and recently by the Arab nations to promote and justify antisemitism.

Sabra: Native-born Israeli. Named for sabra cactus – tough on outside, soft on inside. (Quite accurate description).

Seder: "Order." The Passover celebration held in Jewish homes on first & sometimes second night of Passover, *Pesach* in Hebrew.

Shabbat: Sabbath, Saturday. Day of rest in Israel. Buses stop, stores close by mid afternoon Friday. From sundown Friday to sundown Saturday.

Shechinah: God's sacred presence.

Shema: "Hear." First word of Deuteronomy 6:4, "Hear, O Israel: The Lord our God, the Lord is one." Part of morning & evening prayer.

Sherut: Hebrew word for service. Singular is a large seven-passenger taxi. (Plural, *sheruteem*, is the Hebrew word for rest room or toilet.)

Shin Bet: Israeli secret service, like CIA in the USA. Israeli *Mossad* is like our FBI.

Shofar: Ram's horn used in Jewish services to call worshippers to prayer.

Shulkhan Arukh: "The prepared table." Law code of Orthodox Judaism. Formulated by Joseph Caro (1488-1575).

Tallit: Four-cornered prayer shawl with fringes worn by adult males during prayer and study of the Torah.

Tefillin: *Phylacteries*. Worn during weekday morning prayers by traditional Jews. Parchments inscribed with Torah, encased in two black leather boxes with long leather straps used to attach the tefillin to left arm and head.

Talmud: Encyclopedia of Jewish law. 1) Mishnah – *repetition* compiled by Judah ha-Nasi (c.200 CE.), earliest code of Jewish law & foundation of Talmud. 2) Gemarah – *Completion*. Commentaries on the Mishnah by scholars known as the *Amoraim* (interpreters). Babylonian Talmud is longer and more scholarly than Jerusalem, sometimes called the Palestinian Talmud. Mishnah contains 6 sections or orders: ‹ Zeraim – seeds ` Moed – festivals ´ Nashim – women ˆ Nezikin – damages ˜ Kodoshim – sacred things ¯ Tohorot – purifications

Torah: The Bible – used of the whole Old Testament or just the Pentateuch – the first 5 books. Old Testament also called *Tanakh*:, an acronym for *Torah* (5 books of Moses), the Prophets, *Neviim* and the Writings, *Ketuvim*. Torah means "gracious instruction" and should not be translated simply as "Law."

Ulpan: Plural – *Ulpanim*. Hebrew language courses set up by the Jewish Agency to teach Hebrew to new immigrants as quickly as possible. Total immersion in the language.

West Bank: Biblical Judea and Samaria, territory located on west bank of the Jordan River. Biblical Israel occupied land on both sides of the river. The East Bank is now occupied by the Kingdom of Jordan.

Yeshiva: Plural – *Yeshivot*. Word means "sitting." Place of Jewish study of Torah & Talmud.

Yishuv: Jewish Community in pre-statehood Palestine.

Yom Ha'atzmaut: Israel Independence Day, Hebrew date: Iyyar 5; May 15 on Gregorian Calendar.

Zionism: Concept of the return to Zion, originated with the Babylonian exiles. Modern Zionism owes much to Theodor Herzl, a Viennese journalist who recognized the dangers of rising antisemitism and the need for a Jewish State while covering the Dreyfus trial in Paris, 1892.

Site Descriptions

Note

Christians are in the habit of referring to the Bible as the Old and the New Testament.

Judaism commonly uses the term Tanakh for the First Testament. Many Jews consider the term "Old Testament" biased or derogatory, as it implies that the Tanakh has been supplanted by a "New" testament. We live in a culture that tends to see "new" as better than "old." "Original Testament" is a less-derogatory alternative. In academic circles, terms such as Hebrew Bible or Hebrew scriptures are commonly used to refer to Tanakh.

The term The Old Testament refers to all versions and translations of the Hebrew Bible and is the first major part of the Bible used by Christians. It is usually divided by Judaism into the categories of law: Torah; prophecy: Neviim; and writings: Ketuvim (history, poetry, wisdom books); as denoted by the acronym Tanakh.

The Protestant Old Testament is for the most part identical with the Jewish Tanakh. The differences between the Tanakh and the Protestant Old Testament are minor, dealing only with the arrangement and number of the books. For example, while the Tanakh considers Kings to be a unified text, the Protestant Old Testament divides it into two books. Similarly Ezra and Nehemiah are considered to be one book by the Tanakh.

The differences between the Tanakh and other versions of the Old Testament such as the Samaritan Pentateuch, the Syriac, Latin, Greek and other works, are greater as some include books not in the Tanakh and even in the books included, some have sections that the others do not.

All of these books were written before the birth of Jesus of Nazareth, whose teaching and immediate disciples' deeds and teachings are the subject of the subsequent writings of Christian New Testament. The scriptures used by Jesus were according to Luke 24:44-49: "the law of Moses, and in the prophets, and in the psalms ... the scriptures." According to most Bible scholars, the Old Testament was composed between the 5th century BCE and the 2nd century BCE, though parts of it, such as parts of the Torah, and the Song of Deborah (Judges 5), probably date back much earlier.

In this book I have generally used Hebrew scriptures, and occasionally First Testament, rather than Old Testament, in order to sensitize my readers the a form our Jewish colleagues prefer.

Alphabetical Index of Sites

Table of Contents ~ Site Descriptions

JERUSALEM ~ 4000 Years of History

No city has been coveted and fought over as often as Jerusalem – City of Peace. Jerusalem has been the scene of thirty-six wars. She has been reduced to ashes seventeen times. She has been rebuilt eighteen times. Babylonians, Macedonians, Ptolemies, Seleucids, Romans, Byzantines, Persians, Arabs, Seljuks, Crusaders, Mongols, Mamlukes, Turks, British and Jordanians are only some of the conquerors whose names have fluttered across the pages of her bloody and anguished past. Jerusalem is a sacred city – a city that has played a role in history out of all proportion to her economic importance and size.

Jerusalem's story begins some 4,000 years ago when Melchizedek, King of Salem, welcomed Abraham with offerings of bread and wine (Genesis 14:18). One thousand years later, David captured the city from the Jebusites and brought the Ark of the Covenant to Mount Moriah. David's son, Solomon, enshrined the Ark in a beautiful Temple which made Jerusalem the eternal spiritual center of the Jewish people.

Upon Solomon's death in 922 BCE, the United Kingdom of Israel split into two realms – Israel in the north and Judah in the south. In 721 BCE, the Assyrians captured Samaria, the capital of the Northern Kingdom, taking 30,000 Israelites into captivity and settling foreigners in their place.

The Southern Kingdom of Judah held out until 587 BCE when Nebuchadnezzar, the Chaldean ruler of Babylon, destroyed Jerusalem and carried away 10,000 captives. Thus began the famous Babylonian Exile of the Jews (Judeans), which lasted until 537 BCE when King Cyrus, the Persian, having conquered Babylon, allowed them to return to Jerusalem where they rebuilt the Temple on the ruins of the First Temple. This was completed in 517 BCE, but was a disappointment to those who remembered Solomon's original.

Persian rule was followed by that of the Hellenistic Greeks. In 332 BCE, Alexander the Great came to Jerusalem. Greek rule was initially benign until 169 BCE, when Seleucid King Antiochus Epiphanes tried to enforce the worship of Greek gods and the sacrifice of swine in the Temple. The Jews rose in furious revolt under the leadership of Judah Maccabee and his brothers. The revolt succeeded and the Temple was purified. From 167–63 BCE, Judah's Hasmonean descendants ruled from an independent Jerusalem.

In 63 BCE, under Pompey, the golden eagle of Rome settled on the land and in 37 BCE an Idumean, Herod the Great, was appointed king. Despite his cruelty, Herod was a brilliant architect and magnificent builder. He rebuilt Jerusalem and extended and embellished the Temple so that it became one of the wonders of the world. Jesus was born in the twilight of Herod's reign and was crucified in 30 CE in Jerusalem.

Roman brutality fed the flames of discontent and in 66 CE the people rose in revolt. In 70 CE, Titus' Roman legionnaires stormed into Jerusalem after one of the most terrible sieges ever recorded (Josephus–The Jewish War). The Temple was razed, the city ruined and the State of Israel ceased to exist. This event marks the beginning of Jewish dispersion, diaspora. In 132 CE, the Jews rallied to the desperate banners of Bar Kokhba, but in 135 CE, the Roman general Hadrian marched into Jerusalem, destroyed it completely and built a Roman colony – Aelia Capitolina – in its place.

When Constantine's mother, Helena, arrived in the city in 326 CE, it became the center of the "New Faith," Christianity. Constantine crowned many of Christendom's holiest sites with beautiful edifices, ushering Byzantium into the Holy Land. In 614 CE, a savage Persian invasion left the county in ruins. The Byzantines recaptured the city in 629 but in 637 Caliph Omar took Jerusalem and Islam's star and crescent rose over Moriah where the Ark of the Covenant once stood.

In 1099, the Crusaders captured Jerusalem, slaughtered its inhabitants and established the Latin Kingdom. The Crusaders restored Christendom's holiest shrines, but in 1187 Saladin took the city. Jerusalem returned to Islam.

For 267 years the Egyptian Mamlukes held sway, then in 1517 the city passed to the Ottoman Turks. Except for Suleiman the Magnificent, who rebuilt the walls in 1538 and did much to restore Jerusalem, the 400 years of Turkish rule were a sad progression from neglect to decay and oblivion.

In 1917, following the collapse of the Turko-German armies, General Allenby declared British rule from Jerusalem. Upon the termination of the British Mandate on the May 14, 1948, war between the Arabs and Jews broke out. All Jewish inhabitants were driven out of the Old City and the Jewish Quarter razed to the ground by the Arab Legion who tore down 27 extremely venerated and ancient synagogues. For 19 years Jerusalem lay divided.

The Six-Day War in June 1967 resulted in Jerusalem's unification under the nation that had given it greatness. Today the Star of David flies from its scarred ramparts. Jerusalem has become a sacred symbol to more than one billion people. On this hallowed ground stand shrines venerated by the monotheistic religions.

ISRAEL TIMELINE

BC (BCE)	**THE BEGINNING**
about 2000	Abraham offers Isaac for sacrifice on Moriah (Canaanite Period)
1000-961	King David establishes Jerusalem as Capital of the United Kingdom of Israel
961-922	King Solomon builds the First Temple
922	United Kingdom split into Israel (North) and Judah (South)
715-687	King Hezekiah of Judah builds tunnel from Gihon Spring to the Pool of Siloam and strengthens the city walls
721	Fall of Kingdom of Israel – Assyrian captivity under Sennacherib
701	King Hezekiah successfully withstands Sennacherib's assault on Jerusalem
587-86	King Nebuchadnezzar of Babylon conquers Jerusalem, destroys the Temple and exiles Jews to Babylon

537-332	**THE PERSIAN PERIOD**
537	King Cyrus of Persia conquers Babylon and allows Jews to return to Jerusalem
515	Completion of the Second Temple
about 440	Nehemiah returns from Babylon as governor of Judea and rebuilds the walls of Jerusalem
about 435	Ezra the Scribe comes from Babylon and joins Nehemiah in rebuilding the city of Jerusalem

332-167	**THE HELLENISTIC PERIOD**
332	Alexander the Great conquers Jerusalem – Greek Rule is established
312-198	Rule of the Ptolemies (Egypt)
198-167	Rule of the Seleucids (Syria)
169	Seleucid King Antiochus Epiphanes desecrates the Temple and forbids the practice of Judaism

167-64	**THE HASMONEAN PERIOD (MACCABEES)**
167-141	Maccabean War of Liberation
165	Purification and rededication of the Temple

63 BCE-324 CE	**THE ROMAN PERIOD**
63	The Roman General Pompey conquers Jerusalem and destroys the Temple
40-37	Romans ousted briefly by Jewish Zealots
37 BCE-4 CE	Reign of King Herod the Great who rebuilds the Temple in Jerusalem

CE (AD)*	**THE COMMON OR CHRISTIAN ERA**
26-36	Pontius Pilate named Roman Procurator of Jerusalem
30	Crucifixion of Jesus
66-73	First Jewish revolt against Roman rule
67	Zealots take over Jerusalem
70	Destruction of the Second Temple by Titus and the fall of Jerusalem
73	Siege and ultimate fall of the Zealots at Masada
132-135	Second Jewish revolt against Roman rule, Bar Kokhba's War of Liberation
135	Emperor Hadrian destroys Jerusalem and rebuilds a new Roman city called *Aelia Capitolina*, Jews banned from city

324-638	**THE BYZANTINE PERIOD**
326	Emperor Constantine declares Christianity state religion – his mother, Queen Helena, visits Jerusalem
335	Emperor Constantine begins building the Church of the Holy Sepulcher
614	Persian conquest of Jerusalem
629	Byzantium recaptures Jerusalem

638-1099	**THE MOSLEM PERIOD**
638	Caliph Omar enters Jerusalem – Arab rule is established
688-91	Dome of the Rock built by Abdal- Malik
996-1020	Church of the Holy Sepulcher destroyed by Caliph Hakim
1037	Church of the Holy Sepulcher rebuilt

1099-1187	**THE CRUSADER PERIOD**
1099	Crusaders capture Jerusalem – Jews and Moslems banned
1099-1187	Jerusalem established as Capital of Latin Kingdom
1141	Yehuda Halevi goes to Jerusalem
1165	Moses Maimonides (Rambam) visits Jerusalem

1187	Saladin conquers Jerusalem from Crusaders
1192	Richard the Lionheart fails to conquer Jerusalem
1212	300 English and French Rabbis settle in Jerusalem
1229	Christian Emperor Frederic II gains Jerusalem by treaty
1244	Jerusalem sacked by Tartars
1259	Jerusalem sacked by Mongols

THE MAMLUKE PERIOD

1260-1517	**THE MAMLUKE PERIOD**
1260	The Mamlukes, Egyptian slave kings, capture Jerusalem
1267	Rabbi Moshe ben Nachman establishes Jewish community in Jerusalem

THE OTTOMAN TURKISH PERIOD

1517-1917	**THE OTTOMAN TURKISH PERIOD**
1517	Ottoman conquest of Jerusalem
1538-1540	Sultan Suleiman the Magnificent rebuilds the walls of Jerusalem (the same walls which surround the Old City today)
1700	Rabbi Yehuda he-Hassid begins building the "Hurva" Synagogue
1831	Jerusalem conquered by Mehemet Ali of Egypt
1838	First British Consulate opened in Jerusalem
1840	Jerusalem again under Turkish rule
1844	First official census confirms Jewish majority —7,120 Jews, 5,760 Muslims, 3,390 Christians
1859-60	Mishkenot Sha'ananim—first Jewish settlement built outside Old City walls with assistance of Sir Moses Montefiore This was followed by Nahlat Shiva (1869)
1873-5	Mea Shearim built
1892	Yemin Moshe established
1898	Theodore Herzl meets Kaiser Wilhelm just outside Jerusalem

THE BRITISH OCCUPATION AND THE MANDATE PERIOD

1917-1948	**THE BRITISH OCCUPATION AND THE MANDATE PERIOD**
1917	November 2 – Balfour Declaration; December 11 – British conquest, General Allenby enters Jerusalem
1923	British Mandate confirmed by League of Nations
1932	King David Hotel opened, first issue of "Palestine Post" (later becomes "Jerusalem Post")
1947	United Nations' resolution recommending the partition of Palestine into Arab and Jewish states

THE DIVIDED CITY

1948-1967	**THE DIVIDED CITY**
1948, May 14	British Mandate ends, State of Israel proclaimed, Arab armies invade
1948-1949	Israel's War of Independence – Old City falls to Jordan – City divided; West Jerusalem declared Capital of Israel
1967	June 5-10 – The Six-Day War – Israeli troops capture the Old City from Jordanians On June 7, Jerusalem is reunited and is now under Israeli control

THE UNDIVIDED CITY

1967–to date	**THE UNDIVIDED CITY**
1973	October 6-22 – The Yom Kippur War – Syria and Egypt attack Israel
1977	President Sadat of Egypt visits Jerusalem
1979	Camp David Peace Treaty establishing peace between Egypt and Israel was signed by Sadat, Begin and Carter
1980	The Knesset (Israel's Parliament) voted Jerusalem as the undivided capital of Israel
1985	Extensive excavations by Yigal Shiloh in the City of David
1987-1993	Outbreak of the Palestinian uprising (intifada) in Gaza, West Bank, and eastern Jerusalem
1989-1991	330,000 immigrants from Soviet Union, 14,200 immigrants from Ethiopia
1990	US Senate & House pass resolution confirming Jerusalem as capital of Israel
1991	Gulf War, Iraqi scuds fall on Israel
1991	At Madrid Peace Conference Arab delegates state position that Jerusalem is to be the capital of proposed Palestinian state
1993	Israeli-Palestinian accord – "Oslo Agreement"
1994	Israeli-Jordanian treaty
1995	Sept. 28, Oslo Accords
1995	Nov. 4, Prime Minister Yitzak Rabin assassinated
1996	Election of Binyamin Netanyahu as Prime Minister
1999	Election of Ehud Barak as Prime Minister
2001	Election of Ariel Sharon as Prime Minister
2006	Election of Ehud Olmert as Prime Minister

Gates of the Old City

The walls and gates of the Old City are primarily those built by Suleiman the Magnificent in 1538-41 C.E. Today's walled city includes approximately the same area as Hadrian's *Aelia Capitolina* (135 CE) and includes remains of walls from earlier periods, mainly Herod (37 BCE), Agrippa (41 CE) and Saladin (1187 CE). The wall which encircles the Old City offers many breathtaking views of Jerusalem from its ramparts. It is four kms long (two and a half miles) with seven open gates. Walking the walls is often an exciting feature of our tours.

Jaffa Gate is known as *Bab el Khalil* (Gate of the Friend) because of an Arabic inscription over the entrance which reads: "There is no god but Allah and Abraham is his friend." When Kaiser Wilhelm II visited Jerusalem in 1898, the Turks filled in the moat between the Jaffa Gate and the Citadel to allow for his entry in a mounted procession. Today, this same passage serves as the main thoroughfare for motorized traffic into the Old City.

New Gate was specially opened in 1889 by Sultan Abdul Hamid to facilitate access between the Christian Quarter of the Old City and the expanding Christian properties west of the gate. The New Gate was closed from 1948 to 1967, as well as the Zion and Jaffa gates.

Damascus Gate (*Shaar Shechem* in Hebrew), at the start of the road to Damascus, is Jerusalem's most ornate gate, a monument to the workmanship of Suleiman's artisans. The gate stands on the remains of two earlier entrances into the city. The first gate to stand here was a Herodian structure, while the second dates from 135 CE when it formed the northern entrance into Hadrian's Aelia Capitolina. According to the 6th century Madeba map of Jerusalem, a large column stood just inside this gate, a detail that is still recalled by the Arabic name *Bab el Amoud* (Gate of the Pillar).

Herod's Gate faces the modern post office and busy commercial center of Sheikh Jarrah. The gate received its name from medieval pilgrims who fought in this vicinity, and thought it was near the house of Herod Antipas where Jesus was sent by Pilate. Although it is much more likely that Herod Antipas resided in the old Hasmonean Palace on Mount Zion (Upper City), the name "Herod's Gate" has remained.

Lion's Gate is named after the two lions carved in relief on either side of the entrance and thought to represent the coat of arms of Sultan Beybars. There is also a story about Suleiman dreaming he would be devoured by lions if he did not rebuild the walls of Jerusalem. Arabs call this gate *Bab Sittna Miriam* (St. Mary's Gate) because the road through it leads to the Virgin's Tomb. Since the middle ages, Christians have named this gate after St. Stephen, who was traditionally martyred nearby.

Dung Gate is the nearest city gate to the Western Wall and Mount Moriah. It was so named because the city's refuse has been carted through this gate to be dumped outside the walls since the second century.

Zion Gate leads to Mount Zion. Arabs know it as *Bab en Nabi Daoud* (Gate of David the Prophet) because it gives access to the traditional tomb of King David. In 1949, the Palmach blasted a way through the gate to reach the besieged Jewish Quarter, leaving it as one of the most badly marked sections of the city wall. Repairs were finally carried out on the walls after the Six-Day War although some of the scars of battle were purposely left exposed – Jerusalem's history is written in its stones.

The Topography of Jerusalem

In order to understand the Biblical and historical events that occurred in Jerusalem, it is important to have a comprehensive knowledge of the topography (terrain) of Jerusalem.

Scripture tells us that Jerusalem is surrounded by mountains (Psalm 125:2), and in other places, we read about the tribes *going up to Jerusalem* (Psalm 122:4). In fact, Psalms 120-134 are called Songs of Degrees or Songs of Ascents, "ascents" being the correct rendering of the word translated "degrees." The view most generally accepted is that these Psalms were sung by worshippers from all parts of Israel as they went up to Jerusalem for the great festivals (Deuteronomy 16:16). Is this a contradiction? How can Jerusalem be surrounded by mountains in one verse and be at the top of the mountains in another verse? No, there is no contradiction, and your study and visit to Jerusalem will show this to you.

Jerusalem is located about 2,700 feet above sea level and just east of the main ridge (highest point) of the mountain range that runs north and south in this region of Israel. As a result, anyone traveling to Jerusalem from the east must go "up to Jerusalem" to reach their destination. On the other hand, because Jerusalem is just east of the main ridge, it finds itself in a small saucer-like depression surrounded by mountain tops.

The topography on which the ancient city of Jerusalem is built is very important to our understanding. Look at the following topographic map as we discuss the terrain.

Jerusalem occupies three fingers, or small ridges. They run north and south and are separated by valleys which also run north and south.

Let's look at the Ridges:

• The eastern ridge is the Mount of Olives.

• The middle ridge is Mount Moriah (the Temple Area) running south under the City of David. The middle ridge is also known as the eastern hill.

• The western ridge is the present-day Mount Zion, also known as the western hill.

Note: In biblical days, Jerusalem occupied only the middle and western ridges which were known as the eastern and western hills. Don't get confused. The eastern hill refers to the middle ridge and the Mount of Olives, located on the eastern ridge, will always be called the Mount of Olives in the Bible.

Let's look at the Valleys:

• East of the Mount of Olives, the terrain slopes downward dramatically to the Dead Sea and Jordan Valley. This is the *Judean Desert.*

• Between the middle ridge and western ridge, we find the *Tyropeon Valley*, also called *Cheesemakers Valley* or the *Central Valley.*

• West of the western ridge (Mount Zion), we find the *Hinnom Valley* which runs south and ultimately curves east to meet the *Kidron Valley.*

Please refer to this description and to the map as you read the course material that details significant Biblical and historical sites and events that have occurred in Jerusalem.

Relief Map Of Jerusalem

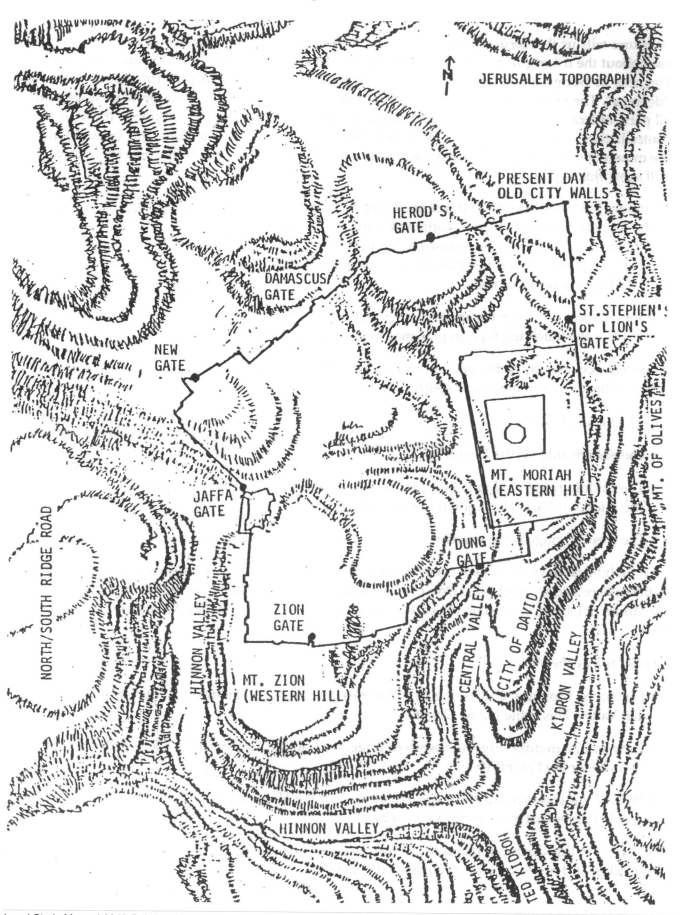

Jerusalem Area Sites

Mount of Olives

I. Background

The Mount of Olives lies between the Old City of Jerusalem and the Judean Desert. Topographically, the mountain consists of three summits stair-stepping from north to south and an east and west face. In order to give you a better feel for the significance of the whole mountain, we will review the main sites and their locations in general, and then discuss the specific points of interest in detail.

On the northern summit lies Viri Galilaei, which is believed to be the place where the two men in white apparel appeared to the disciples as Jesus ascended into heaven (Acts 1:9-12).

The center summit is of special interest to us because from the top of it down the western face to the Kidron Valley, we find the sites for most of the Biblical references concerning Jesus on the Mount of Olives. This whole area overlooks the ancient city of Jerusalem. Beginning at the top, we find the Mosque (Church) of the Ascension, the Church of the Pater Noster (Our Father), Dominus Flevit, Church of St. Mary Magdalene, the Garden of Gethsemane and Basilica of the Agony (Church of All Nations), and the Cave of Betrayal. All of these sites are located along the "Palm Sunday Road" which begins on the back side of the Mount of Olives in Bethphage and descends the western face of the center summit to the Kidron Valley on its way into the Old City of Jerusalem (Luke 19:29-48). Also located on the central summit are the tombs of the prophets Zechariah, Malachi and Haggai.

The southern summit is covered with Jewish tombs and reaches southwest as far as the village of Silwan. This is the largest and oldest Jewish cemetery in the world and dates back to Biblical times. Among the Jewish community, it is believed to be the place where the Resurrection of the Dead will take place at the end of time and therefore, a very desirable place to be buried (Zechariah 14:1-11). This southern hill has also been called the "Mount of Offense" (I Kings 11:7) where Solomon built "high places" of worship to pagan gods for his many wives.

On the back or eastern face of the Mount of Olives, facing the Judean Desert, we find Bethphage, which is over the center summit, and Bethany, on the road to Jericho as it travels around the Mount of Olives from Jerusalem eastward into the Judean Desert and the Jordan Valley to Jericho.

We will now discuss specific points of interest in greater detail.

II. Northern Summit

A. Tower of Ascension

The Tower of Ascension, on the northern summit of the Mount of Olives, is located within the Russian Orthodox Compound of Viri Galilaei (Acts 1:9-12). The exact origin of how this place came to be called Viri Galilaei is not known. One explanation is that it was the place where the men from Galilee camped when they came to Jerusalem for the Jewish feasts. St. Stephen's Gate, also known as the Lion's Gate, was called the Galilee Gate at one time because it faced this place on the Mount of Olives. According to the Russian Orthodox, this is the place where the Ascension of Jesus took place, and within the compound there is a stone believed to be the place where Mary, the mother of Jesus, stood at the time of the Ascension.

The tower itself has six stories and 214 steps. It presents the most beautiful and extensive view of Jerusalem. The church, bell tower and hospice were built from 1870-1880. The huge bell, brought from Russia, was dragged from Jaffa by Russian women. The church stands on the ruins of a 4th-century Byzantine structure and the head of John the Baptist was supposedly found there at the time of Constantine, the first Christian Roman Emperor in the 4th century CE.

III. Center Summit

A. Mosque (Church) of the Ascension

On the top of the center summit, we find the Mosque (Church) of the Ascension, the more traditional site of the event of Acts 1:9-12. The church was built in 387 CE over the place believed to be where Jesus left a footprint in a rock as he ascended into heaven. The octagonal outer wall of the church so impressed the Arabs that they fashioned the Dome of the Rock after it.

In 1187 CE, the church was converted into a mosque and the Church of the Ascension, originally built open to the sky, was covered with a cupola. Every year on the Feast of the Ascension, the Franciscans, Greek Orthodox, Armenians, Coptics (Egyptians) and Syrian Orthodox churches erect tents around the octagonal structure and celebrate the event.

Recent excavations around the property have revealed that the area was uninhabited at the time of Christ. In the early years of Christianity, many monasteries were built around the property, but they were all destroyed in 614 CE by the Persians who killed over 1,200 Christians during the invasion.

The exact spot from which Jesus ascended is questionable and most supporting data for each site comes mainly from tradition. The important fact to remember is that he did indeed ascend into heaven, where he is now. Nevertheless, the general area where the ascension occurred can be verified in the book of Acts by using a mathematical calculation. In Acts 1:12, we find that the place was on the Mount of Olives, a sabbath-day's journey from Jerusalem. According to the Rabbis, this distance would be 2,000 cubits or 1,392 meters, which is the approximate distance that separates Jerusalem from the top of the center summit of the Mount of Olives.

B. Church of the Pater Noster (Our Father)

The Roman Emperor Constantine (fourth century CE) built a church that came to be known as the Church of Eleona, the site where Jesus foretold the destruction of Jerusalem and his second coming. This church was destroyed in 614 CE by the Persians, but rebuilt, probably by Modestus. The church fell into ruin after the departure of the Crusaders (14th century CE). Saladin (the Turk) gave the Mount of Olives to the two families of Waliddin and Abou'l Hasan. In 1868, the land surrounding the church was purchased by the Princess de le Tour d'Aunergul and she ordered the construction of the present church and cloister. During the excavations in 1910-11, an earlier church was uncovered and was identified as the Eleona.

The present Church of the Pater Noster (Our Father) is a place commemorating the events that took place in Matthew 24 (the Olivet Discourse), and the giving of the Lord's prayer found in Matthew 6:9-13. In the church, the entrance, and the cloister, the Lord's prayer is found written on panels of ceramic tile in 60 different languages. On the grounds there is the unfinished Basilica of the Sacred Heart and below the church is the Crypt of the Credo.

C. Other Points of Biblical Interest

The top of the center summit of the Mount of Olives:

- was a place of worship during the time of David (II Samuel 15:30-32)

- was the place where the burning of the red heifer took place at the time of the Second Temple (37–70 CE), as described in Leviticus 16 and mentioned in Hebrews 9:13

- was used to signal the beginning of the Jewish month before the days of calendars

- was the place where the glory of the Lord stood upon the mountain when it departed from Jerusalem in Ezekiel's vision in Ezekiel 11:23

- is the place of the Lord's return in the "day of the Lord" and where the mountain will split in two (Zechariah 14)

IV. Southern Summit

The Southern Summit of the Mount of Olives is discussed in the description of the Kidron Valley in Section III. E. – The Village of Silwan.

V. Western Face

A. Church of Dominus Flevit (The Lord Wept)

As we walk down Palm Sunday Road descending the western face of the Mount of Olives towards Jerusalem and the Kidron Valley, we first come to the Church of Dominus Flevit. It is the traditional site where Jesus stopped and wept over Jerusalem while on the way of the triumphal entry into Jerusalem (Luke 19:37-39). Inside the church, we find on the altar a mosaic depicting a hen with her brood under her wings reminding us of the love and compassion of Jesus. This commemorates Jesus' lament over the city in Matthew 23:37-39 and Luke 13:34. The present church is built over the ruins of a Byzantine church and monastery dating back to the sixth century CE. During the excavations in 1953, many other historical facts came to light such as a tomb from the Late Bronze period (1000 BCE) which provided artifacts and information about the civilization of Jerusalem at the time of its conquest by the Israelites.

Even though this is a traditional site, it does give us a beautiful view of the Old City of Jerusalem. From here we can look directly at the spot where the Temple was located at the time of Jesus.

B. Church of St. Mary Magdalene

Continuing our descent down Palm Sunday Road, we come to the Russian Orthodox Church of St. Mary Magdalene. It was built in 1888 by Czar Alexander III in memory of his mother, Empress Maria Alexandrovna, and dedicated to St. Mary Magdalene. The church is a beautiful example of the old Russian/Moscow style of architecture of 16th-17th century, displaying seven golden onion-shaped cupolas. In the garden, on a slope below the church, there is a part of the ancient stairs which lead from the Kidron Valley to the top of the Mount of Olives. There are also many Jewish tombs along this path.

C. Gethsemane

Towards the end of Palm Sunday Road, we come to Gethsemane. Gethsemane means oil press or oil stores. The Hebrew name is "gat shemanim." It is a place where ancient olive trees, olive presses and storage areas have been found.

Gethsemane is the place of many events in the life of Jesus: his betrayal, teaching of his disciples, and time spent alone with his Father. Luke 21:37 tells us that Jesus slept here at night; Luke 22:39 tells us that it was his custom to go here, and John 18:2 tells that Jesus often met his disciples here. The present location fits the description of Gethsemane at the time of Jesus and this tradition has been maintained since about 330 CE. In this area, we find the Garden of Gethsemane, the Basilica of the Agony, and the Cave of Betrayal.

D. Church of All Nations

1. Garden of Gethsemane

The Franciscan Church of All Nations contains the Garden of Gethsemane outside and the Basilica of the Agony within. In the garden, there are eight olive trees that may well be over 2,000 years old. These trees were there at the time of Christ and witnessed many important events. The olive tree does not die, but continues to live even if cut down by producing new shoots from its roots. This is a beautiful and well-cared for garden.

The Garden of Gethsemane is the place where Jesus left his disciples and asked them to sit while he went to pray (Matthew 26:36). He then took Peter and the two sons of Zebedee (James and John) and began to be sorrowful and very heavy. He asked them to wait there and keep watch for him as he went a little farther where he fell on his face and prayed (at the rock in the Basilica of Agony) (Matthew 26:37-46). It is interesting to note that Peter, James and John were the three who witnessed the transfiguration of Jesus and the glory of it, and now they were witnessing the agony and the perfect submission of Jesus to the will of his Father.

2. Basilica of the Agony

The Basilica of the Agony, within the area of Gethsemane, was built to commemorate the place where Jesus prayed on the eve of his betrayal and arrest (Luke 22:39-44). The agony that he was experiencing was so great that "His sweat was, as it were, great drops of blood falling down to the ground." In front of the altar is believed to be the rock where he prayed and the drops fell to the ground (Luke 22:42). We recall the prayer of Jesus, "Father, if thou be willing, remove this cup from me; nevertheless, not my will but thine be done." After this prayer, an angel appeared to him from Heaven, strengthening Him.

The first Basilica was built by Theodosius in 393 CE, and it was one of the first churches destroyed by the Persian conquest in 614 CE. The Crusaders built a modest chapel over the site in the 12th century and later it was enlarged and named the Church of St. Savionus. It was also destroyed.

The early Byzantines cut away all of the rock around the place of agony leaving the limestone floor and wall where it is believed that Jesus prayed. Excavations in 1909 revealed the Church of St. Savionus, and in 1920, while building the foundations of the present church, the remains of the Theodosian church of 393 CE were discovered at a lower level. Today, the darkness within the church is intentional to produce a sense of prostration before the Rock of Agony. The present church was finished in 1924 and was built with funds from Roman Catholics from many nations, thus the name – the Church of All Nations. The domes in the ceiling of the church are mosaic and each represents a different nation who contributed gifts to build the church.

E. Cave of Betrayal

The Cave of Betrayal, also known as the Grotto of Gethsemane, is an important spot in the path of Jesus to the cross. It is located in the same area as the Garden of Gethsemane and the Basilica of Agony. Today it is separated from the Garden and Basilica by a small roadway. This is believed to be the spot where Jesus was when they came with lanterns, torches and weapons to arrest and take him to first to Annas and then to Caiaphas, the high priest (John 18:1-14). This is the place where Judas Iscariot betrayed the Lord with a kiss (Luke 22:47-48). Tradition also has it that three Apostles – Peter, James and John – slept here.

The Cave itself is 55 feet long, 29 feet wide and 11 feet high at its highest point. The historian Eusebius describes this same cave at the foot of the Mount of Olives as the site of the betrayal in his writings in the year 330 CE. For a time, the Agony and Betrayal were commemorated at the cave until the church was built at the site of the Basilica of Agony in 393 CE. The tradition that this cave was the Cave of Betrayal continued so that the Crusaders accepted it without question.

VI. Eastern Face

A. Bethany

1. Tomb of Lazarus

According to John 11:18, Bethany was situated about two miles from Jerusalem. It is a little village on the southeast of the Mount of Olives where Jesus went many times to be with friends that he loved (John 11:5; Luke 10:38-42). It was here that Jesus raised Lazarus from the dead (John 11:1), and it was here that Mary anointed Jesus at the house of Simon the Leper before the Passover (John 12:1-8; Mark 14:3-9). The village of Bethany must have been a special place to Jesus.

New Testament Bethany was situated somewhat northwest of the present day town called Al-Azariyeh (Arabic form of Lazarium), which grew up around the church that has been built over the Tomb of Lazarus. This appears to verify the authenticity of the tomb of Lazarus, for Jewish custom required that tombs be located outside the city. The tradition associating this tomb as that of Lazarus dates to the fourth century CE when a church was erected over the site. This church was destroyed by an earthquake and rebuilt. Subsequently, after frequent damage and many alterations, it was attached to a neighboring church in the twelfth century. The tomb could then be visited from the crypt of the second church. In the sixteenth century, the second church was converted into a mosque and the Moslems bricked up the original entrance to the tomb. The Franciscans later made a new entrance from the street leading down into the tomb. Today, the tomb itself lies over 16 feet below the street. At the time of Jesus, the area was a garden and the tomb was a cave with a stone laid over it. The antechamber is 10 feet square and three steps lead down through a small opening to the mortuary room which measures 6.5 feet square. The three niches indicate that the tomb was intended for three bodies.

B. Bethphage

The two disciples went from Bethany to Bethphage to get the colt that Jesus was to use for what is known as the Triumphal Entry into Jerusalem (Mark 11:1-6). Bethphage is usually accepted as meaning "house of the unripened, juiceless fig," and this is where Jesus may have been when he cursed the fig tree (Mark 11:12-14).

The present-day Bethphage has been accepted as the Bethphage recorded in the New Testament. The location of Bethphage has been determined by reference to Matthew 21:1 and Luke 19:29, although the exact location is no longer known. Early Christians placed it just south of Kfar et Tur. Why? It is supposed that Jesus, coming from Jericho, followed the old road from Jericho directly to the Mount of Olives to meet the road from Jerusalem to Bethany at Kfar et Tur (Mark 11:4). In rabbinic literature, there are numerous references to Bethphage in connection with the exact definition of the limits within which a sacred object could be prepared or used. The Franciscans, in a church built in 1883, have a stone claimed to be the one Jesus stepped on as he mounted the colt. The stone has been painted with scenes commemorating the events that took place in the vicinity. On Palm Sunday, a procession begins here and travels down the western face of the Mount of Olives, through the Kidron Valley, and into the Old City of Jerusalem to commemorate the Triumphal Entry.

Mount Zion

I. Background

The present-day Mount Zion, located on the western ridge or western hill of Jerusalem, commemorates many Christian events, as well as many sites of pre-church days. Mount Zion, as we know it today, is not the original Mount Zion.

- Originally, Zion was the Jebusite fortress that David conquered (the eastern hill). It later became known as the City of David (II Samuel 5:7).

- When the Ark of the Covenant was transferred to the Temple, Mount Moriah became known as Mount Zion.

- One thousand years later, King Herod constructed a palace on the western hill (the present-day Mount Zion), and the name City of David (Zion), which means political and administrative center, moved there also. This is also how the Tower of David, on today's Mount Zion, got its name.

- The tradition of the western hill being called Mount Zion was held firmly since the fourth century CE. Many believe it is also because the early Christians called themselves New Testament Zion and had their first meeting place there.

II. Significant Sites

A. Upper Room (Cenacle)

The Upper Room, or Cenacle, commemorates the place where the Last Supper was eaten and Holy Communion was instituted. This is also the site where the outpouring of the Holy Spirit occurred on the Day of Pentecost (Mark 14:12-16, Acts 1:12-14; 2:1-4). Both of these events have been located here by tradition, for the Gospels tell us nothing of the location of the house where the Last Supper was held nor of the place of the outpouring of the Holy Spirit. The wording of the Gospels indicates that a particular room was intended. More specifically, an upper room, which probably belonged to a wealthy man since an upper room was most likely an additional story.

In Acts 1:12-14, we find several of the Apostles were abiding in an upper room which could have been the same one used on the Day of Pentecost. Part of the reason that present-day Mount Zion received its name was because the first Christians, who called themselves New Testament Zion, were meeting there. It was at this site where the first church was built, and it must have survived the destruction of 70 CE. Bishop Epiphanius wrote of how the Emperor Hadrian made an inspection tour of Jerusalem in 130 CE and found "everything razed except for a few houses and a certain small church of the Christians which stood on Mount Zion in the place where the disciples returned after the ascension." This report shows us that in those days this place on the western hill was considered to be the place where the disciples lived and where the Holy Spirit descended at Pentecost.

It was not until nearly 400 CE that this location was also considered to be where the Last Supper was eaten and Holy Communion instituted. The "certain small church of the Christians" was destroyed and rebuilt many times,

121

finally to be handed over to the Franciscans who restored the room of the Last Supper giving it its present appearance (Gothic). The most important thing for Christians to remember is what Jesus did for us, and what he is telling us in Matthew 26:26-29 and John 13. This is also thought to be the site of the upper room where the Holy Spirit came on the Day of Pentecost (Acts 2:1-4).

B. Tomb of King David

The Tomb of David is located below the Cenacle (Upper Room) in the same building. It is a place highly respected by the Jewish community. However, the location of the site was chosen by a tradition dating back to the 9th and 10th centuries CE – as are most sites of the Christians, Jews and Moslems.

Although the Tomb of David is commemorated on present-day Mount Zion, there are Biblical and non-Biblical indications of other locations. Most scholars believe the tomb was located on the eastern hill, not the western hill. Many non-Biblical sources speak of a monument to David, well known in Jerusalem, located on the eastern hill. At the time of Jesus, the historian Josephus writes that David's tomb was opened by the High Priest Hyrcanus and by King Herod who built a monument of white stone at the mouth of the tomb. This might have been what Peter referred to in Acts 2:29 when he speaks of the tomb of David. *Tosefta Baba Bathra*, a Jewish source, reports that it was not permitted to leave tombs within the city of Jerusalem, except the tombs of the House of David and the Prophetess Hulda. This statement would indicate that the tomb was within the ancient city, i.e., the eastern hill on which the ancient city was built. Bishop Epiphanius writes that Isaiah was buried at the fountain of Siloam "near to the tomb of King David." Siloam is a spring-fed pool in the city of David coming forth from the eastern hill. The Bible tells us in I Kings 2:10 that David was buried in the City of David, which in Scripture, could refer to Bethlehem (six miles south of Jerusalem), or the eastern hill. Today, the exact location of the tomb is not known, and the site on the present-day Mount Zion is respected as the commemorative location.

C. St. Peter in Gallicantu

The St. Peter in Gallicantu Church, meaning cock-crow, commemorates Peter's three denials of Jesus and his repentance. It lies on the eastern slope of present-day Mount Zion. This site also commemorates the illegal trial of Jesus staged by Annas and Caiaphas, the High Priest, and the imprisonment of Jesus (Matthew 26:57-75). Outside the existing church is an ancient stairway (Scala Sancta), which is actually a main walkway up the side of Mount Zion. It is possible that Jesus, after being taken prisoner, was led up these stairs on his way from the Garden of Gethsemane to the House of Caiaphas. According to archeological reports, the stairs were in

existence in Jesus' day and probably date from an even earlier period. Currently, some scholars are debating the date of the stairway and believe it is from a later period. Whatever the date of these exact steps, they are at the location of the ancient pathway up the side of Mount Zion.

This location for the House of Caiaphas was determined by reports from Christian pilgrims from the 3rd century CE. The reports state that this site "was known by all." About the year 460 CE, it is said, the Empress Eudoxia built a church on the ruins of the House of Caiaphas to commemorate Peter's denial and repentance. Reports from the sixth to the ninth century confirm that a basilica was built on the site, but was probably destroyed in 614 CE by the Persians. The present-day church is thought to have been built over the remains. Archaeologists hold to the belief that the House of Caiaphas was located higher up on the summit of Mount Zion and that the remains on which the present-day church is built upon are from a Byzantine church commemorating only the repentance of Peter.

D. Other Points of Interest

- Christian Cemeteries of the Catholic, Protestant, Orthodox and Armenian faiths are located on Mount Zion.

- The latest archeological excavations have uncovered an ancient gate dating from the time of Jesus which is the Gate of the Essenes. There are also first century CE Jewish mikva (Jewish ritual baths) at the site. The Essenes, ultra-religious Jews from Qumran near the Dead Sea, would symbolically cleanse themselves before entering the Holy City of Jerusalem.

- The Institute of Holy Land Studies, today known as Jerusalem University College, is located on Mount Zion. The Institute, as well as Bridges for Peace, was founded by Dr. G. Douglas Young, who is buried in the Protestant Cemetery.

Kidron Valley

I. Background

The Kidron Valley is located between the middle ridge and the Mount of Olives (see map). The Kidron Valley is a place where many Biblical events have taken place. The Valley begins north of the Old City of Jerusalem and runs in a southeasterly direction, then makes a slight bend to the south so that it passes parallel with the eastern wall of the Old City. The level of the bed of the valley has been raised considerably with debris from the Temple, which was destroyed on several occasions and cast into the deep valley. In spite of the many sieges upon Jerusalem and the many times the city has been destroyed, the Kidron Valley has kept its basic form for the past 3,000 years. We will look at the Kidron Valley traveling from the north to south.

II. Biblical and Historical Significance

Jesus was led through this valley on the night of his arrest for it is believed that the House of Caiaphas was on the western hill (Mount Zion). Therefore, Jesus would have been taken from the Garden of Gethsemane down through the Kidron Valley and up to the House of Caiaphas (see Matthew 26:57; Mark 14:53; Luke 22:54; John 18:12,13). In order for Jesus to get to Jerusalem from the Mount of Olives, Bethany and Jericho, he had to pass through the Kidron Valley.

The portion of the Kidron that separates the Old City of Jerusalem from the Mount of Olives has been called the Valley of Jehoshaphat since the 4th century CE. The Hebrew name Jehoshaphat means "God shall judge" and it is believed that this is where the Last Judgment will take place (Joel 3:1,2). An "old tale" says that the Judgment Seat will be on Mount Moriah and all the nations of the world will be gathered together in the valley on the day of resurrection. Only those who cross the valley on a certain bridge will be saved. Beliefs of this nature account for the desire of many Jews, Moslems and Christians to be buried in this area.

III. Significant Biblical and Historical Sites

A. Second Temple Tombs (1st Century CE)

In the area of the Valley of Jehoshaphat, below the Old City wall and Gethsemane, we can find many ancient tombs. There is a monument called the Pillar of Absalom. It was erected during the period of the Second Temple (Herod's). Popular tradition attributes it to Absalom as referred to in II Samuel 18:18. Just behind the Pillar of Absalom is a tomb called the Tomb of Jehoshaphat, probably getting its name from the valley. These two monuments were cut out of the same piece of rock and were originally a tomb and a stele for one person. During the Middle Ages, passersby stoned the Pillar of Absalom because Absalom had rebelled against his father David. The people of Jerusalem would also bring their disobedient sons to the tomb and tell them that this is what comes to a rebellious son. The tomb and stele have nothing to do with Absalom of II Samuel. It is only a tradition, albeit an ancient one.

The third monument in the valley is just a few steps from the Pillar of Absalom, and is known as the Tomb of St. James. Tradition says that St. James hid himself here at the time of Jesus' arrest. Inscriptions on the tomb tell us that it is the tomb of the family of Beni Hezir (I Chronicles 24:15).

The fourth monument is a tomb called the Tomb of

Zechariah. To the local Arab villagers of Silwan, it is known as Qabr Joze Faraoun (Tomb of the wife of Pharaoh). The top is built like a pyramid and three pillars have been carved out of the rock in relief on the side. Jewish tradition says this is the tomb of Zechariah and refers to the Biblical references concerning the stoning of Zechariah found in II Chronicles 24:20,21. Many believe that these tombs are the ones Jesus referred to when he rebuked the Pharisees in Matthew 23:29-33. These tombs and monuments were in the Kidron Valley at the time of Jesus.

B. Gihon Spring

Further down the Kidron Valley about 200 yards, we find the Gihon Spring, also known as the Fountain of the Virgin and Umm el Daraj (Mother of Stairs, in Arabic). Today, the water gushes out from rock into a natural cavern 25 feet in circumference, then it flows through an aqueduct cut through the solid rock (Hezekiah's Water Tunnel), and empties into the Pool of Siloam 1/3 of a mile away.

The Gihon Spring is the place where David captured Jerusalem, then known as Jebus, the Jebusite capital. At the time of David's conquest (1000 BCE), the Jebusites were retrieving water from the spring by means of a vertical shaft leading to the spring. David's captain, Joab, went up the water shaft vertically into the Jebusite city (II Samuel 5:8). The Gihon Spring is also where Solomon was anointed King of Israel (I Kings 1:38, 39).

C. Hezekiah's Water Tunnel

At the end of the 8th century BCE, Sennacherib and the Assyrian army conquered all of the Northern Kingdom of Israel which had separated from Judah after the death of Solomon. Sennacherib then marched to Jerusalem, the capital of the Southern Kingdom, and besieged the city. In 701 BCE, King Hezekiah prevented the besieged city of Jerusalem from falling into the hands of Sennacherib by cutting a long aqueduct to bring the water from the Gihon Spring into the city to the Pool of Siloam. It was a brilliant engineering feat as he had a tunnel cut 1,733 feet long (1/3 mile) through solid rock from two ends and meeting in the middle. There was a Hebrew inscription commemorating the event at the place where the two stone-cutting crews met. The inscription can be found in a museum in Istanbul, Turkey. By cutting this tunnel, the people within the city walls had water to drink. This allowed them to hold out as God performed a miracle to save them (II Chronicles 32:9-23, 30; II Kings 20:20). The entire event was also found inscribed on an ancient Assyrian stele (memorial stone) depicting the conquests of Sennacherib. It tells how the God of Hezekiah protected Jerusalem and the Kingdom of Judah. This is quite an admission for Sennacherib to make considering he amassed the greatest empire up to that date. In the middle of his empire was tiny Judah and its capital Jerusalem – protected by God.

D. Pool of Siloam

The Pool of Siloam is joined to the Gihon Spring by Hezekiah's Water Tunnel. It is located in the middle of a piece of land with many trees. The Pool of Siloam is familiar to us because this is where Jesus told the man born blind to go and wash. After anointing his eyes with clay made with spittle, the man came away seeing (John 9:1-17). A church was erected here in the 5th century CE, but was destroyed in 614 by the Persians and never rebuilt. The present-day pool is 52 feet long and 12 feet wide. On the Jewish Feast of Rosh Hashana (New Year), Jewish people throw crumbs into the water to symbolize the casting away of one's sins.

In the days of Jesus, during the feast of Simhat Beir Hashoeva, which was celebrated during the Feast of Tabernacles in the fall of each year, a golden pitcher was filled with water from the Pool of Siloam. It was then poured into a conduit at the altar of the Temple on Mount Moriah along with a libation of wine, eventually flowing into the Kidron and out into the desert, symbolizing the washing away of sin. This is significant to us when we read John 7:37, "In the last day, the great day of the feast, Jesus stood and cried, saying, 'If any many thirst, let him come unto me and drink'." The Tower of Siloam referred to in Luke 13:4 could have been located in this area as well.

E. Village of Silwan

We find the modern village of Silwan in the area of the Gihon Spring and the Pool of Siloam. The village covers the ridges on both sides of the Kidron Valley, the City of David on the west and the southern summit of the Mount of Olives on the east.

On the east side of the valley (the southern summit), we find sharp cliffs with Jewish tombs carved into them. Some of these tombs date back to the days of Solomon. From the fourth to the seventh centuries CE, and then again in the 12th century CE, all of these tombs were inhabited by Christian monks. In the 16th century, Arab families began to settle in the area and the present village of Silwan developed.

F. Hinnom Valley

Further down the Kidron Valley to the south, we meet the intersection of the Kidron and Hinnom Valleys (discussed in the Topography of Jerusalem section, page 5). The Hinnom Valley runs west from this point and then north and separates Mount Zion (the Western hill) from the main ridge (highest point) of the mountains to the west (See map, 6).

In Hebrew, the Hinnom Valley is called "Gehenna." In First Testament days, an altar was erected here to the pagan god Molech of the Ammonites, and many babies were burned as human sacrifices. This altar was finally thrown down by King Josiah, but the memory of what took place lived on. This may be the reason that Gei-Hinnom became synonymous with hell (Matthew 18:9). The name of the valley was the "Valley of the Sons of Ennon" and the high place was called Tophet, an object of loathing (II Kings 23:10; Jeremiah 7:31; 19:6; Isaiah 30:33). This was probably the place where the refuse of the city was burned at the time of Jesus, and it bore the name of Gehenna, which became a common expression for hell.

The southern limit of the Hinnom Valley is a ridge called the "Mount of Evil Counsel."

From this point, the combined runoff of water through these valleys travels southeasterly into the Judean Desert on its way to the Dead Sea.

Western Wall

I. Background

The Western Wall, Wailing Wall or Kotel Hamaarvi in Hebrew, is the holiest shrine of the Jewish world. In ancient times, this wall was part of the defense rampart and retaining wall which encircled the Temple Mount. Because the southern slope of Mount Moriah is extremely steep, a level platform or court could only be achieved by constructing a huge box on which the platform could be built. It is the western side of this box-like structure that is the Western Wall. Inside the box, and under the buildings on the court, is a honeycomb of vaulted rooms. It is not solid.

Current excavations which have surveyed the entire length of the wall, have revealed stones upon the lower bedrock dating back to Solomon's Temple (950 BCE). Upon these stones lie stones from Herod's Temple, which was still under construction at the time of Jesus. In 70 CE, Herod's Temple was destroyed by the Roman General, Titus. The Jewish people believe that the Divine Presence withdrew from the Temple to rest upon this wall at the time of the destruction of the Temple. They have special services on the eve of Tisha b'Av (late summer), which is the remembrance day of the destruction of both the First and Second Temples. This wall was also the scene of the climax of the Six-Day War in June 1967 when various Israeli forces captured this area and said prayers...something they were prevented from doing between 1948-67.

The wall is now the scene of perpetual prayers by Jews from all parts of the world. You can see weddings, bar and bat mitzvas (the ceremony marking passage into adult responsibility for Jewish boys and some girls, at age 13), and dancing before the Lord. Small pieces of paper with prayers written on them can be seen stuffed into the cracks in the stone. Many people feel that this is the place where one is closest to God here on earth.

II. Significant Structural Finds

A. Wilson's Arch

Wilson's Arch is a subterranean structure situated perpendicular to the northern side of the Western Wall. This arch is actually part of a great bridge built to link the Temple Mount with the Upper City over the deep Tyropeon Valley (Central Valley). Due to the many destructions of Jerusalem, the valley had become full of debris and the bridge was underground. There are still buildings on top of the arch, even though excavations have cleared away the debris under the arch. It is named after Charles Wilson, the British officer who first explored this site in the middle of the 19th century. The large area under the archway is used as a place of prayer.

B. Robinson's Arch

Robinson's Arch was first discovered by Edward Robinson, an American scholar, in 1838. It is situated adjacent to the southern corner of the Western Wall. Recent excavations in the area have shown how this archway supported a massive stairway leading down into the markets of the Tyropeon Valley (Central Valley). Six levels of stone below the center of the arch, we find a Hebrew inscription of Isaiah 6:14, "And when you see this, your heart shall rejoice, and your bones shall flourish like an herb; and the hand of the Lord shall be known toward his servants, and his indignation toward his enemies."

C. Western Wall Tunnel

In recent years, the entire western wall of the Temple Mount in Jerusalem has been completely revealed for the first time since 70 CE. Excavations have uncovered all 490 meters of the wall that once formed the western girder of ancient Jerusalem's great Temple and the entire stonework that formed the basis of the original Temple mount is now exposed. An ancient Hasmonean water tunnel, built about 120 BCE and later blocked by Herod's builders is also visible for the first time and is one of the rare Hasmonean finds uncovered to date in Jerusalem. One of the most unexpected archaeological finds disclosed by the excavation is that Herod did not complete the entire construction of the Temple Mount as historians and archeologists believe to this day. A change in the type of masonry used at the northern end of the western wall is evidence that Herod built all but the last stages of construction of the Temple Mount. Instead of the polished stones with characteristic Herodian masonry marks, part of the original stonework is roughly hewn. One of the mysteries uncovered during the excavation is the presence of massive stones that measure some 14 meters in

length, three meters in height, and are estimated to be two meters thick and to weigh over 300 tons. No one can explain how these gigantic rocks were transported to the site. Walking along the tunnel, you can see the rock escarpment of the long-lost Antonia Fortress at the northern end of the western wall built by the Maccabees. This imposing building complex existed for only a few decades before it was demolished by the Romans following the fall of the Temple. The Tunnel is wide enough for one person to pass at a time, leading to a one-way route exiting at the beginning of the Via Dolorosa. The opening of this exit was blamed for rioting that occurred in 1996.

Temple Area

I. Background

The Temple Area or Temple Mount is actually a large court or platform resting on a box-like structure which surrounds the steep slopes of Mount Moriah (See Western Wall, Section I). The Temple Area spreads over the sacred Mount Moriah famed for its role in the life of Abraham. Here the Patriarch was ready to sacrifice his son Isaac to the glory of God (Genesis 22:2). The Sages of Israel asked, "Why is this called the mountain of Moriah? Because the word Moriah is derived from Mora, which in Hebrew means awe. From that mountain went forth the fear of the Lord to all mankind. Another reason is that the word Moriah may also be derived from Orah, which means light, and when the Almighty commanded, 'Let there be light,' it was from that mountain that light first shone forth upon all mankind." On this site, stood many Biblical and historical structures. Let's look at them through history.

II. Biblical Structures

A. First Temple

On Mount Moriah stood the first Temple, or Solomon's Temple. It was completed in the year 960 BCE (II Chronicles 3:1). Solomon's Temple was destroyed by the Babylonians in 587 BCE. It is at this point that we lose track of the Ark of the Covenant that had been carried through the desert and finally brought into Jerusalem by David in 1000 BCE.

B. Second Temple

The Second Temple was completed in 520 BCE by Nehemiah. It was very unassuming, yet remained in this state until the days of King Herod. Herod enhanced this hill and the Sages of Israel commented, "He who has not seen the building of Herod has never seen a handsome building." It was in this splendid Temple that we find Jesus in the gospel accounts. The historical period, called the Second Temple period, refers to the time of the magnificent Temple embellished by Herod, 30 BCE – 70 CE. Herod's Temple was totally destroyed by Titus in 70 CE.

III. Historical Structures

A. Dome of the Rock

After the destruction of Herod's Temple, the Romans erected a temple to Jupiter where they put up statues of their emperors. The Byzantine Christians ultimately built a church in 536 CE (See El Aksa Mosque).

With the Arab conquest of Palestine in 638 CE, the Caliph Omar came to Jerusalem. He had a temporary house of worship erected in the Temple Area. After more than 50 years, the existing mosque (Dome of the Rock) was built by Caliph Abd al-Malek in 691 CE.

The Dome of the Rock encloses a rock that formed the natural summit of Mount Moriah. According to Moslem belief, Mohammed, riding on a winged horse with a woman's face and a peacock's tail, and accompanied by the Archangel Gabriel, came from Mecca to Jerusalem to this rock. This was before his ascent into the seventh heaven. According to the legend, as Mohammed began to ascend, the rock itself rose under his foot and was stopped by the Archangel Gabriel, who left his hand print on the rock. Beneath the outcropping of rock is a grotto referred to as the Well of Souls where the spirits of the dead meet twice a week for prayer.

There are many other legends concerning this area from the Moslems, as well as the Jews. One Jewish tradition says that this rock is the foundation of the earth, which was thought to be round and flat. In Hebrew, the stone is called Even Hashettiya (the stone of foundation). Maps from the Middle Ages placed Jerusalem at the center of the world. Spiritually, this is true. Let us remember our roots in the events of the Bible that occurred on this spot. Traditionally, this is the place where Abraham offered Isaac (Genesis 22:2). It is also the area of the threshing floor of Araunah or Ornan the Jebusite which David bought so he could sacrifice unto the Lord. He did this after he repented for numbering the people, which God had forbidden (II Samuel 24). From this time forward, it became a sacred spot where the Temples were built.

Many people incorrectly call the Dome of the Rock the Mosque of Omar. Caliph Abd al-Malek built the Dome of the Rock with materials from the ruins of Byzantine churches destroyed in 614 CE by the Persians. The workmen who did the construction were descendants of Byzantine (Christian) craftsman still living in the city. Since its construction, the mosque has undergone many changes. From 813 to 835 CE, the Abbasid Caliph El Ma'mum made repairs to the building and he inserted his name in the place of Ad al-Malek but forgot to change the date.

In the year 1009 CE, the Crusaders transformed the mosque into a Christian church and renamed it Templum Domini in honor of Jesus. With the capture of Jerusalem by Saladin, a Moslem, in 1187 CE, it was again changed back into a mosque. Many repairs and restorations have been carried out since the days of Saladin, each leaving traces of the different works behind.

The exterior of the mosque is a regular octagon with each side measuring 62.5 feet. The building has a diameter of 178 feet. The dome is mounted on a cylindrical drum and rises to a height of 107 feet. The outside of the mosque is faced with slabs of marble and multicolored mosaics. The mosaics have quotations from the Koran written in Arabic. The inside of the Dome of the Rock is beautifully decorated with colored tile, mosaics on a field of gold, veined marble columns and Persian carpets.

B. Dome of the Chain

Leaving the Dome of the Rock, you see to the east a small building which resembles it. It is called the Dome of the Chain (Qubbet es Silsileh) after the iron chain that is suspended from its cupola. It is also called the Tribunal of the Prophet David. This is a structure that is a hexagon enclosing a polygon and it has a combination of seventeen pillars situated so that all of the pillars can be seen at one time from any angle! Moslem legend says that at the time of Solomon a chain was suspended from heaven at this spot which could only be grasped by the righteous.

The structure was built in the 8th century CE and the Crusaders used it as a chapel dedicated to St. James.

C. Other Significant Structures (Dome Area)

Other significant structures surround the Dome of the Rock in the court area:

Northwest of the Dome of the Rock is another dome called the Dome of the Ascension (Qubbet el Mi'raj). This may have been the baptistery chapel of the Templum Domini at the time of the Crusaders.

Near the flight of steps at the northwest is the Dome of St. George (Qubbet el Kadr) which is said to be the site of Solomon's tormenting the demons.

The nearby Dome of the Spirits (Qubbet el Arwah) is, according to Moslem tradition, the spirits of departed Moslem saints meet there at night for worship. At the bottom of the main flight of steps on the west side, exactly opposite the Dome of the Rock, stands the Sabil Qait Bai. It is a beautiful fountain built in 1487 CE.

A Minbar, or pulpit, erected in 1456 by Birhan ed-Din is the south side of the Dome of the Rock. It is also called Minba Omar and is used as a summer pulpit for outside preaching by the Moslem priests.

Also on the south side, between the Dome of the Rock and the Al Aksa Mosque, is a large round basin called El

Kas. The water from the basin is used by the Moslem faithful who are required to wash before they can pray.

The Temple Area contains a large number of spacious underground cisterns which have a combined capacity of 10 million gallons. This is near a cistern called the Sea, or King's Cistern, which is 725 feet in circumference and 39 feet deep. In ancient days, the cistern was supplied with water from "Solomon's Pools" beyond Bethlehem (10 miles south) by a stone conduit. In 1901, iron pipes were installed.

D. Al Aksa Mosque

The Al Aksa Mosque is the third most holy site in the Moslem world. The Kaaba (black stone) in Mecca and the Tomb of the Prophet in Medina (both in Saudi Arabia) are more important. In every Moslem's lifetime he must make the effort to complete the Haj (Pilgrimage) which includes a visit to each of these three sites. Once a Haj is completed, the individual earns the title of Haj (m.) or Haja (f.), which is used before their name like Mr. or Mrs. The doorway of a Haj's home will also be painted with scenes from his pilgrimage, and will usually include the three holy shrines. Look above the doorways and see how many Haj paintings you can see as you walk through the Old City of Jerusalem.

The present-day Al Aksa Mosque, which is located on the southern end of the Temple Mount, was originally a Christian basilica in honor of St. Mary. The basilica was built in 531 CE and was in the form of a cross. The church and its adjacent hospital were sacked by the Persians in 614 CE. In the late sixth century, there were many repairs and expansions to the building by the Moslems, and in 715 CE, the Caliph al-Walid completed what is known as the El Aksa Mosque. Parts of the original Al Aksa Mosque, as well as a portion of the original basilica, remain.

The Al Aksa Mosque was destroyed by an earthquake in 746 CE, then rebuilt but destroyed again by another earthquake. The next rebuilding was ordered by the Caliph Al-Mahdi who made it a little shorter but wider. Another earthquake in 1034 CE, caused the Mosque to be rebuilt again – this time as a five-aisled building.

From the days of the Crusaders, who made it into a church, to the present, the Mosque has changed hands several times and each group of people made modifications, additions and repairs to the structure. It has finally ended up with seven aisles, with the central aisle being larger and higher than the others. The present-day mosque is 260 feet long and 17 feet wide.

Within the mosque, west of the minbar (pulpit), are two places of prayer. One is dedicated to Moses and the other to Issa (Jesus). In the east section are the columns of ordeal and the Moslems say that if you can pass through these, you will enter Paradise. There are some very beautiful stained-glass windows which date back to the days of the Crusaders. It is also completely carpeted with Persian carpets.

Underneath the Al Aksa Mosque is a stairway that led outside the southern exterior walls in the days of Jesus. Although the entrance has been walled up, the stairway is still there. The original arches and staircase outside the wall have recently been uncovered and restored in an extensive archaeological excavation and restoration. Undoubtedly, these steps were used by Jesus, as it was the main entrance to the Temple Area from the south.

E. Other Significant Sites (Southern Mount Area)

Underneath the southern end of the Temple Area is a network of substructures. One of these substructures located under the southeast corner of the Temple Mount is known as Solomon's Stables. Legend has it that these were the stables used for the horses of King Solomon's chariots and mounted warriors. The way in which the horses came into the king's house is mentioned in II Kings 11:16. The Crusaders used these stables for their horses. The Order of the Templars had its headquarters in the Temple courtyard which is how they came to be called Templars.

On the southeast corner of the Temple Mount you will notice a small dome erected over a hallowed stone called the "Cradle of Christ." It probably got its name because there was a crypt here that could have been dedicated to the infancy of Jesus.

An important area mentioned in the New Testament is the Pinnacle of the Temple (Luke 4:9) where Satan said to Jesus, "If thou be the Son of God, cast thyself down from hence." The pinnacle is believed to have been at the southeast corner of the wall. Look over the side and down into the deep Kidron Valley and remember the Scripture from Luke. Also consider that the valley was even deeper in the days of Jesus.

Recent Excavations on the Southern End of the Temple Mount

The work on the Southern Excavations was begun in 1968 under the guidance of Benjamin Mazar. The first project continued for about ten years. Archeologist Ronny Reich resumed the work in the 1990s. These excavations opened up insights to the world of the Second Temple period long buried under massive stones. Indeed, the dig involved a earth-moving project. The recently opened Davidson Exhibition Center at the Archeological Park gives you the chance to take a virtual tour of the Temple Mount as archaeologists believe it might have appeared to a pilgrim in Herodian times (late 1st c. BCE until the Roman destruction of Jerusalem in 70 CE).

First Century Street

This street was fully uncovered in the mid-1990s and dates to the decades before the destruction of the city by the Romans in 70 CE. The street is 30 feet wide and was paved with large slabs up to a foot thick. The street was covered with massive stones pushed down by the Romans at the time of the attack on the city.

Trumpeting Stone

The top stone on the southwest corner of the Temple Mount bore an inscription which read in part, "to the place of trumpeting." The priests would blow the shofar from this point to signal the start of Shabbat and festival days.

Southern Steps

The western flight of stairs leading to the main entrances of the Temple Mount was 200 feet wide. Excavators uncovered the easternmost part of this staircase with its alternating long and short steps. Some suggest that the fifteen long steps may have been one of the locations where pilgrims sang the fifteen Psalms of Ascent (120-34) as they went up to worship.

Double Gate

The Double Gates and Triple Gates provided access to the Temple Mount through subterranean passageways. Half of the lintel stone and arch of this Herodian gateway is visible above the later protruding arch.

Mikveh

A series of public ritual baths were found on the south side of the Temple Mount. The laws regarding purity required a ritual bath before entering holy places. Therefore the demand for mikvot was high and many have been discovered from first century Jerusalem. Larger mikvot have separate entrances and exits.

F. Golden Gate

We find the Golden Gate, or Eastern Gate, in the eastern wall of the Temple Area. Tradition says that Jesus entered into Jerusalem through this gate when he made his triumphal entry on Palm Sunday. This is very possible because that is the day, under the Law, when the Passover Lamb had to be presented to the Priests for inspection. Christians see Jesus as our Passover Lamb who sacrificed his life for our salvation. This is the entrance of the Temple Area from the Mount of Olives where Jesus came riding on a colt. The Temple Area is where you would find the priests. It is also the gate that some connect with the closed gate of Ezekiel 44:1-4, which will be opened when Messiah comes.

In 629 CE, the Emperor Heraclius entered the city through this gate, bearing what was said to be the true cross which he had taken from the Persians who had destroyed the city in 614. The gate got its present form probably from the Emperor Justinian before 629,

although the foundations belong to a previous structure. The gate was completely blocked up in 1530 by the Turks, and Sultan Suleiman incorporated it into the city wall in 1540. Legend has it that Suleiman did this because of the Christian belief that Jesus would open this gate in his Second Coming. He blocked the gate to prevent this event.

Christians attach the memory of Acts 3:1-3 when Peter, in the name of Jesus, healed the man who was lame from birth at the gate of the Temple which was called "Beautiful." The Greeks called this the Beautiful Gate and it was later rendered into Latin which was translated Golden Gate. (Actually, the Beautiful Gate was an eastern gate of the interior court of the Temple.) Inside of the Golden Gate, we find a beautiful structure of two arched entrances. The north arch is called Bab et Tauba (Gate of Repentance), and the south arch is called Bab er Rahma (Gate of Mercy).

Church of St. Anne – Pool of Bethesda

I. Church of St. Anne

To the north, outside of the Temple Mount and near St. Stephen's Gate (Lion's Gate), is the Church of St. Anne (the mother of Mary). The church is built over the house where, by tradition, Mary was born. This is one of the most well-preserved examples of Crusader architecture. Archeological evidence shows that there had been a church standing on this site since the beginning of the 3rd century CE. The present Crusader structure is over 800 years old. Various churches on this site have been destroyed, either by earthquake or conquest, and rebuilt.

The site was known as the Basilica of St. Mary. It is speculated that when the Crusaders rebuilt the church, they changed the name to the Church of St. Anne. While standing in front of the church, you can notice that it leans slightly to one side. This is an architectural device used to represent Jesus on the Cross. There is a flight of stairs that takes you down under the altar to a crypt. Through this crypt you can enter into the house where Mary was born. It is likely that this is a commemorative rather than an actual location.

II. Pool of Bethesda

We find the Pool of Bethesda on the grounds just west of St. Anne's Church. It was here that most believe the events of John 5:1-9 occurred. On the Sabbath, Jesus healed the man crippled for 38 years. The Pool of Bethesda is mentioned only in the Gospel of John and according to John, the pool lay near the Sheep Gate. While it is no longer possible to determine the location of the Sheep Gate, from the description which John gives us of the Pool of Bethesda with its five porches, etc., we can feel sure this is the likely location. The early Christians also considered this to be the location. The debris and ruins of the Pool of Bethesda are about 65 feet below the present ground level and the structures of the porches can be clearly seen, as well as the water. Because of local underground rock formations, rainwater collects at this spot. The depth of the structures also gives us a good indication of the level of the city in the days of Jesus, as well as the many times that Jerusalem has been destroyed to create so much debris.

The Church of the Paralytic was built on this site in 450 CE, but was destroyed in 614 CE by the Persians. It was not rebuilt until 1100 CE when the Crusaders built a chapel on this site. The chapel of the Crusaders was probably destroyed in 1187 when the Crusaders were defeated by armies of Saladin. The remains of the Pool of Bethesda and the churches were not rediscovered until 1873. The White Fathers, an order of Greek priests, acquired the site in 1878 and have excavated it.

St. Stephen's Gate – Lion's Gate

I. Background

Leaving the grounds of the Pool of Bethesda and St. Anne's Church, you turn east on the roadway 150 feet to reach St. Stephen's Gate. The gate is located on the north portion of the eastern wall of the Old City of Jerusalem.

This gate has been called St. Stephen's Gate because tradition says that it was in this vicinity where St. Stephen was stoned (Acts 6:8 - Acts 7:60, primarily Acts 7:57-60). It is more likely that Stephen was stoned in the area north of the Damascus Gate. The Greeks call this gate the Gethsemane Gate because it leads to the Garden of Gethsemane across the Kidron Valley at the base of the Mount of Olives. Historically, the gate has been called the Galilee Gate because it faced the place on the Mount of Olives where the Galileans encamped when they came up to Jerusalem. This gate is also known as the Lion's Gate for there are a pair of lions carved in the stone on the outward portal. An ancient tale says that Sultan Suleiman the Magnificent dreamed that four lions leapt upon him from the Jordan thickets and tore him to pieces. His magicians explained the dream as an expression of God's wrath because Jerusalem was lying in waste. The Sultan then gave orders for the restoration work to begin and this gate was erected with the lions carved upon it.

It was through this gate that the Israeli Army penetrated the Old City on June 7, 1967.

New Jerusalem

Hakirya — The Government Center

Hakirya, a Hebrew word which literally means "the city," is the name of the Government Center. The Government Center is located in Jerusalem on a hillside commanding a view of the whole area and facing Mount Herzl, the burial place of the prophet of the State of Israel, Theodore Herzl. The many buildings in the Government Center house the various ministries and agencies of government which keep Israel's vibrant democracy working.

I. Knesset

The Parliament (Knesset) of Israel is housed in a prominent building known by the same name, the Knesset. The Hebrew word Knesset means "assembly." The parliament has 120 seats (members) who are elected by the citizens of Israel on a proportional-representation system.

The State of Israel is a democratic parliamentary republic. The Knesset has the sole power to make or amend the laws. The Knesset building was inaugurated in 1966 and is open to the public.

II. The Menorah (Candelabrum)

The Menorah with the olive branch is the emblem of the State of Israel, symbolizing light and peace. A beautiful and very large menorah stands opposite the entrance to the Knesset. A plaque by its side carries the following inscription:

> Following the visit of the British Parliamentary Delegation of Israel, friends and well-wishers of the young State, members of both Houses of Parliament and others evolved the idea of presenting this menorah as a gift from Britain to the Parliament of Israel, as a token of goodwill and friendship.

The Menorah stands 16 feet high and 13 feet wide and is the work of sculptor B. Elkan. It is executed in massive bronze and its seven branches are decorated with 29 panels. These panels depict, in relief, figures and events which are highlights in the history and revival of the Jewish people. (Take the time to study these relief scenes along with the following descriptions.)

A. The Central Pillar

The Central Pillar carries the words: "Hear O Israel," the first words of the fundamental Jewish proclamation of faith written in the Torah, "Hear, O Israel; the Lord our God, the Lord is One." On the two lower branches are the words of the prophet Zechariah, "Not by might nor by power, but by My spirit, saith the Lord of hosts." On the central pillar, from top to bottom, we see: a) **Moses** lifting up his arms blessing Israel before the battle against the Amalekites; b) the **Tablet**s with the Ten Commandments; c) **Rachel** mourning for her lost children; d) **Ruth**, the mother of David's dynasty; e) the Prophet **Ezekiel,** visualizing the raising of the dead bones, receiving the breath of life and marching back to the homeland; f) the battle of the **Warsaw Ghetto** against the Nazis; g) the words "**Hear, O Israel**," and on the bottom, h) the

Halutsim (pioneers) in the land of Israel tilling the soil, sowing and reaping corn and fruit, building houses and bridges, drilling for water and blowing up rocks.

Now we will look at the scenes depicted from top to bottom on the branches of the Menorah, one branch at a time.

B. The Left Branches

1. Facing the menorah from the outside we have Branch #1 showing: a) the Prophet **Isaiah** surrounded by wild beasts grazing together with lambs, gazelle and other small creatures. It is a vision of peace and harmony, the ideal set forth in Isaiah 11:6,7 and 65:25; b) Rabbi **Yohnan Ben Zakkai** leaving a burning Jerusalem (70 CE) and opening a school of learning in Yavne, an act symbolizing the survival of the spirit of Israel; c) Jews in **Spain**, the golden era of its Jewry; d) in **Babylon**, Jews crouching by the bank of the river, weeping and longing for their homeland.

2. Branch #2: a) **Ezra** the Scribe reading the Torah to his people; b) **Job** with his friends — the eternal discussion of good and evil, faith and doubt; c) the **Talmud**, the commentary of the learned rabbis representing the strict observance of the law; d) the **Haggada** — King Solomon amid flowers listening to singing birds.

3. Branch #3: a) **David** the shepherd, after killing Goliath the Philistine, a triumph of simple faith over mighty armor; b) **Fulfillment**, landing on the shore of Israel; and, c) the Patriarch **Abraham** prostrating himself when he hears the voice from heaven, and answering, "Here am I!"

C. The Right Branches

1. From the outside, we have Branch #1: a) the Prophet **Jeremiah** crying out in despair against the wickedness of his people; b) the **Maccabees** fighting their enemy (165 BCE); c) the **Hasid** (ultra-Orthodox) symbolizing the worshipping of God everywhere and in every living form; d) **Nehemiah** restoring the walls of destroyed Jerusalem (440 BCE) under the protection of defenders carrying spear and shield.

2. Branch #2: a) **Hillel** the Elder expounding to a stranger the whole content of Jewish law in three words: "V'ahavta lere' akha kamokha"… "Thou shalt love thy neighbor as thyself." b) **Rabbi Hanina**, son of Teradion, teaching the Torah in the open, in spite of the Roman prohibition. He was arrested and condemned to death. He said, "The Rock, his work is perfect, for all his ways are Justice," c) **Kabbalah**, the Jewish mystics' flight into the mysteries of the conception of the world and man; d) **Halakha**, the application of the incorruptible law, (literally, the way to walk).

3. Branch #3: a) **Bar-Kokhba** after the collapse of his revolt against the Romans (135 CE); b) **Messianic hope**, people praying in ecstatic abandon for the realization of the age-long dream – the return to Israel and the coming of Messiah; and c) **Jacob** wrestling with the angel and conquering – the struggle for blessed confirmation.

Yad Vashem

I. Why Christians Should Care

Yad Vashem is a memorial to the six-million Jews who perished in the Holocaust during the 12 years of Nazi tyranny over Europe (1933-1945); to the hundreds of European Jewish communities which were destroyed; and to the spirit of the Jewish resistance which, despite overwhelming odds, fought for human dignity and freedom. The Holocaust marks the first time in history that a people was singled out for extermination by a political party in power. Its consequences are of decisive significance for the Jewish people – now and for future generations.

The Holocaust was a result of antisemitism (hatred of Jews), within the so-called "Christian" country of Germany. Historically, antimitism was found and even promoted in the Church throughout history. For this reason, it is important that we, as Christians, understand the sin of antisemitism and its results, as well as the specific details of the Holocaust. Antisemitism has no place in the Christian's life, and we should do everything in our power to uphold the Jewish people, God's covenant people. This is why we visit Yad Vashem and take Christians on pilgrimage to Auschwitz. The Nazi Holocaust could not have occurred if Christians had been alert to their responsibility. We cannot undo the past but we can make sure that our generation is aware and prepared to prevent such a thing from happening again.

The Judeo-Christian goal is to "Love the Lord your God with all your heart, all your soul, all your strength, all your mind and love your neighbor as yourself," (Deuteronomy 6:5; Luke 10:27). A contradiction to this commandment is prejudice in all forms because it denies God's desire to reach out in love, through us, to all. Unfortunately we find prejudice creeping into the lives of individual Christians and even into whole church groups. Antisemitism is a particularly virulent form of prejudice which ignores the teaching of Romans 11 and cuts Christians off from their Jewish roots.

Antisemitism, according to Webster's Dictionary, is "prejudice against Jews, or the discrimination against or persecution of Jews." The term antisemitism was coined by Willem Marr, a German who wanted to give the concept of "Jew-hatred" a scienctific name, but the activities of prejudice, discrimination and persecution of the Jewish people have been around for thousands of years. The earliest indications of anti-Jewish discrimination and prejudice can be found in the writings of pre-Christian pagan societies of the Middle East, and in Hellenistic and Roman literature. This was basically because of their rejection of Israel's relationship to God. The Hebrew Scripture presents Israel as God's ambassador to the world (Genesis 12:13).

During the past 1900 years, Christian antisemitism (that prejudice originating from Christian teaching) emerged from the Christian societies of Europe and their many colonies, e.g., Australia, South Africa, Canada, the U.S., South America, etc. As the Jewish communities migrated to Europe and the colonies, they were confronted with a "built-in" prejudice that, unfortunately, became the norm of Western society.

Biblically, Christianity has a responsibility to uphold the Jewish people as the seed of Abraham and the covenant people of God – "the apple of His eye" (Zechariah 2:8). Yet, historically, Christian faith became confused in political and economic struggles which resulted in a prejudice against anyone not coming from the Christian-controlled society. This Christian system became very antagonistic towards the Jewish people who maintained a strict social and religious distinction of their own (some of it being imposed upon them by the majority Christian society around them).

Blatant and overt Christian discrimination against the Jewish community can be found in all periods of Christian history. It began with early Church prohibitions against Christians associating with Jewish people. Then came official government edicts first initiated in the fourth century by the Christian Emperor Constantine, medieval dress codes for Jews, the Russian pogroms, all culminating in the Holocaust. While the latter outbreaks of the pogroms and the Holocaust were not specifically Christian activities, they were certainly the results of centuries of prejudice that used the Jewish people as a scapegoat for social, political and economic problems. This scapegoating could have been averted by the majority "Christian" society – yet it was not. This paved the way for a society that produced an Adolf Hitler and then sat silently by while millions of Jews were being murdered…including over 1,500,000 children!

II. Activities Before and During the Holocaust

The Jewish people lost independence in their own land after the destruction of the Second Temple in Jerusalem by the Romans in 70 CE. Since that time, the majority of Jews have lived dispersed throughout the world. In some places they integrated into the life of the host country, but in many others they were confined to ghettos and frequently were subjected to restrictive regulations, persecution and pogroms.

However, only with the coming to power in Germany (1933) of the Nazi (National Socialist Workers) Party,

headed by Adolf Hitler, did a government ever officially adopt racist antisemitism as a concrete program. Its attitude was popularly expressed in the slogan, "Deutschland erwache – Juda verrecke!" ("Germany, wake up – Jews drop dead!"). In the words of the Nazi anthem, "Wenn das Judenblut vom Messer spritzt, dann geht's nochmal so gut!" ("When Jew-blood spurts from the knife, then things will go twice as well").

The twelve years of the Nazis' anti-Jewish campaign constituted an uninterrupted progression towards making German and German-controlled areas *Judenrein* (free of Jews), accompanied by vicious anti-Semitic propaganda and an escalating barbarization of methods. Until the outbreak of World War II, in September 1939, German policy was to make life so unbearable for Jews that they would be forced to emigrate. The 1935 Nuremberg Laws deprived Jews of their German citizenship and excluded them from public office, the professions and the intellectual, economic and artistic life of the country. The hatred ignited by the Nazi anti-Jewish propaganda resulted in acts of degradation and violence against Jews throughout Germany, culminating in the *Kristallnacht* (Night of Broken Glass) – during which some 25,000 Jews were arrested, 7,000 Jewish shops and businesses vandalized and looted and many synagogues burned down.

About 300,000 of Germany's half-million Jews (representing 0.8% of Germany's total population) did succeed in leaving the country between 1933 and 1939. Some 55,000 settled in what was then called Palestine, the land of Israel, at that time under British control. Others found refuge in Great Britain and other European countries, in the United States and in Latin America.

As the Nazi armies swept through Europe in 1939-40, they instituted anti-Jewish policies in one country after another. Young or old, rich or poor, educated or unschooled – every Jew was condemned. Everywhere, Jews were rounded up and herded into ghettos, tortured, killed at random, rationed at starvation level, systematically deported to camps where the strong and healthy were selected to serve the Nazis as slave labor – and the rest were condemned to death before firing squads or in the gas chambers.

In some places, the local population actively co-operated with the special German units charged with the organization and implementation of the Nazi goal "The Final Solution of the Jewish Problem." In other places, they passively accepted the Nazi actions, and did nothing to prevent them.

In only a few places were Jews helped by their non-Jewish former neighbors, colleagues and friends. Some were hidden from the Nazis by courageous individuals, over 3,000 of whom have been honored as "Righteous Gentiles" by Yad Vashem. Trees are planted in their honor.

(Corrie ten Boom and her family have been so honored. Her tree had to be replanted – it died shortly after she did!) Others managed to join local partisan groups dedicated to sabotaging the Nazis whenever and however possible. In heroic and unparalleled actions, almost the entire Jewish population of Denmark – some 7,000 men, women and children – were smuggled to safety in Sweden by the Danish underground. This story is told in an interesting film called, "The Only Way." (Look for it on Amazon.)

Very few Jews found ways to escape the Nazi machine created to annihilate them. However, within the ghettos and camps, despite inhuman conditions and constant fear, many Jews resisted and fought for survival by organizing underground groups, by smuggling emissaries to the outside world to report their plight and by many thousands of acts of personal self-sacrifice. From April 19 to May 16, 1943, the Jews of the Warsaw Ghetto revolted, holding out for over three weeks against massively reinforced German troops. The Warsaw revolt was followed by similar actions in the ghettos of Bialystock and Vilna. Although these uprisings were crushed by the Nazis and most of the resistance fighters were killed, they were the first and largest armed revolts to occur in occupied Europe.

Meanwhile, most of the desperate efforts of Jewish and Zionist organizations in the free world to rescue the Jews of Europe ended in frustration and failure. Nevertheless, Jews from many countries – including those of Israel (Palestine) – valiantly served the Allied cause in its war against the Nazi regime.

When the Allied armies finally vanquished the third Reich in May 1945, most of the Jews of eastern Europe and large numbers of those in western Europe (excluding Great Britain) had been killed. One-third of the Jewish population of the world had been murdered! The remnants of what once was the most highly cultured and stable Jewish community in the world emerged from the concentration camps and forests – some 250,000 survivors out of a pre-war Jewish population of nearly seven million – starved, haunted by nightmares of what they had experienced and divested of trust and faith. All that remained was a strengthened sense of their Jewish identity and a longing to begin a new life in freedom and peace.

III. Yad Vashem Memorial

In 1953, the Knesset voted to create the Yad Vashem Martyrs and Heroes Remembrance Authority, whose task was to commemorate those who died in the Holocaust; to preserve records of the organizations and institutions of the destroyed Jewish communities; to honor the Jewish resistance fighters; and to commend non-Jews who risked their lives to save Jews.

To house Yad Vashem, a complex of buildings – including a museum, a library and the Hall of Remembrance – was built on a hilltop near Mount Herzl in Jerusalem. Every year on Holocaust Remembrance Day (Nissan 27, six days after the end of Passover), surviving representatives of Jewish communities destroyed in the Nazi era stand guard at the 70-foot high memorial pillar which dominates the site.

On April 12, 1951, the Knesset (Israel's parliament) proclaimed Yom Hashoah U'Mered HaGetaot (Holocaust and Ghetto Revolt Remembrance Day) to be the 27th of Nissan. The name later became known as Yom Hashoah Ve Hagevurah (Devastation and Heroism Day) and even later simplified to Yom Hashoah.

Hundreds of visitors daily encounter the tragedy of the Holocaust as it unfolds before them in the halls of the Yad Vashem. Memorial flames are lit by school children and visiting dignitaries alike in the Hall of Remembrance, whose structure recalls aspects of the concentration camps and whose floor is inscribed with the names of the 22 largest camps. More than two million "Pages of Testimony," bearing the names of Jews who died or who fell in the resistance, have been filed in the Hall of Names by surviving relatives or friends.

Yad Vashem's research center deals with ongoing investigations of Nazi crimes. Its library contains more than 45,000 volumes, and its archive systematically stores documents pertaining to the Holocaust. In co-operation with the Ministry of Education and Culture, Yad Vashem sets up mobile exhibitions to bring the Jewish experience of the Holocaust into classrooms throughout Israel.

Yad Vashem stands not only as a memorial, but also as a symbol of hope. It attests not only to the past and potential richness of Jewish community life, but also the will of the Jewish people for survival and reconstruction. It not only expresses horror at the ultimate inhumanity of the Nazi design, but also proclaims that the Jewish people stand determined to be victims no more.

"And to them will I give in my house and within my walls a memorial and a name (a "yad vashem")... that shall not be cut off." (Isaiah, chapter 56, verse 5. *Yad* is the Hebrew word for *hand* but it is also used for a memorial. *Shem* is the Hebrew word for *name*.

Yad Vashem, the Holocaust Martyrs' and Heroes' Remembrance Authority, was established in 1953 by an act of the Israeli Knesset. Since its inception, Yad Vashem has been entrusted with documenting the history of the Jewish people during the Holocaust period, preserving the memory and story of each of the six million victims, and imparting the legacy of the Holocaust for generations to come through its archives, library, school, museums and recognition of the Righteous Among the Nations.

Located on Har Hazikaron, the Mount of Remembrance,

in Jerusalem, Yad Vashem is a vast, sprawling complex of tree-studded walkways leading to museums, exhibits, archives, monuments, sculptures, and memorials.

The new Holocaust History Museum occupies over 4,200 square meters, mainly underground. The New Museum was dedicated on March 15, 2005 at Yad Vashem in Jerusalem.

A decade in the making, the New Museum combines the best of Yad Vashem's expertise, resources and state-of-the-art exhibits to take Holocaust remembrance well into the 21st century. Both multidisciplinary and interdisciplinary, it presents the story of the Shoah from a unique Jewish perspective, emphasizing the experiences of the individual victims through original artifacts, survivor testimonies and personal possessions.

The Art Museum is a testimony to the strength of the human spirit and holds the world's largest and most important collection of Holocaust art. It includes works of art that were created under the inconceivably adverse conditions of the Holocaust and a selection of works done after the war by Holocaust survivors and by other artists.

The Hall of Remembrance is a solemn tent-like structure which allows visitors to pay their respects to the memories of the martyred dead. On the floor are the names of the six death camps and some of the concentration camps and killing sites throughout Europe. In front of the memorial flame lies a crypt containing ashes of victims. Memorial ceremonies for official visitors are held here.

The Children's Memorial is hollowed out from an underground cavern, where memorial candles, a customary Jewish tradition to remember the dead, are reflected infinitely in a dark and somber space. This memorial is a tribute to the approximately one and a half million Jewish children who perished during the Holocaust.

The Valley of the Communities is a 2.5 acre monument that was dug out from the natural bedrock. Engraved on the massive stone walls of the memorial are the names of over five thousand Jewish communities that were destroyed and of the few that suffered but survived in the shadow of the Holocaust.

Old Jerusalem

Jesus' Trial to Resurrection

I. Background

We will look at the alternative routes from Jesus' trial to the place of his burial and resurrection. We say alternative, because there are two sites commemorating the place of Calvary and the Tomb of Jesus. Don't let this disturb you, for there are often two and sometimes three or more sites commemorating Biblical events. We can know the actual location of an event only when the Bible gives us a definite geographical location. Even when we know this, we have, in some cases, lost track of where these locations were to be found in Jerusalem because of the many destructions of the city in history. Sometimes, the general area is known, and at other times there is no way of knowing. The important thing to remember is that the Biblical events did, in fact, occur. Perhaps it is better that we do not know the exact locations because humankind tends to venerate and worship holy places more than the Lord who made the place holy by his presence or work there.

In relation to Jesus' trial and route to his crucifixion, burial and resurrection, we will walk two routes. First, we will walk the traditional Via Dolorosa (Way of Sorrows), where we will discuss each of the traditional Stations of the Cross as we go from the place of Jesus' trial to the Church of the Holy Sepulchre (Route #1). Then we will walk on the path to Golgotha and the Garden Tomb through the Damascus Gate on the north side of the Old City of Jerusalem (Route #2). Both routes begin at the same place but finish in different locations due to a controversy over the real site of the tomb of Jesus.

II. Biblical And Spiritual Significance

The information relating to the history of the Via Dolorosa, the Church of the Holy Sepulchre, Calvary, and the Garden Tomb are only significant because of the actual events of the trial, crucifixion, burial and resurrection of Jesus. Therefore, let us look together at a summary of these events and their spiritual significance before we consider their historical and traditional sites of commemoration.

A. In the Garden

After the Passover meal (the Last Supper), Jesus and his disciples left the upper room and went out to the Mount of Olives (Matthew 26:30; Mark 14:26). The site was located just across the Kidron Valley (John 18:1) where there was a garden known by the name of Gethsemane. Leaving the group, Jesus took Peter, James and John with him a bit further into the garden; then he left them and went still further to pray alone. Soon Judas came leading a multitude – carrying swords, clubs and lanterns – and guided officials to Jesus, whom he identified with a kiss. Jesus readily admitted his identity, was arrested and led away to be subjected to a series of hastily arranged, illegal trials. His followers left him and fled (Matthew 26:47-56).

B. The Arrest and Preliminary Trial

After his arrest, Jesus was taken first to the house of Annas, the father-in-law of the high priest Caiaphas. In the presence of Annas, Jesus was asked about his disciples and his teaching. When he answered, Jesus was struck by one of the soldiers standing nearby. Annas sent him bound to Caiaphas (John 18:12-27).

Jesus was then tried before Caiaphas, the high priest, and the scribes and elders who were gathered. To accuse Him, they hired false witnesses, but the testimony of the witnesses was contradictory. Unable to make their case with false witnesses, they began to question Jesus. His replies threw them into a frenzy. They decided he had blasphemed and was worthy of death. They spat in his face and beat him with the palms of their hands, and then asked him to identify the person who had done the striking (Matthew 26:57-68).

C. Before Pilate

The next morning Jesus' accusers took him to Pilate, the governor, who was staying in the Antonia Fortress at the northern end of the Temple Mount When they arrived at the counsel hall (Praetorium), the accusers didn't want to enter because they would defile themselves for the Passover. Pilate came out to them and exchanged remarks concerning Jesus. Finally, Pilate told them to try Jesus themselves. They replied that he deserved death and this required Roman approval. At this point, Jesus was asked by Pilate if he were the king of the Jews. After the examination, Pilate told the Jews outside he could find no reason to condemn the man (John 18:28-38).

When Pilate learned that Jesus was from Galilee in the northern part of Israel, he sent him to Herod Antipas, tetrarch of Galilee, who happened to be visiting in Jerusalem. Herod was glad to see him because Jesus had acquired a reputation and Herod wanted to see a miracle. Herod also had a number of questions for Jesus, which Jesus refused to answer. All during the trial, the crowds outside kept up a steady stream of accusations. Soldiers mocked Jesus, dressing him in royal robes (Luke 23:6-11).

Jesus was sent back to Pilate who announced that he had decided Jesus was innocent and that Herod agreed. He indicated that Jesus would be chastised and then released (Luke 23:13-16). Since the governor usually released one prisoner at Passover, Pilate offered the people a choice between the notorious Barabbas and Jesus. He knew that the accusations were brought against Jesus because of the envy of the Jewish religious leaders (Matthew 27:15-18).

About this time, Pilate's wife sent a message that she had a bad dream about Jesus and warned Pilate against harming Him. The chief priests and elders stirred up the crowd, and when Pilate made his offer, the people asked for Barabbas. When Pilate asked what to do with Jesus, the crowd cried, "Crucify Him! Crucify Him!" (Matthew 27:19-23). Pilate made his appeal three times, but the crowds were insistent that Jesus should be killed (Luke 23:22-24).

D. The Scourging

Pilate saw that a riot was developing so he took a bowl of water and symbolically washed his hands of the affair in full view of the crowds. Pilate then had Jesus scourged. The scourge was a whip made of leather thongs, studded with sharpened pellets of lead, iron or bone. The victim was stripped and tied in a bent position to a pillar, or stretched on a frame; his back was literally ripped to pieces. The soldiers on duty with Pilate stripped Jesus, scourged him and arrayed him in a scarlet robe. Then they plaited a crown of thorns for his head, placed a reed in his right hand for a scepter and mockingly bowed in front of Him, spat on him and hit him with the reed as they saluted Him, "Hail, King of the Jews!" (Mark 15:15-20; Matthew 27:24-31).

The account of the trial of Jesus in the Gospel of John indicates that after the scourging, Pilate continued in his efforts to have Jesus released. He thought the scourging would have satisfied the crowds, but they wanted more. After the scourging Pilate went back out to the crowd and indicated that he had found nothing wrong in Jesus. The soldiers brought Jesus out and Pilate presented Him, "Behold the man!" During Pilate's conversation with the crowd he became aware of the fact that Jesus was claiming to be the Son of God. This worried Pilate and he went back into the palace to talk more with Jesus. The more they talked, the more Pilate wanted to release Him. But, when he confronted the crowd with his renewed intentions to release Jesus, they accused Pilate of not being loyal to Caesar. He brought Jesus to the Pavement called Gabbatha in Hebrew, or Lithostrotos in Greek, and decided to crucify him (John 19:4-16).

When we think of the scourging of Jesus, it should bring to mind what Isaiah prophesied about the Messiah in Isaiah 53:5, "But he was wounded for our transgressions, he was bruised for our iniquities; the chastisement of our peace was upon Him; and with his stripes we are healed." The word stripes can also be translated as wounds. Sickness is a curse of the law on a sinful world (Gal.3:13). The fact that Jesus bore our sickness is confirmed to us in I Pet. 2:24, "He Himself bore our sins in his own body on the tree, that we, being dead to sins, should live unto righteousness, by whose stripes you were healed." Traditionally, a scourging was 40 stripes save one, leaving 39 for the bearer. It is interesting to note that there are also 39 different classifications of diseases, which some theologians understand to represent Christ's payment for the healing of humankind. These verses refer to the death of Christ as an atoning death, the result of which provided healing.

E. Road to Calvary

Then the procession toward Calvary began. The Greek word for the place was kranion, which we have in English as cranium. The Latin term is calva, which means a bare head or skull and accounts for the word Calvary (Luke 23:33). In Aramaic, the place of the skull was called Golgotha. For the procession, the criminal was placed in the center of a square of four Roman soldiers. A board was carried before Him, probably whitened with gypsum, with the charge against him painted in black letters. The inscription for Jesus read, "This is the King of the Jews" (Luke 23:27,28).

The victim was expected to carry the cross, or a part of it. The upright beam may have already stood from previous crucifixions, but the crossbeam had to be carried. Jesus, weakened by the scourging, fell under the weight of the cross. Simon of Cyrene, a passerby, was forced to help Jesus carry the cross (Luke 23:26). A multitude of people followed, including some women who "bewailed and lamented Him." Jesus spoke to them and said, "Daughters of Jerusalem, do not weep for me..." (Luke 23:27,28).

F. The Crucifixion

When they reached the place of crucifixion, the cross would be laid flat, and the victim laid on top. Jesus was offered medicated wine (an anesthetic) to drink. This would dull the pain; Jesus tasted and refused it (Matthew 27:34).

Halfway up the upright beam, there was usually a ledge of wood which projected as a saddle on which the body could rest. Otherwise, the nails would tear through the flesh from having to bear the victim's full weight. The nails were driven and his body suspended. Instead of the usual curses from the victim, Jesus said, "Father, forgive them for they know not what they do" (Luke 23:34).

Research on the mode of Roman crucifixion indicates that before the victim was nailed to the cross, he was stripped except, perhaps, for a loincloth, and his clothing fell to the soldiers as incidental income. There were probably six articles of clothing: a belt, sandals, girdle, turban and tunic — all of about equal value — and a robe, which was used as a cloak by day and a blanket at night. Jesus' robe had no seams, making it valuable. Therefore, the soldiers cast lots for it (Matthew 27:35; Psalm 22:18).

The robe was the only thing of value he possessed. Robes were ordinarily made at home, usually a mother's gift to her son as he left home. Soldiers gambling for the robe may have caused his thoughts to turn toward Mary, his mother who stood near the cross. Jesus said to John, "Behold, your mother!" John understood and took Mary to his own home (John 19:25-27).

The cross was near a highway. People going to and from the city taunted Him, "You who would destroy the temple and build it in three days, save yourself! If you are the Son of God, come down from the cross." (Matthew 27:40) The priests, the rulers and the soldiers all joined in the ridicule (Psalm 22:16,17).

Jesus was crucified at nine in the morning, and at noon darkness came over all the land for three hours. About three in the afternoon, he cried with a loud voice, "My God, my God, why hast Thou forsaken me?" (Matthew 27:46; Psalm 22:1)

He was thirsty. When they held a sponge full of vinegar to his mouth, Jesus said, "It is finished!" John 19:30). He prayed a brief prayer, Psalm 31:5, "Father, into Thy hand I commit My spirit!" (Luke 23:46). Then he bowed his head and died.

At that moment, the curtain of the Temple was torn in two, from top to bottom; the earth shook and the rocks were split; the tombs also were opened, and many bodies of the saints who had died were raised. (Matthew 27:51,52). The centurion who was supervising the crucifixion said, "Truly, this was the Son of God!" (Matthew 27:54)

Christians believe that the crucifixion of Jesus was not only a physical and historical event, but a spiritual act, the ultimate sacrifice for human sin.

To get a better understanding of what Jesus experienced and did for us, read Psalm 22. Some people believe that Jesus may have repeated this Psalm while on the cross. It has also been said that Jesus died of a broken heart. In Psalm 22:14, we find that the heart of Messiah would melt into the midst of his bowels. In fulfillment, we find in John 19:34 that as the soldier pierced Jesus' side, blood and water came out. This can be explained. When his heart rent, blood from all parts of his body poured into the cavity which holds the heart. As the body cooled off, the red corpuscles coagulated and settled to the bottom as the clear serum rose to the top. When the soldier's spear pierced his side, it pierced that heart cavity, "and forthwith came there out blood and water." John saw this happen (John 19:34,35). We cannot fully realize what Jesus did us for at the Cross. Isaiah tells us in Isaiah 52:14 that, "His visage was so marred more than any man, and his form more than the sons of men," so that the people present were stunned at his appearance."

This was all a result of what he allowed himself to go through as the ultimate sacrificial atonement, once and for all, for all mankind. II Corinthians 5:21 states, "For he has made him to be sin for us, who knew no sin; that we might be made the righteousness of God in him." Jesus was not only dying physically, but he was taking on the sin nature to pay the price for Adam's sin so as to redeem us.

Jesus was then taken down from the cross. John 19:38-42 relates to us that Joseph of Arimathaea was joined by Nicodemus who brought the anointing ointments for the burial. Together, they laid the body of Jesus in the tomb. The tomb belonged to Joseph of Arimathaea and was closed with a rolling stone (Matthew 27:60). It was later sealed at the request of the Pharisees, and a guard was set by Pilate to guard the tomb, "lest his disciples come by night and steal him away" (Matthew 27:62-66).

While Jesus' body was in the tomb, his soul descended into hell for three days. (Read Psalm 16:10, Psalm 22, Matthew 12:40 and Psalm 88:4-7.) Jesus was plunged into the lowest, deepest and darkest part of that pit but he was not to stay there long. Psalm 16:10 tells us, "For you will not leave my soul in hell neither will you suffer your Holy One to see corruption." We can also see these sufferings reflected in Psalm 22. Even Jesus told the Pharisees where he was going to go (Matthew 12:40), but also that he was not going to stay there! (John 2:19). Praise the Lord! He is risen indeed!

G. The Resurrection

The most exciting aspect about the tomb where Jesus was buried is that it is empty! It was also the place where Jesus was resurrected! On the first day of the week, Mary Magdalene came early in the morning to the garden and saw that the stone had been rolled away from the front of the tomb. She ran to get Simon Peter and another disciple and when they came to the tomb they saw it was empty, and the burial clothes folded and in place. Mary was grieved because she thought the body had been stolen. Then two angels asked her why she was weeping. When she told them why, she turned and saw Jesus (John 20:1-81).

It is interesting to note that the main evidence of Jesus' resurrection was not the empty tomb. Mary Magdalene was grieved, and when Peter saw that the body was missing, he wondered what had happened (Luke 24:12) and the women trembled and were bewildered (Mark 16:8). The main evidence of Jesus' resurrection is his appearances to the disciples. Jesus appeared first to Mary and the women with her (John 20:10-18; Matthew 28:9-10); to the two disciples on the road to Emmaus (Luke 24:13-35); then to the disciples (Mark 16:14, Luke 24:36, John 20:19-23); then to Thomas (John 20:24-30). He then ascended into heaven as witnessed by the disciples and others (Acts 1:9-10, Luke 24:51).

In I Corinthians 15:3-7,20, the apostle Paul shares this account of the resurrection appearances, "For what I received I passed on to you as of first importance: that Messiah died for our sins according to the scriptures, that he was buried, that he was raised on the third day according to the Scriptures, and that he appeared to Peter, and then to the Twelve. After that, he appeared to more than five hundred of the brothers at the same time, most of whom are still living, though some have fallen asleep. Then, he appeared to James and then to all the apostles. But Messiah has indeed been raised from the dead, the first fruits of those who have fallen asleep" (1 Cor. 15:3-7,20).

Acts 2:24 states, "Whom God has raised up, having loosed the pains of death; because it was not possible that he should be held by it." Jesus had paid the sacrificial price for redemption. He came forth as a Conqueror. Colossians 2:15 states, "And, having spoiled principalities and powers, he made a show of them openly, triumphing over them in it." Hebrews 2:14 adds, "through death, he might destroy him who had the power of death, that is, the devil."

Jesus came for a reason. "For God so loved the world that he gave his only begotten Son, that whosoever believes in him should not perish but have eternal life" (John 3:16). We who were born in sin deserved death, but Jesus paid the sacrificial price for our redemption. "This righteousness from God comes through faith in Jesus the Messiah to all who believe. There is no difference, for all have sinned and fallen short of the glory of God, and are justified by his grace through the redemption that came by Jesus the Messiah. God presented him as a sacrifice of atonement, through faith in his blood" (Rom. 6:22-25). "For the wages of sin is death, but the gift of God is eternal life in Messiah Jesus, our Lord"(Rom. 6:23).

Jesus now is at the right hand of the Father with his work completed, making intercession for us. Jesus testifies of his death and resurrection to John, "I am he that liveth, and was dead; and, behold, I am alive forevermore, Amen; and have the keys of hell and of death"(Revelation 1:18). Thank God for the victory, and for the tomb that is empty! (Cf. I Corinthians 15 for further evidence and fuller meaning of Jesus' resurrection.)

H. God's Gift And Calling To Us All

When Martha was in sorrow at her brother Lazarus' death, Jesus said to her, "I am the resurrection and the life; he who believes in Me, though he die, yet shall he live, and whoever lives and believes in Me shall never die. Do you believe this?" At that point Martha said to Jesus, "Yes, Lord, I believe that you are the Messiah, the Son of God, he who is coming into the world." (John 11:25-27)

Ask yourself the same question Jesus asked of Martha. Make this walk a special walk of faith!

III. Via Dolorosa, Way of Sorrows (Route #1)

A. Background

The Via Dolorosa is the most ancient and traditional route of Jesus from his trial in the Praetorium to Calvary, dating back to the year 326 CE. This was when the Emperor Constantine of Rome, a new convert to Christianity, had the Church of the Holy Sepulchre built in the same location where we find it today. There are fourteen Stations of the Cross along the Via Dolorosa. Some stations are related to events in the Gospels, and others are based on post-biblical traditions.

B. Stations of the Cross

The First and Second Stations of the Cross are found at the site of the Antonia Fortress of the Romans. It was here that Jesus was condemned to death, scourged, mocked and crowned with thorns (Matthew 27:2, 11-30; Mark 15:1-5; Luke 23:1-7, 13-25; John 18:28 - 19:16).

The Antonia Fortress was built by Herod the Great in 36 BCE and named in honor of his friend Mark Anthony. The fortress was a huge quadrangular structure with massive towers at each corner and had, according to the historian Josephus, "the largeness and form of a palace, it being parted into all kinds of rooms and other conveniences such as courts and places for bathing and a broad square for camp." The western third of Antonia was covered by an impressive paved square (lithostrotos in Greek) which was used by Rome's legionnaires for training, parades and games. Under the fortress were large cisterns which can still be seen today. The actual location of the fortress was on the northern wall of the Temple Mount, which allowed the Roman authorities to have a clear view of Jewish activities in the Temple Area, and thus quiet any potential disturbances.

Today, we find the area of the Antonia Fortress on the same road just west of the Church of St. Anne (Pool of Bethesda) and the Lion's Gate.

1. The **First Station** is found at the site of the Praetorium, or Pilate's Judgment Hall, which was part of the Antonia Fortress. The Praetorium is where the private discourses between Jesus and the Roman Governor, Pontius Pilate, took place. The public portion of the trial was held in the courtyard of the fortress (see the Second Station). Due to the occasion of the Jewish Feast of Passover, the Roman Governor Pontius Pilate resided in the Antonia Fortress to be close at hand in the event of trouble in Jerusalem.

Today, the Praetorium is found within the courtyard of the El Omariyel College. To enter, you must walk up a flight of steps. The original staircase, known as the Scala Santa, was transferred to Rome in the 4th century by Queen Helena, the mother of Emperor Constantine, where it is displayed in a church to this day. As you enter the courtyard, you will notice a small domed building on a higher platform. This was originally the Chapel of the Crowning with Thorns.

2. The **Second Station** is where Jesus received the Cross (John 19:16-17). This station is across the roadway from the First Station, and where you will find the Chapel of the Condemnation. This chapel is built upon the Lithostrotos. The Lithostrotos is a good example of the type of pavement found in the courtyard of the Antonia Fortress where Jesus was presented to the public, scourged, mocked, crowned with thorns, and also where Pilate presented Jesus to the crowds and said, "Behold the Man."(John 19:5) It is probably not the actual street level of Jesus' time.

The Chapel of the Condemnation is next to the Convent of Ecce Homo (Behold the Man), which is of the Catholic order of the Sisters of Zion. In this complex, you will see a large portion of the Lithostrotos and the deep cisterns which were located under the courtyard pavement of the Antonia Fortress. As you look at the pavement, you will see the striated surface of the otherwise-smooth limestone which prevented the horses from slipping; ruts made by the wheels of wagons and chariots; and drainage channels which carried rainwater into the large cisterns below.

The courtyard of the Antonia Fortress was a place where you could always find Roman soldiers. One of the most interesting things found carved into the stone of the Lithostrotos are the games commonly played by the Roman soldiers. One game in particular, called the Game of the Kings (*Basilicus*), involved the scourging, mocking and exile of the loser. It is likely that the Roman soldiers were re-enacting this game when the soldiers mocked Jesus (Matthew 27:27-31).

Walking west on the way to the Third Station, we pass under a semicircular archway that spans the road. This was part of a Triumphal Arch erected by Hadrian in 135 CE and was part of his Roman city of Aelia Capitolina. A triumphal arch is made up of three arches, the middle one being the highest. The right portion of the triumphal arch is located inside the Basilica of the Ecce Homo Convent and is part of their altar. Since the 16th century, the arch has been called the Ecce Homo Arch because it was thought to be the gateway of the Antonio Fortress. But, subsequent excavations located the Lithostrotos of the fortress at a lower level under the convent, indicating that the arch was of a later period.

3. The **Third Station** commemorates a traditional spot where Jesus fell under the weight of the cross. The Gospels do not mention this particular fall, but the tradition arose because of the fact that the Roman soldiers forced Simon, a man of Cyrene, to carry the cross (Matthew 27:32, Mark 15:21, Luke 23:26). Therefore, it must have been heavy and Jesus fell under its weight. John records that Jesus began carrying the cross, and from the other Gospel accounts, we know that Simon was forced to take over somewhere along the way.

NOTE: Up to this point, Alternative Routes #1 and #2 to Calvary and the Tomb have been the same. Now, Route #1, the traditional Via Dolorosa, zigzags left (south), then right (west) on its way to the Church of the Holy Sepulchre. Route #2, the path to Golgotha and the Garden Tomb, turns right (north) at this point and travels on the roadway of the Tyropeon or Central Valley out of the north gate (Damascus Gate). In this study guide, we will continue the Stations of the Cross on the Via Dolorosa (Route #1) and then discuss Route #2.

4. The **Fourth Station** is just a few yards from the Third Station and is traditionally the place where Jesus met his mother. In the process of building the present church, they found a portion of a mosaic floor dating prior to the 7th century. The mosaic is a representation of two feet pointing to the northwest. Tradition says that this is where Mary, the mother of Jesus, stood when she saw Jesus as he fell under the weight of the Cross. The Gospels tell us that Mary was present at the death of Jesus and possibly this is where she first saw him when he was on his way to Calvary.

5. The **Fifth Station** is just a short distance from the Fourth Station and is where Simon the Cyrene began to carry the Cross for Jesus.

6. The **Sixth Station** is a traditional one marking the place where Veronica wiped the face of Jesus. This is located about 80 paces from the Fifth Station. There is a fragment of a column inserted in the wall on the left indicating the traditional site of the house of Veronica. It is believed that when Veronica wiped the face of Jesus, that an imprint of his face remained on the cloth. Tradition also says that Veronica was the woman that Jesus healed who had an issue of blood for 12 years (Luke 8:43-48). However, it is thought that the name, Veronica, was derived from the Latin words, *Vera Icone*, meaning the True Image. There is nothing in the Gospels to confirm this event or the traditions surrounding it.

7. The **Seventh Station** is located where the Via Dolorosa ascends rapidly towards Golgotha (Mount Calvary). A tradition relates that this is where Jesus fell for a second time. During this period of history, a city gate called the Old Gate or the Jeshanah Gate was located here (Nehemiah 12:38-39). It was here that Jesus would have exited the city in this Alternative Route #1. It is also believed that a copy of the death sentence pronounced against Jesus was, according to custom, fastened to one of the exterior columns of the gate.

8. The **Eighth Station** commemorates the place where Jesus spoke to the Daughters of Jerusalem (Luke 23:27-31). The station is marked by a stone with a Latin cross on it. It is good to notice the compassion of Jesus even while on his way to die. He told the women not to be concerned about him, but to worry for themselves. He then prophesied about the destruction of Jerusalem that was coming because of the wickedness of man.

9. The **Ninth Station** is a traditional one where some believe that Jesus fell for a third time before reaching Calvary. The shaft of a column enclosed in the pillar of the doorway marks the Ninth Station.

The Tenth through the Fourteenth Stations are found within the ancient Church of the Holy Sepulchre. For this reason, we will discuss the history of the church before continuing the description of the remaining five Stations of the Cross.

Due to the monumental edifices of the Church of the Holy Sepulchre which cover Calvary and the Tomb within, we cannot see these places as they were in their natural setting.

In 135 CE, the Roman Emperor Hadrian, wishing to stop the Christians from worshipping the God of the Bible and wanting to wipe away the memory of the Christian sites, constructed a pagan temple on the site. The sites of Calvary and the Tomb were covered with dirt, and a great terrace was built over the areas. He then erected a statue of Jupiter over Calvary and a statue of Venus over the Tomb. Contrary to his purpose, he permanently marked the locations.

The Christian historian Eusebius tells us that this area remained covered with these pagan shrines until 326 CE when the newly converted Roman Emperor Constantine ordered them removed. When the Roman works were removed, they found the entire site intact. This was quite a find because the Christians believed that the Romans had destroyed the Tomb before they began their building.

Critics of the authenticity of the Church of the Holy Sepulchre as the correct location for Calvary challenge this account of history. They state that when Hadrian built his Roman city of Aelia Capitolina in 135 CE and forced out the Jews and Christians, he built the Roman temple to Venus and Jupiter in this location because of its centrality within the city. When Constantine came to power in the early 4th century, he was influenced by Christian leaders to build the Church of the Holy Sepulchre in this location to erase the memory of the pagan temple.

Whatever the true story may be, in 335 CE, Constantine began the construction of a beautiful basilica. The position and arrangement of this basilica are still discernible today. The rock of Calvary stood in a garden and had a cross on top of it, yet was protected from the weather by a roof. Just to the west of the garden stood a circular church with the Tomb of Jesus in the center. For some reason, the rock surrounding the tomb and the mortuary chamber were removed, leaving only the place where the body was laid. This church was destroyed in 614 CE when the Persians invaded the land, but was soon restored by the Abbot Modestus on a reduced scale.

When the Arabs conquered Jerusalem in 638 C.E., they protected the city's Christian sites, prohibiting their destruction and their use as living quarters. The Arabs left the Christian sites relatively undisturbed for almost four centuries, with the exception of a riot in 966 C.E.

during which the door and roofs of the Church were burned. In 1009, however, the so-called "mad" Fatimid Caliph al-Hakin ordered the destruction of all churches in Jerusalem, including the Holy Sepulchre. Christians were forbidden to visit the Church's ruins. It took almost forty years for the Byzantine Emperor to negotiate a peace treaty with al-Hakin's successor that granted him permission to rebuild the Holy Sepulchre. It was rebuilt in 1048 by the Emperor Constantine Monomachus. Only the Basilica over the Tomb was restored to its original magnificence, while the other holy sites were marked by small oratories.

The Crusaders decided to unite these scattered sanctuaries under one new building in the form of a cross. The Holy Sepulchre (Tomb) was repaired and an *edicule* (small house) was placed over it. The rotunda was conserved in great part, and an arched opening was added which led to the new church erected over the former garden where Calvary is located. Many other expansions were added to encompass the various little oratories commemorating certain events of the Passion.

The building of the Crusaders, although disfigured by later additions and unsightly restorations, still exists to this day. During the following centuries, the Basilica was preserved by the Franciscans who carried out two important restorations, one in 1555 and the other in 1719. There were other groups who restored portions of the church, some of them doing more damage in the process. At one point in history, the church was dismantled, the pieces numbered, and hidden away. After the dust had settled, the pieces were put back together, thus preserving the structure.

Today, the Church of the Holy Sepulchre is occupied by various denominations: Greek Orthodox, Roman Catholic, Coptic (Egyptian), and Armenian within the church, and Abyssinian (Ethiopian) and Syrian located on the roof. Each denomination maintains strict control or rights over portions of the church with the Greek Orthodox controlling the largest and most important sections. The rights of each community are manifest in their different areas by use of decorations, lamps, pictures, etc., but above all, the right to carry out repairs. Therefore, the reconstruction of a roof, a wall, a chapel, etc., implies the exclusive possession of the community that restores it. This agreement has caused great difficulty in reaching a consensus about restoration, repairs and maintenance and this explains the poor condition of the church.

Even sadder than the condition of the church structure is the obvious disunity among these Christian denominations. Throughout history, these rival groups have even fought to bloodshed over the holy shrines, and it continues even to this day. The post of custodian of the church is hereditary in a Moslem family named the Nuseibeh.

They were given the keys during the time of Saladin (12th century) and they have kept the keys ever since. This is because the Christian groups constantly fought over it. This display of disunity confuses the non-Christian world when we speak glowingly of the unity in the Church, the Body of Christ. They see the historical denominational infighting and fail to see the unity. We who are Christians need to pray and to work to build a measure of visible unity before the watching world.

10. The **Tenth Station** is the place where Jesus is stripped of his garments. This site is located at the top of some stairs which is the top of a rocky knoll, Calvary. It is divided into two naves. The nave on the right, after you ascend the fourteen steps, is the location of the Tenth Station. We have no record of this event in the Gospels, but we do know that it occurred because of the known process of Roman crucifixion, and the Biblical references that indicate the Roman soldiers parted his garments and cast lots for his vesture (Psalm 22:18, Matthew 27:35).

11. The **Eleventh Station** is where they nailed Jesus to the cross. This fulfilled the prophecy of Psalm 22:16, "For dogs have compassed me, the assembly of the wicked have enclosed me, they pierce my hands and my feet." The dogs referred to in Psalm 22:16 were the Gentile soldiers who crucified Jesus, for the Gentiles were always referred to as dogs in that day.

12. The **Twelfth Station** commemorates the place where Jesus was on the cross and where he died to redeem us. This station is located in the left nave on the top of Calvary. There is a disc with an opening in it covering the place where the cross of Jesus was located. On the right is a metal slab covering a great crack in the rock which is believed to have been caused by the earthquake at the time of Jesus' death (Matthew 27:51).

13. The **Thirteenth Station** is the place where Jesus was laid after he was taken down from the cross. It is called the Stone of Unction, located downstairs and just inside the main entrance to the church. Jesus died at about the 9th hour (3:00 p.m.) and the law, as stated in Deuteronomy 21:23, said that the body of one hanged upon a tree shall not remain upon the tree all night. We find in Luke 23:50-52 that Joseph of Arimathaea went to Pilate and begged for the body of Jesus and Pilate consented. Luke 23:53 tells us that Joseph of Arimathaea took his body down, wrapped it in linen, and placed it in the sepulchre in which never before a man was laid.

14. The **Fourteenth Station** is the Holy Sepulchre, after which the church is named. This is the place where Jesus was laid in the tomb. Inside the Holy Sepulchre are two small chapels, one behind the other. The first one is called the Angel's Chapel. At its center there is a stone set in marble which is said to be the one which closed the

door of the sepulchre and which the angel rolled away. Through a low door, you then enter the actual Chapel of the Holy Sepulchre. The burial place is covered with marble.

Behind this small structure is a very small Coptic Chapel (Egyptian). The Coptic priest will show you the Coptic version of the "actual" stone of the tomb, and not just the marble covering. He will also sprinkle you with Holy Water and give you a small wooden cross (a small contribution is appreciated). In an adjacent part of the Coptic Chapel, the priest will also show you ancient rock-hewn tombs which prove that this was an area of burial at one time. This entire Coptic area of the church is in great disrepair. Now, with improved relations between Israel and Egypt, money for restoration should be forthcoming.

Other Significant Sites

Within the Church of the Holy Sepulchre, there are other significant historical sites to be seen. Within the Roman Catholic Chapel, you can see a portion of the column that was used for the scourging of Jesus (taken from the Antonia Fortress). At the opposite end of the church and down many steps, you can see the chapel dedicated to the Finding of the True Cross by Queen Helena, mother of Constantine, in the 4th century CE. It is highly unlikely that she found the true cross at the bottom of this cistern. Nevertheless, there is a chapel to be found. On your way to see this chapel, halfway down the stairway, you will notice the Armenian Chapel with its beautiful mosaic floor. In the center of the Greek Orthodox Cathedral, the main sanctuary of the church, there stands the Catholicon which is a stone chalice, said to mark the center of the earth.

Conflicts over who is responsible for repairs in what parts of the church have always occurred. In 2006, when this book is being edited, the church looks better than it has in some time. Recent repairs were motivated by the visit of Pope John Paul II in 2000.

IV. Pathway to Golgotha and the Garden Tomb (Route #2)

A. Background

The path to Golgotha (Skull Hill) and the Garden Tomb is an alternative to the more ancient and traditional route (Via Dolorosa) of Jesus from his trial in the Praetorium to Calvary. The difference in the routes depends on where you place the location of Calvary and the Tomb of Jesus. If you place them in the Church of the Holy Sepulchre, then the Via Dolorosa will be your route. If you prefer to imagine the crucifixion and burial of Jesus at Gordon's Calvary and the Garden Tomb, then Route #2 will be your path.

Historically, Route #2 is relatively new. This possible route has only been considered during the past 120 years since the declaration of General Charles Gordon, in 1882, that Golgotha and the Tomb of Jesus were outside the Damascus Gate, north of the Old City of Jerusalem. While the Via Dolorosa is an established and sacred route to the Catholic and Orthodox Christians, Route #3 is merely the roadway between the Praetorium and the Garden Tomb. There are no stations or chapels along the way, nor is it considered sacred.

Route #2 follows the Via Dolorosa for the first three Stations of the Cross (the first two stations commemorate events that occurred in the Antonia Fortress). Then, just at the Third Station where the Via Dolorosa turns south for a short distance, Route #2 turns north and follows the roadway which travels along the ancient Tyropeon or Central Valley. You will continue north out the Damascus Gate (outside the Old City walls) a short distance to the site of Golgotha (Gordon's Calvary) and the Garden Tomb.

B. Golgotha and the Garden Tomb

1. History of Discovery

There are many today, generally Protestants, who believe that the Garden Tomb, rather than the Church of the Holy Sepulchre, is the true site of Jesus' burial. This controversy is not new. Between 1840 and 1876, there were sixteen theories concerning the site of the death and burial of Jesus. Twelve argued in favor of the Holy Sepulchre and four against it. In 1840, Otto Thenius first suggested that the hillock outside the Damascus Gate, with ancient cisterns dug into its side, was the authentic Calvary.

In 1882, the British General Charles Gordon was sitting on the roof of the Spafford Children's Center which is built into the northern section of the Old City wall, high above on a cliff. Outside the wall and at the bottom of the opposite cliff was a roadway, a field, and another cliff face, just as high and facing him. The area between the wall and the opposite cliff had been an ancient rock quarry. The stone of the quarry was removed long ago, perhaps at the time of King Solomon for his great city and Temple and also by King Herod the Great. General Gordon noticed that the cliff face was shaped like the eye sockets of a skull. (Today this cliff face is behind the Arab bus station.) Knowing that the place of the crucifixion had to be near a garden and a tomb, he went to find out this possibility. He found it. In 1867, 15 years earlier, a Greek doing work at the foot of the hill had found a rock-hewn tomb there. The tomb was cut from solid rock with a channel carved for a rolling stone. Its construction had been dated to the Roman period by some scholars and to the Byzantine period by others. Because of this and other evidence, the discovery became known as Gordon's Calvary and the Garden Tomb.

No tradition earlier than the nineteenth century regards the site of Gordon's Calvary as authentic. The site of the Garden Tomb is 650 feet north of the present Damascus Gate, a part of the modern north wall of Jerusalem. The tomb is cut into solid rock and is 14 feet wide, 10 feet deep, and 7-1/2 feet high. The controversy as to whether the Church of the Holy Sepulchre or the Garden Tomb is the site of Jesus' death and burial continues to be debated.

2. Biblical Description Comparing the Two Sites

Scripture tells us that Jesus and his captors arrived at Golgotha for the crucifixion. Golgotha is an Aramaic word meaning the place of the Skull. "And when they were come unto a place called Golgotha, that is to say, a place of a skull…"(Matthew 27:33). The word appears only three times in the Bible (Matthew 23:33, Mark 15:22, John 19:17), and is also known by the term Calvary. We know that Gordon's Calvary was discovered because of its resemblance to the face of a skull. But the Golgotha in the Church of the Holy Sepulchre is also an outcropping of white stone resembling the top of a skull protruding from the ground.

Paul tells us in Hebrews 13:12 that this place was "without the gate" meaning outside the gate on of the city wall. However, it was not far outside the walls, but "near the city" (John 19:20). Matthew's statement, "And those who passed by…" (Matthew 27:39), may indicate that Golgotha was by a well-traveled road. Gordon's Calvary would have been located outside the north gate of the city of Jerusalem near the road north to Damascus and east to Bethany and Jericho. On the other hand, the Calvary in the Holy Sepulchre would also have been outside the Old Gate (see Section III, B7) where the road would have forked west to Jaffa and south to Bethlehem and Hebron.

It was also visible from some distance, as indicated by the expression, "women looking on from afar" (Mark 15:40; Luke 23:49). This has led some to think it was a hill, but nowhere does the Bible indicate that the crucifixion took place on a hill. Nevertheless, the Calvary in the Holy Sepulchre was on a rocky knoll; and Gordon's Calvary could have been on top of the cliff, but more likely at the bottom in the rock quarry… a place for execution and easily visible.

Only in John 19:41 is there an indication that the tomb was near the site of death and that it was in a garden, "Now in the place where he was crucified, there was a garden; and in the garden a new sepulchre wherein was never man yet laid." This is another proof that the place of crucifixion was outside the walls. This is because the Jews would never have a sepulchre within the city limits (it is against Mosaic Law), and the Tomb of Jesus was originally that of Joseph of Arimathaea, a member of the Sanhedrin (Jewish religious court) and also a secret disciple of Jesus the Messiah. We know that area of Calvary in the Holy Sepulchre was a place of tombs, but not an area of gardens. On the other hand, we know that the area of the Garden Tomb was, in fact, a garden where a private tomb had been hewn in the face of a cliff. Located in the area of the Garden Tomb was an ancient wine or oil press, indicating it was an orchard and a cistern which held 1,000,000 gallons of water.

Walking two alternative routes from Jesus' trial to place of death, burial and resurrection should not confuse the significance of the event. My personal opinion is that God, who is the Ultimate Teacher, loves visual aids. I suspect that He allowed the discovery of the Garden Tomb so modern visitors could see a rolling stone tomb and a skull-faced hill. I am inclined to think that the Church of the Holy Sepulchre is the original site.

But let's remember that, for those of us who believe the Christian story, it is not exactly where Jesus Christ was crucified, buried and raised from the dead that matters, but the fact that it happened. Actually, it matters little whether the site of the Holy Sepulchre or the Garden Tomb is correct. Perhaps both are wrong. The point of supreme importance is that Jesus lived, died and lives again. This is a part of the solid evidence that he is the divine Son of God and our Savior. Hallelujah!

Sites Outside Jerusalem

Bethlehem

I. On the Road to Bethlehem, Valley of Rephaim, Rachel's Tomb

Bethlehem is located six miles (10 kilometers) south of Jerusalem. The road you travel is the ancient ridge route which Abraham and the patriarchs would have traveled thousands of years ago. This "Road of the Patriarchs" follows the Valley of Rephaim where the Philistines encamped against David (II Samuel 5:17-25; 23:13). The Lord fought for David and the battles were won.

As we near the outskirts of Bethlehem, we come to the Tomb of Rachel. We find in Genesis 35:16-20 that Jacob and Rachel were on their way from Bethel (north of Jerusalem) to Ephrath. Just outside of Bethlehem, Rachel went into labor and gave birth to Benjamin, but died in the process. Jacob set a pillar on her grave and it is believed to be at this site.

II. Bethlehem

A. Biblical and Historical Significance

In Hebrew, Bethlehem is called Beit-Lechem, or House

of Bread. This is significant because of the wheat fields which still fill the valleys around Bethlehem. These fields are the site of many of the Biblical accounts involving Bethlehem, e.g., the story of Ruth, and the shepherds watching their flocks by night at the time of Jesus' birth. Bethlehem, like Jerusalem, is just east of the central mountain ridge overlooking the dry Judean Desert.

Bethlehem is the place of the birth of our Lord Jesus. However, the history of Bethlehem does not begin here. Bethlehem is first mentioned in the Bible in Genesis 35:19 in connection with the death of Rachel, the wife of Jacob. Later, we see the story in the Book of Ruth that takes place in Bethlehem. The story should come alive in our hearts as we realize that the "line of the Messiah" was once more set into motion by Kinsman Redemption, as set forth in Deuteronomy 25:5-10. It was in Bethlehem that Naomi, a widow, returned from the Land of Moab, east of the Dead Sea, with her widowed Gentile daughter-in-law Ruth. Years before, a famine in the Land of Israel had driven Naomi and her husband Elimelech to Moab, where Elimelech and their two sons (who had married Moabite women) died. Boaz, a kinsman of Naomi's husband Elimelech, accomplished the kinsman redemption according to the law (Leviticus 25-34; Deuteronomy 25:5-10). Boaz, having redeemed the dead man's inheritance, married Ruth and they had a son named Obed who was the grandfather of David. Outside of Bethlehem is a field where these events are believed to have taken place. The area is known as the Field of Ruth. It is also believed to be the same Shepherd's Field where the angel appeared when Jesus was born.

Boaz was the only one who could meet the requirements of kinsman redemption. He was a kinsman, he was willing to redeem the property and he was able to redeem it. This means something to us when we realize that Jesus, born in Bethlehem, was the only one able to redeem us. Jesus became one of us when he was born in Bethlehem. John 1:14 says the Word was made flesh and dwelt among us. Therefore, Jesus was our kinsman according to the flesh. Jesus was willing, he willingly left Heaven and its glories and came to earth to die on the cross for our salvation. John 3:16 shows us this willingness in God's love. Jesus was also the only one able to redeem us and pay the required price. We find in Revelation 5 that the Lamb of God is the only one able to redeem us.

Samuel went to Bethlehem after Saul had been rejected by God. He assembled the ancients of the city to a solemn sacrifice and in obedience anointed David to be king over Israel (I Samuel 16:1-13). David became Saul's armor-bearer and calmed him by playing the harp when Saul fell under demonic control. When the Philistines invaded Israel, David's father sent him from Bethlehem with food for the Israelite camp. While David was there, the giant, Goliath, came out taunting and insulting the Israelites. David killed Goliath with his sling and a small stone (I Samuel 17). This took place in the Elah Valley on the road from Bethlehem to the seacoast.

Later, Bethlehem fell into the hands of the Philistines (II Samuel 23:14), and David desired a drink from the well of Bethlehem, his home town. David's friends broke through the Philistine line and got him the drink, but David, realizing they had risked their lives for his pleasure, poured it out unto the Lord (II Samuel 23:14-17).

The birth of Jesus makes Bethlehem an important site for Christians. Micah prophesied about 750 years before the event, "But thou, Bethlehem Ephrata, though you be little among the thousands of Judah, yet out of thee shall he come forth unto me that is to be ruler in Israel; whose goings forth have been from of old, from everlasting" (Micah 5:2). We know from Luke 2:1-20, that Jesus was born in Bethlehem. This was a result of a decree from Caesar Augustus declaring that all should be taxed and everyone had to return into his own city to register and pay the tax. Joseph was of the lineage of David, and David was born and raised in Bethlehem. Joseph and Mary went from Galilee to Bethlehem to register and pay the tax, and during their stay, Jesus was born. When Joseph and Mary arrived in Bethlehem, it was crowded and they couldn't find any room in the inn, but found a cave where Mary gave birth. She wrapped him in swaddling clothes and laid him in a manger.

B. Church of the Nativity

The Church of the Nativity was constructed over the site of the birth of Jesus by the Emperor Constantine in 326 CE. The site was determined by local tradition which says that the Roman Emperor Hadrian (117 – 138 CE) tried to obliterate all memory of the Christian tradition associated with the site of the Nativity by planting a grove of trees in honor of the god Adonis. However, the grove did exactly the opposite because it permanently marked the spot.

The Church of the Nativity, which Constantine built, was said to have been his most magnificent work. This church survived the many destructions that other churches experienced in the Holy Land. In 529 CE, the Samaritans damaged it badly, but it was restored the same century under Justinian. In 614 CE, the Persians invaded the Holy Land and destroyed most of the churches, but spared the Church of the Nativity because they recognized their own national costumes in the mosaic of the pediment depicting the Nativity scene with the Magi, the traditional three wise men from the east. (The scriptures do not tell us how many wise men there were, but the mention of three gifts – gold, frankincense and myrrh – has given rise to the idea of three kings.) The church also escaped the destructions of later centuries and is now a

Greek Orthodox Church.

Over the course of time, the three large portals of the basilica were bricked up to prevent people from entering the church on horseback. Today there is only a very small doorway in one of the portals and you must stoop to pass through it into the church. Passing through the narthex, we come to the main sanctuary. The rows of columns appear to be of marble, yet are actually of wood and made to look like marble. The Grotto of the Nativity is located beneath the High Altar at the end of the sanctuary and can be reached by stairs on either side. Within the grotto, we find the traditional spot where Jesus was born. Across from it and three steps lower, we find the place where Jesus was wrapped in swaddling clothes and laid in the manger. The manger was actually a fodder trough hewn out of the rock.

Below this structure and the adjacent Roman Catholic church, there are many other grottos. It was within these grottos where St. Jerome, beginning about 382 CE, translated the First Testament from the original Hebrew into Latin. It was known as the Vulgate and was an early step in the process of bringing the Bible to the common people.

The Herodion

I. Background

We find the Herodion on the fringes of the Judean Desert to the southeast of Bethlehem. The Herodion is named after King Herod the Great who built a fortress on this hilltop. Flavius Josephus describes it as follows, "An artificial rounded hill in the form of a breast...the crest he crowned with a ring of round towers, the enclosure was filled with gorgeous palaces, the magnificent appearance of which was not confined to the interior of the apartments, but outer walls, battlements, and roofs all had wealth lavished upon them in profusion...and provided an easy ascent by two-hundred steps of the purest white marble..." (*The Jewish Wars*, 1,21,10).

After the death of the king, his body was buried here. "The bier was of solid gold, studded with precious stones and had a covering of purple, embroidered with various colors. On this lay the body enveloped in a purple robe, a diadem encircling the head and surmounted by a crown of gold, the scepter beside his right hand. Around the bier were Herod's sons and a large group of his relations; these were followed by the guards...armed, and in orderly array, led by their commanders and subordinate officer...the body was thus conveyed to the Herodion, where, in accordance with the directions of the deceased, it was interred" (*The Jewish Wars* 1,33,9).

The body and riches of Herod the Great have not been found. The Herodion is one of many fortress palaces of King Herod, another being Masada on the Dead Sea.

Because Herod was so paranoid for his life, he built these palaces in various locations as potential retreats in the event of a conspiracy or threat to his life in Jerusalem. As with Masada, this fortress was a shelter for Jewish rebels until it fell into the hands of the Romans in 70 CE. Excavations conducted here by the Franciscan Biblical Institute of Jerusalem have uncovered many remains of ancient Herodion which are strewn over the area.

Just to the south and within clear view rises a large tel, the site of the Biblical city of Teko'a, the birthplace of the prophet Amos (Amos 1:1). Ruins of an ancient church with a large front can be seen on the top of the tel.

Hebron

I. On the Road to Hebron

A. Valley of Berachah

There are two routes from Bethlehem to Hebron. One route is via the Herodion, and the other is on the Road of the Patriarchs along the central ridge for 10.5 miles (17 kilometers). This road winds over the mountains and across the Valley of Berachah (Blessing).

At the time of King Jehoshaphat, nomads from Transjordan invaded Judah and the Lord utterly destroyed them (II Chronicles 20:20-30). "And when Judah came toward the water tower in the wilderness, they looked unto the multitude, and, behold there were dead bodies fallen to the earth and none escaped. When Jehoshaphat and his people came to take away the spoil of them, they found among them in abundance both riches with the dead bodies, and precious jewels, which they stripped off for themselves, more than they could carry away, and they were three days in gathering of the spoil, it was so much. And on the fourth day they assembled themselves in the Valley of Berachah, for there they blessed the Lord. Therefore, the name of the place was called the Valley of Berachah, unto this day" (II Chronicles 20:24-26).

B. Ein-Dirwa – Beit-Zur

Further down the road, we pass a spring on the left which is named in Arabic Ein-Dirwa. Here we find the place where Philip baptized the Ethiopian Eunuch (Acts 8:26-40). Afterwards, Philip was miraculously transported to another location where he continued his ministry of evangelism, ultimately arriving in Caesarea on the Mediterranean seacoast.

Close by the spring on the mountainside, we find the ruins of Beit-Zur, an important city of Judah. It is related that "Rehoboam dwelt in Jerusalem and built cities of defense in Judah; he built (fortified) even Bethlehem ... and Beit Zur ... and Hebron" (II Chronicles 11:5-12).

II. Hebron – the Town

A. Background and Biblical Significance

Hebron is one of the oldest towns in the Middle East. According to the Bible, it was founded seven years before Tanis, the capital of Lower Egypt (Numbers 13:22). The ancient city was situated southwest of the present town.

Abraham pitched his tent in Hebron (Genesis 15:18) at the Oaks of Mamre. It is also where he met the three messengers of God and where he interceded for Sodom and Gomorrah (Genesis 18). In the division of the Promised Land the town of Hebron went to the Tribe of Judah and was given to Caleb (Joshua 14:13). Hebron was also designated as one of the Cities of Refuge (Joshua 20:7) and assigned to the sons of Aaron (Joshua 21:11). After David was anointed king, he made Hebron his capital for 7-1/2 years (II Samuel 11:11). Absalom, David's rebellious son, made Hebron the center of his revolt (II Samuel 15:7).

In Arabic, the name for Abraham is al-Khalil er-Rahman, the "Friend of the Lord" (Genesis 20:7; Isaiah 41:8; James 2:23), hence the Arabic name for Hebron is Khalil. During the many centuries of its existence there has always been a Jewish community living there. However, in 1929 most of the Jewish community was brutally massacred during a period of Arab rioting. Today Jews once again live in this sacred city, although the vast majority of the population is Arab Moslem. The two main industries of the area are glass-blowing and clay pottery making.

B. Cave Of Machpelah

The Cave of Machpelah is one of the major sacred shrines in Israel. Inside are cenotaphs (empty tombs honoring persons who may be buried elsewhere) of Abraham, Isaac and Jacob, and their wives, Sarah, Rebecca and Leah. An old Hebrew tradition has it that this cave is also the burial place of Adam and Eve, who lived in Hebron after their banishment from Eden. Since Hebron is also known as Kiryat-Arba (the Town of Four) some Hebrew sages have explained, "This alludes to the four conjugal pairs who were buried here." However, Joshua 15:13-15 indicated that the town was named for Arba, the father of Anak.

Abraham's purchase of the burial place for Sarah is related in Genesis 23. Sarah died at age 127 while they were living at Hebron. Abraham asked the Hittites, the sons of Heth, to sell him a burying place since he was a stranger and a sojourner among them. They offered him the sepulcher of his choice after a typical Middle Eastern bargaining session. Abraham chose the cave of Machpelah which was owned by Ephron, the son of Zohar.

Over the cave there now stands a Moslem mosque surrounded by a wall. The foundations and exterior of the walls date from the period of the Second Temple and were built by Herod, making them 2,000 years old. Hebron was burned by Titus during the first Jewish revolt. As with the Temple Mount area, this shrine has been in the hands of Jews, Christians and Moslems, each adding their own architectural adornments. The walls of the mosque were originally a Crusader church, and there are inscriptions within that indicate initial construction by the Byzantines. The graves of the patriarchs are covered by the cenotaphs – house-like structures – which are draped with green tapestries embroidered with pious inscriptions.

All access to the cave itself is strictly forbidden, even to the guardians of the mosque. The Crusaders opened the cave in 1119 CE to examine it and then closed it up again. In June 1119, a man named Arnulf opened the cave, found bodies, put them in coffins, and left an entrance to visit. However, after the Crusader era the place was closed and sealed. Today the structure is a place of worship for both Moslems and Jews.

During the years 1964-67, Dr. Philip Hammond and an American expedition excavated on the slope just west of the Mosque of Abraham. They discovered thousands of pieces of ceramic materials, a wall 36-feet thick built before 1728 BCE, and a house dating to a time before the pyramids of Egypt (3500 BCE). Hebron may be the oldest continuously occupied, unwalled city in the world.

Judea

Today we will visit the eastern area of Judea. The general area covered by Judea is the tribal area of Judah as designated by Joshua (c.1300 BCE). After the death of Solomon, when the kingdom was divided in two sections, this area became known as the kingdom of Judah or the Southern Kingdom. Its capital was Jerusalem, and its inhabitants were known as Jews.

In 722 BCE, the Assyrians, under the leadership of Sargon II, defeated the Northern Kingdom, known as Israel. In 701 BCE, the Assyrians, under the leadership of their new King Sennacherib, attempted the defeat of Judah but failed. Judah was protected by God and the leadership of King Hezekiah (I Kings 18:13-19:37; II Chronicles 32:1-12; Isaiah 36:1-37:28). The Southern Kingdom remained intact until 586 BCE when the Babylonians under the leadership of King Nebuchadnezzar defeated Judah and took its inhabitants captive as slaves. It was at this time that the area became known as Judea, a province of the Persian Empire. This geographical term, Judea, first appears in the Bible in Ezra 5:8 in connection with the return of the Jews from Babylon (beginning in 537 BCE) and the rebuilding of the Temple (520 BCE). The Jewish population dominance over the area was finally re-established in 445 BCE when Nehemiah returned to rebuild the walls of Jerusalem.

During the New Testament period, King Herod the Great served as a puppet king under the Romans. In 6 CE, Judea was annexed to the Roman province of Syria and Archelaus, the son of Herod the Great, was deposed as king. Rome ruled Judea, as well as Galilee in the north, with governors and procurators appointed by the Roman Emperor. Their immediate superior was the Proconsul of Syria who ruled from Antioch (Luke 3:1). The official residence of the procurators was Caesarea. This governmental rule remained in force during the ministry of Jesus.

Geographically, Judea covers about a 55-mile square from north to south and east to west and extending from the Mediterranean Sea east to the Dead Sea; from Jaffa south to Gaza along its western border of the Mediterranean Sea; and from Jericho south to the southern end of the Dead Sea along its eastern border. These are approximate borders because exact boundaries were never fixed. Jerusalem was always considered in Judea.

Judea's terrain and climate are greatly varied from west to east. This is due to a 3,000-foot high mountain range running north to south about 30 miles inland from the Mediterranean Sea. Because most of the moisture in the air is "squeezed" out as it rises 3,000-feet, the climate is vastly different on the western and eastern slopes of the mountains. This is also true of the terrain for the soil types are different on both sides of the mountains. On the western (Mediterranean Sea) side of the region, we find a fertile, wide plain and a good climate for agriculture. The western side of the mountain range was also tree-covered. Along the top of the mountain range, we find a terraced landscape etched into limestone hillsides suitable for grape growing. (Jerusalem is located on top of these mountains.) The eastern side of the mountain slopes precipitously to 1,300 feet below sea level at the Dead Sea. The soil is chalky and dry, supporting only a little grass during the winter months. While the western plain and slopes could support cities, the eastern slope could support only nomadic tribes who could move in search of water, unless there was a spring, as is the case with Jericho.

Biblically, Judea is rich in history. In it we find the cities of Jerusalem, Bethlehem, Hebron, Jericho and the land of the Philistines. The activities of God in the lives of the patriarchs – Abraham, Isaac, and Jacob – through the judges, kings, prophets, and Jesus can be seen in Judea. Historically, it is a land that was dominated at different times by Canaanites, Jebusites, Philistines, Egyptians, Assyrians, Babylonians, Greeks, Romans, Byzantines, Persians, Arabs, Crusaders, Turks and the British. It is important to remember that this is part of the land that was given by God to the descendants of Abraham, Isaac and Jacob as an everlasting possession. Therefore, we see the dominance by the Jews in biblical days, as well as today … a fulfillment of prophecy and an example of God's steadfastness to keep his promises.

The Wilderness of Judea

As we travel east on the road from Jerusalem to Jericho, you will notice an almost immediate change in the vegetation, terrain and climate. As you drive up to Jerusalem from the west (Mediterranean Sea), you see beautiful forests of trees and terraced mountainsides of fruit trees and grapes. As you drive east into the Wilderness of Judea from Jerusalem towards the Dead Sea, the trees and terraced landscapes disappear. They are replaced by chalky, brown mountain tops and steep valleys (wadis) with little or no vegetation except for sparsely growing grasses. Even the grass is brown and dry unless it happens to be early spring, for the climate is hot and dry most of the year. The Wilderness of Judea actually comprises the eastern one-third of the region of Judea (from the edge of the central mountain range east to the Dead Sea).

You will travel from 3,000 feet above sea level to 1,300 feet below sea level, a drop of 4/5 of a mile into the Jordan Rift Valley. You can actually see and feel the solitude of the Wilderness of Judea that is referred to so often in Scripture. As the children of Israel marched "up to Jerusalem" for feasts, they sang Psalms while walking through this wilderness (Psalm 120-133, called Psalms of Ascent). Read Psalm 121 and imagine the call for God's protection in this hot, parched, and rocky region with many hiding places for robbers.

This is the area frequented by John the Baptist (Matthew 3:1-6); where Jesus was brought by the Holy Spirit to be tempted by Satan (Matthew 4:1-4, Mark 1:12-13, Luke 4:1-8); and the setting for the story of the Good Samaritan (Luke 10:30-37). This is also an area frequented by David when he was fleeing from Saul (I Samuel 23-24); a solitary place where we find the religious sect of the Essenes; the army encampments of Bar Kokhba, leader of the Second Jewish Revolt (135 CE); and cave dwellings and monasteries of the Christian Byzantine hermits. On the western edge of the Wilderness of Judah, on the top of the central mountain range, we find Hebron, the burial place of the Patriarchs; Teko'a, the home of the prophet Amos; and Bethlehem, the home of David and the birthplace of Jesus.

The Dead Sea

I. Description and Composition

The Dead Sea is at the lowest spot on earth – 1,300 feet below sea level! It is part of the Great Rift Valley which extends from Lebanon south through the Red Sea into Africa. The lowest part of this long rift valley is the region of the northern Dead Sea. The depth of the sea at the northern end reaches 1,300 feet (2,600 feet below sea level), while the southern end of the sea averages only 10 feet deep. The Dead Sea is 47 miles long and 10 miles wide at its widest point. It has a shoreline circumference of 124 miles and a surface area of approximately 300 square miles.

The water is clear and blue and looks like the perfect place for swimming, boating, fishing and a picnic. While you can swim (don't put your face in the water!) and picnic, it is not a freshwater lake but a highly concentrated chemical lake. The Dead Sea water contains between 24-26% solid matter in the form of dissolved salts. The minerals deposited in the Dead Sea have been estimated as follows:

22,000,000,000 tons magnesium chloride

11,000,000,000 tons sodium chloride (common salt)

7,000,000,000 tons calcium chloride

2,000,000,000 tons potassium chloride

1,000,000,000 tons magnesium bromide

This high percentage of dissolved salts gives the Dead Sea some unusual properties. Its specific gravity is 1.166 which is the reason the human body floats. It is virtually impossible to sink, and the more fat your body contains the higher you float. You can actually relax on the surface and read a newspaper just as though you were in a lounge chair. The water has a bitter taste due to the magnesium chloride, while the calcium chloride makes it smooth and oily to the touch. The water is heavy and feels like swimming in Karo syrup. Fish cannot live in the Dead Sea water, which destroys practically all organic life. (Recently, small, one-celled red microorganisms were discovered in shallow pools along the Dead Sea. Their tiny bodies are a valuable resource for beta-carotene, glycerol, and protein. Because they can reproduce daily, they are easily grown for their by-products…a valuable resource for desert countries where these microorganisms can be cultivated in shallow salt ponds.)

The high concentration of the salts is caused by the fact that the Dead Sea has no outlet. The only way water leaves the Dead Sea is by evaporation. When this occurs, the salts are left behind, thus accumulating into the high concentration. The sea gets its salts from tributary streams and salt springs that frequent the Jordan River Valley between the Sea of Galilee and the Dead Sea. This is called the Ghor. The Jordan River and the other tributaries and springs add approximately 6-1/2 million tons of water daily! Most of this evaporates daily, leaving only enough for the sea to rise very gradually over the years. Since Israel and Jordan began utilizing the fresh water of the Jordan River in agriculture, the surface level of the Dead Sea has dropped dramatically over the past 30 years.

The salts in the Dead Sea are mined. Work was first begun in 1930 on the northern shore of the Dead Sea. But, when this area was captured by the Jordanians in 1948-49, a new plant was constructed at the southern end of the Sea in 1952. The Dead Sea Works, Ltd. currently mines common salt, carnallite, bromine, magnesium chloride and calcium chloride. They even produce a balanced composition of Dead Sea salts as bath salts for medicinal purposes for home use. Doctors from around the world send their patients to resort hotels along the sea for treatment of various diseases and ailments because of the curative properties of the water.

Construction on the Mediterranean/Dead Sea Canal (Med/Dead Canal) has been planned and some work has been done. However, lack of financing and some political considerations has halted the project at this time. The decision to attempt this canal was motivated by two factors. The first was that the level of the Dead Sea has been falling over the past 30 years because Israel and Jordan have channeled off all the fresh water from the Sea of Galilee, Jordan River and Jabbok River into agricultural uses. Because the southern end of the Dead Sea is so shallow, it is rapidly drying up, making it difficult to get water to the Dead Sea Works for processing. Secondly, because the Dead Sea is 1,300 feet below sea level, the movement of the water as it falls could produce hydroelectricity as it passes through a series of generator stations. It is estimated that electricity can be generated equivalent to Israel's current total usage. The future of the Med/Dead Canal is uncertain at the time of this writing.

II. Biblical Significance

The Biblical reference to the Dead Sea can be found first in Genesis 14:3, where it is mentioned as the Salt Sea in connection with a major war in the Valley of Siddim. Lot was captured and Abram had to rescue him. Even though it is referred to as the Salt Sea, we know that Lot chose this area when Abram and Lot separated. Abram lived in Canaan near Hebron and Lot chose the plain of Jordan and pitched his tent toward Sodom. Lot chose this area because then it was "even as the garden of the Lord before God destroyed Sodom and Gomorrah" (Genesis 13:10-13, c. 2090 BCE). We later find in Genesis 19:24-28 that God did destroy the cities of Sodom and Gomorrah "and all the plain" which laid at the southern end of the Dead Sea with fire and brimstone. Recent research has verified every detail of this account. This area must have been beautiful and fruitful prior to this destruction.

The Dead Sea was also called the Salt Sea in Numbers

34:12, the Sea of the Plain (Deuteronomy 3:17; 4:49; Joshua 3:16), the East Sea (Joel 2:20) and the Former Sea (Zechariah 14:8).

The sea has also been called the Asphalt Sea by early writers because of great chunks of asphalt that would float to the surface which could be used for fuel. It has been called the Dead Sea since about the second century CE because of its obvious lack of fish and the foul-tasting water that cannot be drunk.

Scripture indicates that changes are coming for the Dead Sea. In Ezekiel. 47:8-11, the prophet foretold the day when the waters will be healed. 2,500 years ago, Ezekiel wrote that fishermen would fish from the shores of the sea from Ein Gedi to Eneglaim. The fish will be "as the fish of the Great Sea" (Mediterranean Sea). These verses also speak of lush vegetation and trees which indicates that the entire area will be purified by God. This miracle has yet to take place!

Masada

I. Location and Description

Masada is located on the southwest shore of the Dead Sea. On our way to Masada, we will travel east from Jerusalem on the road to Jericho. After descending in the Jordan Rift Valley, below sea level, we turn south (right) and follow the western shore of the Dead Sea, passing the 2,000 year-old Essene settlement of Qumran, and Ein Gedi. These are two sites to be visited later in the day. While driving along the Dead Sea, you will notice impressive 1,000-foot cliffs rising out of the sea, pockmarked with numerous caves. These caves were used for protection by David, the Essenes, the Zealots in 70 CE and the army of Bar Kokhba in 135 CE. Valuable artifacts and ancient manuscripts from this period have been found in these caves.

As we come to Masada, you will notice it as a large, diamond-shaped plateau rising 1,300 feet in massive isolation from the salt flats of the Dead Sea valley. Masada (Hebrew: *Metsada*, Metsuda, means stronghold, fortress) is totally cut off from the surrounding mountains by deep gorges.

Masada comes to mind more from history than from the Bible. It is a mountain fortress which has come to symbolize Jewish freedom … a place where the last of the Jewish Zealots held out against the Romans for three years and ultimately put themselves to death rather than fall into enemy hands. Masada fell in 73 CE and marked the end of Jewish independence until May 1948.

II. History of Masada

Archeological excavations carried out in 1963-1965 CE at Masada revealed much about the history of the Jewish people during the Roman occupation and the lifetime of Jesus.

Masada was first occupied in the Chalcolithic Period (Late Stone/Early Bronze Age) and there are traces that it was occupied during the 10th–8th centuries BCE. History tells us that it was first fortified by the High Priest Jonathan (103-76 BCE), but the main work on the summit was carried out by Herod the Great from 40 BCE–4 CE.

In 40 BCE, Herod the Great, king of Judea, fled south from Jerusalem with his family to escape subjugation by the Parthians who had invaded the country from the north. He took sanctuary at Masada, which had been fortified some years earlier by Jonathan the High Priest. Herod left for Rome to obtain a mandate for his kingship, but his entourage remained with an 800-man garrison under the command of his brother Joseph. Upon his return from Rome, Herod relieved the siege and took his family to safety in another place. Herod then ordered the fortification of Masada as a refuge for himself. At this time he also ordered the building of the Herodion, the man-made mountain palace stronghold in the desert near Bethlehem (cf. Chapter 1– Herodion).

The structures built by Herod on Masada, described by the first-century historian Josephus, and verified by archeological findings, included a double-casement wall 12 feet high. It enclosed the entire 20-acre, diamond-shaped plateau on the rock's summit, and in it were incorporated some 70 rooms used mostly as living quarters and stores, 38 towers and four gates. Special attention was paid to the construction of enormous water cisterns cut into the mountainside and summit of Masada. Rainwater runoff from the Judean mountains to the west was channeled through a network of plastered aqueducts. The capacity of these cisterns was 40,000 cubic meters, which ensured a water supply for many years and the ability to grow crops on the plateau's surface.

The main group of buildings, concentrated on the northern half of the plateau, included massive rectangular storehouses for food and other supplies, barracks for soldiers, one large and two smaller palaces and a synagogue. The royal living quarters were richly decorated with frescoes and the floors of the bathhouses were paved with colorful mosaics. Beneath the fortifications on the north face of Masada, Herod's builders constructed a three-tiered palace-villa, designed presumable for the pleasure and comfort of Herod and his family. Josephus tells us that "Herod had furnished the fortress of Masada with provisions in great quantities… corn, oil, wine, all kinds of pulse (lentils, peas, beans), dates, etc.… enough to sustain men for a long time. There was also found here a large quantity of all sorts of weapons of war, which had been treasured up by that king (Herod), and were sufficient for ten-thousand men; there was cast iron, and brass, and tin, which shows that he had taken much pain to have all things here ready for the greatest occasions; for the report shows how Herod prepared this fortress on his own account as a refuge against two kinds of danger: the one for fear of the multitude of the Jews, lest they should depose him and restore their former kings to the government; the other danger was greater and more terrible, which arose from Cleopatra, queen of Egypt, who did not conceal her intentions, but spoke often to (Mark) Antony, and desired him to cut off Herod, and entreated him to bestow the kingdom of Judea upon her." For a more complete description of the place and events, refer to the *Works of Josephus*, Volume I, Book 7, Chapters 8 & 9. Modern archeological excavations of 1963-65 proved Josephus to be quite accurate in his descriptions.

After the death of Herod in 4 BCE, historians assume that a Roman garrison was stationed at Masada. In 66 CE, at the beginning of the First Jewish Revolt against Roman rule, Masada was captured by a group known as the Zealots – a Jewish resistance movement which had arisen at the beginning of the century in opposition to repressive measures imposed by Rome on the Jewish population. After the fall of Jerusalem to the Roman general, Titus, in 70 CE, in the battle which virtually marked the end of the Jewish Revolt, the Jews on Masada were joined by other people fleeing to safety… a few of them Essenes from Qumran. In the Bible, we find where Jesus spoke about the destruction of Jerusalem as he prophesied in Matthew 24:2, "And Jesus said unto them, 'See you not all these things? Verily, I say unto you, there shall not be left here one stone upon another that shall not be thrown down'." The historian Josephus wrote that the Romans destroyed the city of Jerusalem and the Temple only after they had slaughtered all of the Jews. The destruction of Jerusalem was so complete that there was nothing left that would convince anyone who came there that the city was ever inhabited. (*Works of Josephus*, Volume I, Book 7, Chapter 1). The Zealots knew exactly what the intentions of the Romans were and they were not going to allow this to happen without a fight. There were 967 Jewish men, women and children on Masada under the leadership of Eliezar ben Yair, who held out on Masada until 73 CE.

The Jews altered some of Herod's luxurious buildings, to meet the requirements of their religious way of life, by remodeling the synagogue, incorporating two ritual baths into existing rooms in the outer casement wall, as well as converting the palaces into simple living quarters and defense posts. According to Josephus, much of the food provisions left by Herod were intact and available for use by the Zealots … 70 years after they were stored! In fact, both Josephus and Pliny confirm that provisions would last intact on Masada for at least 100 years. They also had much of the arms left by Herod.

While the Roman army was subduing all of Palestine, the Jewish leader Eliezar ben Yair and his men launched raids against the Romans from the security of their mountain fortress. In 72 CE, the Roman governor, Flavius Silva, dispatched his powerful Tenth Legion to camps encircling the base of Masada in order to crush this last outpost of Jewish resistance. Jewish slaves were used to build a retaining wall four miles long with 12 towers and eight encampments around the base of Masada. The wall was to prevent anyone from escaping from the mountain top, or resupplying food and ammunition. The siege was on…

Flavius Silva also began the building of a ramp on the western flank of the mountain on which he set up his catapults and eventually his battering rams with the objective of knocking a breach in the walls of Masada. The ramp was 600 feet in length and made of stone and beaten earth, reinforced by wooden ties. The ramp and wooden ties can be seen today – 1,900 years later!

One day in the following year, the Romans finished with the ramp and began to pound the defense wall on the western side of the summit of Masada. The Jews realized that the battle was going to be won by the Romans. Eliezar met with his people to discuss their desperate situation. Only two alternatives remained: surrender or death. They knew that when the Romans entered Masada, the men would be slaughtered, their wives raped and children taken into slavery, which would mean eventual death after hard labor. They knew what their fate would be at the hands of the Romans after watching the slaughter of Jerusalem three years before.

Rather than suffer this fate, they decided that the 967 men, women and children of Masada would end their own lives. Before they died, they gathered up their belongings and set fire to them and then set fire to most of the buildings. But they did not destroy their provisions – they wanted it to be clear to the Roman conquerors that they were not forced into this decision because of lack, but because they chose not to be Roman slaves. The men, women and children of Masada died by their own hand. Two women and five children survived by hiding in a cave. They related the story to Josephus. Concerning the death, Josephus writes, "Then, having chosen by lot ten of their number to dispatch the rest – these, having unswervingly slaughtered all, ordained the same rule of lot for one another, that he on whom it fell should slay first the nine and then himself last of all!" In this way, only one had to commit suicide – a practice forbidden in Judaism.

When the Romans broke through the walls the next morning, they were met by charred piles of personal possessions and total silence – a hollow victory, overshadowed by what Josephus described as "the courage of their [the Jews'] resolution, and at the contempt of death which so great a number of them had shown…."

In modern times, many new recruits for the Israel Defense Force (IDF) have been sworn in on top of Masada. During the ceremony they are told the story of the Jewish Zealots of 73 CE and they take an oath that "Masada Shall Not Fall Again!"

After this tragic chapter of history, Masada remained virtually uninhabited. Byzantine Christian hermit monks lived there in the 5th and 6th century CE. They built a church and made cells in the upper level of the Northern Palace of Herod. Except for the monks, the site lay dormant until modern Israelis began excavating in the 1950s and 60s. Masada has been aptly described as looking "curiously like an aircraft carrier moored to the western cliffs of the Dead Sea."

III. Archeological Findings

Today you can reach the summit of Masada by modern cable car or you can hike the ancient Snake Path (used by the Zealots) on the eastern side (about 45 minutes for those in good walking condition) or you can hike the Roman ramp on the western side (about 20 minutes). Once on top, you can view the remains of Herod's magnificent architecture and honor the courageous spirit of those Jewish fighters who defended their freedom more than 1900 years ago. The pledge "Masada shall not fall again" reflects the will of the Jewish people to preserve Israel's independence for all time.

Under the direction of Professor Yigael Yadin, the excavation of Masada was carried out by volunteers from all over the world between October 1963 and April 1965. Many of the artifacts, as well as remnants of Biblical and apocryphal scrolls found at the site, are now on display at the Israel Museum's Shrine of the Book in Jerusalem.

Among the ruins of Masada, we find the palace villa on the northern point of the mountain, which is the highest point of the summit. This palace villa was the smaller of two palaces Herod built on the summit, the second and larger palace being more administrative. The palace-villa hung over the northern cliff on three terraces, the second terrace being 60 feet below the summit, and the third terrace being 48 feet below the second. Originally, there was an internal stairway leading to the different levels of the palace-villa. This was a fantastic example of the architecture, technology and wealth Herod lavished on his buildings. Being on the northern face of the cliff, the palace would be shaded in the afternoon for coolness, and commanded a breathtaking view of the Dead Sea and the mountains of Moab.

The main group of buildings immediately to the south of the palace-villa is a complex which housed the storage warehouses, the Administration building, and hot, warm and cold baths. In front of the bathhouse was a large courtyard with a mosaic floor. In the storage warehouses, jars were found with goods and money still in them from 2,000 year ago! To the west of this complex is a synagogue built by Herod and remodeled during the occupation of the Zealots.

Just to the south of the synagogue are the ruins of regular living quarters used by Herod's officials, and later by the Zealots. A large collection of shekels was found in these rooms. Excavators also found ten pieces of pottery (potsherds) with names on them, presumably the lots cast by those who carried out the deaths of the people in 73 CE.

To the south we find the ruins of a Byzantine Chapel dating from the 6th century. The mosaic floor which can still be seen. The walls were covered with plaster and broken pieces of pottery left by the Zealots were used to make a design.

Next we find the second palace built by Herod, called the Western Palace, and located just west of the center of the summit. This is the largest structure on Masada and was the administrative palace of Herod, used for official visits and entertaining foreign dignitaries. There are three different blocks of ruins: 1) living quarters, 2) services, including another complete bathhouse, and 3) stores, including a tannery along the western edge of the summit so that the prevailing winds could blow the bad smell into the desert. Nearby are five small villas for Herod's family and a swimming pool.

The walls around the edge of the summit are double-casement walls in which rooms were located. Ruins of a mikve (ritual bath) of the synagogue were found there. Within the mikve were found parts of the Books of Ezekiel and Deuteronomy. Parts of the Books of Psalms, Ecclesiastes, Leviticus, and the letters of Ben Sira were found in other rooms of the casement wall. Through research, it is clear that some of these scrolls belonged to the Essenes, who very likely joined the Jewish Zealots. All of the scrolls date from about 50 BCE and are housed at the Israel Museum in Jerusalem. While on the summit, you can also see the many large water cisterns dug into the solid rock. They were supplied by aqueducts that collected rainwater from the surrounding mountains.

The Spring of Ein Gedi

The Spring of Ein Gedi is located along the western shore of the Dead Sea at about the halfway point. Everything about the spring is the antithesis of the surrounding area. The water that pours forth from the spring is fresh, cold and sweet in contrast to the salty water of the Dead Sea. As the spring water flows down the ravine, there is lush green vegetation teeming with birds, ibex (wild goats), small animals such as conies, and even the leopard. This is in contrast to the parched, chalky and rocky landscape devoid of much animal or plant life. For these reasons, Ein Gedi is literally an oasis in the desert and the example for that which is good and abundant in the Bible and other literature.

The name Ein Gedi is Biblical and in Hebrew it means "Fountain of the Kid." It is first mentioned in Joshua 15:62 when the list of the cities of Judah was set forth. Later, we find that David the shepherd found shelter from King Saul at Ein Gedi, "And it came to pass, when Saul was returned from following Philistines, that it was told him, saying, 'Behold, David is in the wilderness of Ein Gedi.' Then Saul took three thousand chosen men out of all Israel, and went to seek David and his men upon the rocks of the wild goats… and David and his men went up into the stronghold" (I Samuel 24:1-22). In II Chronicles 20:2, Jehoshaphat receives the bad news that the Ammonites were in Ein Gedi and on their way to battle with the Israelites.

Ein Gedi was famed for its fruitful vineyards which covered the sides of the surrounding mountains. They are extolled in the Song of Solomon, "My beloved is unto me as a cluster of henna blossoms in the vineyards of Ein Gedi…" (Song of Solomon 1:14). To Ezekiel, Ein Gedi was a symbol of fertility and abundance: "And it shall come to pass that the fishermen shall stand beside the sea from Ein Gedi to Eneglaim; it will be a place for the spreading of nets; its fish will be of very many kinds, like the fish of the Great Sea." (Ezekiel 47:10). Even the 1st century CE Roman historian Pliny in his book, Historia Naturalis, laments the wasted fertility of Ein Gedi, "Its groves of palm trees are now like Jerusalem, a heap of ashes."

Today an Israeli kibbutz named Ein Gedi is located at this site. They have replanted the vineyards and acres of date palms. They have also developed the area of the spring into a nature preserve which is open to the public. While walking through the nature reserve, you will be delighted by the surrounding lush vegetation and beautiful scenery as you climb to the waterfall at the source of the spring. You will also see wild goats (ibex) wandering through the reserve. If you look carefully, you may see the coneys making their houses in the rocks, as Proverbs 30:26 describes. And don't worry about the leopards, they stay high in the rocks above the waterfall.

The kibbutz has also developed a restaurant on the shore of the Dead Sea with changing rooms, fresh water showers and a beautiful guesthouse high on the cliffs above the sea. It is a beautiful and restful place to stay.

In April 1970, a Jewish synagogue dating from the 4th-6th century CE was found at Kibbutz Ein Gedi. It was located in a field overlooking the Dead Sea. Eusebius, a Christian writer of the 4th century, wrote about a large Jewish community living at Ein Gedi during his lifetime. The synagogue was burned in the 6th century and not rebuilt. Many ritual implements were discovered along with 5,000 coins near the niche for the Ark of the Law.

According to the archeologist Mazar, a thriving town existed at Ein Gedi during the time of Ezra and Nehemiah. The evidence of jars and other artifacts indicates that a perfume industry existed there until it was overrun by the Greeks in the 4th century BCE.

Some of the earliest known settlements in history were also found at Ein Gedi. High above the sea are the foundations of pagan temples dating back to the Chalcolithic Period (Stone Age).

Ein Gedi is an exciting and beautiful place with a wealth of ancient and Biblical history.

Qumran

I. The Settlement and the Essenes

After our exploration of Ein Gedi, we will drive north along the Dead Sea to its northwest shore and visit the Qumran community and caves. We will see where the Essene community lived and the nearby caves where the Dead Sea Scrolls were found.

The site of Qumran was a fortress during the Iron Age (1200-600 BCE), but was abandoned until the Essenes occupied it during the 2nd century BCE. The Essenes installed an elaborate water collection system because they had to rely entirely on sparse rainfall for their fresh water. The people of the community abandoned it from 31 BCE – 4 CE, probably because of an earthquake which caused damage. Upon their return, they restored the community buildings and remained there until the Romans sacked Qumran in 69 CE. When the Romans came, the Essenes hurriedly hid their entire library in the nearby caves where they remained hidden for 1,900 years. The Essenes fled, some of them to Masada about 30 miles to the south.

The Essenes were a religious sect in Judaism at the time of the Second Temple. They lived a communal life, some of them tilling the soil. Much of their time was spent studying the Bible and relevant religious literature. Trade was forbidden to them because they were convinced that the occupation contained the seed of corruption and moral decay. They condemned slavery, avoided sacrifice and abstained from taking oaths. They loved the tranquil expanse of the desert over which they had wandered. These are the people who wrote the famous Dead Sea Scrolls. Their theology was very simple, believing in the Spirit of Truth and the Spirit of Falsehood. This is what motivated their ascetic lifestyle which separated them from Jewish life of the day. Their strict regulations and isolationism were enforced to assure their relationship to God and truth, and away from sin and falsehood.

Archeological excavations of the Essene settlement at Qumran revealed a small fort which guarded the settlement, a large room where writing tables and small clay inkpots were found, ritual baths (Hebrew: mikve), well-plastered water reservoirs, a dining hall and several rooms. You can even see the repaired earthquake damage, nearly 2000 years old. The layout of the settlement shows clearly their monastic lifestyle of simplicity and religious study.

II. Dead Sea Scrolls

Qumran has become synonymous with the Dead Sea Scrolls because of an accidental find by two Bedouin shepherd boys in 1947. Nine jars were discovered in a cave on the side of the cliff overlooking the Dead Sea. The boys were throwing stones in the cave and heard a strange sound like the rocks hitting clay pottery. The jars were all empty except one which contained sheepskin scrolls and about 600 fragmentary inscriptions. The scrolls were written in Hebrew and Aramaic and one of the scrolls was the Scroll of Isaiah. The scrolls and fragments were offered for sale in Bethlehem for almost nothing. The enterprising merchant, realizing what he had was valuable, cut the scrolls in pieces and sold them for a great price. Parts of the scrolls turned up all over the world and the Israel Museum is still trying to purchase back all the pieces.

In 1948, some of the manuscripts were taken to America to be photographed and studied. In 1949 this area was occupied by the Jordanian army and the Director of Antiquities in Jordan excavated Cave 1 and found many small fragments of scrolls and a good quantity of pottery. There was some linen found in the cave dating to 33 CE, ±200 years by the Carbon 14 dating method. Altogether, 900 pieces of manuscript on skin and papyrus were found and taken to Amman by the Jordanian government.

In 1951, the decision was made to excavate Khirbet Qumran (the Essenes' settlement) in order to determine the place of origin of the scrolls. The excavation discovered jars of the same type found in the original find and in Cave one. But this time there was also a coin dating to 10 CE!

The local Bedouin were now aware of the value of the scrolls and searched for more caves. In 1951 Cave two was discovered near Qumran, as well as other large caves located 15 miles south of Qumran. A man named Harding examined 37 caves in the area and in Cave three found two rolls of copper with Hebrew inscriptions visible on the outside. These scrolls also went to Amman, Jordan.

In 1952, the Bedouin made their greatest discovery in Cave 4, which produced the largest quantity of manuscript material. It was located only 100 yards from the Essenes' settlement – the ruins of Qumran.

In 1954, four Dead Sea Scrolls that were taken to America were purchased for $250,000 and taken back to Israel. Presently, the exact location of the many manuscripts is not known, but most are in Jerusalem at the Israel Museum; some in Amman, Jordan; and others in the Louvre Museum in Paris.

The finds in the caves of the Qumran community of Essenes have been of great value in the study of the Hebrew scriptures. These manuscripts predate the earliest previously known Hebrew manuscripts by 1,000 years! Aside from the virtually complete manuscript of Isaiah, there are portions of the five books of Moses (Genesis, Exodus, Leviticus, Numbers and Deuteronomy), plus the Psalms, Ruth and parts of other texts from the Hebrw scriptures.

Extra-Biblical writings, documents and letters were also found which shed light on the inter-testamental period and the development of sectarian Judaism.

The background of the New Testament will also be illuminated with results that are already affecting New Testament criticism. For example, before the finding of the Dead Sea Scrolls, the Gospel of John was regarded by some critics as being written after 150 CE because they felt its conceptual imagery was of a later period of thought. However, the Dead Sea Scrolls prove that the contents of John's Gospel can be of an earlier writing as it reflects the authentic Jewish background of John the Baptist and Jesus, as well as ideas and influences illustrated in intertestamental literature.

The two copper scrolls found in Cave 3 turned out to be a collection of traditions revealing where ancient treasure was supposed to be hidden.

The translation of most of the manuscripts has not even begun. We can look with excitement for the eventual revelations from the Dead Sea Scrolls which will further substantiate our confidence in the historicity of the Bible, the Word of God, as well as give us greater knowledge about a very important time of history.

In 2006 archaeologists, Yizhak Magen and Yuval Peleg of the Israel Antiquities Authority, published their research questioning the prevailing belief that Qumran was the home of the Essene community. Much research remains to be done.

Jericho

I. Background

Jericho is the oldest known city in the world. This site is thought to have been continuously inhabited by someone for at least 9,000 years.

Jericho is located below sea level in the Jordan Rift Valley, five miles west of the Jordan River and seven miles north of the Dead Sea. There are three Jerichos in the same general area. The city referred to in the Bible was located on a mound now called Tel es-Sultan which is a mile northwest of the present-day Jericho. The Jericho mentioned in the Christian scriptures is located on a higher elevation about a mile to the south at the mouth of Wadi Kelt (a dry riverbed which fills with water from Jerusalem when it rains in the winter).

In ancient times, Jericho was a strategic site because you could ford the Jordan River at Jericho and have access to the hill country of Canaan/ Israel/Palestine. (Note: These three names refer to the same place at different times.) It is also significant because the mountain range that runs like a spine through Israel is at its lowest altitude just to the west of Jericho. This would make an easier route for those traveling west to the Mediterranean Sea. For these reasons, all of the ancient trade routes from the east were controlled by Jericho. Another important reason for Jericho to have been continuously inhabited is its fresh water springs which are needed to sustain life in this hot and dry desert wilderness. Jericho is literally an oasis in the desert.

II. First/Old Testament Jericho

Archeological excavations at the ancient site of the Jericho of the Hebrew scriptures revealed an unexpected find. Excavators uncovered a tower built by people who inhabited the city in 7000 BCE. It is the oldest man-made structure ever found. The city continued to be inhabited through the late Stone Age and Early Bronze Age, although evidence of at least five cities existed on this site from 3000 BCE until 1400 BCE. At this time, Joshua led the Children of Israel into the Promised Land and they were directed by God to "utterly destroy" Jericho (Joshua 6).

The first mention of Jericho in scripture is in connection with the advance of Israel to Canaan; they "encamped in the plains of Moab on this side of the Jordan by Jericho" (Numbers 22:1). From the manner and frequency in which it is referred to, it would seem to have been the most important city of the Jordan valley at that time (Numbers 31:12; 34:15; 35:1, etc.). God even spoke of Jericho when he showed the Promised Land to Moses from Mount Nebo and defined the borders of the tribal territories (Deuteronomy 34:15).

The spies sent by Joshua were housed and protected in Jericho by Rahab. In return they promised her protection when the city was destroyed; the promise was kept when the city was conquered (Joshua 2:1-21; 6:25). The miraculous capture of Jericho, the sin and punishment of Achan and the curse pronounced upon anyone who should attempt to rebuild it, are graphically recorded (Joshua 6:1-7:26). Jericho was given to the tribe of Ben-jamin (Joshua 18:21), and from that time a long interval elapses before Jericho appears again upon the scene. In Judges 1:16; 3:13, Jericho is mentioned only in passing as "a city of palm trees." It is only incidentally mentioned in the life of David in connection with his embassy to the Ammonite king (II Samuel 10:5).

In I Kings 16:34, it is recorded that Hiel the Bethelite and his sons began the process of reconstructing Jericho. Once actually rebuilt, Jericho rose slowly into prominence. Opposite Jericho, across the Jordan River, Elijah "went up by a whirlwind into heaven" and Elisha "healed the spring of the waters" while seeking retirement from the world (II Kings 2:1-22). In the plains of Jericho, Zedekiah fell into the hands of the Chaldeans (II Kings 25:5; Jeremiah 39:5).

In the return from Babylonia under Zerubbabel, the "children of Jericho" (345 in number) are counted (Ezra 2:34; Nehemiah 7:36); and it is even implied that they moved back to Jericho when they returned from Babylonia, because the men of Jericho assisted Nehemiah in rebuilding the part of the wall of Jerusalem that was next to the sheepgate (Nehemiah 3:2).

III. New Testament Jericho

The New Testament Jericho was excavated in 1950 and it was discovered that much of the city was built by King Herod the Great as his winter capital. It was a magnificent Roman-style city with pools, villas, a palace, a hippodrome, and other buildings. King Herod died here in 4 BCE.

Jericho is mentioned in connection with Jesus restoring sight to the blind (Matthew 20:30; Mark 10:46; Luke 18:35), and his being entertained by Zaccheus, the tax collector (Luke 19:1-10); and was introduced in the parable of the Good Samaritan, which, if not a real occurrence, derives interest from the fact that robbers have always been the terror of the road from Jerusalem to Jericho.

IV. Present-Day Jericho

Today you can visit the archeological sites of both First and New Testament Jericho. But our love for history and the Bible should not overshadow the remarkable fact that Jericho is still alive and well today after 9,000 years of continuous habitation! Present-day Jericho and the surrounding plains are very fertile, being fed by natural freshwater springs. The climate is tropical and the city becomes a winter resort for people fleeing the cold winter weather in the hill country. There is very little rainfall in Jericho (less than two inches per year), but the springs provide the life to this green oasis in the middle of the dry Jordan Rift Valley.

From Jerusalem to Galilee

From Jerusalem to Galilee there are two main routes. Both have been traveled since before history began to be recorded.

One is the Ridge Route, also known as the Road of the Patriarchs. It is called this because it was traveled by Abraham, Isaac, Jacob and other notable Biblical and historical figures. This route is located along the ridge of Israel's Central Mountain Range which runs south to north, from the Negev Desert to the Jezreel Valley like a backbone. Refer to your Hammond Bible Atlas. Significant cities and regions along this route from south to north are: Hebron, Debir, Bethlehem and Jerusalem (in the Hill Country of Judah); Gibeah, Geba, Ramah, Mizpah and Bethel (in the Central Benjamin Plateau); Shiloh (in the Hill Country of Ephraim); and Shechem, Samaria and Dothan (in Samaria). On our trip to Galilee, we will be concentrating on the portion of the Ridge Route from Jerusalem to the north.

We know that Jesus traveled this route many times, first with his parents when they traveled from Nazareth to Jerusalem for the Jewish high-holiday feasts, and later during his ministry. In John 4, Jesus encounters the Samaritan woman at the well (Jacob's Well) located in Shechem.

The road is rugged, winding and difficult to travel as it passes through the mountains. This was especially true in the days before modern highways. There is vegetation and water along this route which is important for travelers. The route is particularly rugged between Mizpah and Shiloh as it passes through a deep valley with high rock walls on both sides. All through history, this stretch of road was called the Valley of the Robbers. It made a perfect place for an ambush because there is nowhere to run. It was at about this place on the route (a day's journey from Jerusalem), that Mary discovered Jesus was not with them when they were traveling home to Nazareth (Luke 2:44). Actually, it is not unusual that Mary didn't notice him missing. Due to the difficulty in traveling, people traveled with family clans and groups for safety. It would have been easy to miss Jesus as the group from Nazareth happily made their way home after the feast in Jerusalem.

The mountains are hard limestone and terraced. Any flat areas are cultivated with wheat and fields of onions in the spring. You will notice olive groves growing everywhere, even out of the cracks in the rock. In fact, the olive tree is green all the time, no matter what the conditions…hot, cold, wet, dry, rocky, etc. Even if you burn an olive tree or cut it down, new green shoots will come up out of the roots. It is almost impossible to kill. The olive trees in the Garden of Gethsemane may be over 2,000 years old. Psalm 52:8 says, "But I am like a green olive tree in the house of God; I trust in the mercy of God forever and ever." This is how we should be before God. No matter what the conditions are around us, we should remain "green," faithful and steadfast before God.

The second route from Jerusalem to Galilee is the Valley Route which passes through the Jordan River Valley from Jericho to the Sea of Galilee. But first, you have to travel via Bethany, through the Judean Desert to the northeast of Jerusalem, to Jericho. The main cities on this hot and dry desert route are cities with springs of water: Bethany, Jericho and Beit She'an (also known as Scythopolis during the New Testament/Roman Period).

The route is easier to travel because the terrain is relatively flat compared with the Ridge Route. But, it can be more risky and difficult due to a lack of water in the Judean Desert and the southern part of the Jordan River Valley. When in Jericho, notice how green it is — an oasis surrounded by a dry and dusty landscape. Water is very important, especially to the traveler.

Provided there are no problems of travel through the mountains, we will be traveling the Ridge Route. Otherwise, we will take the Valley Route via Jericho.

The Land of Benjamin & the Hill Country of Ephraim

Traveling north from Jerusalem to Galilee along the Ridge Route we first pass through part of the area allocated to the Tribe of Benjamin. This includes the Central Benjamin Plateau and the Hill Country of the area allocated to the Tribe of Ephraim. Although it is a relatively small area, it was very significant in Biblical history.

There are many cities of particular Biblical interest located on the actual Ridge Route, also called the Road of the Patriarchs, and others located just to the east or west of this route which we will be traveling. Although we will not see each site, it is important that you are aware of their locations and of the exciting Biblical events which took place in the land you will be passing through on your travel to Galilee. This description will follow their appearance from south to north: Nob, Gibeah, Ramah, Gibeon, Geba, Michmas, Mizpah, Bethel, Ai and Shiloh. Please refer to your maps for orientation.

I. Nob

Nob was a city of Benjamin that was a city of priests. Its exact location is uncertain, although it lay somewhere between Anathoth (the city of the prophet Jeremiah) and Ananiah (believed to be ancient Bethany). That would place it just north of Jerusalem. In fact, we have a Biblical reference that indicates Nob was situated on the heights overlooking Jerusalem (Isaiah 10:28-32). Today, it has been located just north of the Hadassah Mount Scopus Hospital and south of the modern Jewish community of French Hill. You will be able to see it from the road.

Here was a shrine, the service performed by a family of priests headed by Ahimelech, a descendant of Eli (I Samuel 14:3). David came to this shrine in his flight from Saul and asked for bread and was given "holy bread" (showbread) c. 1012 BCE (I Samuel 21:1-9).

Nob was called "the city of priests" for there were 85 priests serving here (I Samuel 22:18-19). They had apparently located in Nob after Shiloh was destroyed about 1050 BCE (I Samuel 4:11). Saul brutally massacred the priests of Nob for helping David (I Samuel 22:9-23). It is believed that Nob was the residence of the Temple gatekeeper Obed-Edom, who kept the Ark of the Covenant before it was brought to Jerusalem (II Samuel 6). After the return of the Jews from the Babylonian Captivity (5th century BCE), a company of Benjamites settled in Nob (Nehemiah 11:32).

From Nob, the Assyrian King Sennacherib "shook his fist at Jerusalem" (Isaiah 10:32). This too was the military operation headquarters for the Babylonian King Nebuchadnezzar (58 BCE), the Roman General Titus (70 CE) , the Crusaders (12th century CE), and the British General Allenby after World War I (1917).

II. Gibeah (of Saul)

Gibeah is located along the east side of the Road of the Patriarchs about three miles north of Jerusalem and over the hill from Nob. A modern town called Shu'afat is now located on this site.

Gibeah is first mentioned in the Bible in connection with the bizarre murder of the concubine of a Levite from Bethlehem when he was spending the night in Gibeah. The murder was at the hands of the men of Gibeah and resulted in the near extermination of the Benjamites by the other tribes of Israel (c. 1375 BCE, Judges 19 and 20).

Saul was selected from a prominent family of Gibeah and anointed as the first king of Israel (II Samuel 9 and 10). With the establishment of the monarchy, Gibeah became the first capital of Israel, hereafter referred to as Gibeah of Saul (I Samuel 11:4). In the audience chamber of Saul's castle, the young David played his harp to soothe the demented spirit of the king (I Samuel 16:23; 19:9-10). It was here that David courted Saul's daughter Michal (1025-1010 BCE).

The noted archeologist, W.F. Albright, excavating at Gibeah, unearthed Saul's crude fortress palace, the second of a series of four fortresses built on this same site during subsequent periods. Albright's findings showed that the first fortress was burned between 1150 and 1100 BCE. He believes this was the time when Israel decimated the Benjamites (Judges 20:40). Other sources date this much earlier. The second fortress, with its double-

casemate walls and corner towers, was erected between 1020 BCE and 100 CE and seems to be that of the rustic chieftain Saul. When compared to the architecture of the glorious period of King Solomon about 100 years later, Saul's royal residence was more like a dungeon than a palace. The Gibeah fortress was later partially rebuilt by kings Asa and Uzziah, only to be soon destroyed in the ambitious advance of the powerful young Assyrian, Sennacherib in 722 BCE. Isaiah graphically describes the terror of his coming, "Ramah trembles, Gibeah of Saul is fled" (Isaiah 10:29).

A fifth palace was almost built on this site, that of King Hussein of Jordan. Its construction was interrupted by the Six-Day War in 1967, and the unfinished palace can be seen from the road.

III. Ramah

Ramah is located along the Road of the Patriarchs several miles north of Gibeah. Today this area is known as Ram and it is very near and just south of the Jerusalem Airport.

Ramah is first mentioned in the Bible as a city of Benjamin (Joshua 18:25). Samuel was born to Hannah and Elkanah in Ramah (c. 1080 BCE) (I Samuel 1:19). Samuel resided in Ramah during his judgeship (I Samuel 7:17). All the elders of Israel gathered here to ask Samuel for a king (c. 1030 BCE) (I Samuel 8:4).

Narrowly escaping Saul's assassination attempt, David fled to Samuel in Ramah. Saul's servants, sent to take David, were overcome by the Spirit in prophesying, as was Saul (I Samuel 19). Samuel died and was buried here (c. 1017 BCE) (I Samuel 25:1).

Ramah is situated at the main roadway intersection of the road from the Sharon Plains (along the seacoast to the west) to Jerusalem and the Road of the Patriarchs running north and south. As such, control of Ramah insured control of the Central Benjamin Plateau and east-west trade. This is also true today in the control of the West Bank.

In 894 BCE, Baasha, king of Israel, fortified Ramah (I Kings. 15:17-22) which alarmed Asa, king of Judah, to intervene. In 586 BCE, Babylonian King Nebuchadnezzar brought the Jewish captives, including Jeremiah, to Ramah and slaughtered those not worth transporting to Babylon (Jeremiah 40:1, 39:8-12,15). The descendants of the captives from Ramah rebuilt the town upon their return from the Babylonian Captivity (Ezra 2:26).

NOTE: Although we will continue to travel north on the Road of the Patriarchs towards Galilee, there are significant Biblical cities to the west (Gibeon) and east (Gebah and Michmas) of Ramah which will be described so that you will know more of the exciting events that occurred in this area.

IV. Gibeon

If we were to turn west from Ramah along the ancient road that linked Jerusalem to the seacoast, we would come to Gibeon, the central city of the four Hivite cities: Gibeon, Chephirah, Kiriath-jearim, Beeroth (Joshua 9:17). By resorting to trickery, this confederation of Hivite cities made a covenant with Joshua (Joshua 9:3-27), in contrast to the military alliance formed by the Amorite kings against the Israelites (1300 BCE) (Joshua 9:1,2). Gibeon was a great city, greater than Ai, a royal city where all the men were mighty (Joshua 10:2). Gibeon was also strategically located along the main road. When the Amorite kings heard of the peace treaty between the Gibeonites and the Israelites, they conspired to capture Gibeon to prevent further advances by Joshua's army (Joshua 10:1-6). This tested the treaty and Joshua brought forth his army against the Amorites. Having broken the Amorite encampment against Gibeon, the Israelites could pursue them down the Valley of Ayalon (Joshua 10:1-14) which opened the way of access to the city-states of southern Canaan along the coastal plain (Joshua 10:10-35).

Gibeon was allotted to the tribe of Benjamin and was made a Levitical town (Joshua 18:25, 21:17). The Tabernacle was erected here after the destruction of Nob and it remained here until the building of the Temple (II Chronicles 1:3,4).

By "the great pool which is in Gibeon" (Jeremiah 41:12), in the territory of Saul's son Ish-bosheth, the servants of David penetrated and here met Abner's men. The hand-to-hand combat by a chosen number of champions resulted in full-scale war (c. 1004 BCE) (II Samuel 2:12-3:1).

At "the great high place" in Gibeon, the young King Solomon worshipped, offering 1,000 burnt offerings. At night in a dream, the Lord appeared to Solomon with the gift of an understanding mind of wisdom so as to discern and judge his people rightly (I Kings 3:4-15).

Joshua's covenant to spare the Gibeonites appears to have been broken by Saul in a general massacre which was atoned for in David's reign by the hanging of Saul's descendants "before the Lord" in Gibeah of Saul (c. 975 BCE) (II Samuel 21:1-9). The Gibeonites were numbered among the Nethinim who were appointed for service in the Temple (I Chronicles 9:2).

V. Geba

Geba was chosen as one of the four Levitical cities in the territory of Benjamin (Joshua 21:17). It is located just east of the Road of the Patriarchs and was one of a chain of towns serving as a defense line against the cities of the Hivites (Gibeon, Chephirah, Baalah and Beeroth) to the west.

Following the defeat of the Israelite tribes in the battle between Aphek and Ebenezer in 1050 BCE (I Samuel 4), Geba became a Philistine garrison (see Michmas). In a daring raid, Jonathan took this stronghold. This launched a major struggle between Israel and the Philistines (I Samuel 13:3-14:52) in which the Philistines were finally subdued under David who smote them from Geba to Gezer in 1003 BCE (II Samuel 5:25).

In 894 BCE, when Baasha (king of Israel) invaded Judah, Asa (king of Judah) fortified Geba (I Kings 15:16). Eventually, the border of Judah stretched "from Geba to Beersheva" (II Kings 23:8).

In 722 BCE, Geba was conquered by Sennacherib (Isaiah 10:28-32), and was later resettled after the return of the Jews from the Babylonian captivity (Ezra 2:26).

VI. Michmas

Michmas is located in the hills east of the Road of the Patriarch and north of Geba. It is high on a hilltop on the edge of a steep and deep valley. The modern Arab village of Mishmish is located here today.

In the days of Saul, the Philistines had penetrated deep into Israelite territory, destroyed Shiloh, and occupied key positions in the hills. The Philistines also occupied Geba, and Saul came against them. Saul took 2,000 men and encamped in Michmas and Bethel (north and east of Geba), and Jonathan took 100 men and stationed them in Gibeah. Jonathan first routed the garrison of the Philistines from Geba. This angered the Philistines and they concentrated their attack and took Michmas with their 30,000 chariots, 6,000 horsemen, and innumerable foot-soldiers. Crossing the deep Michmas valley, Jonathan and his armor bearer made a daring sortie up the steep cliff, surprising the Philistines. A sudden earthquake, coupled with the attack by the Israelites, resulted in the flight of the Philistines westward through the Valley of Ayalon to the seacoast (c. 1035 BCE) (I Samuel 13 and 14).

VII. Mizpah

Mizpah is located on the main north-south highway, the Road of the Patriarchs, just a few miles north of Ramah. Its archeological remains, known as Tel Nasbe, are just north of the Jerusalem Airport.

During the time of the Judges, a center of worship was located at Mizpah where several significant oaths were made (Judges 21). After the fall of Shiloh in 1063 BCE, Mizpah became the gathering site for Israel under the prophet Samuel (I Samuel 7). Here, following the defeat of the Philistines through divine intervention, Samuel set up the "stone of help," calling it Ebenezer (II Samuel 7:12). Mizpah was within Samuel's circuit as he judged

Israel. Here began the Hebrew monarchy, as Saul was crowned king (I Samuel 10). It was later fortified by Asa, king of Judah, against incursions from the northern kingdom (I Kings 15:22). After the destruction of Jerusalem by the Babylonians, Mizpah became the residence of Gedaliah, the governor appointed by Nebuchadnezzar (Jeremiah 40:10).

VIII. Ai

As we travel north on the highway on our way to the ancient site of Bethel, we should note that off to the east and out of sight is the archeological site believed to be ancient Ai. After Jericho, located to the east in the Jordan Valley, Ai was the second city which fell before the Israelite conquest (c. 1300 BCE). It was east of Bethel (Genesis 12:8, Joshua 7:2). The Israelites were permitted by God to take spoils of Ai, and thereafter to destroy it (Joshua 8:27). Joshua's first contingent of 3,000 was defeated due to Achan's sin in the conquest of Jericho (Joshua 7). In the second attack on Ai, Joshua planned a diversionary offensive with 30,000 men. The king of Ai and 12,000 defenders were killed and the city set ablaze, being turned into a heap of ruins (Joshua 8).

IX. Bethel

Bethel is located about twelve miles north of Jerusalem next to the Arab village known as Beitin. Except for Jerusalem, no other city is mentioned more often in the Bible. Throughout history, this site has been holy ground. It was originally a Canaanite town known as Luz (Genesis 28:19), but became known as Bethel or Beit-El (House of God) when Jacob renamed this place.

It was here that Abraham camped and built an altar to God when he entered the land (Genesis 13:1-3). On his journey northward to Laban's country, Jacob rested at Bethel and dreamed of a ladder reaching to heaven with angels ascending and descending upon it and the Lord standing above. It was at this time that the Abrahamic Covenant was confirmed in Jacob. When Jacob rose up in the morning, he took the stone where he had laid his head and turned it up and poured oil upon the top of it. Jacob renamed the town Beit-El (House of God) (Genesis 28:11-22). About 30 years later, Jacob returned to Bethel at the command of God who called himself "the God of Bethel" (Genesis 31:13). Nearing Bethel, Jacob ordered his family to destroy all their foreign gods (Genesis 35:1-4). At Bethel, Jacob's name was changed to "Israel," and the Abrahamic Covenant was renewed (Genesis 35:10-15).

Bethel was the earliest location for the Ark of the Covenant (Genesis 20:18). After the conquest by Joshua, Bethel was given to the tribe of Benjamin. The Benjamites were apparently unable to take or keep it, because from this time on, Bethel was under the possession of different Hebrew tribes, e.g., taken by the sons of Joseph (Judges 1:22-30), and engulfed by the tribe of Ephraim from the north. During the period of the Judges, the Ark of the Covenant was kept in Bethel.

Bethel was within the circuit of the prophet Samuel (I Samuel 7:15). It declined in importance under the monarchies of Saul, David and Solomon, but gained new importance under Jeroboam after the death of Solomon when the kingdom divided in 931 BCE. Jeroboam made Bethel the new, albeit pagan, sanctuary which rivaled Jerusalem as a spiritual center (I Kings 12:26-33). In fact, Bethel and Dan (far to the north) became the cultic centers with non-Levitical priests officiating at the shrines of the golden calf (931 BCE). About 85 years later (845 BCE), there resided a school of the prophets in Bethel who met Elijah and Elisha (II Kings 2:2-3). Here Elisha was mocked by the children who were slain by bears (II Kings 2:23-24).

Amos focused his prophetic message upon Bethel and was ordered out of town by the sanctuary priest, Amaziah (Amos 7:12,13).

In 722 BCE, Assyrians invaded the northern kingdom and took the population captive while bringing in foreigners from Babylon and other regions of the east to repopulate Israel. When some of the newcomers were killed by lions, the Assyrian governor ordered a Hebrew priest from Samaria to Bethel to teach the people how to worship the God of Israel and thus remedy the judgment (II Kings 17:25-28). This was the beginning of the Samaritan people discussed in the section on Samaria (the region).

As Assyrian rule waned, King Josiah of Judah moved north and annihilated the Bethel sanctuary, wiping out the priesthood (I Kings 23:15-20). Bethel was destroyed under the Babylonians (586 BCE), but both Ezra and Nehemiah record how some of the inhabitants returned to Bethel after the Babylonian Captivity (Ezra 2:28; Nehemiah 7:32).

Bethel never again became a city of significance. Perhaps this is in fulfillment of the prophecy spoken by Amos who lived at the time of Jeroboam, who put up the golden calf in Bethel. He says to "seek not Bethel...Bethel shall come to nothing" (Amos 5:5). Archaeologists have had difficulty finding the definite site of Bethel.

X. Shiloh

Once again traveling north on the Road of the Patriarchs, we leave the Central Benjamin Plateau and enter the land of the tribe of Ephraim. You will notice more and more groves of olive trees. You will also pass through the Valley of the Robbers, mentioned in the introduction to this section, "From Jerusalem to Galilee."

Shiloh is located about twenty-five miles north of

Jerusalem and three miles east of the main road. It is centrally located, which is one of the reasons it was chosen by Joshua as the site for erecting the Tabernacle of God after the Israelites entered the land (c. 1300 BCE). Shiloh became the most important religious center for the tribes following the conquest (Joshua 18:1). The tribes made regular pilgrimages to Shiloh to offer sacrifices and to commemorate their festivals (Judges 21:19). During one such festival, the remnants of the decimated tribe of Benjamin were permitted to hide in the surrounding vineyards while the maidens of Shiloh came out to dance, and then each to kidnap a dancer for a wife to take back to the land of Benjamin to the south (Judges 21:16-25). To this day, the Arabs call the adjacent valley Marj el-Id, the Valley of the Feast.

Elkanah of Ramathaim went up annually to Shiloh with his family and here his wife Hannah prayed for a son. When the child Samuel as born he was "lent to the Lord" to assist the elderly priest Eli (I Samuel 1). A massive destruction at Shiloh in 1050 BCE is believed to be that of the Philistines when the Ark of the Covenant was taken (I Samuel 4). A small settlement must have survived at Shiloh for here Jeroboam's wife sought out the prophet Ahijah when her son was mortally ill (c. 915 BCE) (I Kings 14:1-6).

The ancient Biblical site of Shiloh was excavated by a Danish Expedition, and today there is a modern Israeli settlement developing next to this site – still called Shiloh!

Samaria (The Region)

I. The Region of Samaria (Background)

From Shiloh, still traveling north on the Road of the Patriarchs, we soon come to some sharp hairpin turns as we descend into the deep and fruitful Valley of Luban (Biblical Lebona). At this point, we pass from the Hill Country of Ephraim into the region of Samaria.

Mount Gerizim and Mount Ebal are the mountains where Joshua divided the tribes and had six read the blessings on Mount Gerizim while the other six read the curses on Mount Ebal. An altar of sacrifice was built on Mount Ebal (Joshua 8:30-35). It seems appropriate that the altar is built where the curses were read reminding God's people of the need for sacrifice where sin is committed. In 1982, Dr. Adam Zertal of Haifa University was digging at Mount Ebal and found what he believes to be an ancient altar of sacrifice and large collections of animal bones. We are not sure that this is Joshua's altar but the dig reminds us of the significance of the site.

The name of Samaria for this region came into usage after the division of the Kingdom of Solomon by his two sons, Rehoboam, king of Judah – the Southern Kingdom; and Jeroboam, king of Israel or Samaria, the ten tribes in the Northern Kingdom. The expression "cities of Samaria" (I Kings 13:32) is used for the building of the city of Samaria as the capital of the kingdom and the residence of the kings of Israel (I Kings 16:24). This term also includes all the tribes over which Jeroboam made himself king, whether east or west of the Jordan River.

In the Book of Hosea, we find Israel, Ephraim and Samaria used interchangeably as equivalent terms. In Amos 3:9, the "mountains of Samaria" are spoken of and we find the expression in Ezekiel 16:53, the "captivity of Samaria and her daughter."

In the New Testament, we know that Jesus passed through Samaria and met the woman at the well (John 4:1-42). Peter, John and Philip preached and ministered "in the villages of Samaria" (Acts 8:14-25).

Today, the region of Samaria covers the entire Central Mountain Range from Shiloh north to the Jezreel Valley.

II. The Biblical Capitals of the Northern Kingdom (Israel)

After the death of Solomon (931 BCE), his kingdom was divided into two kingdoms, the Northern Kingdom (Israel) under Jeroboam, and the Southern Kingdom (Judah) under Rehoboam. The various capitals of the Northern Kingdom (Israel) were always in Samaria.

Jeroboam put his capital in Shechem although he lived in Tirzah, his royal city not too many miles to the north. After the death of Jeroboam and his successor Nadab, Baasha (king of Israel) moved the capital to Tirzah which was easier to defend. Asa, King of Judah had turned a military alliance with the king of Syria against Baasha and this prompted the move (I Kings 15:16-21). Tirzah remained the capital through Baasha's dynasty and for the first six years of Omri's reign (909-880 BCE). In the conflagration that followed the treason of Zimri against King Elah (son of Baasha), Tirzah was severely damaged (885 BCE) (I Kings 18:8-20). This may have been the reason that Omri eventually transferred the capital from Tirzah to Samaria, nine miles northwest of Shechem (I Kings 16:9-24). For a more complete description of Shechem and Samaria (the city), refer to those sections in this chapter.

III. The Samaritans

The inhabitants of this region are called Samaritans. In the Hebrew scripture, the term is found only in II Kings 17:29. It is customary to refer to the Samaritans in this passage as the colonists brought by the kings of Assyria in place of the deported Israelites, but the text seems to infer that these colonists put their gods into the houses of the high places which the Samaritans, i.e., the former inhabitants of Samaria, had made for their own religious use. But the Samaritans of subsequent history and of the New Testament are the descendants of the colonists brought in by King Sargon of Assyria in 721 BCE. "The King of Assyria came up through all the land, and went up to Samaria and carried Israel away to Assyria. And the King of Assyria brought men from Babylon and from Cuthah ... and placed them in the cities of Samaria instead of the children of Israel, and they possessed Samaria and dwelt in the cities thereof" (II Kings 17:24). A century later, Jeremiah 41:5 implies that a remnant of true Israelites remained in the area so we must assume that they intermarried with the new inhabitants creating a composite population which took on the general name of Samaritans.

The invasion of Samaria by Sargon of Assyria left the area so desolate that it became overrun with wild animals (II Kings 17). The people complained and concluded that "the god of the land was angry at their presence and ignorance of his propitiatory rites." They asked the Assyrian monarch to select a priest from among the deportees to instruct them in the necessary ritual worship. The king granted this and a knowledge of God was introduced, although they continued to serve their own gods as well. This attempt to purify the Samaritans did not reconcile them with the Jews, however.

After the return of the Jews from the Babylonian Captivity (5th century BCE), enmity arose between the two peoples. Since the Samaritans were worshipping Jehovah, they sought a share in the rebuilding of the Temple in Jerusalem, but were not allowed to participate. Sanballat of Samaria was apparently the one who had the most dealings with the Jews in Jerusalem and he was obviously rejected (Nehemiah 2:10, 19). Sanballat's son-in-law was Manasseh, grandson of the Jewish high priest Eliashib. Nehemiah's drive for racial purity led to the expulsion of Manasseh from Jerusalem (Nehemiah 13:28). When Manasseh left Jerusalem, he took with him a large band of dissident Jews, and went into Samaria. Thus the rift between the peoples was made permanent.

According to tradition, Manasseh persuaded the Samaritans to abandon many of their idolatrous practices and a sect was established on Mount Gerizim in a temple built by Sanballat. It was also from this time that Samaria became a refuge for malcontent Jews, with the consequent use of "Samaritan" as a term of abuse for a dissident rebel (John 8:48). The animosity between the Samaritans and the Jews was at its greatest during the time of Jesus.

This is the background for the conversation between Jesus and the woman at the well (John 4:5-9) (see Jacob's Well), and the dramatic example of Jesus' parable of the Good Samaritan (Luke 10:30-37). For a Samaritan to stop and help a Jew on the road to Jericho was indeed an act of great mercy and kindness that broke through the established prejudice between the two groups. And Jesus was illustrating the mockery of reli-giosity when he showed that a priest and a Levite passed the beaten and robbed man... and the Samaritan stopped to help.

Today a small sect of Samaritans still live and worship on Mount Gerizim just as separated as they were 2,500 years ago. They still worship in a form of Judaism, although they are not considered Jewish by blood or by faith. In fact, during Passover, you can go to Mount Gerizim and see the sacrifice of the Passover Lamb. (The Jews cannot sacrifice a Passover Lamb because the Temple in Jerusalem was destroyed in 70 CE.)

I. Shechem

A. Biblical and Historical Significance

The city of Shechem is the geographical center of the whole country. It is situated between Mount Ebal and Mount Gerizim and was originally a flourishing Canaanite city as early as 2000 BCE. The sacred Canaanite grove of oaks in Shechem received particular mention in the stories of the Patriarchs (Genesis 12:6, 35:4), as well as later generations (Joshua 24:26; Judges 9:6,37). This sacred spot was designated "a sanctuary of the Lord" in Joshua's day. It was so special to the patriarchs that Joseph was carried out of Egypt and buried in Shechem (Joshua 24:32), even though Abraham, Isaac and Jacob were buried in another family burial tomb in Hebron.

During Jacob's encampment here and the defilement of his daughter Dinah by prince Shechem, Levi and Simeon slaughtered the men of the city (Genesis 34). During the conquest of Canaan by Joshua, Shechem was chosen as the site for welding the tribes together (Joshua 24). It was assigned to the Levites as a "city of refuge" (Joshua 21:20). Shechem's location in the valley between Mount Gerizim and Mount Ebal made it the site for many of the activities involving these two Biblical mountains.

Archeological finds revealed a strongly built shrine with two high turrets which evidently served also as a fortress built in the Late Bronze Age and continuing into the time of the Judges (1600-1125 BCE). This was likely the "tower of Shechem" which Abimelech set ablaze, burning it down with the 1,000 citizens who had taken refuge inside it, following their conspiracy against him. Abimelech destroyed the city of Shechem, killed the inhabitants and salted the fields. He then went to the nearby city of Thebez to destroy them in a similar manner. From the burning tower of Thebez, a woman tossed a millstone which struck King Abimelech, breaking his skull 1126 BCE (Judges 9:22-57).

The destruction of Shechem and the death of Abimelech were the result of a judgment pronounced from Mount Gerizim upon the men of Shechem and Abimelech. Why did Jotham pronounce this judgment? When Gideon (Jerubbaal) died, his son Abimelech came to Shechem and arranged to be made king over the area in his father's stead. The people agreed and gave him money from the house of the pagan god Baalberith. Abimelech hired worthless and light persons who followed him. Then he went to his father's house at Ophrah and killed the 70 sons of Gideon, his brothers, except for the youngest named Jotham, who hid himself. It was Jotham who chastised them in his speech and concluded with these words, "If you have dealt truly and sincerely with Jerubbaal (Gideon) and with his house this day, then rejoice ye in Abimelech and let him also rejoice in you. But if not, let fire come out from Abimelech and devour the men of Shechem and the house of Millo; and let fire come out from the men of Shechem and from the house of Millo and devour Abimelech." (Judges 9:1-2). Thus the dishonor of Abimelech and the men of Shechem against the house of Gideon became their downfall. "Thus God rendered the wickedness of Abimelech, which he did unto his father in slaying his seventy brothers. And all the evil of the men of Shechem did God render upon their heads; and upon them came the curse of Jotham, the son of Jerubbaal (Gideon)" (Judges 9:56-57).

After the death of Solomon (931 BCE), all Israel assembled at Shechem to inaugurate Rehoboam as king (I Kings 12). Soon afterward, the ten tribes renounced Rehoboam, transferring their allegiance to Jeroboam, his brother, who made Shechem the capital of the northern kingdom, Israel (I Kings 12:16-20,25).

The significance of Shechem declined following the Babylonian Captivity and the influx of strangers under Esar-hadden, becoming part of the history of the Samaritans (II Kings 18:9; Ezra 4:2).

During the period of the Romans, Shechem was called by the Latin name Neapolis (New City) and was a garrison of the Roman army (Acts 16:11). Today, the city is still called Shechem by the Jews and Nablus by the Arabs. Interestingly, there is no letter "P" in Arabic and the Arabs could not pronounce the ancient name Neapolis when they conquered the area in the 7th century CE. Thus, they called it Nablus by replacing the letter "B" for "P" in pronunciation.

B. Mount Gerizim and Mount Ebal

One of the first acts of consecration for the congregation of Israel upon entering into the land was the recitation of the blessings and curses of the Law as instructed by Moses (c. 1406 BCE) (Deuteronomy 11:29). There were two amphitheaters opposing each other across the Valley of Shechem. Six tribes were to stand on Mount Gerizim to bless the people and six tribes on Mount Ebal to hear the curses for disobedience. The Levites with loud voice recited first the curses, followed by the blessings, with the people solemnly intoning the "Amen." (Deuteronomy 27 and 28; Joshua 8:33-35). Here, immediately following the conquest of Ai, Joshua assembled the people to renew the covenant, building an altar atop Mount Ebal, writing upon the stones a copy of the Law (Joshua 8:30). Again, just prior to his death, Joshua reassembled Israel to these sacred environs before these mountains for his final solemn address consecrating the nation to the service of the Lord (Joshua 24).

When Jotham, Gideon's youngest son, heard that Abimelech, the murderer of his brothers, had been crowned king in Shechem, he climbed Mount Gerizim and with a loud voice recited his famous parable of the trees crowning the bramble bush (Judges 9:7-21). Manasseh built a temple atop Gerizim after the Babylonian Captivity by permission of Alexander the Great, and here the Samaritans joined idolatry and monotheism (II Kings 17:33).

During the period of the Maccabees (167-37 BCE), John Hyrcanus destroyed this temple (c. 128 BCE). To this sacred high-place the Samaritan woman alluded in her question to Jesus, "on this mountain… or in Jerusalem men ought to worship?" (John 4:20).

The 1st century CE historian Josephus writes about the siege of the Samaritans on Mount Gerizim by the Romans in 67 CE. Vespasian sent Cerealis, the commander of the Fifth Legion, to Mount Gerizim to put down any revolt from the Samaritans. Cerealis, fearing for his men, did not want them to go up the mountain because the Samaritans were on higher ground and that presented a threat. So he besieged the mountain. Due to the great heat, many of the Samaritans died for lack of water and some of them surrendered to become Roman slaves rather than die. The others continued to hold their position, so Cerealis sent them an ultimatum to lay down their arms in peace and he would not harm them. They refused, so he attacked the Samaritans and killed all 11,600 of them! (*The Wars of the Jews*, Book III, Chapter VII, Section 32).

II. Jacob's Well

After Jacob was reconciled with his brother Esau, he moved his family to Shechem "and he bought a portion of a field where he had spread his tent" just east of the city (Genesis 33:18-20). It was here that Jacob set up an altar to God, calling El-Elohe-Israel, "God, the God of Israel" and dug the well for his family and flocks that is still called Jacob's Well to this day. It was also on this plot where the children of Israel buried the bones of Joseph which they brought up from Egypt (Joshua 24:32).

About 1,700 years later, this area around the well grew into a small village known as Sychar. It was located on the Road of the Patriarchs just a few miles east of the main city of Shechem (Neapolis). While Jesus was traveling from Jerusalem to Galilee, he stopped at Jacob's Well for a drink. It was at this well that he had a life-changing conversation with the Samaritan woman from Sychar. She, being a Samaritan was surprised that he, a Jew, would even talk with her. Jesus used the image of well water and living water as a reference point to illustrate the deeper meaning of true salvation and faith in God versus a life of sin or even religiosity. The woman understood and received salvation and a change from her former life of sin. She also realized that Jesus was the promised Messiah and ran into town to tell everyone. They also came out to hear Jesus' message, received salvation and urged him to stay and teach them more (John 4:1-42).

Jacob's Well is located under an unfinished Greek Orthodox church with a roof. You can still draw fresh water from the well. The town around the well is called Askar by the local Arabs, which is a derivation of the town Jesus visited 2,000 years ago, Sychar.

Samaria (The City)

The capital of the northern kingdom of Israel was in the tribal area of Manasseh in the region of Samaria, first at Shechem (931-909 BCE), then transferred by King Baasha to Tirzah (909-880 BCE). But the district of Manasseh could very easily be invaded and their early history was taken up in securing their approaches and building for defense. There was no obvious site for a naturally safe capital in Manasseh. The only locations with a focal point of convergence needed by a capital were in valleys which were indefensible. Thus, King Omri decided to build atop a natural stronghold nine miles northwest of Shechem, and purchased the hill of Shemer for two talents of silver (I Kings 16:9-24). Commanding several major highways, the hill of Shemer, also known as the hill of Samaria, had natural defenses and was a strategic location for the new capital. The new capital was called Samaria, the same as the regional name, sometimes making the distinction hard to determine when reading the Bible. Samaria was the capital of the northern kingdom for 168 years (880-722 BCE), after which Israel (the ten northern tribes) was taken captive by the Assyrians.

During this time, Samaria was a byword for wealth, luxurious living, cosmopolitanism and idolatry (Isaiah 9:9; Jeremiah 23:13-14; Ezekiel 16:46-55; Amos 3:12, 15; 4:1; 6:1). Here was the pleasure-loving and iniquitous court of King Ahab and his brilliant queen, Jezebel, and here Ahab built a temple to Baal (I Kings 16:32-33). His taste for splendid building projects was indulged by building an ivory house and several cities (I Kings 22:39). Here in the streets of Samaria, the prophet Elijah suddenly appeared before Ahab and proclaimed the vengeance of Jehovah for the apostasy of the king (I Kings 17:1).

Ben-hadad, king of Syria twice besieged Samaria.

Through strategy outlined by a prophet, Ahab succeeded in defeating Syria in the first siege in 863 BCE (I Kings 20). The second siege resulted in a cruel famine, and Elisha's prophecy of plenty was fulfilled miraculously by the flight of the Syrians (II Kings 6:24-7:20). Ahab's family was killed in Samaria by Jehu in 841 BCE. Jehu also destroyed the temple of Baal (II Kings 10:17-28). Samaria was destroyed in 722 BCE by Sargon, king of Assyria, and the ten tribes of the northern kingdom of Israel were deported (II Kings 18:9-10).

In 331 BCE, Alexander the Great stopped by to punish the Samaritans who had murdered his governor appointed for the district. The rebuilt city of Samaria was dismantled by Ptolemy Lagos to prevent revolt, and having been rebuilt again, it was destroyed fifteen years later. The Hasmonean leader, John Hyrcanus, took the city after a siege of one year (129 BCE). During the Roman period, Pompey's successor, Gabinus, rebuilt Samaria and Augustus gave it to King Herod. Herod the Great completely rebuilt Samaria and called it Sebastia in honor of the Roman Emperor Augustus – Sebastos being Greek for Augustus. The name is still retained by the village built over part of the site, today populated by Arabs. Herod's Sebastia was rated one of his most impressive architectural monuments. His huge temple of Augustus was built over an early Baal shrine.

When visiting the site today, you will see the remains from each period of Samaria/Sebastia's active history. Leaving the main highway, we travel to the east and up a steep hill. First, you will see an ancient gate with round towers dating back to the Roman Period. The stones of the threshold still show the marks of the hinges of the heavy doors that at one time locked the gate. On both sides of the gateway stretch the foundations of the rampart which surrounded the city, having been besieged by numerous foes throughout the ages.

After passing through the gateway, you will drive along what used to be the main thoroughfare, traversing the city from west to east. It was a place buzzing with activity and humming with life. You can still see many columns that lined the street which also had shops on each side. Today, this magnificent thoroughfare has become a narrow trail which takes you due east to the modern village of Sebastia. Beside the houses of today's village, stands the Moslem mosque with its minaret built inside a Crusader cathedral dating from about 1160 CE. In the center of the mosque's courtyard, there is a small subterranean cave. In the Middle Ages, the tombs of the prophets Elisha and Obadiah were said to be here. Elisha spent much of his life in Samaria and Obadiah concealed 100 prophets from Jezebel by hiding them in a cave and feeding them bread and water (I Kings 18:4,13). Christian tradition is that the head of John the Baptist was buried in Sebastia, having been requested by the daughter of Herodias, who hated John and tricked Herod Antipas into executing him (Matthew14:1-12; Mark 6:14-29; Luke 9:7-9).

Having arrived at the main part of the ancient city, you can walk around and see much of what was excavated by the combined archeological teams from Harvard University, the Palestine Exploration Fund, the British School of Archaeology and the Hebrew University of Jerusalem. The first building structure is a hall of magnificent workmanship, the ruin of a 3rd century CE Roman basilica, with many pillars and the foundations still visible. Standing at the base of the hill and looking east, you see the hippodrome where the remains of several columns can be distinguished. Close by, the basilica part of the Israelite city wall was uncovered, probably dating from the time of Ahab (870 BCE). Proceeding along a pathway to the summit of the ancient city you see a splendid semicircular tower and a beautifully preserved Roman amphitheater. Then reaching the top of the hill, you see the foundations of several buildings including those of the palace of Omri and Ahab, kings of Israel. There are broad steps built by the side of the ruins near which once stood the huge statue of Emperor Augustus. Many ostraca (broken pieces of pottery [potsherds] with writing on them) were found with Hebrew inscriptions dating from the Israelite Period. The excavations also unearthed various pieces of carved ivory, perhaps the remains of the ivory palace of King Ahab. All of this was destroyed as prophesied by the prophet Amos. He talks of the people who "rest in the mountains of Samaria… that lie upon beds of ivory," and goes on to say, "And he shall bring down thy strength from thee and thy palaces shall be spoiled… and the houses of ivory shall perish and the great houses shall have an end, saith the Lord." (Amos 6:1-4)

Close by these ruins, on the summit, are the remains of an ancient Christian church dating from the Byzantine period.

Valley of Dothan

After leaving Samaria/Sebastia, we will join the main road and wind our way north in the mountains of northern Samaria. You will notice many small Arab agricultural villages on either side of the road. After about 15 miles we will enter the beautiful and fertile Valley of Dothan where we find the site of the ancient city of Dothan.

It was here, that Joseph, wearing his coat of many colors, found his brothers with their flocks. They threw him into a pit and later sold him to the Ishmaelite caravaneers who brought him to Egypt (Genesis 37). "And Joseph went after his brothers and found them in Dothan… and they… sold Joseph to the Ishmaelites… and they brought Joseph into Egypt." In an attempt to seize the prophet Elisha (c. 845 BCE), King Ben-hadad of Syria laid siege to Dothan, surrounding the fortified city with horses, chariots and a great host. Panic-stricken, Elisha's servant informed the prophet who prayed that the Lord would open the young man's eyes. The youth saw the mountain full of horses and chariots of fire around Elisha. As the prophet prayed, the army was smitten with blindness and the prophet led the blinded Syrians from Dothan to Samaria where he commanded King Joram to give them provisions and send them home to King Ben-hadad (II Kings 6:11-23). The city of Dothan evidenced continuous occupation from 3000 BCE to 300 CE.

The Valley of Dothan was also the site of one of the most crucial battles of the Six-Day War in 1967 between Israel and Jordan. A monument on the east side of the road immortalizes Israel's victory.

We will continue on this road to the north into the Jezreel Valley passing through the Arab town of Jenin, probably the site of ancient Ein Gannim, Spring of the Gardens, of Biblical times.

Jezreel Valley

As we pass into the Jezreel Valley, you will immediately notice the vastness of this broad, fertile plain. Historically, the Jezreel Valley was the name of a smaller portion of this bigger valley lying on the north side of the city of Jezreel between Mount Gilboa and the Hill of Moreh. The name eventually extended to the whole plain (Joshua 17:16; Judges 6:33; Hosea 1:5).

Actually, the plain is known by several other names depending on the Biblical or historical reference: Plain of Esdraelon, the Greek modification of the name Jezreel (God sows); the Valley of Megiddo, named after the city of Megiddo located on the southern border of this valley; and Armageddon, the location of the last battle in which God intervenes, "They go forth unto the kings of the earth and of the whole world to gather them to the battle of the great Day of God Almighty… And He gathered them together unto a place called in the Hebrew tongue Har Mageddon" (Revelation 16:16). Har Mageddon literally means hill or city of Megiddo.

The Jezreel Valley is a large plain about twenty miles long and fourteen miles wide. It is famous for its fertility due to soil washed down from the neighboring mountains of Galilee and the highlands of Samaria. The valley is ringed by mountains and shaped like an arrowhead pointing northwest directly to the Mediterranean Sea and Haifa. This arrowhead-shaped valley also has a shaft which is a long, narrow valley called the Harod Valley. The Harod Valley originates below sea-level in the Jordan Valley by the ancient/modern city of Beit-She'an and passes northwest where it connects with the "arrowhead" near the ancient city of Jezreel.

The Jezreel Valley is drained by the Kishon River into the Mediterranean Sea, and the Harod Valley is drained by the Brook of Harod which empties into the Jordan River. Historically, much of the runoff water was trapped in both of these valleys, creating marshes. These marshes were also caused by the presence of natural springs. Today, this excess water has been channeled into ponds for the production of freshwater fish and water storage for watering crops. Biblically, we find the rivers and marshes playing particular roles in some of the battles reounted in the Hebrew scriptures. For example, the River Kishon was used in the battle of the Israelites, led by the prophetess Deborah and Barak against the army of Jabin, king of Canaan. The Israelites won because God intervened and caused a great rain to swell the river Kishon, entrapping the enemy in the mud (Judges 4). We also find that after Elijah and the Lord defeated the prophets of Baal at Mount Carmel, he had them taken down to the river Kishon and executed (I Kings 18:40).

The Jezreel Valley was always a target of the ancient world's mightiest. The main trade routes – north and south, east and west – had to pass through this valley. Therefore, to control the Jezreel Valley was to control world trade and commerce and it has always been either the warpath or the battlefield of empires.

There are five main entrances to the Jezreel Valley, each guarded by a fortress-city:

1. the pass from the Mediterranean at the point of the arrowhead was guarded by Haroshet Hagoiim through which Sisera entered (Judges 4:13).

2. the main southern pass from the coastal plain and Egypt, used by Egyptians and Philistines, was controlled by the most efficient fortress-city, Megiddo.

3. the pass from Samaria at the tip of the southern "wing" of the arrowhead was guarded by the city of Jezreel.

4. the Harod Valley, the main pass from Gilead and peoples of the east (Midianites, Ishmaelites, Amalakites, etc.) was guarded by Beit-She'an where the Harod Valley joins the Jordan Valley.

5. the pass from the Sea of Galilee used by the kings of the north (Syrians, Assyrians, Babylonians, etc.) was guarded by an ever-present fortress on Mount Tabor. The occupation levels of these fortresses and cities mark the cavalcade of history which made this plain the classic battleground of Scripture.

Initially, these important fortress cities, Jezreel, Megiddo, and Beit She'an, were built by Canaanite chariot kings to guard incursions into the plain, as well as other parts of the land. Here in about 2350 BCE, the Egyptian Pepi I landed near Mount Carmel on the sea and looted the cities of this area. The great Egyptian Thutmose III fought the confederate princes of Syria and Canaan in

1468 BCE, conquering the plain. Here also, the conquering Israelites faced the Canaanite kings in about 1290 BCE. Near the city of Jezreel, Gideon faced the Midianites (Judges 7), and later, King Saul was slain by the Philistines (I Samuel 31:1-3).

Jezreel (The City)

Ein Harod — Spring Of Gideon

I. Geographical Overview

The ancient tel of the city of Jezreel commands a breathtaking view of the valleys below. The location of Jezreel is near the junction of the entire Jezreel Valley (the arrowhead) and the Harod Valley (the shaft). It is easy to see how a fortress city in this location could protect and control the area.

Standing in the city you can see many geographical points that relate to many Biblical events. To your left (northwest) you are looking directly across the length of the Jezreel Valley – Armageddon, toward the spear point. Directly in front of you is the original Jezreel Valley from which the whole plain gets its name. To your right (southeast), is the Harod Valley, the long, narrow valley that passes below sea level to the Jordan Valley and the city of Beit-She'an.

The city of Jezreel is located at the base of Mount Gilboa near a spring which gave the city and valley its name. Jezreel means "God sows." Behind you and over your right shoulder you can see Mount Gilboa. Looking north, across the valley in front of you, is the Hill of Moreh.

At the base of the Hill of Moreh you can see the modern Arab village of Sulem, which is the site of the ancient Biblical town of Shunem. There is also a modern Jewish kibbutz called Merhavya, a name taken from Psalm 118:5, "I called upon the Lord in distress, the Lord answered me, and set me in a large place (merhav ya)… ." Shunem was the site for the mustering of the Philistines to fight against King Saul who had the Israelite army by Mount Gilboa (I Samuel 28:4). Shunem was the home of the beautiful Abishag, nurse of David in his old age (I Kings 1:3). The prophet Elisha stayed in the house of a wealthy woman whenever he came to Shunem. The family even constructed a special room on the roof for the man of God, furnished with articles customary for Israelite notables: a bed, table, chair and a lamp. In reward, Elisha promised that she would have a son. When the child had grown, while in the field among the reapers, he died of a sunstroke. The Shunemite woman hurried to Mount Carmel to bring Elisha, who, stretching himself upon the lad, restored him to life (II Kings 4:8-37).

To your right (southeast), along the base of Mount Gilboa, is the location of Ein Harod, the Spring of Gideon, about two miles away, while directly below and closer to Jezreel is the location of the vineyard of Naboth, coveted by King Ahab. Now that we have an orientation for this area, we will review the very exciting Biblical history of this location. Please refer to your maps and Bible Atlas.

II. Biblical and Historical Significance

The location of the city of Jezreel was chosen some distance above the marshes of the plain below. The Canaanites, with their chariots of iron, lived here (Joshua 17:16). Following the conquest under Joshua, Jezreel was included in the territory of the tribe of Issachar (Joshua 19:18).

A. The Period of the Judges (1303-1200 BCE) and Ein Harod

In the period of the Judges, the Midianites and Amalekites had completely overrun the plain of Jezreel (Judges 6:33), which led to battle for control of the territory between the Midianites and Israel, under the leadership of Gideon (c. 1170 BCE).

At the foot of Mount Gilboa, several miles to the east of Jezreel, flows the spring of Harod (Ein is spring in Hebrew). After Gideon had laid his fleeces before the Lord to make sure he was to go into battle against the Midianites, he and his 32,000 soldiers encamped at Ein Harod while the camel-riding Midianites mustered in the plain by the Hill of Moreh across the valley to the north. The Lord was concerned about the number of soldiers in Gideon's army and said to Gideon, "The people who are with thee are too many for me to give the Midianites into their hands, lest Israel vaunt themselves against me saying, 'mine own hand has saved me.'" So, at the Lord's command, Gideon dismissed a fearful 22,000 men who returned home. The remaining 10,000 he brought down to the spring to drink. The posture of drinking revealed the Lord's choice: those who lapped water from their hands were to be separated from those who bowed down on their knees to drink. Those lapping would go into battle. Only 300 did so and these were the ones the Lord chose to go into battle and confront 135,000 Midianites. The battle was the Lord's; the blast of the war-trumpets, the smashing of the pitchers, the flash of the blazing torches by the 300 Israelites shattered the night's stillness, and shocked the Midianites into panic, killing their own... right in their own camp. The Midianites retreated eastward through the Harod Valley, and the Israelites pursued them all the way across the Jordan River. God wanted everyone to know, including the Israelites, that he was their protector and sustainer ... the God of Israel. Gideon also made this fact clear to his own people when they asked him to rule over them. "And Gideon said unto them, I will not rule over you, neither shall my son rule over you, the Lord shall rule over you." (Judges 8:23).

The period of the book of Judges was a time when the

Lord groomed his people through blessing and chastisement. He always raised up a judge to help when the people had sinned, felt God's chastisement and cried out to him for mercy. Each judge illustrates, both physically and spiritually, a different character and style as God moved during this period of growth in Israel's history. It is comforting to see God's covenant-keeping faithfulness, love and power in the face of the repeated theme: "Israel again did evil in the sight of God." As we come to places of spiritual dryness after times when "every man did what was right in his own sight," it is good to know the God of the Judges is still forgiving and showing mercy to his people today if we will also repent and come before his throne of grace.

B. The Period of the Kings (1030–931 BCE)

In the time of King Saul, the Philistines intended to cut off the regions of Judah and Samaria from the plain of Jezreel and Galilee and thus control the entire region through which passed the Via Maris, The Way of the Sea — the main trade route of the ancient world. Thus the Philistines would effectively control world trade and commerce and be on their way to subjugating and possibly forcing the Israelites out of the land given to them by God. There was a constant series of attacks and counter-attacks between the armies of Israel and the Philistines throughout Saul's reign. The final battle of Saul with the Philistines (c.1010 BCE) took place in the plain of Jezreel at the foot of Mount Gilboa. Incidentally, this is the same battle area where Gideon fought the Midianites 160 years earlier.

With the Philistines encamped at Shunem, the town at the foot of the Hill of Moreh on the north side of the valley, Saul gathered all Israel together and mustered at the foot of Mount Gilboa near Jezreel. From the heights of Mount Gilboa, King Saul could see across the valley the hosts of the Philistines encamped at Shunem, and "he was afraid, and his heart greatly trembled." In desperation, because "the Lord did not answer him, either by dreams, or by Urim, or by prophets," Saul determined to seek out a spiritual medium (a witch). Hearing that there was a medium, a witch, among the numerous caves in the hillside of the Hill of Moreh at En-Dor, Saul disguised himself, crossed the eight miles of terrain to the north side of the Hill of Moreh at night so as not to be seen by the Philistines. He begged the witch of En-Dor to divine for him a spirit to communicate with the prophet Samuel. The communication was made and Saul was told that the Lord had taken the kingdom of Israel away from him and he was no longer anointed because he did not obey the Lord. He was also told that the battle with the Philistines would be lost by Israel and that Saul and his sons would be killed. Shattered by the experience and information, Saul returned to the Israelite camp to face his fatal battle the next day on the slopes of Mount Gilboa (I Samuel

28).

On the following day, the battle was lost; Saul's sons Jonathan, Abinadab and Malkhishua were killed; and Saul killed himself rather than fall at the hands of the Philistines. When the Philistines found their bodies, they cut off Saul's head and paraded it through the Philistine cities, ultimately fastening his head in the temple of the pagan god Dagon; took his armor and put it in the house of the pagan god Ashtaroth; and hung Saul's headless body and the bodies of his three sons on the wall of the city of Beit-She'an for all to see. When the Israelites heard this, they retrieved the bodies by night, cremated them and buried the bones under an oak tree at Jabesh (across the Jordan), then fasted seven days. "So Saul died for his transgression which he committed against the Lord, even against the Word of the Lord, which he kept not, and also for asking counsel of one that had a familiar spirit, to inquire of it; and inquired not of the Lord; therefore he slew him and turned the kingdom unto David, the son of Jesse" (I Samuel 31, I Chronicles 10).

During the reign of King Solomon (970-931 BCE), Jezreel was one of the cities in the Fifth Administrative District under the authority of Baana, the son of Ahilud, one of his twelve princes (I Kings 4:12).

During the reign of King Ahab (874-853 BCE), he had a winter palace in Jezreel, overlooking the valley below. The climate is much warmer at Jezreel and he held court there away from the cold climate in the mountains of central Samaria, in the capital city of Samaria. There was also a temple of Baal and other pagan gods at Jezreel.

Elijah was no stranger to Jezreel. Because Ahab had built houses of worship to the pagan god Baal, this provoked the God of Israel who sent Elijah to proclaim to Ahab that there would be a prolonged drought. After three years of drought and the death of many of God's prophets at the hand of Ahab's wife Jezebel, Elijah challenged Ahab and the prophets of Baal on Mount Carmel. God was victorious, Elijah had the prophets of Baal executed at the river Kishon and then God sent rain. Elijah told Ahab to take his chariot and hurry home to Jezreel and then Elijah ran faster than Ahab's chariot to the gates of Jezreel where Ahab told Jezebel what Elijah had done (I Kings 17:1; 18:17-19).

At another time (c. 854 BCE), when Ahab and Jezebel were residing in Jezreel, Ahab coveted the vineyard of Naboth which was close by the royal palace. Ahab tried to buy the vineyard, but Naboth would not sell. Ahab was so disappointed by this that Jezebel plotted the death of Naboth through false accusation. With Naboth dead, Ahab took the vineyard for himself. As Ahab was going down to take possession of his new vineyard, he confronted by Elijah who prophesied doom over the house of Ahab for this act. Included in the prophesy against Ahab were the following, "in the place where dogs licked the blood of Naboth, shall dogs lick thy blood...I (the Lord) will bring evil upon thee, and will take away thy posterity and will cut off from Ahab every male...and of Jezebel, the dogs shall eat Jezebel by the wall of Jezreel." Ahab repented in sackcloth and ashes and the Lord showed mercy and said, "Because he humbled himself before me, I will not bring evil in his day; but in his son's days will I bring evil upon his house" (I Kings 21). About a year later, in 853 BCE, Ahab and Jehoshaphat, King of Judah went into battle against the Syrians. Ahab was killed by an arrow due to the great loss of blood which "ran out of the wound into the inside of the chariot." He was taken to the city of Samaria to be buried and "the dogs licked up his blood...according to the word of the Lord" (I Kings 22:29-39; II Chronicles 18:28-34).

In 841 BCE, twelve years later, Elisha sent a prophet with a message from the Lord to Jehu, son of Jehoshaphat. Jehu was anointed king over Israel and told to smite the whole house of Ahab including every male (Ahab's sons were still ruling Israel), "and the dogs shall eat Jezebel in the portion of Jezreel, and there shall be none to bury her." Jehu went to Jezreel to carry out the judgment of the Lord, which was the result of the prophecy of the Lord by Elijah against the house of Ahab for the wanton murder of Naboth so many years before, and for the death of so many of God's prophets at the hand of Jezebel (II Kings 9:1-13).

Jehoram, king of Israel (Ahab's son), was killed by Jehu's arrow in the vineyard that had once belonged to Naboth. He also killed Ahaziah, king of Judah, who was visiting King Jehoram in Jezreel at the time (II Kings 9:14-29).

Jehu then rode his chariot through the gates of Jezreel and ordered Jezebel to be thrown from her chamber window to the ground. As a result, "her blood sprinkled on the wall," and Jehu ran over her with his chariot. He then went into the palace to eat and drink and later told men to go and bury Jezebel. When they went to her, "they found no more of her than the skull, and the feet, and the palms of her hands." When Jehu was informed of this, he said, "This is the word of the Lord He spoke by his servant, Elijah the Tishbite, saying, 'In the portion of Jezreel shall dogs eat the flesh of Jezebel'" (II Kings 9:30-37).

Jehu had 70 of Ahab's sons killed wherever they were found in Israel and their heads sent in baskets to Jezreel. He had the heads piled in two heaps at the entrance gate of the city until the next morning. Jehu then killed all of Ahab's remaining family in Jezreel (II Kings 10:1-11).

Jehu's lust to kill was not satisfied. He proceeded to the

city of Samaria where he first met the relatives of King Ahaziah of Judah. He captured them in the pit of the shearing house and had them killed (II Kings 10:12-14). Then he took his chariot up into the city of Samaria and killed all that remained of the house of Ahab. "Thus Jehu destroyed Baal out of Israel" (II Kings 10:18-28).

It seems that the Lord was not pleased by Jehu's lust to kill even though the house of Ahab deserved judgment. Hosea foretells divine vengeance upon the house of Jehu for his slaughters, especially those at Jezreel (Hosea 1).

Mount Tabor

Possible Site of the Mount of Transfiguration

I. Background

Mount Tabor is located at the northeastern tip of the north wing of the arrowhead-shaped Jezreel Valley. It is six miles east of Nazareth and about four miles northeast of the Hill of Moreh, creating a valley between them which is one of the main passes into the Jezreel Valley from the northeast. Mount Tabor was the boundary pivot between three of the tribes of Israel: Zebulun to the west, Issachar to the south and Naphtali to the north.

The mountain is conical and quite symmetrical in shape. It literally rises alone out of the floor of the surrounding plain 1,350 feet to an altitude of 1,843 feet above sea level. The mountain is hard limestone and is covered with vegetation. Mount Tabor grows a great variety of trees and bushes. Deserving special notice is a species of oak named the Tabor Oak. In the spring, the mountainsides are covered with a colorful carpet of wild plants and flowers. Wild barley, called Tabor barley, is commonly found among them.

The ascent to the top of the mountain is made up the west side, passing through the Biblical village of Daberath, mentioned in Joshua 19:12 as a town in Zebulun. Today, Daberath is an Arab village called Daburiya. From this point the road becomes a series of sharp hairpin turns climbing the steep side of the mountain to the summit. From the summit, there is a magnificent vista of the surrounding landscape. To the west you see the expanse of the Jezreel Valley and its prosperous settlements and agriculture. To the south are the Mountains of Samaria extending before you from Mount Gilboa on the east (left) to Mount Carmel on the west (right). To the east can be seen the Jordan Valley and the mountains of Gilead (Transjordan). To the north are the mountains of Galilee, with the Sea (Lake Kinneret) glimpsed between them. Crowning all, rises the majestic Mount Hermon far to the north, recalling the song of the Psalmist praising the majesty of the Lord, God of Hosts, "The north and the south, thou hast created them; Tabor and Hermon shall rejoice in Thy name" (Psalm 89:12).

I. Biblical and Historical Significance

A. History from the Hebrew Scriptures

Mount Tabor holds great Biblical and historical interest. It has always been the point of protection, guarding the northeast entrance into the Jezreel Valley and the land of Canaan to the south. Fortresses from every period, from Canaanite to today, are evidenced either on or near Mount Tabor. Because of its prominence, the summit of Mount Tabor was the place where the Canaanites erected altars to their pagan gods. Even in the days of the prophet Hosea (8th Century BCE), he upbraids the people for building altars to heathen gods, "Hear ye this, O priests and harken house of Israel, because you have been a snare on Mizpah and a net spread upon Tabor... " (Hosea 5:1).

We know from II Chronicles 6:72-77 that Daberath and its pastures, and Tabor and its pastures were given to the priests and Levites as Levitical cities, indicating the presence of a city on the summit of Mount Tabor.

In the early period of the Judges (c. 1200 BCE), the Jezreel Valley fell into the hands of Jabin, king of the Canaanites who reigned in Hazor, the main city of the Hulah Valley north of the Sea of Galilee. The entire region from the Mediterranean to the Jordan Valley was controlled by the Canaanite army under the leadership of Sisera who was based in Haroseth Hagoiim at the point of the arrowhead-shaped Jezreel Valley. This Canaanite oppression effectively cut off the northern tribes of Zebulun and Naphtali from the southern tribes of Manasseh, Ephraim, Benjamin and Judah while paralyzing the tribal area of Issachar, in which the Canaanites took control, and Asher on the coast.

This oppression by the Canaanites was allowed by God because "the children of Israel again did evil in the sight of the Lord." After twenty years of this, they repented, cried out to God and he sent the prophetess Deborah to end the Canaanite occupation. Deborah lived "under the palm tree of Deborah, between Raman and Bethel in Mount Ephraim, and the children of Israel came up to her for judgment." (Judges 4:5)

Deborah called her military leader, Barak, to meet her. He lived in Kedesh of Naphtali, in the mountains of Galilee. Barak assembled 10,000 men and proceeded to the place of muster on the slopes of Mount Tabor. Beneath them they watched the lengthening line of Sisera's 900 chariots stretching out toward Megiddo and Taanach on the other side of the Jezreel Valley. At Deborah's command, as guided by the Lord, she told Barak, "Up; for this is the day in which the Lord has delivered Sisera into your hand." In a fierce charge, Barak's men rushed into the valley. Simultaneous with the charge, a storm broke, like an attack from heaven and a miraculous intervention from the Lord. Slaughter was mingled with drowning as the bogged-down chariots were caught in a flash flood of the Kishon River.

Sisera jumped from his chariot and fled eastward past Tabor toward the Sea of Galilee, first stopping at Meroz, and then to the tent of Heber the Kenite. Meanwhile, the Canaanite army fled westward toward Harosheth where Barak and his men caught up with them "and the host of Sisera fell upon the edge of the sword; and there was not a man left."

Barak pursued Sisera and came to the tent of Heber where Jael, Heber's wife, came out to meet him. Sisera lay down to rest and, as he slept, Jael drove a tent peg through his temples, fastening his head to the ground. When Barak arrived, Jael displayed the enemy – dead on the ground.

In her song of victory, Deborah summons chiefs and travelers to praise God for His victory through his people. The inhabitants of Meroz, who allowed Sisera to escape, earned Deborah's curse and Jael received a blessing for her deed. This story is found in Judges 4 and 5.

B. History from the Christian Scriptures

Mount Tabor is also known as the Mount of Transfiguration because it is the traditional site for the Transfiguration of Jesus, although some scholars place this event on Mount Hermon, far to the north. "And after six days, Jesus took Peter, James and John his brother and brought them up into a high mountain apart and was transfigured before them, and his face did shine as the sun and his raiment was white as the light. And behold, there appeared unto them Moses and Elijah talking with him. Then answered Peter, and said to Jesus, 'Lord, it is good for us to be here; if you will let us make three booths; one for you, and one for Moses and one for Elijah.' While he yet spoke, behold, a bright cloud overshadowed them, and, behold, a voice out of the cloud, which said, 'This is my beloved son, in whom I am well pleased; hear ye him.' And when the disciples heard it, they fell on their faces, and were very much afraid. And Jesus came and touched them, and said, 'Arise, and be not afraid.' And when they lifted up their eyes, they saw no man except Jesus only." (Matthew17:1-13; Mark 9:2-13; Luke 9:28-36).

During the First Jewish Revolt against the Roman Empire (66- 70 CE), Josephus fortified the top of Mount Tabor, providing material and water from below, since no water except rain water existed on the summit of the mountain. The insurgent Jews took refuge there, and the Roman Vespasian sent Placidus and 600 horsemen to remove them. Placidus could not ascend the mountain, so he invited the Jews to make peace, planning to take them captive when they came down off the mountaintop. The Jews agreed, planning to take Placidus when they were within reach. When the fight began, Placidus pre-

tended to be fleeing, drawing them further into the plain. Placidus finally encircled the Jews, cut them off from a retreat to the mountaintop, and killed many of them. Those that remained fled to Jerusalem, giving up the area to the Romans. (Josephus, *The Wars of the Jews*, Book 4, Chapter 1, Section 8.) These fortifications can still be found on the summit of Mount Tabor.

Apparently, Mount Tabor remained an outpost until the Christian Church began to grow in strength and position. The belief that Mount Tabor was the Mount of Transfiguration made it the focus of those on pilgrimage to the Holy Land. We find the remains of numerous churches dating as far back as the Byzantines in the 6th century CE and the Crusaders of the 12th century. Today, it is still considered the Transfiguration site and there are two churches on the summit to commemorate this event.

III. Present–Day Structures on the Summit

The Basilica on the summit of Mount Tabor belongs to the Franciscans – the Custodians of the Holy Land. It was erected between 1921-23 on the remains of older churches of the Byzantines of the 6th century and of the Crusaders of the 12th century. The ancient parts are incorporated in the new construction.

The Greek Orthodox Church stands close to the Franciscan basilica. It was built in 1911 next to the Cave of Melchizedek, king of Salem, who welcomed Abraham on his return from war (Genesis 14:18). According to legend, this cave was the site of their meeting. Most scholars agree that the meeting took place in Salem (Jerusalem), not on Tabor.

The remains of structures from every period of habitation can be found on the summit of Tabor, e.g., Canaanite altars to their pagan gods, fortresses of the Canaanites, Israelites, Jews from the First Jewish Revolt and the Crusaders. On driving into the present-day complex of buildings on the summit, you pass through a Crusader arch, left from the 12th century CE. We know of the presence of church buildings on this location since the Byzantines of the 6th century CE.

Mount Tabor is a very interesting and beautiful place to visit. There is no doubt that future excavations on this site will reveal even more of the exciting history of this mountain.

Nazareth

Located in the hills of Galilee, about 1,230 feet above sea level, the home town of Jesus, Mary and Joseph is today home to Israel's largest Arab Christian community. The only Jewish population lives in a newer suburb called Nazareth Ilit – Upper Nazareth.

The town is not mentioned in the Hebrew scriptures but archaeologists have found evidence of settlements in the area from the middle Bronze Age. It is located in the tribal area of Zebulun. The name Nazareth is probably related to the Hebrew word meaning "to blossom or flower." The modern Hebrew word for Christian is "Notzrim."

Nazareth was destroyed by the Romans during the Jewish Revolt. After the collapse of Bar Kokhba's rebellion in 132-135 CE, the town became home to many Jewish refugees from Judea. Some of the Jews sided with the invading Persians in 614 BCE and were therefore expelled when the Byzantines came to power again. Nazareth's Christian shrines were identified and the first churches built here during Constantine's time. The Moslems destroyed the city but the churches were rebuilt by the Crusaders. Sultan Beybars destroyed the city completely in 1263 CE and it lay desolate for about 400 years. Under the rule of the tolerant Druse the Franciscans returned and began to rebuild. It was briefly controlled by Napoleon's troops in 1799 and later reclaimed by the Turks. Nazareth was the German headquarters for Palestine before World War II. It surrendered to the British in 1918. Nazareth fell to the Israelis two months after Independence.

Today it is a busy tourist center with many industries such as an auto assembly plant and textile and furniture manufacture – apparently there are still carpenters in Nazareth. There are over 40 churches, convents, monasteries, orphanages and parochial schools in the town where Jesus spent his first thirty years. However in recent years many Arab Christians have been leaving traditionally Christian areas because of unrest, primarily due to Muslim pressure.

As with most holy sites and the Holy Land, there are two churches of the Annunciation – the place where the Archangel Gabriel appeared to Mary to announce the birth of the Messiah. The Greek Orthodox Church is Nazareth's oldest church, the original church was built in Constantine's time over a spring which feeds Mary's Well nearby. The present church is over 300 years old. The Basilica of the Annunciation is the largest church in the Middle East and was built by the Franciscan Friars between 1955-65. The church features art from many different Christian communities and painting and mosaics depicting Mary as perceived by Christians in different lands.

In the market area there is a Greek Catholic Church called the Old Synagogue which some believe to be the place where Jesus preached his first recorded sermon in Luke 4:16. It is a nice place to stop and read Luke 4, but remember, the current building is no older than Crusader times. Another well-known site is the Mount of Precipitation southeast of the city. Local myths have grown up around the story in Luke 4:28-30 which recounts the residents trying to throw Jesus off the cliff after he had applied the Isaiah scripture to himself. Today many think Jesus made his escape by leaping from mountain to mountain but the Bible simply says he walked right through the crowd and went on his way.

Nazareth was not a prestigious address according to Nathanael who said, "Can any good come out of Nazareth?" (John 1:46). However it was the place where God chose to train his son and it reminds us not to despise the day or the place of small things. Certainly Jesus must have sat on the hillside and watched the Roman legions march back and forth through the Megiddo pass. He grew up knowing what happens to those who do not choose to serve the kingdoms of this world. He would have seen crucifixions long before he went up to Jerusalem. Yet he continued to choose to do "that which he saw his Father doing."

References:

- Annunciation by Gabriel – Isa. 7:14; Luke 1:26-38; Matthew 1:18-25

- Joseph and Mary leave for Bethlehem – Luke 2:1-7

- Joseph, Mary and Jesus return from Egypt – Matthew 2:21-23

- Jesus' childhood home – Matthew 2:23; Luke 2:39, 51-52

- First sermon – Luke 4:16-30

- Unbelief in Nazareth – Matthew 13:53-58; Mark 6:1-6

Cana

Four miles northeast of Nazareth we find the little town where Jesus, his disciples and his mother, Mary, attended a wedding and Jesus performed his first miracle by turning water into wine. It is interesting that John 2:1 tells us the wedding was on the third day which is Tuesday by Hebrew reckoning. This is the traditional day for Jewish weddings. In the Genesis account of creation, the third day is the first time God looks at his creation and says, "It is good."

Cana was also the home town of Nathanael who questioned whether anything good could come from Nazareth. He became a faithful disciple and was one of the group who met Jesus on the shores of the Sea of Galilee after the resurrection.

Yodfat

About eight miles northeast of Cana are the ruins of a fortress also known as Jotapata or Yotapata or Yodefat. During the great Jewish Revolt against the Romans, in 66-9 CE, the caves in this area sheltered many Jewish freedom fighters. For 47 days the defenders of Yodfat held out against overwhelming odds. About 40,000 Jews may have died in this battle, many preferring suicide to surrender. The commander, Yosef ben Matityahu, surrendered to the Romans. When he was brought to the Roman commander, Vespasian, Yosef predicted that the general would become emperor of Rome. Yosef was spared, sent to Jerusalem to encourage the population there to submit to Rome. He is better known to us as Josephus Flavius, his Roman name. While he was something of a traitor, his contribution to historical understanding is invaluable. Without his books, *The Antiquities of the Jews* and *The Jewish War*, we would know very little about the Second Temple period and the beginning of the Christian era.

Sepphoris

The Hebrew word *tsippori* means bird and this town, three miles northwest of Nazareth, perches like a bird on the top of the mountain. It was the largest and most important city in Galilee during the first four centuries CE. It was a major place of refuge for the Jewish scholars after the destruction of Jerusalem. Rabbi Yehuda Hanasi compiled and edited the Mishna here. There is also a tradition that Mary, the mother of Jesus, was born and grew up here. Archaeologists have uncovered a synagogue mosaic, a Byzantine church and a Crusader basilica. The Crusader forces set out from Sepphoris on their ill-fated journey to the Horns of Hittin where they were soundly defeated by Saladin in a famous battle on July 4, 1187.

Sea of Galilee – Lake Kinneret

I. Background Description

In Scripture, the Sea of Galilee is referred to by four different names: the Sea of Chinnereth (Numbers 34:11; Joshua 12:3; 13:27), the earliest designation named after the walled town on the northwest shore called Chinnereth (Joshua 11:2; 19:35); the Lake of Gennesaret (Luke 5:1), called after the plain of Gennesaret on the northwest shore between the Arbel and Chinnereth (Matthew 14:34, Mark 6:53); the Sea of Tiberias (John 6:1, 21:1), named from the city of Tiberias on the western shore; and the Lake of Galilee (Matthew 4:18, 15:29), a name derived from the region of Galilee where the lake is found. Today, it is referred to as the Sea of Galilee, primarily by Christians; and Lake (yam) Kinneret, primarily by Jews. Both names are Biblically derived. The Hebrew name Kinneret means harp-shaped. A legend says: "From all the seas which God created, He chose for him only the Sea of Kinneret. And why is it called Kinneret? Because the voice of its waves is pleasant as the voice of the harp." Kinnor in Hebrew means harp. Others say it is because the shape of the sea resembles that of the harp.

The sea is actually a subtropical, freshwater lake. It is 13 miles long and eight miles wide at its widest point. It is more shallow at its northern end, attaining a depth of 155 feet at its southern end. The sea is 680 feet (212 meters) below sea level which is why the area surrounding the sea is subtropical. The water is blue and sweet, being carried on a steep descent by the River Jordan from the

heights of Mount Hermon over 25 miles away. While the sea looks placid and calm, it is subject to sudden tempests during the winter months, due to the strong winds that blow between the mountains over the sea, and its relatively small size which creates a sloshing effect.

The region immediately surrounding the sea has always been an active center of Galilean life. Both travelers and merchants converged on this area because it was on the main trade route between Damascus and the sea, as well as the Via Maris trade route between Egypt and the empires to the north and east, e.g., Assyria, Babylonia and Syria. It also attracted people because of its fantastic climate, its abundance of fresh water (a scarce commodity in the area) and its industry.

II. The Sea of Galilee at the Time of Jesus

A. Historical Description

At the time of Jesus the area was very active. There were nine cities surrounding the sea, each with a population of not less than fifteen thousand. Multitudes were attracted to the pleasant climate of the area, the fresh water, the hot springs for health reasons and the industries. There was agriculture, fruit growing, dyeing, tanning, import and export trading, and the main sea-based industries of boat-building, fishing and fish curing. The Galilean technique of fishing and fish curing spread far and wide throughout the Roman Empire even before the time of Jesus. The fishing trade provided employment for thousands of families, as there was no monopoly on the fishing grounds which were best at the northern end of the sea where the Jordan streams entered. It was free to all and a very profitable trade.

B. The Ministry of Jesus

The area around the northern half of the sea became the setting for much of the ministry of Jesus and many of his most wonderful miracles took place here. Eighteen of the thirty-three recorded miracles of Jesus were probably performed in the immediate neighborhood of the Sea. In the city of Capernaum alone, ten of his miracles occurred.

Jesus' move from Nazareth to Capernaum signaled a major change in his life (Matthew 4:13; Mark 2:1). Situated in the center of the Galilean fishing industry on the northern shore, Capernaum was the gravitational focus of the region, to which came Nathanael from Cana, near Nazareth; Mary from Magdala, near Tiberias; and Simon and Andrew from Bethsaida, a city just east of Capernaum.

It was in this area that Jesus called his first disciples: Simon Peter, Andrew, the sons of Zebedee, James and John, all fishermen (Matthew 4:18-22; Mark 1:16-20; John 1:35-42). In fact, the family of Zebedee of Capernaum, together with Simon and Andrew of Bethsaida, were associates in a large fishing partnership, employing assistants (Mark 1:20), and owning at least two boats. When Jesus challenged them to "launch out into the deep, and let down your nets for a draught" their catch was so big that the nets began to break and the boats to sink under the weight of so many fish. As a result of this, they realized he was Messiah and followed him to become fishers of men (Luke 5:1-11). It was into the waters by Capernaum that Simon Peter cast his hook and took a fish in whose mouth was a coin. With this coin, he paid the tax for Jesus and himself (Matthew 17:24-27).

It was in this area that Jesus found and called Matthew (Levi), a tax collector at the custom house, which was an important job in this well-traveled area (Matthew 9:9; Mark 2:14; Luke 5:27-29). Jesus also called Philip of Bethsaida, and Nathanael, who was sitting under a fig tree near Bethsaida (John 1:43-51).

In this same northern part of the shoreline, we find an isolated area a short journey from Bethsaida (Mark. 6:45) and from Capernaum (Mark 6:32), there occurred the feeding of the 5000 who had followed Jesus to hear his teachings (Matthew 14:13-21; Mark 6:30-44; Luke 9:10-17; John 6:1-14). The ancient site commemorating this event is called Tabgha. The disciples, departing by boat, encountered a storm during the night. Jesus came to them walking on the water (Matthew 14:22-33; Mark 6:45-52; John 6:15-21). On an earlier occasion, leaving Capernaum, Jesus set sail with his disciples on a longer journey to Gergasa, the eastern shore. While Jesus was asleep, a great tempest arose, and when he awakened, he rebuked both the storm and the sea and all was calm. He asked the disciples, "Why are you fearful, O ye of little faith?" (Matthew 8:23-27; Mark 4:36-41; Luke 8:22-25).

The southeastern shore was part of the Decapolis and identified as the territory of the Gadarenes. Not being Jewish, they owned swine, which are not kosher. Here we have the setting for the healing of the demoniac and the stampede of swine that rushed down the cliff and drowned in the sea (Matthew 8:28-34, Mark 5:1-20; Luke 8:26-39).

Jesus was also on the northwestern shore of the plain of Gennesaret where he healed people from all that country round about, even those who only touched the hem of his garment (Matthew 14:34-36; Mark 6:53-56). The city of Magdala, hometown of Mary Magdalene, was in the plain of Gennesaret, below the Arbel hill.

We know that Jesus "went about all the cities and villages, teaching in their synagogues, and preaching the gospel of the kingdom, and healing every sickness and every disease among the people" (Matthew 9:35).

III. The Sea of Galilee Today

Today the Sea of Galilee is still teeming with activity.

The main city is Tiberias, which has grown beyond its historical limits to cover the surrounding mountainsides. Tiberias has become the center of influence 2,000 years later, replacing Capernaum. Its hot springs are still in use and one of the main attractions for visitors to Tiberias.

Around the sea we find numerous archeological sites of Biblical cities, e.g. Magdala, Chinnereth, Capernaum, Chorazin, Gadara and Hippos, as well as holy sites commemorating Biblical events, e.g., Tabgha, site of distribution of the loaves and fishes to the 5,000; the Church of the Beatitudes; and St. Peter's house and the synagogue at Capernaum.

You can also see modern kibbutzim (collective farms) producing an abundance of fruits such as citrus, bananas, avocados and dates. These kibbutzim are near ancient cities that once inhabited these sites for the same reasons: fresh water and rich land. Some of the larger kibbutzim are: Nof Ginnosar in the plain of Gennesaret at the foot of the Arbel; Ein Gev on the southeast shore, known for its St. Peter's fish; and Degania, located on the southern shore, founded in 1911, and the first kibbutz in Israel. It is also the place where the Syrian tank column was stopped in 1948.

The sea is the major source of fresh water for all of Israel. A national water-carrier system of canals distributes the water as far south as the Negev Desert! The sea is also a great source for water recreation. Swimming across the Sea of Galilee, between Tiberias and Ein Gev, is a relatively new competitive sport. The first crossing was made in 1943. The sea is still an abundant source of fish, particularly the Galilean Comb, or St. Peter's fish, indigenous to this body of water. This would have been the type of fish caught by Peter, thus the name. This very tasty fish is served in the local restaurants (usually with the head still on!). There is domestic farming of fish in ponds created in the marshy areas around the sea and the Jordan River. Israel now boasts the largest variety of farm-grown freshwater fish in the world.

Today, one of the largest industries for the region is tourism. The attraction is the climate, the water, the beauty of the area and its history for both Christians and Jews. It is particularly sought out by Christians on pilgrimage, who want to visit the places where Jesus walked and ministered. The Israeli Government has built a baptismal site at the picturesque spot where the Jordan leaves the Sea of Galilee.

Tiberias

Joshua 19:35 lists Hammat, Rakkat and Chinneret as fortified cities in the tribal area of Naphtali. It is thought that Tiberias, built in approximately 20 CE by Herod Antipas, stands on the ruins of ancient Rakkat. Antipas, son of Herod the Great, is the Herod who executed John the Baptist and was described as "that fox" by Jesus. He apparently continued the family custom of currying favor with the Romans since he named his new city in honor of Emperor Tiberius. It was a Hellenistic city, avoided by observant Jews in the time of Jesus and his followers. Peter lived just a few miles away but probably never visited the place in view of his comment in Acts 10:28. Ironically, Tiberias became the center of Jewish learning after the destruction of Jerusalem. Some of the sages suggest that the name is related to the Hebrew word Tabur which means navel, and it certainly became the seat of Jewish intellectual life. Sometime before the year 220 CE the Jewish scholars of Tiberias wrote the Mishna, the collection of civil and ritual laws, under the direction of Rabbi Yehuda HaNassi. The Jerusalem or Palestinian Talmud was completed here around the year 400 CE. A century later the Babylonian Talmud was completed in the academies of Mesopotamia and it overshadowed the shorter Palestinian Talmud. The use of vowel points and punctuated Hebrew script also originated in Tiberias.

The modern city is a bit north of the hot springs which have made the city a health spa in ancient and recent times. The hot springs, mentioned by historians such as Pliny and Josephus, are probably at the site of biblical Hammat. Recent archaeology has discovered a beautiful mosaic floor depicting the ark of the covenant between two menorahs. It is thought to be from a synagogue of the 4th century CE.

In Byzantine times Tiberias was the seat of a bishop. It fell to the Moslems in 637 CE. Many famous rabbis are buried here including the great philosopher and physician, Maimonides, also called Rambam from the initials of his full name: Rabbi Moshe Ben Maimon. Tiberias was left in ruins following the series of battles fought between the Crusaders and Moslems in the 12th century. When the Turks came to power in the 16th century Suleiman the Magnificent gave the city to Don Joseph Nassi and his mother-in-law, Donna Grazia who encouraged industrial development and restored the Jewish community. In 1837 the city was destroyed by an earthquake and was rebuilt as a Jewish town.

Magdala/Migdal

About four miles north of Tiberias is the home town of Mary Magdalene – Mary from Migdal – a devoted follower of Jesus, out of whom he had cast seven demons. Migdal means tower in Hebrew and was probably an area where a watchtower was placed. When Josephus was governor in Galilee he fortified the city – before he defected to the Romans. Titus defeated the Jewish defenders of Migdal and killed 6,700 of them (Luke 8:2; Mark 16:9).

Plain of Gennesaret

A fertile plain or valley on the northwest corner of the Sea of Galilee, marking the border between Lower and Upper Galilee. (Remember, Galilee is the area, not the lake.) Jesus and his disciples often traveled and ministered in this area. The Hebrew name Ginossar is the name of a prosperous kibbutz which is the home of the "Galilee Boat." This 2,000 year old fishing boat was found during a dry spell in 1986 and was housed for some years in a special tank at the Kibbutz. Recently the Kibbutz has built a modern visitor center with a high-tech museum to display the boat and tell the story. Do include this stop on your travels in Galilee. Nearby is the Kinneret Pumping Station where water from the Sea of Galilee is pumped into a pipe and transported south to water the Negev.

Tabgha

Tabgha is an Arabic contraction of the Greek word Heptapegon which means seven springs. It is the traditional site of the feeding of the 5,000, although Luke 9:10 places the event near Bethsaida, farther to the northeast, near the spot where the Jordan enters the sea. A new church has been built over the 4th century Byzantine mosaic floor. Another traditional site in the area is the Chapel of the Primacy where it is thought that Jesus told Peter that the keys of the kingdom of heaven were to be given to him.

Capernaum

Located on the northwestern shore of Sea of Galilee, in what was the region of Zebulun and Naphtali. (Matthew 4:13-16). Capernaum is not mentioned in the Hebrew Scriptures. The name could mean "the village of Nahum" but this is not necessarily the prophet Nahum. In Jesus' time between 3,000 to 5,000 people lived there, making it one of the largest towns in the area. Industries included a fish market, millstone production and a large salted fish industry. In the Second Temple period the main diet consisted of fish and chicken. (During the First Temple period lamb and beef were major dietary items.) The town was a custom station where Levi, also known as Matthew, sat to collect taxes (Mark 2:14).

All apostles were Galilean except for Judas Iscariot, who came from a town in the south. Peter and Andrew were from Bethsaida; James and John, sons of Zebedee, were from Capernaum. Jesus taught throughout the Galilee and his fame spread. Many sick and crippled who came to him were probably drawn to the local hot springs for a cure.

The house of St. Peter's mother-in-law was Jesus' headquarters and the site of many of his miracles. The house is actually what is known as an insula—an extended family dwelling. Here we see one of 40 rooms, able to house up to 200 relatives! Peter's mother-in-law may have had quite a project on her hands. The center kitchen was open to the sky and there were plenty of storerooms.

This house is the first known house-church in world. Where events happened, people met to worship. There are 134 examples of graffiti in Hebrew, Greek & Aramaic, including Hebrew prayers in the name of Jesus.

Today the Franciscans who control the site have built a modern church over the traditional site of Peter's mother-in-law's house.

Biblical Significance

1. Roman military post. Matthew 8:5-13

2. Seat of tax collector. Mark 2:1,4

3. Jesus made his headquarters here and referred to it as his own city. Matthew 4:13; 9:1

4. Jesus performed many miracles here:

   – Centurion's palsied servant - Matthew 8:5-13

   – Peter's mother-in-law - Matthew 8:14-17, Mark 1:29

   – Man sick with palsy - Mark 2:1-13

   – Man with withered hand - Mark 3:1-6

   – Nobleman's son - John 4:46-54

   – Many diseased and demon possessed people. Matthew 9:9-13

5. Other significant events.

   – Jesus preached on Bread of Life, John 6:24-71 (Possibly in synagogue)

   – Matthew/Levi called to discipleship, Matthew 9:9-13

   – Jesus predicted terrible judgment on Capernaum, Matthew 11:23-24

Mount of Beatitudes

No one knows with certainty where Jesus spoke the Sermon on the Mount. It is quite possible that this was a message that he gave many times in different ways. However, the traditional Mount of Beatitudes may well be one site where he spoke. Next to the Franciscan chapel is a hillside sloping down to the sea which forms a natural amphitheater. This is a lovely spot to stop and read the Beatitudes while sitting on the hillside, listening to the bleating of the neighboring sheep in the background. The octagonal chapel is attractive if you overlook the fact that it was paid for by the Italian dictator Mussolini in 1937. Lovely architecture built by nasty dictators has been characteristic of the Holy Land since the days of Herod. This peaceful garden, overlooking the Sea of Galilee is a great place to pause and meditate on what it means to be among the "blessed." The verses of Matthew 5 through 7 take on special meaning here.

Korazin & Bethsaida

In Matthew 11:20-24 Jesus pronounces a curse on three of the cities on the shores of the Sea of Galilee. Capernaum, Bethsaida and Korazin are told that if the miracles they had seen were performed in Sodom or Tyre and Sidon those cities would have repented in sackcloth and ashes. None of these cities are alive and functioning today. Korazin is about 3 miles north of Capernaum. It was a Jewish town until the Talmudic era and one can see ruins of a 3rd or 4th century synagogue. Ancient Korazim spread over 25 acres and was partitioned into five sections with a synagogue in the middle. It is mentioned in the Talmud and was famous for its grain.

The site of biblical Bethsaida is somewhat uncertain. It is thought to be at Tel Beit Zaida, about a mile and a half north of the point where the Jordan enters the Sea of Galilee. Bethsaida was the birthplace of Peter, Andrew and Philip, (John 1:44; 12:21-22) and the place where Jesus healed a blind man (Mark 8:22-26).

Kursi or Gergesa

Luke tells us that Jesus sailed across the Sea of Galilee to the region of the Gergesenes. There he met a demon-possessed man who lived among the tombs and often broke his chains and injured himself. Jesus cast out the demons and sent them into a neighboring herd of swine. The pigs rushed down the steep hill and drowned in the sea. This site has the features described in the biblical account and a large Byzantine convent has been discovered here. As you climb the hillside and look back toward the sea you can easily visualize the events of Luke 8:26-39.

Other places of interest near the Sea of Galilee

Ein Gev

Ein Gev was founded in 1937 by German and Czechoslovakian pioneers and was the first settlement on the eastern shore of the sea. It has a large amphitheater where a musical festival draws large crowds during the Passover holiday. Former Jerusalem mayor, Teddy Kollak, was a member of Ein Gev. The restaurant features St. Peter's fish, a tasty white fish which is served with the head still intact so you can make eye contact while eating it.

Hamat Gader

If you have time for a swim, Hamat Gader is worth an hour's stop. It is an ancient Roman hot bath located in the Yarmuk Valley near the borders of Israel, Jordan and Syria. There are five pools, one sweet water and four mineral pools. In addition to the pools, there are picnic areas, archaeological finds and an alligator farm. There is something for everyone.

Golan Heights and Hula Valley

I. Background

The biblical city of Golan was in Bashan, in the tribal area of Manasseh, east of the Jordan River. It was a Levitical city of refuge (Deuteronomy 4:43; Joshua 20:8; I Chronicles 6:71). Today the name Golan is given to the whole territory east and northeast of the sea of Galilee, the mountainous tableland of volcanic rock running northward along the upper Jordan and the Hula Valley as far as the Mountains of Hermon. In ancient times the fertile volcanic soil made the Golan one of the richest farming areas in the Fertile crescent. Biblical Bashan was known for its particular breed of fat cows, great oak forests and fruit orchards. Be sure to try the Golan apples!

The natural boundaries of the Golan are: on the west, the Sea of Galilee and the Jordan River; on the north, the slopes of Mount Hermon; on the south, the Yarmuk River; and on the east, the Rakkad River. The area is 15 to 20 miles wide.

Many ruins of 2nd and 3rd century CE synagogues have been found, testifying to a significant Jewish population in those years. In the early years of modern Jewish settlement in Israel a few settlements were established here but the remoteness and difficulty of transportation and communication kept the area sparsely populated. At the end of World War I the Golan was given to Syria under the French Mandate. The Syrians built fortifications throughout the Golan Heights and used their superior position to keep up constant warfare against the Jewish agricultural settlements, shelling workers in the fields. The Syrian bombardment of Kibbutz Ein Gev was a major cause of the Six Day War in 1967. With great difficulty and the loss of many Israeli lives, Israel finally defeated the Syrians and now control the Golan Heights.

The pressure of world opinion is on Israel to return the Golan to Syria. While we certainly believe Jesus' words about the blessing to the peace-makers, we also hope that the decision-makers will remember that Israel occupied this area since the days of Joshua which does pre-date the French Mandate by a few years. Today there are 33 Jewish communities (27 kibbutzim and moshavim, five communal towns, one city) and fourDruse villages on the Golan Heights.

Hula Basin

The Hula basin is located between the southern foothills of Mount Hermon and the Bridge of Jacob's Daughters. It is five miles wide and 15 to 20 miles long. Lake Hula was the most northern, the highest and the smallest of the three bodies of water in the Jordan rift valley. The Jordan flows into the Hula from the north and on to Yam Kinneret (the Sea of Galilee). The Hulah Valley or Hula Valley is an agricultural region in northern Israel with abundant fresh water.

Lake Hulah or Lake Hula (the Biblical Lake Merom) and its surrounding swamps were drained in the 1950s as an attempt to alter the environment to suit agricultural needs. Though initially perceived as a great national achievement for Israel, with time it became evident that the benefits from transforming the "wasteland" of Lake Hula and its swamps were limited. In the past few years, following nearly 50 years of an unsuccessful struggle to utilize the drained valley's resources, the Israeli government has finally recognized that successful development can endure only if a balanced compromise between nature and development is reached. Thus, a small section of the former lake and swamp region was recently reflooded in an attempt to prevent further soil deterioration and to revive the nearly extinct ecosystem.

Gamla

Gamla is often called the "Masada of the North." It is a ruined city situated on a strange mountain ridge shaped like a camel's hump – from which it takes it's name – gamel is camel in Hebrew. During the Jewish Revolt against Rome in 68 CE, Josephus was commander of this area. In his, *Wars of the Jews* he describes the city and tells of its courageous defense and its tragic fall: "From a lofty mountain there descends a rugged spur rising in the middle a hump, the declivity from the summit of which is of the same length before as behind, that in form the ridge resembles a cleft all round by inaccessible ravines, but the tail end, where it hangs on the mountain, is somewhat easier of approach. The inhabitants, by cutting a trench across it, had rendered difficult of access. The houses were built against the steep mountain flank and astonishingly huddled together, one on top of the other, and this perpendicular site gave the city the appearance of being suspended in the air and falling headlong upon itself!..."

Katzrin

Katzrin is a development town and the administrative center of the Golan. The local Field School is a valuable source of information on the area. The local rubble includes Roman chariot wheels, Crusader artifacts and Suleiman's tea cups. The Golan Field School has a wealth of information on the area and is worth a visit if you have time. South of the city a large synagogue from the Talmudic period has been found. Many synagogues have been discovered in the Golan. Some were found in the last century by Sir Lawrence Oliphant, a somewhat eccentric Christian who believed whole-heartedly in Zionism.

Nimrod's Castle

Kalat Nimrud, the Crusader castle said to be named for Nimrod, the son of Cush, grandson of Ham. He is described as "a mighty hunter before the Lord" (Genesis 10:8). Tradition says he challenged God himself and was defeated by a mosquito! During the Moslem era this area was populated by the Ismailiya sect who drugged some of their people with hashish and sent them out on murder missions. They became known as the Hashishin or the assassins. This sect made an agreement with the Crusaders in return for shelter and protection. This fortress was fortified by the Crusaders and later taken over by the Mamlukes led by Beybars. Much of the castle was built in the 1200s and a tunnel system has recently been discovered. The view from the top of the fortress in unique. You can see Mount Hermon to the north and the Huleh Valley to the southeast. The Crusaders used this area as a rest camp and built on the crag above the castle which commanded the approaches to Banyas and the road to Tyre. The castle fell to the Saracens in 1164 CE.

Birket Ram

Beyond Banias the road reaches the southern ridge of the anti-Lebanon range at the Druse village of Mas'ada. On the slopes of Mount Hermon is the large Druse town of Majdal Shams (Tower of the Sun). Just beyond Mas'ada is the mountain lake of Birket Ram (the High Pool) probably a large volcanic crater. Josephus tells the story of Herod Philip who had chaff thrown into the lake believing that it would appear down at Banyas confirming his theory that the lake was the highest source of the Jordan River. His courtiers made sure he was not disappointed by throwing chaff in the river at Banyas.

Tel Dan

Dan marked the northern border of the biblical land of Israel. Joshua assigned the tribe of Dan to the coastal plain south of Jaffa. The Danites were unable to hold their territory against the Philistines and, apparently believing that discretion was the better part of valor, they moved to the extreme north and occupied the Canaanite city-state of Laish (Joshua 19:47).

After the death of Solomon, Jereboam created two rival shrines in his northern kingdom. Dan in the north and Bethel in the south established the religious independence of the northern kingdom from the Temple in Jerusalem.

The saying, "From Dan to Beersheba," I Samuel 3:20, indicated the length of the Land of the Bible. In a later period Dan was a center of idolatry and one of the golden calves stood here. I Kings 12:30 says, "And this thing became a sin , for the people went to worship before the one, even unto Dan." Jeremiah describes the invasion of the enemy from the north – "The snorting of his horses is heard from Dan, at the sound of the neighing of his strong ones, the whole land trembles."

Caesarea Philippi, Banias

Caesarea Philippi is located at the base of Mount Hermon, northeast of the Sea of Galilee. The Greek name Panias probably indicates that the Greek god of forests, meadows and flocks was worshipped here during the Hellenistic period. In 20 BCE Herod the Great built a temple to Pan. The city was rebuilt by Herod's son Philip the Tetrarch and named in honor of Augustus and Philip. The site was called Neronica by Agrippa II. The city was destroyed in 1157 CE by Syrian Muslim forces battling against the Crusaders.

The Hermon River branch of the Jordan rises just north of the town. Matthew 16:13 tells of Jesus' journey to this area on his second trip north. This was the place where Peter made his confession "You are the Messiah, the Son of the living God," and where Jesus predicted his death. The heights of Hermon above Caesarea Philippi is one possible site for the transfiguration.

Jordan River Sources

The melting snow and ice which cover Mount Hermon flow down to form underground springs which then flow out in various places in the foothills of the mountain. There are four main sources of the Jordan:

1. The Banias, fed underground by the lake at Birket Ram, is the eastern source. About 5 1/2 miles long, it springs forth at the base of a large, red limestone cliff at Caesarea Philippi,

2. The Dan, which springs from a fountain near Tel Dan at the foot of Mount Hermon, the shortest but strongest of the four sources,

3. The Snir, also called Hasbani, is the longest source – 24 miles. At one point it parallels the Litani River in Lebanon,

4. The Ayun River, also from Lebanon, enters Israel via the lovely Hatanur waterfall.

Druse Settlements

There are a number of Druse villages in the Mount Hermon area and also some near Haifa. Daliyat el-Karmel, Isfiya, Majdal Shams, Beit Jann, Rama, Bi'na and Mas'ada are some of the main ones. (Do not confuse Mas'ada with Masada, the famous Zealot fortress near the Dead Sea.) The Druse religion is an off-shoot of Islam, dating from the 10th century CE. They believe they are the descendants of Jethro, the father-in-law of Moses. Their beliefs are secret and they have been persecuted by the Muslim establishment. Since the birth of the State of Israel the Israeli Druse have been loyal citizens and have fought in many of Israel's battles. They have their own courts and representatives in the Knesset.

Metulla and Good Fence

Metulla is the border town where, until recently, you could visit the "Good Fence," Israel's gateway to Lebanon and the place where the IDF set up a medical station to help sick and injured Lebanese in the 1980s. The town is 1,722 feet above sea-level and provided visitors with a scenic mountain view as well as a view in the distance of Beaufort Castle, originally a Crusader fortress, more recently a PLO spotting base. Metulla was founded in 1896 with money from the Rothchild family.

Kiryat Shmona

This town of about 18,000 people, six miles from the Lebanon border is named for "the eight"– six men and two women who held the Tel Hai colony against a force of attacking Arabs. The eight, including Joseph Trumpeldor (1880-1920), died here. Trumpeldor, the leader of Revisionist Zionism, is regarded as an Israeli Nathan Hale. He, too, regretted having only one life to give for his country. Kiryat Shmona has been on the receiving end of many katyusha rocket attacks over the years and bomb shelters are a notable feature of the local architecture. But the local residents are stalwart types and new industry is flourishing. However in July of 2006 most of the town had to be evacuated due to bombing from the Hezbolla in Lebanon.

Hazor

As you drive toward Safed you will see the ruins of Hazor, pronounced more like "Hatzor" just across the road from Kibbutz Ayelet Hashahar, a good place to stop for lunch or a snack. Hazor, Megiddo and Gezer were ancient chariot cities of the Israelite kings, Solomon and Ahab. They each guarded an important pass through a strategic valley: the Huleh, the Jezreel and the Ayalon. In the 19th century BCE Hatzor appeared on the list of cities which rebelled against Egyptian rule. In the 14th century the kings of Tyre and Ashtarot complained of the treachery of the King of Hatzor. When Joshua led the Israelites into the land he captured Hazor and burned it. After the defeat of the northern kingdom, Assyria controlled Hazor. Later Jonathan, youngest of the Maccabean brothers, fought here against the generals of the Seleucid king, Demetrius II.

Then Hazor faded from the scene, existing just as a tel, a large mound filled with history awaiting the modern archaeologists and their spades and brushes. Yigal Yadin, famous Israeli archaeologist, brought his team to Hazor in 1955. Hazor and Masada provided the most exciting finds in modern Israeli archaeology. Yadin found strong evidence for the Biblical account in Joshua 11:10-13, the burning of a major Canaanite city by Joshua. In addition to Canaanite temples, Solomon's casemate walls, stone pillars of Israelite store-houses and a myriad of small arti-

facts, the most spectacular find of all was the deep shaft and tunnel built by King Ahab in the 9th century BCE. As you walk down 123 steps of the spiral staircase leading to the tunnel, you will be awestruck by the technological ability of Ahab's builders. This underground water system – the largest of its kind and more than twice the size of the one at Megiddo – was discovered during the summer of 1969. The tunnel is 82 feet long, 13 feet high and 13 feet wide. Twenty-one levels of civilization were uncovered at Hazor, (Joshua 11:1-14; Judges 4; I Kings 9:15; II Kings 15:29.)

Upper Galilee

General Description

Upper Galilee was unexplored territory until the 1930s. The height, vegetation and poor roads made it difficult to visit and more difficult to settle. In centuries past it served as a refuge for various groups: Druse, Christians, Circassians – many of whom came here fleeing each other in their home countries. When the Bible refers to "Galilee of the Nations," this is the territory referred to.

The northern road was built by the British as an entrance into the Galilee. Jewish settlement brought new roads and settlements on the northern border and central Galilee. The draining of Lake Huleh made the area more desirable, at least temporarily. Later it created something of a ecological nightmre and efforts are now under way to recreate the lake. The rocky ridges of the upper Galilee produce dramatic sunsets. The dense cedar forests of the nature reserves provides a home for this areas ancient and exotic wildlife.

Rosh Pinna

Rosh Pinna was established in 1882 on deserted rocky land and was the first settlement in Galilee. The name comes from the words of Psalm 118:22, "The stone which the builders rejected is become the head of the corner." (Rosh Pinna means head of the corner.) Here is the main cross-road to the Golan, Tiberias and the Jordan River bridge.

Safed, S'fad, Sefad, Zefat or Tsefat

The various spellings of the name are not the only confusing things about Safed. This lovely center of mystical Kabbalism presents one with many ideas to sort out. Some of the mystical truths have much to recommend them, some come close to occultism. Let the buyer beware – of ideas as well as merchandise.

Jewish settlement in Safed dates back to the Second Temple period but the Jewish presence has not been continuous. Plundered by the Romans and later the Crusaders, the Jewish community reemerged only in the Middle Ages when refugees from the Spanish Inquisition began to build the synagogues of today's Spanish Quarter. Other mystical sects settled here including Rabbi Isaac Luria (1534-72). His followers refer to him as Ha'Ari, "the Lion." He is known for his teaching on tikkun – restitution of the right order of the universe.

By the late 19th century the town became predominately Arab and was bitterly contested during the 1948 War of Independence. James Michener tells the story in his book, *The Source*. Safed is the highest city in Israel (2,737 feet above sea level) and may be the city Jesus had in mind when he said, "a city set on a hill cannot be hid."

Rosh HaNikra

This is the place where Israel and Lebanon meet, one of the world's most controversial borders. The Lebanese-Palestine border lines were drawn in 1915 by Sir Mark Sykes of Great Britain and the Frenchman, George Picot as part of their secret agreement outlining the dismantling of the Ottoman Empire, to take place after the defeat of Turkey. They drew a line from Rosh Hanikra eastward toward Syria and it has remained the border ever since.

Nikra means crevice or cavern and you will understand why if you take the cable car down to the sea-side caves. The chalk-white limestone cliffs have been carved into natural grottos by centuries of lashing waves. During the British period the caves were enlarged to accommodate a tunnel intended for a train line between Haifa and Beirut. The tunnel is no longer open but the caves and the water are beautiful. Just to the north is the ancient Phoenician city of Tyre and the cliffs at Rosh Hanikra are called the Ladder of Tyre.

Akko

Akko is a 4,000 year old Canaanite and Phoenician port city. It is nine miles north of Haifa and 12 miles south of the Lebanon border in the tribal area of Asher, with a population of about 20,000. It is mentioned in the early Egyptian records in the 18th and 14th centuries BCE. Assyrians conquered it in 701 and 640 BCE, In the 3rd century BCE, under the Greeks, the name was changed to Ptolemais, the name by which it was known in Acts 21:7. It played a role in the history of the Maccabees and Cleopatra of Egypt held it for a time. Herod the Great entertained Caesar in Akko. During the Middle Ages many Jewish pilgrims including Maimonides landed at Akko on their way to Jerusalem. The Crusaders called it St. Jean d'Acre. The huge, subterranean Crusader city lies directly under old Akko. The network of tunnels and rooms built by the Crusaders in the 12th century were too strong for the Turks to destroy so they simply filled it with sand and built on top. The city that survives today was built by an Albanian adventurer, Ahmed, who ousted the previous Bedouin residents and became the Turkish pasha El-Jazzar – the butcher. Napoleon tried to con-

quer it in 1799 but he failed and it was held by the Turks until Allenby's victory in 1918.

A citadel built by the Turks and used as the central prison by the British during the Mandate houses the English hanging room, where members of the Israeli underground forces were put to death. The mosque of El Jezaar is claimed by some to be the largest and most beautiful in Israel. It was built in 1781 on the ruins of the Knights church. The Khan or caravansary is open to visitors. You can walk on the city walls and get a great view of the sea and the city, Joshua 19:24-31; Judges 1:31, Acts 21.

Haifa

Haifa is a modern city, but the area has an ancient history. Relics of stone-age communities have been found on the western seaward slopes of the Carmel. The meaning of the name is uncertain. It may be from Ha'yafah, the beautiful one, which is certainly a accurate description. From the 14th century BCE, Tel Abu Hawam, a small port in the vicinity, flourished until Hellenistic time. By the 3rd century CE Haifa and Shiqmona were established Jewish communities which probably expanded and became one. Haifa was a thriving Jewish center by the 11th and 12th centuries CE, when the local Jews and Moslems joined together in an unsuccessful attempt to fight off the attacking Crusaders. After a period of decline the local ruler Dahr el-Omar destroyed and rebuilt it in the 18th century. In the 19th century the returning Jews brought serious expansion to Haifa. It became a modern port and Herzl called it "The City of the Future." Today it is a major industrial center and home to over a quarter of a million people. It has its own university, theater, museums, symphony orchestra and is home to the Technion – Israel's well-respected institute of technology.

The first section to be built was the lower town by the sea. European immigrants founded Hadar Hacarmel halfway up the mountain. More recent settlers have built farther up the mountain in Har Hacarmel. The various levels are linked by the Carmelit, Israel's only subway. The harbor lies in a wide and well-sheltered bay providing access to ships of many sizes and carrying many flags. An annual seabed cleaning operation keeps the basin clear of the Nile silt washed in by undercurrents of the Mediterranean.

Haifa is in the tribal area of Zebulun and the valley north of Haifa is called Emek Zevulun. The name is not mentioned in the Bible, but many biblical events occurred in this area.

Mount Carmel

Carmel is a range, not just a peak. It stretches for about 16 miles south and west of Haifa. It varies from 470 to 1,790 feet and is noted for its vineyards. The name comes from the Hebrew Karem-El which means Vineyard of God. Two Carmelite monasteries on the mountain commemorate the famous confrontation between Elijah and the 450 prophets of Baal (I Kings 18). Elijah's famous challenge needs to be sounded again for our casual generation: "How long will you waver between two opinions? If the Lord is God, follow him; but if Baal is God, follow him." The prophet Amos spoke of Carmel and Isaiah referred to the "glory of Carmel and Sharon." The Carmelite monastery at Muhraka, the place of burning, is located on the traditional site where Elijah called down fire from heaven. As with most biblical sites in Israel, we do not know with certainty that this is the exact spot but it is very near and the view from the roof of the church gives you a spectacular look at the Jezreel Valley. On a clear day this is one of the best places to get oriented to the geography of the Galilee.

Megiddo

Megiddo is one of the largest archeological tels in Israel. During the 6,000 years of its existence towns have been built and rebuilt leaving layers of history for archeologists to uncover. The tel was excavated by the Oriental Institute of the University of Chicago between 1925 and 1939. It is located about 22 miles north of Shechem and 15 miles southeast of Haifa, on the southern edge of the Valley of Megiddo (II Chronicles 35:22; Zechariah 12:11). One of the most significant finds was the water system, consisting of a vertical shaft 120 feet deep connected by a tunnel 215 feet long to a spring located outside the city walls, built during the mid-9th century BCE to protect the city's water supply in war time.

Historians believe that more battles were fought at this location than anywhere else on earth. The Assyrians, Canaanites, Egyptians, Greeks, Israelites, Persians, Philistines, and Romans all fought major battles in this valley. Megiddo stands near the point of entry into the Jezreel Valley at one of the most important passes through the Carmel range, (Wadi `Ara). It controlled the "Way of the Sea" or Via Maris.

This important highway was the ancient trade route between Egypt and Mesopotamia. Megiddo was mentioned in historical documents over 3,000 years ago. It figures in the lives of some famous biblical characters: its king was among those who fought against Joshua; it was here that the prophetess Deborah overcame Sisera's army; it was one of three chariot cities of kings Solomon and Ahab. It is the site where the Judean kings, Ahaziah and Josiah, fell in battle. In 1918 the British defeated the Turkish forces at Megiddo, and in the 1948 War of Independence the Arab forces who attacked Mishmar Ha'emek were defeated here.

Many Christians believe in a view of biblical prophecy that sees a major place for the valley of Megiddo at the end of the age. This view expects that this valley, also known as the valley of Jezreel, will serve as the gathering place for an immense army which will engage the returning Messiah, Jesus Christ, and his supernatural army in the Day of the Lord (Revelation 1:10; 16:12-16; 19:19; 1 Thessalonians 5:2; Joel 1:15; 2:11, 31).

Christian tradition identifies Megiddo with "Armageddon" or Har Megiddo, the site of the last great battle on earth. Armageddon, the mount of Megiddo, according to the New Testament book of Revelation, is once again to host one of the world's major confrontations between East and West (Revelation 16:16). The idea of Megiddo being the site of humanity's apocalyptic finale, the "final" battle in this war called the "Battle of Armageddon," is probably incorrect. The actual battle is to occur at Jerusalem and called "the war of the great day of God, the Almighty" (Revelation 16:14 NASB) or the "Battle of That Great Day of God Almighty" (KJV).

There are various interpretations of just how this struggle for global dominion will work out. Many expect an alliance of Israel and the western powers to battle against a union of armies, probably Islamic nations and their Eurasian allies, from the East (Revelation 16:12). The setting is a time of warfare where nuclear exchanges between West and East have already occurred. In the aftermath of a surprise nuclear first strike by the West (Revelation 9:1-11), and a nuclear response by the East (Revelation 9:13-21), both sides move major military forces into the Middle East.

The book of Revelation implies that it is Satan's demons, influencing key political and military leaders, who are responsible for inciting this concentration of forces (Revelation 16:13-16). Without the intervention of God, the destruction of all living things would occur, possibly in a final nuclear holocaust and its aftermath (Matthew 24:22).

The valley is a large flat plain ideal for the assembling of military equipment and personnel. Armageddon could serve as the gathering place, a natural staging area about 15 miles from the Mediterranean port and industrial area of Haifa, for the western forces. From this staging area western forces advance southward toward Jerusalem where a horrendous battle will take place. Rather than proceeding east against Islamic forces the leaders of the western forces would turn to the south to bolster their forces at Jerusalem, about 55 miles away, and to engage advancing eastern forces. The armies ultimately clash at Jerusalem.

The focal point of the battle is the Valley of Jehoshaphat (Joel 3:2, 12), also called the Valley of Decision (Joel 3:14) situated between the Old City of Jerusalem and the Mount of Olives, now known as the Kidron Valley. This valley is a deep ravine with very steep sides. Jehoshaphat means "Judgment of YHWH." Here the Messiah and his supernatural force will engage all enemy forces in battle when he returns and stands, just east of the old city, on the Mount of Olives (Zechariah 14:1-4). A description of the battle is given in Revelation 19:11-21. In the figurative language of Revelation, the carnage is to be so great that the blood of the casualties, flowing "without the [old] city" in the Valley of Jehoshaphat, will rise as high as horses' bridles (Revelation 14:20).

We are probably wise to avoid being too specific as to how all this will work out historically. Suffice to know that there has been a battle between the forces of good and evil from time immemorial and we who see God's hand in history can confidently expect good to win out in the end.

Excavations at the site have uncovered over 25 distinct historical periods. Among the findings are the remains of palaces and temples, gates, walls, a grain silo, horse stables and an intricate water system from the 9th century BCE.

Coastal Plain and the Shephelah

General Description

The strip of flat land between the mountains and the Mediterranean Sea is called the Plain of Sharon. The plain is about 8 to 12 miles wide and 30 miles long – from Mount Carmel to Jaffa. King David's herds were pastured here (I Chronicles 27:25,29) and Isaiah spoke of its beauty (Isaiah 35:2, 65:10). Today it is heavily populated with a string of cities, towns and agricultural settlements all along the coast. In biblical times it was a less popular place to settle since it was part of the Via Maris, the "Way of the Sea," where armies marching through presented a real danger to civilians. The highway follows the coast up from Egypt and turns inland to the strategic pass at Megiddo. The Sharon has always been a lovely and fertile area. Today it is famous for its orange groves.

Sites

Ancient Dor

A tel south of Haifa and eight miles north of Caesarea is thought to be the biblical city of Dor. A harbor and remains of a fortress and a Byzantine church have been discovered. King David captured it from the Philistines and Solomon gave it to his son-in-law. It was one of the 12 regions charged with providing the royal household with food for one month each year. It was famous for producing the purple dye known as royal purple. The purple-red color came from a little sac in a mollusk found along the coast. The king of Dor was killed in battle with Joshua, (Joshua 11:2,8; 12:7, 23).

Caesarea

Caesarea is the spectacular Mediterranean port built by Herod the Great. He intended to create a city equal to Athens and he probably achieved his goal. The city was named for Augustus Caesar and statues of the Emperor stood in a huge temple dedicated to him. It became the largest city in Judea, the major port and the official governor's residence. However, Caesarea was not the first city to occupy this site. About 300 BCE a port was constructed here by colonists from Sidon and named after King Sharshan.

The name was later changed to Straton and the town became known as Strato's Tower. About 90 BCE the town was conquered and rebuilt by Alexander Jannaeus, the Hasmonean king of Judea. Rome annexed all of Judea in 63 BCE and the city was much enlarged and embellished during the reign of Herod the Great (37–4 BCE).

Caesarea was the home of Philip the evangelist, and the headquarters of Cornelius, the Roman centurion who became one of the first Gentile converts to Christianity and the place where the Holy Spirit came to the Gentiles (Acts 10-11). The Apostle Paul spent two years in prison here after his arrest in Jerusalem and before his last journey to Rome – in chains. Paul testified here before the Roman governors, Felix and Festus and before Herod Agrippa II and his sister-mistress, Bernice. (Herod Agrippa I died here in a spectacular manner, Acts 12:19-23.)

The Roman occupation brought persecution to both Jews and Christians and many were imprisoned in Caesarea. In 66 CE, according to Josephus, 20,000 Jews were brutally massacred in the Caesarea theater. This led to the Jewish revolt which ended with the destruction of Jerusalem and the seige at Masada. Bar Kokhba's rebellion in 132-135 CE brought more destruction upon the Jews. Nearly 500,000 Jews died throughout the country and many great Jewish scholars, including Rabbi Akiva, were tortured and burned alive in the theater at Caesarea. It was in Caesarea that the victorious Romans minted the famous coin marked "Judaea Capta" – Judea captured. When the modern state of Israel was established they minted a coin inscribed, "Yisrael Hameshuhreret" – Israel Liberated.

The Byzantine Christians headquartered here in the 3rd and 4th centuries CE. The scholar, Origen, established the school of Caesarea, and Eusebius, the church historian, was bishop of Caesarea from 313-340 CE. He was the author of the lexicon of biblical geography known as the Onomastikon. During the 400s Caesarea became the seat of the metropolitan bishop responsible for all the Christian communities of the eastern Mediterranean. A small Jewish community also co-existed here at that time. The

Arab invasions ended the growth of Caesarea in 640 CE. The Muslim leaders – caliphs – ignored this port city.

The Crusader occupation began with the conquest of the city by Baldwin I in 1101. Louis IX of France fortified the smaller city with the walls and moats you see today. Baldwin's troops discovered what they thought to be the Holy Grail – the cup from which Jesus supposedly drank at the Last Supper. The Crusaders began to build a cathedral but they did not have time to finish it. In 1265 Sultan Beybars captured and destoryed the city and it was not repaired until the 19th century under the Turks. In the 1700s Ahmed Jezzar Pasha, the Ottoman governor, sent his workmen to take many of the Carrara marble columns and capitals to his capital at Akko.

In 1884 Muslim colonists from Bosnia came to Caesarea and tried to form a fishing village. Malaria and the shifting sands forced them inland and they became farmers. In 1940 Kibbutz S'dot Yam, "Fields of the Sea," was founded and its members discovered much of Caesarea's remains. The World War II Jewish heroine, Hannah Senesh, who parachuted behind German lines to help the Hungarian Jewish Community, was a member of this kibbutz. She was captured, tortured and killed by the Nazis. She wrote this famous poem,

> "Blessed is the burning match that kindled a sea of flames, Blessed is the flame, glowing in the hearts of men, Blessed are the proud hearts that knew when to stop beating"

The Sites Today

The ruins of Caesarea stretch for about two miles along the Mediterranean beach. Kibbutz S'dot Yam is at the southern end. North of the bungalows is the Roman theater and beyond that is the walled Crusader city. Just inland from the city is the Byzantine street and about a kilometer north is the Roman aqueduct.

The Theater

Constructed during the time of Jesus and Pontius Pilate, the theater as restored in the 20th century seats 5,000. Concerts are held here in the summer and the acoustics are amazing.

The Crusader City

Enter the city via the bridge across the moat and through the gatehouse with its Gothic vaults. The fortified town is impressive, but small by Herodian standards.

The Port

Herod's harbor was completed in 10 BCE. It was named Sebastos and extended about three times as far out to sea as what is visible today. The *National Geographic* of February 1983 has a very good article about the harbor with diagrams and pictures. An exhibit called, "Herod's

Caesarea" visited many U.S. museums in recent years. The harbor was not discovered until 1960 when aerial photography and underwater archeological explorations revealed the ancient offshore ruins. It is possible that an earthquake in the 3rd century CE sank the harbor structure.

The Byzantine Street

The street of statues is really part of a 5th century CE forum. The headless statues are headless because the heads were made to be replaced as new emperors replaced old one. The white marble statues are 2nd century and the red porphyry is from the 3rd century. They were discovered by the kibbutzniks while they worked in the banana fields in 1954.

The Aqueduct

The present construction dates from about 100 CE. There was an earlier one, which was somehow destroyed. It was six miles long, beginning near Mount Carmel. Much of it has been buried by the shifting sands (Acts 8:40, 21:8-9; 10; 9:30; 18:22; 25:3-6; 12:19; 23:22-26:32; 26:28).

Hadera

Established in 1891, Hadera was the center of the citrus growing area. It is not a biblical town but is an important junction and a number of industries are located here. The area was plagued by swamps in the 19th century CE and owes much of its fertility to Baron Edmond de Rothschild's wise plan of importing eucalyptus trees from Australia. These trees draw up great quantities of water and are very effective in drying the soil.

Herzliya

Named for Theodore Herzl, father of modern Zionism, Herzliya is a pleasant sea-side resort town. Many foreign diplomats live here to avoid the noisy activity of Tel Aviv.

Tel Qasila

Just north of Tel Aviv, on the campus of today's Tel Aviv University, stands an ancient fortress that guarded the Yarkon port at the time of King Solomon. It is possible that the cedars of Lebanon were sent by King Hiram of Tyre to this point and then hauled overland to Jerusalem for use in the Temple. Another possiblity is that the cedars were sent to Jaffa (II Samuel 5:11; II Chronicles 2:3-16).

Petah Tikva

The oldest Jewish agricultural settlement in Israel, founded in 1878 by settlers from Jerusalem. The name comes from Hosea 2:17: "the Valley of Achor (trouble) will be a door of hope."

Aphek, Antipatris

The ancient site of Antipatris is about two miles northeast of Petah Tikva. It was built on the ruins of Aphek in about 35 BCE by Herod the Great in memory of his father, Antipater. The remains seen today are Crusader. Here the Philistines captured the ark of the covenant which had been brought from Shiloh to bring good fortune in the battle. Paul stopped here on his way to Caearea after his arrest (I Samuel 4:1-11; Acts 23:23, 31).

Tel Aviv

While Tel Aviv is not a biblical city, it has a biblical name. The original Tel Aviv was in Babylon (Ezk. 3:15). The name means the old-new land or the hill of spring. It was founded in 1909 as a suburb of Jaffa. It was originally intended to be a housing project known as Ahuzat Bayit. The founders wanted to build a Jewish neighborhood outside the exclusively Arab town of Yafo, Jaffa. The suburb outgrew the main city quickly and by 1921 it was a separate city. Now Jaffa is a Tel Aviv neighborhood. Today Tel Aviv has a population of nearly 500,000 and is the cultural, business and industrial center of the country. The hotel strip along the Mediterranean coast is Israel's Miami Beach. If you stay overnight in Tel Aviv, walk the beach and visit Dizengoff Street – Tel Aviv's version of Times Square or Piccadilly Circus. The two museums on the campus of the university, Eretz and the Museum of the Diaspora, are well worth a visit. The Shalom tower, in the heart of the financial district, is the tallest building and it's observatory is worth a look on a clear day.

Yafo, Jaffa, Joppa

The history of Jaffa begins in the time of the Canaanites. In 1465 BCE it was ruled by the Egyptian, Thutmose III. It was supposed to be part of the tribal territory of Dan but they were unable to control it. and moved north to the area along today's Lebanon border near Mount Hermon. Jaffa was Solomon's main seaport and is mentioned in II Chronicles 2:16 and Ezra 3:7 as the port where building materials arrived from Lebanon. Jonah 1:3 records the beginning of the prophet's misguided voyage to escape God's command. A statue of a smirking fish is a popular spot in the artist colony along the coast today and many young couples have themselves photographed next to it, as part of their wedding photos. (One wonders what they would do if the Lord called them to go to Nineveh and preach?) Here Peter raised Dorcas to life and at the home of Simon the Tanner had a vision of the sheet containing unclean animals which caused Peter to open his kosher heart to the invitation to visit and preach at the home of Cornelius – and thus the ministry to the gentile world began.

Later Richard the Lion Heart built a citadel in Jaffa. It was captured by Saladin's brother and many Christians were killed. The Crusader citadel was destroyed by Napoleon and rebuilt by the Turks. In the 19th and early 20th century Jaffa was a main port for pilgrims and pioneers. It was not a very safe port and many lost their lives in the landing process. Before the 1948 war, Jaffa was an Arab community and that is why Jewish neighborhoods began in outlying areas. When Israel became a state nearly 67,000 Arabs fled Jaffa and poor Jewish immigrants moved in. Modern Jaffa is a mixed Jewish and Arab city.

It is a quaint and interesting town today. churches, mosques and Jewish sites co-exist in relative peace. The mile between the two cities was filled with rubble for years but clean up is beginning. Our tour groups often spend their first and sometimes second nights in the Tel Aviv/Jaffa area which will enable you to walk the beach and have coffee in Jaffa during an evening stay.

Ayalon Valley & Kiryat Yearim

English-speakers are probably more familiar with this valley as "Ajalon," the place where the sun stood still while Joshua defeated the Amorites in Joshua 10:6-27. This valley, like the Jezreel to the north, has always been an important pass and a common battleground. Gezer is the chariot city in this area. Kiryat Yearim, Kirjath-Jearim or Abu Ghosh, again different names for one city, is located on the edge of the valley and is known as the city where Abinadab lived and kept the ark of the covenant for twenty years while David waited the God-ordained moment to bring the ark to Jerusalem. Pilgrims coming from the west get their first glimpse of Jerusalem at this site.

Sorek Valley

Near the Judean cities of Eshtaol and Zorah, in the wadi which figured in the story of Samson or Shimshon, as his name is pronounced in Hebrew. Delilah lived in this valley as did Samson and his family. Judges 13-16 tells the story of this very human Israelite judge.

Beit Shemesh

Located on the south slope of the Sorek Valley, this Canaanite town was a center of sun god worship. Digs here show evidence of town life as far back as 3000 BCE. Early Iron Age walls may be from David's fortifications. The ark of the covenant was returned here after being captured by the Philistines of Ekron and later King Amaziah of Judah was defeated and captured by King Jehoash of the northern kingdom of Israel (II Kings 14:11-14).

Tel Azekah

This town appears on Joshua's list of Judean towns in Joshua 15:35, "Yarmut and Adullam, Socoh and

Azekah." Azekah is in the western foothills, known in Hebrew as the "shphelah." Just east of Azekah is the Valley of Elah where David slew the giant, Goliath. In I Samuel 17 we learn that the Philistines gathered for war at Socoh and pitched camp at Ephes Dammin, between Socoh and Azekah. Saul and the Israelites camped in the Valley of Elah. We often stop to pick up stones in the valley.

Azekah is also known as one of the last cities to hold out against the Babylonian army and is mentioned in the *Lachish Letters*, a major archaeological find. It was the last stronghold to fall to Nebuchadnezzar's forces before the fall of Jerusalem in 587 BCE. In one of the Lachish letters a statement was made indicating that the lights of Azekah were no longer seen and only Lachish was still resisting.

Beit Guvrin

In this area there are hundreds of fascinating caves. We can visit a different one on each tour and not exhaust the supply for years to come. The Bell Caves at Beit Guvrin date back to Roman and Byzantine times. The caves are shaped like a bell or a beehive and are open at the top. Some think these man-made caves were burial caves. The clay may have been taken to build the walls around Ashkelon. During the early Byzantine times this city was known as Eleutheropolis which means city of liberty, so named because Emperor Septimius Severus granted it special privileges.

Tel Maresha, Marissa

This ancient biblical site is located one mile south of Beit Guvrin and four miles northeast of Tel Lachish. Pottery found here dates back to 800 BCE. This town was a main base of operations by the Seleucids against the Maccabees. It was destroyed by the Parthians in about 40 BCE. Caves are currently being excavated in this area and some of our tourists have worked here on "Dig for a Day." Joshua listed Maresha as one of Rehoboam's fortified cities. Good King Asa defeated the vast Cushite (Ethiopian) army in this area as recorded in II Chronicles 14:9-13. His prayer is a model for all of us who face strong foes: "Lord, there is no one like you to help the powerless against the mighty. Help us, O Lord our God, for we rely on you, and in your name we have come against this vast army. O Lord, you are our God; do not let man prevail against you."

Land of the Philistines

General Description

This portion of the coastal plain, the beginning of the Way of the Sea, begins south of Gaza and extends northward about five miles south of Jaffa. It is an area about 70 miles long and 25 miles wide at its widest point near Beersheva. It is a fertile area but its strategic position made it a dangerous place to live in the ancient world. This trade route from Africa to Asia and Europe saw the armies of many mighty nations marching through its narrow habitat in the Fertile Crescent. One can see the wisdom of the Lord in placing his chosen people, with their commitment to monotheism, on the main highway of the ancient world.

Who were the Philistines?

They were part of the Sea People who probably migrated from the Aegean islands or Crete and were known as early as the time of Abraham. During the Late Bronze Age they were headquartered in five cites on the coastal plain of Israel: Ashkelon, Ashdod, Gaza, Gath and Ekron. (The word "age" is a useful memory device.) The Philistines conquered the Canaanites in part of the land and threatened the Israelites for many years. They are mentioned in Ex. 13:17 where we are told that, "when God brought the Israelites out of Egypt He did not lead them through the land of the Plishtim lest they recoil in the face of war and turn back to Egypt." The name "Palestine" derives from Plishtim, related to the word for migrate. The Philistines controlled the trade of iron working in the early years of the Israelite presence in the land. The Israelites had to go the Philistines for sharpening of utensils and weapons which resulted in a shortage of swords and spears among the biblical IDF. However, as has occurred many times in history, the battles were in the hands of the Lord.

Sites

Ashdod

Eighteen miles south of Tel Aviv stands the ruins of this ancient Hyksos and Canaanite city which became one of the five Philistine strongholds in biblical times. The Anakim prevented the forces of Joshua from controlling it even though it was in the territory assigned to the tribe of Judah. It was the main center of Philistine Dagon worship and the ark of the covenant was placed in the Philistine temple at Ashdod after the sons of Eli foolishly took it into battle. The God of Israel had the last word when the statue of Dagon was found fallen on its face and later broken in pieces (I Samuel 5). King Uzziah's capture of Ashdod is recounted in II Chronicles 26:6. It was also captured by the Assyrians under Sargon, (Isaiah 20:1) and when Nehemiah returned he was very angry to discover the degree of assimilation that had occured with Jews intermarrying with women of Ashdod and producing children who did not speak Hebrew. Later it was ruled by the Greeks, the Maccabees and the Romans. Some twenty levels of civilization have been unearthed in the digs at Ashdod. In Acts 8:40 Philip appeared in Azotus, the Greek name for this city, after baptizing the Ethiopian eunuch.

A modern city was founded in 1957, about three miles north of the ancient site. It is a headquarters for the Israeli navy and a major deep-water port. It is also an industrial center which includes a regional electric power plant, diamond polishing plants and the Leyland bus assembly factory.

Ashkelon

About 18 miles south of Ashdod lies Ashkelon, one of the oldest known Canaanite cities, built around 2000 BCE. Later it became the only Philistine city with a harbor. The tell el'Amarna letters of the 14th century BCE mention the wealthy city of Ashkelon, and Pharaoh Ramses II recorded the capture of the city in a bas-relief in Karnak, in upper Egypt. The carving shows Egyptian soldiers attacking a fortified city, using ladders to scale the walls, while bearded defenders man the walls.

Like Ashdod, it was a center of Dagon worship under the Philistines. Samson, enraged when the Philistines solved his riddle – with the help of Delilah – killed 30 men of Ashkelon and used their possessions to pay his debt.

In II Samuel 1:17 we read of David's lament over the death of Saul and Jonathan, "David took up this lament concerning Saul and his son Jonathan, and ordered that the men of Judah be taught this lament of the bow (it is written in the Book of Jashar): 'Your glory, O Israel, lies slain on your heights. How the mighty have fallen! Tell it not in Gath, proclaim it not in the streets of Ashkelon, lest the daughters of the Philistines be glad, lest the daughters of the uncircumcised rejoice.'"

Herod the Great was born in Ashkelon and, as was his habit, he embellished the city. The archeologists have found many Roman remains here, visible in the park at the southern end of the city. A small Jewish community remained when Ashkelon became a Christian city under the Byzantines. The Crusaders under Baldwin II took the city in 1153 CE and it was finally destroyed by Sultan Beybars in 1270 and never rebuilt until modern times. Today Ashkelon is a resort town and a National Parks site. Nearby is Israel's main oil field – Heletz, discovered in 1955. Perhaps its restoration since 1948 is in fulfillment of Zeph. 2:7, "...it will belong to the remnant of the house of Judah; there they will find pasture. In the evening they will lie down in the houses of Ashkelon. The Lord their God will care for them; he will restore their fortunes."

Ekron

The most northerly of the five main Philistine cities. It is listed in Joshua 15 as one of the boundaries of the tribe of Judah. However when Joshua was old, Ekron still had not been subdued. While the Ark of the Covenant was in Philistine territory, they moved it from Ashdod to Gath and finally to Ekron. As the ark of God was entering Ekron, the people of Ekron cried out, "They have brought the ark of the God of Israel around to us to kill us and our people." After seven months in the area, the Philistines sent it back to Beit Shemesh on an ox cart.

After David killed Goliath (I Samuel 17:52), the Bible tells us that "the men of Israel and Judah surged forward with a shout and pursued the Philistines to the entrance of Gath and to the gates of Ekron. Their dead were strewn along the Shaaraim road to Gath and Ekron."

When King Ahaziah of Israel rebelled against the Lord in II Kings 1:21-4, he sent his messengers to consult Baalzebub, the god of Ekron, to see if he would recover from his injury. Elijah asked them, "is it because there is no God in Israel that you are going off to consult Baal-zebub, the god of Ekron?" In New Testament times Beelzebub was regarded as the prince of evil spirits.

Yad Mordechai

Kibbutz Yad Mordechai, seven miles south of Ashkelon, was founded in 1944 and named for the Warsaw Ghetto fighter, Mordechai Anilevich. A statue of him on a hill overlooking the kibbutz bears the inscription: "My final aspiration in life has been fulfilled – Jewish defense has become a reality. I am happy to count among the first Jewish Ghetto fighters. 23/4/1943." Within five years of his death the kibbutz which bears his name was also deeply involved in the reality of Jewish defense. After six brutal days of Egyptian bombardment, 24 defenders had lost their lives and the whole kibbutz was destroyed. There is a life sized reconstruction of the battle scene showing the Egyptian assault and the meager defense capabilities of the settlers. However, they stalled the Egyptians long enough to allow time for reinforcements to reach Jerusalem and Tel Aviv so their seemingly hopeless battle contributed much to War of Independence. There is also a museum on the grounds of the kibbutz telling the story of the Holocaust and Jewish Resistance movements.

Gaza, Aza

Gaza is probably the oldest and most important of the five Philistine cities. It is 40 miles south of Jaffa and is the last main city on the coast as one travels to Egypt. It is mentioned in Genesis 10:19 in the description of the borders of Canaan which "reached from Sidon toward Gerar as far as Gaza."

Joshua 10:41 says, "Joshua subdued them from Kadesh Barnea to Gaza and from the whole region of Goshen to Gibeon." He reached it but did not conquer it.

Joshua 11:22 refers to the descendants of Anak and says that, "No Anakites were left in Israelite territory; only in Gaza, Gath and Ashdod did any survive."

We find Samson in this area quite often. He removed the

gates of Gaza nearly to Hebron, 40 miles away! He was captured, imprisoned, blinded and finally died in Gaza – taking the temple and many inhabitants with him.

King Hezekiah defeated the Philistines, as far as Gaza and its territory, II Kings 18:8. Jeremiah prophesied the attack of Pharaoh on Gaza, Jeremiah 47. Acts 8:26 reports the story of the conversion of the Ethiopian eunuch: "Now an angel of the Lord said to Philip, 'Go south to the road – the desert road – that goes down from Jerusalem to Gaza.'" When you are in Jerusalem you will notice that one of the main roads through west Jerusalem is called, "Derekh Aza," the road to Gaza.

Gaza has seen many wars. It was conquered by Crusaders, Turks, Napoleon's troops and the British in World War I. It was conquered by Israel in 1956, given back to Egypt and regained by Israel in the Six-Day War. It is currently the home of approximately 500,000 unhappy Arab refugees. Although they are bitter toward Israel, their Arab brethren have contributed little to their support and much to their status as permanent refugees. Many Gazan Arabs worked in Israel until the 1993 closing of the borders.

In February 2005, the Israeli government voted to implement Prime Minister Ariel Sharon's plan for unilateral disengagement from the Gaza Strip beginning on August 15, 2005. The plan required the dismantling of all Israeli settlements there, transferring the lucrative hot house industry to Palestinian control to spur economic development, and the removal of all Israeli settlers and military bases from the Strip, a process that was completed on September 12, 2005 as the Israeli cabinet formally declared an end to military rule in the Gaza Strip after 38 years of control. The withdrawal was highly contested by many on the right in Israel as well as many Israel supporters around the world. Some Israelis now consider the Gaza Strip to be an occupied part of Israel. Following withdrawal, Israel retains offshore maritime control and control of airspace over the Strip. Israel withdrew from the "Philadelphi Route" that is adjacent to the Strip's border with Egypt after an agreement with the latter to secure its side of the border. The future political status of the Gaza Strip remains undecided, and is claimed as part of any prospective Palestinian state. (This paragraph from Wikipedia)

Gath

Gath, pronounced Gat in Hebrew, was the home of the giant, Goliath, who challenged the armies of Israel and was defeated by a young shepherd's sling. Modern Kiryat Gat is located south of Tel Gat where archaeological excavations have revealed homes, palaces, tools and storage areas. David fled to this area when he was hunted by King Saul and he was given refuge in Ziklag by King Achish of Gat. In a later time King Rehoboam of

Judah fortified Gat as the southern outpost of the kingdom and King Uzziah destroyed the walls of Gat after retaking it from the Philistines. This city is in a strategic position. It controls two highways, one from the southern coastal plain to Jerusalem and one from the plain of Beer Sheva to the central region. Kiryat Gat is a modern city with many industries.

The Negev

General Description

The Negev or Negeb, Israel's southern desert area, is not precisely defined. It is comprised of about 4,000 square miles of sand, stone and scrub vegetation which looks rather like a lunar landscape. It begins south of Hebron and extends about 70 miles south. It is bounded on the east by the Dead Sea and the Aravah, on the west by the coastal plain. The area saw much settlement by the Nabataeans in the Second Temple period and later by the Byzantines. The climate is characterized by hot days, cold nights – except in summer – and minimal rainfall. In wet years the northern Negev is quite productive. In the 1960s the National Water Carrier was built to bring water from the north to the Negev. There is also water from underground springs and occasional flash floods. The word negbah also means south, which is the direction you usually go to get there. The general rule in Israel is that the weather gets hotter and drier the further east or south or downhill you go.

Rainfall is a serious concern in a land where precipitation only occurs in the winter months. The north-south pattern of rainfall is usually as follows:

> From north to south:
> Mount Hermon, elev. 9,200 feet, 60 inches
> Mount Meron, central hills, 44 inches
> Jerusalem, elev. 2,800 feet, 22 inches
> Beersheva, Negev, 10 inches
> Eilat, Red Sea, 1 inch

An area which receives less than 10 inches of rainfall per year is technically considered a desert. Here wells are of life and death significance. We can understand why so much emphasis is put on water sources in the biblical account of the Patriarchs.

Beersheva

The southern border of the biblical promised land is near Beersheba or Beersheva, which means the well of the seven or the well of the oath. "From Dan to Beersheva" is the accepted length of the Promised Land. Beersheva is known as the capital of the Negev and is a totally Jewish town today. Abraham, Isaac and Jacob all camped in this area, dug wells, made agreements with neighboring tribes and generally staked out a claim to this land.

Beersheva is 50 miles south of Jerusalem and 35 miles west of the southern end of the Dead Sea. Which of the area wells is the well of Abraham is not known today. The famous Israeli archaeologist, Yohanan Aharoni, excavated from 1969-76 at a site now called Tel Beersheba. A well was found outside the gateway and some ruined houses dating from the 12th century BCE. Some scholars believe this is the site of the well mentioned in Genesis 21:25 and 26:15. However, there is no way to prove that this well is or is not the Genesis well. We cannot be assured that this is the exact spot since there are a number of wells and settlements in the area and others have been found from that period of time. Also, there is no mention of a town in the Genesis account and Abraham may have dug his well in an uninhabited area.

General Allenby captured Beersheva from the Turks in 1917. Lawrence of Arabia blew up the trains on the way to Egypt by bombing the railroad tracks near Beersheva. When Israel captured the town in 1948 there were about 2,700 inhabitants. Today there are over 200,000. Many immigrants have settled here and Beersheva has several good academic institutions, most notably the Ben Gurion University and the Negev Research Institute. An industrial center is growing southeast of the city.

The Israeli government has built a large housing development for the approximately 20,000 Negev Bedouin nearTel Sheva. Some Bedouin still prefer to live in tents but many are becoming farmers as well as herdsmen now that dependable water supplies are more readily available. Many are pursuing higher education and some return as doctors and social workers to help their own people.

Arad

One possible meaning of the name Arad is fugitive. The territory certainly has provided a great hiding place for runaways through all periods of history. Archaeologists have found remains of a 5,000 year old city in this area, establishing that Arad was long a strategic outpost at the southern entrance to Eretz Israel.

Biblical references to Arad:

Numbers 21:1 – When the Canaanite king of Arad, who lived in the Negev, heard that Israel was coming along the road to Atharim, he attacked the Israelites and captured some of them.

Numbers 33:40 – The Canaanite king of Arad, who lived in the Negev of Canaan, heard that the Israelites were coming.

Joshua 12:14 – The king of Arad was one of 3I Kings Joshua defeated.

Judges 1:16 – The descendants of Moses' father-in-law,

the Kenite, went up from the City of Palms with the men of Judah to live among the people of the Desert of Judah in the Negev near Arad.

On the mound at Tel Arad archaeologists discovered a sanctuary built according to the layout of the Holy of Holies in Solomon's temple in Jerusalem.

Modern Arad was founded in 1961. When natural gas was found there it became something of a boom town. Although it is not a particularly attractive city, it is a healthy spot for those who suffer from respiratory ailments. Its height (3,000 ft. above the Dead Sea), and dry climate make it an excellent place for asthma sufferers.

Mamshit

Mamshit is the Hebrew name for the town which the Madeba map calls by the Greek name Mampsis. Several large groups of Nabatean buildings were found here and a Roman military cemetery, mosaic floors and other remains have been excavated. In the gorge which runs at the foot of Mamshit are found three dams dating to the 5th and 6th centuries CE – the golden era of the town under Byzantine rule. The dams were used to store precious water during the rainy season so it would last through the dry, hot summer. Small forts, which guarded the reservoirs, are found on the surrounding hills. Ruins of a British Mandate Police Station are also found in the area. The Arabic name of the town is Kurnub.

Dimona

This town is listed in Joshua 15:22 among the Judean towns facing Edom. It is uncertain if this is the exact site of biblical Dimona but it is definitely in the area. The modern town was built in 1955 and many immigrants came here to work in the textile, diamond and chemical industries. Everyone says that the funny-looking buildings along the highway near Oron are a textile factory but it is a not-very-well-kept secret that they are really part of the nuclear center.

Avdat

Located at the crossroads of the two main caravan routes—from Petra and from Eilat—Avdat became a very important city in the Negev. It was a fortress and toll-house for the caravans traveling the spice route. The Nabateans were a mixed race of Arabs and Edomites and were traders and farmers. Their rule in the Negev lasted from 312 BCE to 106 CE when this region was conquered by the Romans. Their capital was at Petra in Jordan and their main towns in the Negev were Mamshit, Avdat, Shivta, Nitzana, Rehovot and Halutza. They were clever at building, field cultivation and water preservation. They produced lovely pottery made from soft material and decorated by patterns in deep red. They wrote in an alphabet similar to Hebrew. The Hebrew University set up an experimental farm in this region to teach farming methods used by the Nabateans.

Avdat looks down on the valley from its high perch. After the Nabateans, the Byzantine Christians built St. Theodore's Church on the top of the hill. It is well preserved except for its missing roof. You pass through the ruins of a monastery to enter the castle and watchtower.

Shivta

This Nabatean-Byzantine town of the 2nd century BCE is northwest of Avdat. It is about 2,000 years old and is one of the best preserved towns of the area. Three Byzantine churches of the 5th and 6th centuries are here and Nabatean houses with the second stories still intact.

Maktesh Ramon

Fifty miles from Beersheva and 13 miles from Avdat you will see an amazing view! Here is a little town balancing on the edge of a giant crater, called a maktesh in Hebrew. This is the northern boundary of the Wilderness of Zin where the Israelites rebelled against Moses.

Maktesh Ramon is the largest of three round basins. The other two are called Maktesh Gadol and Maktesh Katan. (In Hebrew, gadol means large, katan means small and Ramon means high.) The Makteshim may have been formed by volcanic activity or by subterranean water currents gradually washing away the soil and rock until the upper crust caved in. Deposits of gypsum, quartz, sand, flint and multi-colored sand have been found at Maktesh Ramon and some hope to find oil in this region. In the Maktesh is a pumping station transporting oil from Eilat to Ashkelon. The nearby development town is called Mitzpeh Ramon – the watchtower of the craters.

Wadi Paran

Wadi or Nahal Paran is the longest of the watercourses that drain the southern Negev. It is about 22 miles south of Maktesh Ramon and is the central wadi of the northern Sinai, where the tribes of Israel camped on their way to Canaan. It is mentioned in two scriptures: Numbers 13:1-3, The Lord said to Moses, "Send some men to explore the land of Canaan, which I am giving to the Israelites. From each ancestral tribe send one of its leaders." So at the Lord's command Moses sent leaders of the Israelites out from the Desert of Paran. Deuteronomy 33:2 says: "The Lord came from Sinai and dawned over them from Seir; he shone forth from Mount Paran. He came with myriads of holy ones from the south, from his mountain slopes." Earlier in Genesis 21:21 we find Ishmael camping in Paran after he and his mother, Hagar, separated from Abraham's family.

In 1956 the Israeli army began its Sinai campaign in the Wadi of Paran. The highway crosses the wadi and climbs the steep, rocky side of Ma'ale Paran—Ascent of Paran—where a beautiful view unfolds over the wide, dry river bed. Be careful of wadis after a rain – they can suddenly become raging rivers!

Aravah

The Aravah or Arabah is the Hebrew name of the great rift valley that extends from Mount Hermon to the Gulf of Aqaba and on down to Africa. It is also called the Afro-Syrian rift. In Israel the Aravah refers to the 110 mile area from the Dead Sea to the Red Sea. Moses and the Israelites probably traveled this region as they went to Kadesh-Barnea and when they retreated south in their detour past Edom (Numbers 20:21; 21:4; Deuteronomy 2:8).

Timna

Timna is a national park and is the site of the striking rock formations known as "Solomon's Pillars." It is also the site of ancient copper mines used by the Egyptians.

Eilat

Israel's southern-most city on the Red Sea has been a port since King Solomon's time. We learn about Solomon's navy in I Kings 9:26-8: King Solomon also built ships at Ezion Geber, which is near Elath in Edom, on the shore of the Red Sea. And Hiram sent his men – sailors who knew the sea – to serve in the fleet with Solomon's men. They sailed to Ophir and brought back 420 talents of gold, which they delivered to King Solomon. I Kings 10:22: The king had a fleet of trading ships at sea along with the ships of Hiram. Once every three years it returned, carrying gold, silver and ivory, and apes and baboons.

Biblical Etzion Geber was located near present day Akaba to the east. The ancient port may have been about five miles south of modern Eilat near the Coral Island where there is a natural harbor. The Crusaders built a fortress on the granite rock which they called "Pharaoh's Island." Eilat is Israel's outlet to the Indian Ocean, South Asia and East Africa.

Eilat was always an important outpost and various Judean kings are mentioned as building it up in times of strength or losing it to stronger foes.

"Then all the people of Judah took Azariah, who was sixteen years old, and made him king in place of his father Amaziah. He was the one who rebuilt Elath and restored it to Judah after Amaziah rested with his fathers" (II Kings 14:21-2).

"Then Rezin, king of Aram and Pekah son of Remaliah, king of Israel marched up to fight against Jerusalem and besieged Ahaz, but they could not overpower him. At that time, Rezin king of Aram recovered Elath for Aram by driving out the men of Judah. Edomites then moved into Elath and have lived there to this day" (II Kings 16:5-6).

Now Jehoshaphat built a fleet of trading ships to go to Ophir for gold, but they never set sail – they were wrecked at Ezion Geber. At that time Ahaziah son of Ahab said to Jehoshaphat, "Let my men sail with your men," but Jehoshaphat refused (I Kings 22:48-9).

Now and then Jews returned to Eilat until the time of the Crusaders in the 12th century. Eilat became a Jewish town again in 1949 when the Israelis captured it without firing a shot. While strategically important, the town consisted of two British-built customs houses.

The building of modern Eilat began in 1950 and became serious after the Sinai Campaign in 1956. Oil arrives by tanker ships and flows via a 16-inch pipe to the refineries in Ashkelon. The warm, dry climate and one of the world's most beautiful – and accessible coral reefs makes Eilat a popular tourist center.

East bank of Jordan

In biblical times, the country that is now Jordan contained the lands of Edom, Moab, Ammon, and Bashan. Together with other Middle Eastern territories, Jordan passed in turn to the Assyrians, the Babylonians, the Persians and, about 330 BCE, the Seleucids. Conflict between the Seleucids and the Ptolemies enabled the Arabic-speaking Nabataeans to become part of the Roman province of Arabia. The Romans conquered Petra in 106 CE. The city had a population of about 7,000 at that time. The Byzantines came in the 4th century CE and also maintained similar population number. In 633–636 CE the area was conquered by the Moslem Arabs. The Crusaders ruled during the 12th century. In the 16th century, the territory of Jordan came under Ottoman Turkish rule and was administered from Damascus. Taken from the Turks by the British in World War I, the Palestine mandate in 1920-21 set the stage for creation of a new nation of Jordan under the rule of Abdullah ibn Hussein.

The Decapolis

Original cities probably were:

Scythopolis (Beisan) Beit She'an

Pella (Khirbet Fahil)

Dion (Husn)

Gadara (Um Qais)

Hippos (Fiq)

Gerasa (Jerash)

Philadelphia (Amman)

Kamatha (Qanawat)

Raphana (Al Rafah)

Damascus

All except Scythopolis are on the East bank of Jordan. The cities were not a fixed group of ten. Cities joined and withdrew. Among them were Arbila (Irbid), Capitolias (Beit Ras), Edrei (Dera'a), and Bosra, in Syria. Pella, Dion and Gerasa are thought to have been founded by Greek soldiers. The others were older towns.

At the time of Pompey the Romans formed the Decapolis into a military alliance for protection against the Jews, Nabateans, and desert tribes. Later Emperor Trajan joined Perea, the district between Arnon and the Decapolis, with the latter to create the Province of Arabia (90 CE).

The capital of the new province, Arabia Petraea, was first at Petra and then at Bosra in Syria. The 3rd legion (Cyrenaica) was posted in the north, and the 4th (Martia) in the south of the country. Two great camps built to accommodate the latter, at Lajjun near Kerak and Adhruh near Petra, can still be seen. The great road from Bosra to Aqaba was begun by Trajan and finished under Hadrian.

Christianity gained a foothold in the area between the 2nd & 3rd centuries and spread rapidly after the conversion of Constantine in the 4th century. Byzantine control brought a period of peace and prosperity for 200 years. Under Justinian (527-565 CE) a large number of churches were built and pilgrimage was encouraged. There were approximately 20 bishoprics east of the Jordan.

Local tranquility ended in 614 CE, when the Persians swept through the country.

Petra

Our tours often include an optional day trip to Petra from Eilat. Petra means "rock" in Greek. It has been poetically described as, "A rose-red city, half as old as time." This fortress city is set in a canyon whose only entrance was a long, narrow passage, the "Siq." Inside the canyon the Nabataeans created a city by carving houses and temples out of the variegated rock of the canyon walls.

Prior to the Nabataeans, Petra was probably in the land of the Horites, about 2000 BCE. Later it was known as the land of the Edomites. Petra may be the same as "Sela," which also means rock. The Nabataeans, a Semitic tribe from North Arabia, settled in Petra about 800 BCE. By the 4th century they had occupied the territory astride the main trade route from Arabia to the Fertile Crescent. They became the protectors and toll collectors for the caravans who passed through their lands.

Petra lies about four hours south of modern Amman and about two hours north of Aqaba, on the edges of the mountainous desert of the Wadi Araba. The city is surrounded by towering hills of rust-coloured sandstone which gave the city some natural protection against invaders.

The area is semi-arid and the sandstone provided building materials allowing the Natataeans to carve their temples and tombs into the rock. From the official entrance to the site, a dusty trail leads gently downwards along the Wadi Musa (The Valley of Moses). Situated in small rock outcrops to the left and right of the path are small Nabataean tombs, carved into the dry rock. Beyond these, walls of sandstone rise steeply on the left, and a narrow cleft reveals the entrance to the Siq, the principal route into Petra itself.

The Nabataeans were expert hydraulic engineers. The walls of the Siq are lined with channels to carry drinking water to the city, while a dam to the right of the entrance diverted an adjoining stream through a tunnel to prevent it flooding the Siq.

The Siq narrows to little more than 15 feet in width, while the walls tower 200-300 feet on either side. The floor was originally paved but is now largely covered with soft sand, although evidence of Nabataean construction can still be seen in some places. The Siq twists and turns until abruptly, through a cleft in the rock, the first glimpse of the city of Petra can be seen. Carved out of pale reddish sandstone, ornate pillars supporting a portico jut out from the cliff face ahead. This is the "Khazneh," which means "treasury." Legend says that it was used as a hiding place for treasure. It seems to have been something between a temple and a tomb, possibly both at once or at different times.

A little further on is the giant semicircle of the amphitheatre, which had seats for eight thousand people. Behind it, the rock wall is pitted with tombs.

Close to the theater, a flight of steps marks the start of the climb towards the High Place of Sacrifice, while continuing towards the right, the wadi widens out. Ahead lies the center of the city, while following the cliff face further to the right takes you to the Royal Tombs.

Ammon, Moab

Scripture references:

- Numbers 20:14-21, Obadiah 10, Amos 1:11, Ezekiel 25:12-14, Edomites refused passage to Israelites.

- II Kings 14:1,7, captured by King Amaziah.

- Isaiah 16:1, called "Sela."

Other East Bank Scripture References

- Genesis 19:29-38, Moab & Ben-ammi – father of the children of Ammon.

- II Kings 3:26-27, Leviticus 20:2-5, Deuteronomy 2:19, Ammonites lived on east bank of Jordan River & the Dead Sea, between Arnon & Jabbok rivers. Chief god was Molech to whom human sacrifices were offered.

- Judges 11:4-33, Oppressed Israel, overthrown by Jephthah.

- II Samuel 11, City taken by David. Uriah, husband of Bathsheba, killed in the battle.

- II Samuel 17:27, Showed mercy to David.

- I Kings 14:21, Solomon married Ammonite woman.

- Mark 7:31, Decapolis city

Jabesh-Gilead

- Judges 21:8-14, When men of Jabesh did not come to the meeting of tribes, Israel sent army to kill every living creature. The tribe of Benjamin found wives among 400 virgins who lived in Jabesh.

- I Samuel 11, When men of Jabesh-gilead asked for Saul's aid vs. the king of Syria, Israel rallied behind him and recognized him as king.

- I Samuel 31:11-13, Men of Jabesh-gilead removed bodies of Saul & his sons from the wall at Beit She'an, burned and buried them in Jabesh. David honored them.

- II Samuel 21:12, David took bones of Saul & Jonathan from the men of Jabesh-gilead.

Heshbon

- Deuteronomy 2:30, Numbers 32:27-37, Assigned to tribe of Reuben.

- Nehemiah 9:22, Held by Israel for over 300 years.

- Song of Solomon 7:4, "your eyes like the fishpools in Heshbon."

Medeba, Madaba

20 miles south of Amman on King's Hiway is the city famous for its mosaic map. History back to middle bronze age: 2000-1580 BCE. Map dates from 6th century CE.

- Numbers 21:24-30, Moabite city captured by King Sihon and later by Israel.

How Did A Nice Gentile Girl from Minneapolis Become a Zionist?

When people ask me how I got into all this I have to say, "It was my Grandmother's fault."

Grandmothers can be dangerous! I became a grandmother some years ago and I hope to be as dangerous to my little granddaughters as my grandmother was to me. She did very dangerous things – like praying for me and reading to me from the Bible. If you want to have a neat, orderly life, completely under your own selfish control – don't let anyone start doing things like that!

I have always regarded myself as most fortunate to have spent the first ten years of my life in the home of my paternal grandmother, Ida Emmeline Morgan Gardner. Ida was born the year after the American Civil War ended and died two years after the end of World War II. She was a serious student of history and the Bible and a keen observer of the passing scene. Like many families of the 19th century, Ida and Will Gardner buried three of their six children who died of childhood diseases. Will died accidentally in his mid-40s leaving Ida with two teenagers and four-year-old Walter who later became my father.

Ida was in failing health by the time I was born but, from the perspective of a small child, she seemed to have endless hours to read aloud – one of my favorite activities. I never hear the first chapter of Genesis read without recalling Ida's voice saying, "No matter what anyone tells you remember this: In the beginning GOD created the heavens and the earth."

Ida lived in an aging Victorian setting surrounded by lace curtains and red velvet drapes. She would interrupt reading sessions to point to the sunbeams dancing near the windows. "Oh JoAnn," she would say, "Look, God has sent sunbeams to amuse us while we read His word." I was well on my way to adulthood before I realized that sunbeams are really dust particles which occur in the presence of dusty old draperies. Or maybe that is the skeptic's view, perhaps Ida had it right all along.

Ida was known as "Gram" and occupied a major place in the days of a growing, asthmatic child with boundless curiosity about the world and the meaning of life. After the war began the aging lady and the little girl developed an evening ritual, parking themselves in front of the Silvertone radio to listen carefully to the "war news." Several older cousins were in the U.S. military and prayers were raised on their behalf. Gram often read from the Bible, particularly from the prophet Jeremiah, the portion which says, "This is what the Lord says, He who appoints the sun to shine by day, who decrees the moon and stars to shine by night, who stirs up the sea so that its waves roar – the Lord Almighty is his name: "Only if these decrees vanish from my sight," declares the Lord "will the descendants of Israel ever cease to be a nation before me." This is what the Lord says: "Only if the heavens above can be measured and the foundations of the earth below be searched out will I reject all the descendants of Israel because of all they have done," declares the Lord. *Jer. 31:35-37*

Gram would say to me, "God has a covenant with the Jews that will last as long as the sun, the moon, and the stars. This is a terrible war but Hitler will be defeated and the Jews will be back in their ancient land. We must pray for that." Somehow this left me with a sense of personal responsibility for the success of this project.

Ida died in May of 1947 leaving behind her old Bible underlined at all the points of promise to restore Israel. I read that Bible over the following year, so I was impressed, but not too surprised when I came home from school in May of 1948 to find the Minneapolis Tribune headline shouting, "State of Israel Declared." I thought, "Wow, Gram knew this was going to happen because she read the Bible." That definitely affected my view of the world and the Bible and set me on a path that led to life-long involvement with Israel and the Jewish people.

Many other people have influenced my life. One was my Lutheran pastor during the 1950s and '60s who encouraged me to study biblical languages and church history. My own children have had a major influence on my life. They both went to Israel to work as kibbutz volunteers in the late 1970s which contributed more threads to the interesting weaving that God has made of our lives.

I spent much of the decade of the 1970s working part-time in a small Christian book store and volunteering for an inner city ministry that helped rescue young girls who were caught in the web of drugs and prostitution. My 40th birthday was about to dawn and, even though I was not looking for new things to do, I thought I should make it a matter of prayer as to what the lessons for my 40th year might be. One morning, just before my birthday, I awoke with a clear thought (something I've come to call the SSV – the still, small voice) directing me to read Joshua 14:7. It turned out to be a quote from Caleb, Joshua's right hand man, who said, "When I was 40 years old I was sent to spy out the land." Sure enough, that was the year of my first trip to Israel.

I've been spying out the land ever since. As of this writing, I have led 58 trips to Israel. I am thankful for all the friends who've become tourists and all the tourists who've become friends.

My grandmother had lots of pithy sayings, one of which was,

> "The wise old owl sat in the oak
>
> The more he heard, the less he spoke
>
> The less he spoke, the more he heard
>
> Why can't we be like that wise old bird?"

I've learned a lot by hanging around and listening. I've tried to organize some of that knowledge about Israel and the Jewish people in this book. I pray that it will be useful to those who read it.

Years ago I stood with two English friends in front of the Western Wall in Jerusalem. I noticed that birds were nesting in some of the scrubby vegetation that stubbornly grows from the cracks in those ancient walls. My thoughts turned to the following Psalm.

Psalm 84:1-6

How lovely are Your dwelling places, O Lord of hosts!

My soul longs and even yearns for the courts of the Lord; My heart and my flesh sing for joy to the living God.

The bird also has found a house, And the swallow a nest for herself, where she may lay her young,

Even Your altars, O Lord of hosts, My King and my God.

How blessed are those who dwell in Your house! They are ever praising You.

How blessed is the man whose strength is in You, In whose heart are the highways to Zion!

The highway to God's city runs through my heart and through the hearts of many Christians. We are not ashamed to be called, "Christian Zionists." That term simply means that we are Christians who believe that God keeps His promises and that the descendants of Abraham, Isaac and Jacob are back in their ancient land because God willed it. I say, a resounding "Amen" to that.